Second Edition

RELIGIOUS AND SPIRITUAL GROUPS IN MODERN AMERICA

ROBERT S. ELLWOOD
University of Southern California

HARRY B. PARTIN
Duke University

Prentice Hall, Englewood Cliffs, New Jersey 07632

Library of Congress Cataloging-in-Publication Data

Ellwood, Robert S., (date)
  Religious and spiritual groups in modern America.

  Bibliography: p. 303
  Includes index.
  1. United States—Religion.   2. Cults—United States.
I. Partin, Harry B. (Harry Baxter)   II. Title.
BL2525.E43 1988   291′.0973   87-17464
ISBN 0-13-773045-4

Editorial/production supervision and
  interior design: **Barbara DeVries**
Cover design: **Wanda Lubelska Design**
Manufacturing buyer: **Margaret Rizzi**

 © 1988, 1973 by Prentice Hall
A Division of Simon & Schuster
Englewood Cliffs, New Jersey 07632

Printed in the United States of America

10 9 8 7 6 5 4 3 2 1

ISBN 0-13-773045-4 01

Prentice-Hall International (UK) Limited, *London*
Prentice-Hall of Australia Pty. Limited, *Sydney*
Prentice-Hall Canada Inc., *Toronto*
Prentice-Hall Hispanoamericana, S.A., *Mexico*
Prentice-Hall of India Private Limited, *New Delhi*
Prentice-Hall of Japan, Inc., *Tokyo*
Simon & Schuster Asia Pte. Ltd., *Singapore*
Editora Prentice-Hall do Brasil, Ltda., *Rio de Janeiro*

CONTENTS

3   NEW VESSELS FOR THE ANCIENT WISDOM: GROUPS IN THE THEOSOPHICAL AND ROSICRUCIAN TRADITIONS   73

4   THE DESCENT OF THE MIGHTY ONES: SPIRITUALISM AND UFO GROUPS   111

5   THE CRYSTAL WITHIN: INITIATORY GROUPS   134

6   THE EDENIC BOWER: NEO-PAGANISM   151

PREFACE

Since its first publication in 1973, *Religious and Spiritual Groups in Modern America* has enjoyed a gratifying reception as a guide to the major new or unconventional religious movements in America and the traditions that lie behind them. Significant changes have transpired in this area since the appearance of the earlier edition, however, and a new and updated version is now in order. In preparing this new edition, Harry B. Partin of Duke University joins the original author, Robert S. Ellwood of the University of Southern California, as coauthor.

Together we have endeavored to take into account three important developments in the past dozen years regarding religious and spiritual groups in modern America: a) the mass of new historical and sociological studies which have been done relevant to them since 1973; b) the bitter controversies about "cults," "brainwashing," and "deprogramming" that have arisen around them; and c) developments in the histories of individual groups in the 1970s and 1980s. In a few cases, groups presented in the first edition have disappeared or much diminished, leading us to omit them; others have been added.

At the same time, we have striven to retain the flavor of the first edition in the descriptions of the individual groups, with an emphasis on the empathetic understanding of the spiritual quest of each. No religious or spiritual path, we deeply believe, can be rightly understood without an understanding of why it is appealing to some. In the last analysis, it is not facts or figures which interpret religious life, but patterns in the mind and experience in the heart. Above all, it is essential to retain an empathetic, human-centered approach in examining faiths that have become the topics of heated controversy or which can too easily be dismissed as merely bizarre. They are nonetheless part of American life and of the human experience.

The authors would like to express their thanks to the great number of men and women associated with the groups discussed in this book who generously devoted hours of time in talking with us about their spiritual experiences. We are likewise deeply grateful to the organizations which gave us permission to reproduce literature under their copyright. Invariably we have found officials and members of groups presented in this volume courteous, helpful, and appreciative of our interest.

We alone are responsible for the contents of this book. In a few cases members of groups may find reason to regret wording or emphases we have chosen in discussing them. We sincerely hope, however, that most readers will feel the the tone of our effort reflects the respect we both have for all sincere human spiritual experience, our deep commitment to religious freedom and pluralism, and our gratitude for the friendship and assistance of members of these religious and spiritual groups.

R.S.E.
H.B.P.

INTRODUCTION
In Search of New Religious Movements

America is a land which has long presented two religious faces to the world and, more significantly, to itself. On the one hand, it sees itself as a Christian nation, established by God-fearing patriots and flourishing under divine protection. As such, it continues to have one of the highest rates of church attendance, mostly in conventional Christian denominations, of any Christian country in the world. The Bible remains a best-seller, and according to opinion polls the majority of Americans, largely conventional Christians, say their religious faith is important to them.

Yet on the other hand America appears to the world and to itself as a land of remarkable religious diversity. Its Christians, and likewise its Judaic minority, are divided into an unparalleled number of denominations and sects. Furthermore, virtually every religion of the world, including those quite outside the Judaeo-Christian orbit, can be found on these shores, sometimes in substantial numbers. Today, almost every large American city hosts a Muslim mosque, Buddhist temple, various groups of Hindu background, representatives of other Chinese and Japanese religions, perhaps Sikhs, Jains, and Parsees, and outposts of traditional Native American and Afro-American religions. Nor is this all. While many faiths of the sort just enumerated are ethnic in orientation and the product of immigration, a glance at the religion pages of a large city newspaper or phone book will reveal many more which do not seem to have that background. Some have names which have received a great amount of publicity and are well known

1

despite comparatively small numbers: the "Hare Krishnas," Scientology, the Unification Church ("Moonies"), Transcendental Meditation. Others are far less familiar to most people. Some like Spiritualism and Theosophy go back over a century to the America of another day. Others, including all those in the first set just mentioned, essentially got their start amid the extraordinary spiritual ferment of the 1960s. Yet one thing they have in common, apart from being unconventional in doctrine and practice compared to normative Judaism and Christianity, is that they are not grounded in a special minority ethnic group, but tend to draw adherents, and often leadership, from the American "center"—people of middle-class background and European descent.

Some of these religions are imports to America, some were originated here and—like modern Spiritualism—generously exported around the world. But they all add to the image of America's second spiritual face: that as well as being a staunch redoubt of traditional Christianity, America is also a hotbed of incredible religious diversity, ferment, and creativity. Somehow the two images coexist, and both represent real and important truths about religious America.

Our concern in this book will be with the second face, and in fact only with the second half of the second face as presented above. Without denigrating in any way the importance of "unconventional" American religion brought by immigrants from Asia or elsewhere, or growing out of the Native American or Afro-American experience, for reasons of space and coherence we shall restrict ourselves to those unconventional—that is, not normatively Judaeo-Christian—religions in America, whether of oriental or occidental provenance, which seem to appeal to Americans largely for reasons independent of ethnic identities. (Or if there is such an appeal, it is for *these* adherents more exoticism than familiarity that is the magnet.) It tends, in fact, to be these out-of-the-mainstream spiritualities which nonetheless pull in people of "mainstream" background that are most interesting and important to the average observer.

Why are such new religious movements interesting and why do they seem important? These are two different questions and must be addressed separately.

First, though, a third question ought to be put which may unite those two: Why do we Americans pay so much attention to new religious movements? Why do groups like the "Hare Krishnas" and the "Moonies," which have never numbered more than a few thousand active members in America, fewer than some individual churches of mainline denominations, gobble up so much space in the printed media and on TV? Nearly all the groups in this book are, in truth, very small, despite the impression that certain popular books on "cults" would like to give. Nor, at the time of writing, are most of them growing very much, if at all. Yet they continue to fascinate us.

To be sure, some of these groups have been involved in widely-publicized court cases that have made headlines. Yet that does not answer the question why *these* particular cases made headlines in the first place. The overwhelming majority of cases tried in our civil and criminal courts go totally unreported, unknown to anyone save those concerned. Is it because anything involving a new religion—or "cult"—of this sort is intrinsically fascinating in a way that "ordinary" lawsuits or charges of tax evasion are not?

During the early 1980s, in highly controversial court cases leaders of the Hare Krishnas were convicted of "brainwashing" and retaining a teen-age devotee; the Rev. Sun Myung Moon of the Unification Church was convicted and imprisoned for failure to pay income tax on money he claimed was church funds but that the court said was his personal income; and the Church of Scientology was charged with being a profit-making rather than a nonprofit organization, thus liable to taxation. On the other side, it should be noted that during the same period "deprogrammers"— those who, for a fee, take a member of a religious group from out of its control and seek to bring about the member's deconversion—have been convicted of kidnapping and have been given little legal support. Further, articles in increasing numbers have appeared in popular newspapers and magazines presenting the point of view that "cults," contrary to the asser-tions of "anticult" literature, can be helpful in some persons' quest for who they are, and can be (and are) left by most members voluntarily.[1] (Many studies have shown that more than 75 percent of those who join such a group leave on their own within a year.) This is in contrast to the situation a few years earlier, when mass-media material on "cults" usually gave a highly negative picture.

Again, why do we concern ourselves as a people—not just as under-standably concerned friends and family members of adherents—with the vicissitudes of these tiny but highly visible groups, viewing them in now one light and now another? First, it is because religion is still very important to a great many Americans. We take it seriously. We seek religious solutions to personal and social problems. Nonconformist religions draw our attention, therefore, because on one side they just might have something new and important to offer; on the other they might be "bad" religions that could cause harm to a society that expects a lot from religion.

Any society has its own "social construction of reality," in the expression of Peter Berger and Thomas Luckmann.[2] A prevailing view of God or ultimate reality, the meaning of human society, and how human life ought to be lived is articulated at once in the minds of members of that society and in the visible "symbols" set up by it, in its chief temples, govern-ment edifices, monuments, holidays, social structures, advertising motifs, and on innumerable more subtle levels. The subjective and the outer realm continually interplay: we accept within our minds the view of reality that constantly reaches our consciousness via the symbols—both religious and secular—operative in our society, and as members of the society we our-selves keep constructing the symbols. To say this is not to say that the symbols of a society are untrue; it is simply to note that this is how they work as a self-reinforcing system. When a society is highly cohesive the system operates in such a smooth and subtle manner that most people are hardly aware of how their beliefs and their social/symbolic environment make one another.

But introduce someone else—an intrusively different belief, a wholly new symbol of reality, people obviously living according to quite other values—and the sacred canopy, in another expression of Peter Berger,[3] is shattered. Something else has come in. It does not matter if it is large or small; the mere fact that the alien presence is *there* is enough to challenge—or threaten—all sorts of tacit assumptions.

That is why societies—including ones as pluralistic as American society—cannot ignore even tiny new religions that appear like islands right in the midst of their mainstream. Two kinds of response occur, one positive and one negative.

First, new religions may be seen as horizon expanding. They open up new possibilities for being human besides those of the conventional symbols. If the conventional set says that you best get in touch with ultimate reality by praying in church, these may say you can do it through meditation or chanting, too. If the conventional set says you best fulfill your social role by having an ordinary marriage and family and job, these may hold out the alternative of living off the earth in a commune. Even if one has no personal desire to follow any of these alternatives, and even if the alternative is extolled by no more than a dozen people out of a population of millions, the very fact that *they are there* irreversibly widens your horizons. You have to take their possibility into account; you can reject it, but you can't go back to thoughtless acceptance of the way things are as though nothing new had appeared down the street or on the TV screen.

For some, cracking open the charmed circle like this is exciting, for others it is threatening. The world is divided into people who instinctively feel the new and different is intriguing and quite likely better, and those who—especially in matters of religion and society—instinctively feel protective toward the way things are. Either way, though, they find new religious movements interesting and important for reasons that have less to do with size than the fact of their very existence, sticking pins in the social construction of reality, showing new ways to be human—and perhaps new ways for humans to get into mischief.

We must now look more closely at just what we mean by a new religious movement, or "cult" as they are sometimes called, which is different from the normative religion of the society and also is not based in an ethnic group. As we have already indicated, the term may embrace a wide range of groups—some new, some relatively old. They may also vary from closely-knit groups to very open societies, and the focus of their spiritual attention may run from philosophies out of ancient India to UFOs.

Indeed, it must be noted that our use of the word "religion" in regard to them should not be taken to indicate that all would consider themselves a religion. That is why this book is entitled *Religious and Spiritual Groups in Modern America*. Some groups rightly do not consider themselves religions in any conventional sense, for they do not conduct services of worship or teach particular religious practices, and persons may and do attend their lectures or classes while participating in church worship at other times as well. It is not unknown for yoga and meditation groups cited in this book, for example, to have Christian ministers, priests, and nuns among their attenders; they do not rival the churchly religions directly so much as fill a different niche in American spiritual ecology. (Other groups, of course, make demands of faith and practice much more often seen as incompatible with any other religious commitment on any level.) All are, however, "spiritual" in the sense that they teach about realities other than the purely material, and usually instruct one in some practice for getting in rapport with them.

TRUTH AND EMPATHY

The new religious movements may be important even to traditional faith. Dr. Krister Stendahl, Dean of the Harvard University Divinity School, once suggested that a new "world theology" may be in the making from the "shambles" of modern Christian theology. In contrast to the past tendency to ask what the traditional church or biblical teaching is, he says, "We come to a point where theologians have started to become much more bold, expressing 'straight' theology out of religious experience, rather than the historical approach. This will lead to where contemporary religious experience will be allowed once again to inform theology. Ultimately it will bring us to give much more serious attention to other religious experiences than Christianity alone." This does not mean, Dr. Stendahl explained, that distinctively Christian truth will be lost, but that religious truth will be sought wherever it may be found. "Truth cannot take adjectives. There cannot be a Methodist truth, or a Lutheran truth or a Catholic truth. There can be only—truth."[4]

If this is the case, where do we find these "other religious experiences"? It is not necessary to make Herman Hesse's paradigmatic *Journey to the East* by literally travelling to India or Japan. Nor need we content ourselves with the highly vicarious experience of reading.

We have, in America, a subculture which has long lived to taste these exotic spiritual experiences. Indeed, it has not satisfied itself just with reproducing more or less successfully export versions of the great non-Western faiths. It has also given birth to religious expressions otherwise not known that may also cast a light on some facet of nonadjectival truth.

Our quest in this book will be to investigate many of these religious movements. Sometimes it may be a tour no less strange than the exploration of another planet or a fairyland from out of the mists of childhood memory. But it is also a tour which requires all the discipline of social analysis one can bring to it. This is necessary to see not simply a reflection of one's own fantasy in a movement, but also what it is in itself—why it arose where and when it did, how it works, what sort of people are attracted to it. Only by recreating in this way the world of the movement can we really comprehend what it is in itself, and thus get outside of ourselves and into it for the sake of understanding.

Yet this task simultaneously requires sympathetic human empathy. We need that peculiar, almost indefinable quality which enables one individual to have a flash of insight into what it would *really* feel like to be someone else. We need to be able to make a jump from seeing a member of a "cult" as an intriguing human-sized object "out there" with certain bizarre beliefs and behavior, to saying, "He has the same feelings inside as I do—though he's looking at things with a different pair of spectacles, he could be me and I could be him. By learning about where he is, I'm not just expanding myself intellectually, I'm expanding my *humanness*—my ideas, my feelings, my life style, everything." If we cannot perceive in this way what total human experience, and so what human truth, lies inside a "cultic" experience, how can we contribute to the quest for nonadjectival truth? The question to ask is always, "How would it feel from within to be a part of this religious movement?"

What is a religious movement? To many, the term calls up the image of an unusual wild-eyed individual in the mountains or desert hearing the voice of some new god, and then returning to the city and shouting that it is the divine will that people wear only one shoe or build a temple of pure isinglass. Vast crowds become so possessed as to return the seer's fervor with mob enthusiasm and money.

To others, a religious movement may suggest activity within the institutional religious tradition: the effect of a popular evangelist, the splintering of denominations. On the other hand, there are those who speak of political causes like Fascism and Communism as "religious" in some very important sense.

In this book we will be looking at a number of groups which fall into a certain category. They may be called *new, not normatively Judaeo-Christian, religious movements in America.* The borderlines of any such definition are inevitably hazy. It may help to make a brief preliminary examination of the terms used.

New means groups which have arisen or taken root in America within the last 150 years and are extant today. This time span, going back to the early nineteenth century, may seem overly long. But it is necessary to include in our general purview the beginnings of Swedenborgianism—actually eighteenth century—Spiritualism, New Thought, and Theosophy. These movements have all had continuing interaction to the present day with the cultural milieu of the type of groups we are studying. All are still of some importance today. Groups which have arisen only in the last century and a half, of course, are very "new" in comparison with Judaism and Christianity, even though major American denominations and schools of both are no less recent.

Not normatively Judaeo-Christian means that the group's central symbols or teachings are not directly derived from mainstream interpretations of Jewish or Christian sources. They obviously have a different focus from the Bible, the creeds, and what is considered normal in the church or synagogue down the street. Some of the groups consider themselves Christian according to their own lights. They may claim, as Spiritualists do, that the Bible verifies their views. But here we are mainly concerned with the similarity or dissimilarity of the central teaching (and spiritual experience) which called a group into being to that of the synagogues and churches in the group's actual setting.

The purpose is not to cast doubt on any group's right to the use of Christian or any other term, but to set up categories for comparison. In the case of Spiritualism, for example, the central *raison d'être*, the practice of communication with the spirits of the departed through a medium and belief in the importance of this practice, is obviously at great variance with the Christianity and Judaism found elsewhere. In the same way, even the most Christian-oriented groups in the Theosophical and occult traditions, such as Anthroposophy and the Liberal Catholic Church, seem better understood as a part of an alternative to the ordinary Judaeo-Christian tradition than as a part of that tradition.

The principal test for determining whether a group is not normatively Judaeo-Christian will be the historical continuity of its central teaching and experience with the Judaeo-Christian religion of its actual American setting. Similarity in worship format, symbolism, or type of organization to other American religion will not, however, exclude a group from our study. There is much variation in these matters in groups with non-normative teaching. In some New Thought churches, like the Church of Religious Science, the structure of Sunday morning worship is barely distinguishable from that of any liberal Protestant church. But the teaching, coming down as it does to a "mind is all" philosophical idealism, is really not very dissimilar from that of the Maharishi Mahesh Yogi, the colorful Hindu guru whose involvement with the Beatles and other entertainment figures a few years ago led to considerable publicity for his movement. The Maharishi's cultus, with the offering of fruit and flowers to the teacher, the guru's tiger skin pallet, and secret initiation and silent meditation of adherents, is wildly different from the ambiance of Religious Science. Obviously, followers of Religious Science prefer, in their new teaching, to experience general symbols of continuity with the worship and organization of the churches of their forefathers. In fact, the victory of those with such a preference was an important milestone in the history of that denomination. The generally younger and more "alienated" adherents of the Maharishi's movement clearly want to express their profounder dissatisfaction with much of the whole Western religious tradition by rejoicing in an atmosphere of exoticism.

We thus determine whether a group is or is not normatively Judaeo-Christian by comparing its "reason for being" teaching with "ordinary usage" meanings of "Judaism and Christianity." We ask whether it expresses continuity or discontinuity with its cultural setting. This means asking such questions as, "Does it have a clear lineage in denominational history?" "If most churches emphasize salvationist doctrine and experience, does it emphasize something else?"

A *religion* means a group centrally concerned with "the means of ultimate transformation," which has simultaneous expression in three areas: *theoretical* or *verbal* (myth and doctrine); *practical* or *worship* (ritual, cultus, and other special behavior); and *sociological* (a structure of interpersonal action which enables a continuing group life).

The terms of this definition will be discussed later. It is a definition not so much concerned with the *kind* of teaching or practice of the group (whether about God or not, whether ritualistic or not) as with the *value* and *goal* of the teaching or practice. Does the idea seem to be to work toward an unqualified transformation of oneself and/or society and the cosmos into a final and perfect state in line with the nature of absolute reality? Does one experience in the teaching and practice of the group *means* to accomplish this change? Or is it thought of as just a moderate reform movement, or as interesting and entertaining ideas and activities?

A religion is not just a teaching, like the philosophy of Plato. It produces a corporate expression. In a religion persons are regularly in contact with each other to study, discuss, celebrate, and practice the teaching; these people would presumably not otherwise associate. Probably the group of persons brought together around the teaching—or more precisely, no doubt, around the teacher—come to have some sort of structured interaction. They develop patterns for calling meetings, making decisions, and determining whose words are most weighty.

A real religion—a "means of ultimate transformation"—always takes this kind of social expression. It always manifests a verbal, a worship, and a societal vehicle. It is never just an idea or an inchoate assembly. If it is genuinely concerned with the *ultimate*, it seems to require vehicles for expression in all these areas. Their presence or absence, then, is a good test (and one employed in this book) of whether a group is really a "religion" or not. One can quibble about what is or is not a religion. Some groups included here do not care to be called religions, associating that word with some other definition than the one we have employed. But it has been necessary to establish a yardstick and apply it impartially.

MEANS OF ULTIMATE TRANSFORMATION

In order to have a clear idea of what kind of general phenomena we are dealing with, it may be helpful to digress a moment to further discuss our understanding of the nature of religion. In this section we will also look at some dynamics of religious change relevant to understanding new movements today against their background in the nature of religion.

We have indicated that some political movements, like Fascism and Communism, have been spoken of as "religious," and that religion is defined as a "means of ultimate transformation." If this is the case, it is evident that no particular metaphysical idea, such as the existence of a heavenly god, is necessarily involved in the definition. We in the West tend to forget that there are vast numbers of persons in the world who observe practices involving temples, altars, priests, offerings, scriptures, meditation, and festivals which in all respects look like religion, yet do not make a personal God central. We speak of most Buddhists, many Hindus, and many followers of the Chinese religions. A definition of religion which said it necessarily had to do with God or gods would seem very odd in these cultures. But religion does have to do with something which wants to come out simultaneously in the three forms of expression we mentioned. It has to do with something which impels people to relate certain stories, perform certain stylized actions which would seem quite odd in any other context, and organize themselves into certain groups. This approach on the basis of what looks like religion, judged by similarity to universal patterns, after observing simply the "forms that appear," is called the phenomenological.

Some groups object to being called religions because to them the word implies that they accept their beliefs on authoritarian grounds, rather than out of rational philosophical reflection. Yet this too is a matter which varies greatly in different cultures, despite the consistent appearance of what looks like religion. Our definition is concerned not so much with the basis of the authority of the teaching as with what is done with it—how it is symbolized, how it is acted out, how ultimate its position is, what type of group forms around it.

It seems that religion first of all implies a distinction between two kinds of activity: the ordinary, which we do because we must and look forward to its end; and the special, in which we are joyous and fulfilled in a condition which seems complete and sufficient in itself. An anthropologist once asked a South American tribe what they did. They said, "We work and we dance. But we work in order that we can dance." Undoubtedly dancing exhausts as much energy as working. But it *feels* different. Dancing is not drudgery; it creates a glorious, ecstatic, timeless mood.

Mircea Eliade and others have spoken of these two poles of activity as the sacred and the profane.[5] The sacred indicates place, time, or state of consciousness in which a person feels as totally real and sufficient as he conceives the gods were at the beginning. In this condition one wishes to dwell, but it is hard to bear, and one cannot stay in it all the time. There is also a frightening dimension to the sacred; it may reach out to slay those who presume too much upon it. And one must save time to do the work of the world. The profane is the opposite of the sacred. It is the common everyday world with its dull, continuing sense of enervating meaninglessness.

Religion involves the experience of space, time, or aspects of self as polarized by the sacred and profane. This makes the world of religious man nonhomogeneous. Religion is the process by which one tries to express in symbol, story, and experience this polarized quality of his life and to make as much of it as possible sacred. One builds temples as sacred centers, celebrates festivals which recapitulate sacred time, and endeavors to achieve ultimate identification with the sacred by internalizing it within himself through mysticism.

Frederick Streng proposed "means of ultimate transformation" as a definition of religion which adds an element of dynamism to the sacred and the profane.[6] It is also reminiscent of Paul Tillich's "ultimate concern," of reflection on the deepest questions of meaning one can ask, as the ground of religion. But religion is not just individual musing, or even passionate existential commitment. It is intended to do something.

The Buddhists speak of their faith as *yana,* a ferryboat. It is intended to carry believers from here to the farther shore where the Buddha himself went. That "shore" is not, of course, a geographical place, but a totally transformed state of consciousness as infinite and unconditioned as our present consciousness is limited by our being able to think of only one thing at a time. The journey on the *yana* is thus a radical reversal, an ultimate transformation of man's present state. The "ferry" by this definition is a religion.

The means Buddhism uses are a set of stories the believer hears (about the Buddha and his saints—verbal expression); a set of actions he performs (meditation practices, the cultus of the Buddhist temple—worship expression); and a set of persons he groups himself with (a Buddhist order or denomination—social expression). By these means he builds around himself a sacred world, a world in which everything is conducive to the journey toward ultimate transformation, and operates like a foretaste of it. He puts himself into the middle of that sacred world.

Religion is a set of symbols, words, acts, and social groupings which have this thrust toward *ultimate*, unconditioned transformation of self and/ or world. It does not aim for mere reforms, though these may be part of the path, but for a total, exhaustive change which leaves not the slightest margin for more. Religion is the means of movement between the two poles, the conditioned and profane and the ultimate or sacred or unconditioned. It is the individual's attempt to create in and around oneself the sacred.

New religious movements often originate in periods of great social stress, frustration, or transition. They employ symbols from the prevailing culture, but the symbols are radically rearranged. Symbols—the word is used very broadly to include language, art forms, subjective experience with special meaning, and so forth—are scrambled into new constellations. Perhaps formerly nonreligious symbols—political, technological—will be discovered to have religious meaning, while formerly religious symbols will have lost it. Symbols imported from elsewhere will be discovered to have meaning within the culture. In any case, the use of symbols in the new movement will not be the established usage, since the intention is to express alienation. But the symbols do not spell out the social situation, or the alienation, in a one-to-one way; as soon as they are "released" they acquire a life of their own.

Usually a new movement has a single individual who actually or symbolically sums up its meaning—like H. P. Blavatsky of Theosophy,[7] Bapak of Subud, or UFO contactees. The founder expresses the rearranged symbol system and "style" in his or her personality. Like the symbols, the founder is not one utterly different from his culture, as though descended from an angelic sphere. He or she is a man or woman who lives in the context of the time and place, and may well wear more conventional clothes than traditional religious leaders. (The latter also have to serve as symbols of continuity with earlier cultural eras.) Religious founders and leaders are those who call into conscious expression the deepest latent spiritual intuitions of which their hearers are potentially conscious and can understand. This evocation is possible only because a commonality of experience exists between the founder and the audience. This common experience seems to take into account areas of life as it is now actually lived which the traditional religion leaves out. The way is open for a word which will crystallize a new pattern, a new religious gestalt.

To invent totally new religious notions, to jam new pieces into the puzzle, is usually precisely what is not very successful. The founder is one who can reintegrate a cosmos which is shattered, which already holds too many extra notional and experiential fragments. His genius is to see the possibility of a new pattern which will give integrated value to everything which now has independent value—not merely by rearrangement but by opening a window which casts new, and now harmonious, patterns. A new principle, a different focus, is drawn, but in a way which leads one to say, "This was really true all the time, but we did not realize it." An example is Mary Baker Eddy, who devised in Christian Science a tightly integrated system from pieces of transcendentalism, the Calvinist struggle of light against darkness, and the prestige of science. She had that sort of impact on some of her contemporaries. Christian Science provided, as do all religions, a new means of ultimate transformation.

Saying that once the new symbol is released it acquires a life of its own is not saying that the structural form it takes is entirely unpredictable. There are really only a few basic religious symbols which appear over and over again in many forms. In the center will be the main means of ultimate transformation, hedged about with appropriate signs of special numinosity. One may find an *axis mundi* (central pivot of the world), like the cross in Christianity, or the bodhi tree under which the Buddha found enlightenment in Buddhism. Behind it, as in these cases, may be the even more powerful symbol of the individual who has attained ultimate transformation and bears it to others. Further common symbols are waters of rebirth, an initiating female, the wise old man, the moon as token of regeneration.

The religious group provides foretastes of ultimate transformation as a part of the means to attain it. The group will demarcate sacred time and space as occasions and places where the winds of the ultimate are felt most strongly—in all likelihood, places and times of worship or gathering. In some cases these experiences may be highly individualized. The means of transformation—the *axis mundi*, the sacred space and time—is within the individual's heart. So it is with groups stressing mental transformation, like Christian Science, or those centered on yoga or meditation. But even so, such symbols as it has, or even the very absence of symbol considered as a symbol, is a corporate support of the internalization process.

The new symbol system—the new cosmic constellation of meaning orbiting around the founder and the group—will probably be both external and internal, though the "outer" or "inner" may be stressed. Neither is absolute. One may be given an actual sacred center (mountain or temple), or a metaphorical-internalized one, or both. The symbol system begins by expressing the individual discovery of alienation and goes on to articulate its own cosmos centered on the new means of ultimate transformation. It then winnows out the absolute nature of reality implied by those means.

SHAMANISM

One of the most important religious phenomena is *shamanism*. It is essential to give this phenomenon particular attention when examining aspects of religion relevant to understanding the dynamic of new religious movements. In certain important ways the genius of the primitive shaman is reborn in those individuals, called magi, adepts, masters, mediums, or magicians, or by no such special name, who have been the centers of new religious movements. The example of an illumined and empowered magus offering individual initiation into his mysteries is no new thing, but has roots far back toward the dawn of religion. In many archaic societies, alongside the regular means of initiation of young boys and girls into the sacral matters of adulthood, a few individuals may receive special admission into unusual practices connected with the sacred. They will be those who become shamans.

G. K. Nelson has suggested that, of all religious institutions, the one which most resembles modern spiritualism is primitive shamanism.[8] It has striking parallels not only to spiritualism, but also to all the groups under consideration in this study. The new religions' phenomena could almost be called a modern resurgence of shamanism. It is important, therefore, that we examine some of its characteristics.

Many kinds of religious specialists inhabit the world of primitive society—priests who offer sacrifices, heads of households who perform the family cultus, old men who supervise initiations, sorcerers who cast spells for luck or love, witches who curse, medicine men who heal the sick by natural or supernatural means, sacred kings, and so forth. In the midst of them may be a person who, having probably passed through a severe emotional ordeal, now communicates with gods or spirits by ecstatic means—he is called a shaman.

Mircea Eliade writes, "The shaman begins his new, true life by a 'separation'—that is . . . by a spiritual crisis that is not lacking in tragic greatness and in beauty."[9] The shaman typically passes through an initiatory psychopathy. It will probably begin with a "call" from a god or spirit, perhaps the primordial master shaman, communicated by a seizure, an involuntary trance, dreams, or visions. Thereafter the novice is disturbed by these things until he controls them by acquiring the techniques of shamanizing. This means, as Eliade points out, that the process is not a happenstance matter but follows a traditional model in the culture.

The cultural role of the shaman is not to be despised. Sick he may be by ordinary standards, but he has conquered his sickness and made it a vehicle for the exploration of realms far beyond the everyday perimeters of the human spirit. In him lie the seeds of later culture, seeds of a meaning to human life beyond the struggle to meet basic needs. Indeed, general culture has as yet only begun to claim some of the spiritual terrain marked out by shamanism. Dante in his *Divine Comedy* recapitulated the shaman's journey and made it part of the Western literary heritage. But the *angakok*, or enlightenment-giving spirit, obtained by Eskimo shamans during initiation, suggests an ecstatic opening which is harder for our uninitiated concepts and expectations to deal with.

The *angakok* consists "of a mysterious light which the shaman suddenly feels in his body, inside his head, within the brain, an inexplicable searchlight, a luminous fire, which enables him to see in the dark, both literally and metaphorically speaking, for he can now, even with closed eyes, see through darkness and perceive things and coming events which are hidden from others: thus they look into the future and into the secrets of others."

The candidate obtains this mystical light after long hours of waiting sitting on a bench in his hut and invoking the spirits. When he experiences it for the first time "it is as if the house in which he is suddenly rises; he sees far ahead of him, through mountains, exactly as if the earth were one great plain, and his eyes could reach to the end of the earth. Nothing is hidden from him any longer; not only can he see things far, far away, but he can also discover souls, stolen souls, which are either kept concealed in far, strange lands, or have been taken up or down to the Land of the Dead."[10]

Certainly this is an experience of ultimate transformation. Perhaps this kind of experience of ecstatic vision and power is one origin and ground of all religion, the gods themselves patterned on the model of great shamans.

But contemporary non-normative religious movements are not identical with primitive shamanism. The most obvious difference is that the primitive shaman is part of an integral culture whereas the modern new religionist is expressing a sense of alienation. Sometimes, like the primitive psychopath who is potentially a shaman, he may be going through a half-ritualized process of self-realization with a number of visible precedents. But the modern new religionist also has much in common with those founders of historical religions whose alienation was based not only on existential factors but also on historical experience—a sense that time moves irreversibly and that therefore some symbols are more in tune with the present than the conventional symbols of ultimate transformation. For this reason, unlike the shaman, he or she has no role sanctioned by the established world view. That person is a fragment of a pluralistic culture, not a major prop of an integrated one.

Nonetheless, some of the new movements like to compare themselves to shamanism in one way or another. Perhaps they are looking for roots in those ages when humans were not aware of history, because that is the kind of consciousness they would like to have today—and believe is still valid. Theosophists think of themselves as perpetuating the teachings of "ancient mystery schools" which are said to be preserved in many traditional cultures, such as the Maori, Hawaiian, African, and Mayan. In all of these, the bearers of lore would be shamanistic types of individuals. Indeed, Theosophists talk of dream initiations, expanded states of consciousness, and other mainstays of shamanism. Spiritualists like to call their faith the "oldest religion in the world," which expresses certainly a desire to identify with the mediumistic functions of the shaman. The affinity the spiritual counter-culture feels with Native Americans will be explored in this book. But we do not speak of a new primitive shamanism today, but of a rediscovery of certain motifs of shamanism as effective counters to the values of a technological, rationalistic culture in historical time. The charismatic leaders of the new movements in question have in common certain elements of the shamanistic typology. The elements are, of course, detached from archaic integration, and serve as major constituents of a new constellation with a life of its own.

Whether spiritualist medium, Theosophist, UFO contactee, witch, or orientalizer, on one level of language or another, an experience of initiation into a new ecstatic consciousness is found against the background of a nonhistorical universe of cosmic and spiritual law, through the mediation of personal supernormal helpers. The new shaman's role is to serve as charismatic center of a cultus, around which a new symbolic cosmos, and ultimately transformed world (through processes really mystical or apocalyptic rather than historical), will form itself.

General Characteristics

Shamanism, then, with its complex relation to the traditional and the new, the role of the charismatic individual and the institutions of society, has much in common with the internal life of modern American new religious movements. Indeed, often the new movements share with shamanism not only the general typology of the charismatic seer, but to a remarkable extent details of the pattern, including the spirit band, learned or spontaneous ritual, antihistoricism, bringing wisdom from faraway geographical or supernatural places, healing, and above all, techniques of ecstasy.

Here are some general characteristics of modern American new religious movements.[11] Different examples will, of course, stress or interpret certain characteristics in different ways.

1. A founder who has had, or at least seems to know the secret of, nontemporal ecstatic experience. (It is often not really so much having ecstatic experiences, as being fascinated with their techniques, literature, and meaning, which activates groups and even their founders. It is that which seems faraway which people are driven to quest for.) The founder may be a personality of the magus type, to be discussed later.

2. An interpretation of the experience as possession or marvellous travel. This familiar motif of archaic shamanism is strikingly renewed in Spiritualism and UFO cults and less obviously perhaps in the symbolism of interior mystical exploration and lore from faraway places.

3. A band of supernormal helpers. Again, in Spiritualism, there is a literal re-creation of this shamanistic motif, and scarcely less so in the Theosophical "Masters" and the UFO "space brothers," in the spirits evoked by witchcraft and the gods and goddesses of Neo-Paganism. If the psychological meaning of this phenomena is the subduing of uncontrolled fragments of the psyche, it indicates the emphasis on the understanding and control of subjectivity typical of the whole movement. Its equivalent can be found in other groups which prefer not to use such mythological modes of expression.

4. A desire to be "modern" and to use scientific language. As we have indicated, there is something postscientific about the mood as well, a tendency to disdain as materialistic science and technology for their own sake. But there is an instinctive realization that something in science—especially the broad confident assertion of unchanging natural law more typical of Victorian than of contemporary science—is congenial with the experience of timeless absolute reality and can be used to strengthen it intellectually.

However, when scientists attack the new religionist's use of scientific language, he does not hesitate to respond in kind; the alliance is quite unstable and one-sided. Like the scientist, the religionist also has felt a bitter alienation from much of the West's religious past, and hence much is made of modernity and the hope of a better future.

5. A reaction against orthodoxy. Hard language is often used in opposition to the established churches, and also, when occasion suits, against scientific orthodoxy.

6. Eclecticism and syncretism.

7. A monistic and impersonal ontology. It is impressive how common this metaphysical characteristic is. Groups may populate the "intermediate" cosmos between humanity and the absolute with any number of spirit guides, masters, space brothers, and other quasideities, but the absolute itself is not the personal Judaeo-Christian God, but some more abstract entity, usually capitalized, like "Infinite Intelligence," "Principle," etc.

8. Optimism, success orientation, and a tendency to evolutionary views. This is no doubt a part of the "scientific" and "modern" mentality, reinforced by a feeling that orthodoxy is too much devoted to other-worldly benefits (although the orthodox are also inconsistently accused of praying in church for selfish ends), and that a faith based on present experience ought to be able to produce benefits in this world, here and now, and a better world to come. This is a major argument of groups as sociologically divergent as Religious Science and Nichiren Shoshu. They say that other groups promise pie in the sky after you die; only we can deliver the goods here and now and tomorrow on this earth. Sectarian groups may tend toward apocalypticism; other groups toward a slower and more evolutionary change for the better under the influence of better thinking, though in times of crisis their language too may move in an apocalyptic direction. The groups are usually nonpolitical, and do not do much to advance the course of social evolution by direct political or reformist action. They may use utopian rhetoric, but because they require only tolerance, they function well in a capitalist society because today capitalism usually implies religious pluralism.

9. Emphasis on healing. This is another characteristic of shamanism picked up by modern alternative religions. No doubt it grows out of the sense of total power and vision engendered by the ecstatic experience. Most provide some means for charismatic power to be applied to the healing of mind and body.

10. Use in many cases of magic techniques. Nelson defines magic as the use of nonempirical means for empirical ends, in contrast to pure religion's nonempirical means and ends and science's empirical means and ends.[12] The final purpose may be ultimate transformation, but there is generally a spin-off which can be applied to secondary, finite transformations. Ceremonial magic, another shamanistic motif, is becoming popular. Of course ceremonial magic has also an ultimate transformation usage as a means to mental concentration to attain an altered state of consciousness.

11. A simple but definite process of entry and initiation. The importance of this is obvious. Whatever they say, most groups want a large membership. They also recognize the clear psychological importance in a

group based on a sense of alienation of making membership seem a privilege not lightly granted, involving a definite act of separation, commitment, and study.

12. In some cases, the establishment of a sacred center. Perhaps because of the strong reaction toward universalism, this has been less a feature of new American groups than those elsewhere, but some groups do speak of places of special spiritual power, and afford imposing temples which are like Mecca to scattered members.

13. Emphasis on psychic powers. This is another shamanistic trait which is no doubt taken as evidence of access to the places of ecstatic transformation, although not all psychics are ecstatics.

14. Tendency to attract isolated individuals rather than family groups. This is an obvious but important characteristic of any new religion. Some older groups like Theosophy and Spiritualism maintain this characteristic even after virtually a century of continued existence.

15. Increasing emphasis on participation by all members in the ecstatic experience through group chanting, meditation, and so forth. The ecstasy is not just a display trance by the central figure, but a corporate act.

Taken together, these characteristics suggest a special kind of spiritual group having a particular relationship to its surrounding society, and held together within by distinct kinds of leadership and experience. They imply, in fact, the sort of group often labelled a "cult," a word which immediately calls up certain images and reactions. We must now, therefore, examine more closely that portentous term and, in the process, learn a great deal more about the kind of groups which are the subject of our study.

NOTES

[1]See, for example, Saul V. Levine, "Radical Departures," *Psychology Today* 18, 8 (August 1984), pp. 20–27.

[2]Peter L. Berger and Thomas Luckmann, *The Social Construction of Reality* (Garden City, NY: Doubleday and Co., 1966).

[3]Peter L. Berger, *The Sacred Canopy* (Garden City, NY: Doubleday and Co., 1967).

[4]"World Theology Move Seen by Harvard Dean," *Los Angeles Times*, Sunday, May 31, 1970. Copyright 1970, *Los Angeles Times*. Reprinted by permission.

[5]Mircea Eliade, *The Sacred and the Profane* (New York: Harper & Row, Publishers, 1961).

[6]Frederick J. Streng, *Understanding Religious Man* (Belmont, CA: Dickenson Publishing Company, Inc., 1969), pp. 4–5.

[7]The puzzling and yet human quality of the founder is suggested by these words about the Theosophist Helena Blavatsky by her close associate Colonel Olcott:
"Just because I did know her so much better than most others, she was a greater mystery to me than to them. It was easy for those who only saw her speaking oracles, writing profound aphorisms, or giving clue after clue to the hidden wisdom in the ancient Scriptures, to regard her as an earth-visiting *angelos* and to worship at her feet; she was no mystery to them. But to me, her most intimate colleague, who had to deal with the vulgar details of her common daily life, and see her in all her aspects, she was from the first and continued to the end an insoluble riddle. How much of her waking life was that of responsible personality, how much that of a body worked by an overshadowing entity? I do not know." Henry Steel Olcott, *Old Diary Leaves, Second Series, 1878–83* (Madras: Theosophical Publishing Co., 1900, 1954), p. viii.

[8]Geoffrey K. Nelson, *Spiritualism and Society* (New York: Schocken Books, 1969), p. 44.

[9]Mircea Eliade, *Shamanism, Archaic Techniques of Ecstasy,* trans. Willard R. Trask, Bollingen Series LXXVI (Copyright © by Princeton University Press, 1964), p. 13.

[10]Eliade, *Shamanism,* pp. 60–61. Based on and quoted from Knud Rasmussen, *Intellectual Culture of the Iglulik Eskimos* (Copenhagen: Report of the Fifth Thule Expedition, 1930). Compare the following statement by an individual who had reached the initiatory state of Clear in Scientology:

I am CLEAR! It's really out-of-sight! Distances have no significance to me anymore. I can just see as far as I can see and that's quite a distance. When it happened, going Clear that is, I looked at the stars and the moon. They were within reach of my arm. And oh my gosh, I just realized—it's forever!! (Church of Scientology of California, *Clear News,* May 11, 1970.)

[11]Some items in this list are suggested by the characteristics of the new religions of Japan given in Harry Thomsen, *The New Religions of Japan* (Rutland and Tokyo: Charles E. Tuttle, 1963), pp. 20–29.

[12]Nelson, *Spiritualism and Society,* p. 132.

I _____

THE SEVERAL MEANINGS OF "CULT"

A PROBLEMATIC TERM

The common use of the word "cult" for new religious movements within our own society has entailed certain problems of understanding. This is, first, because the term is capable of several different definitions, and, second, because (like comparable racist labels) it automatically evokes pre-packaged stereotypes and emotional reactions, both usually negative. (No one calls his or her own religious group a cult; this is inevitably a name given a group by an outsider.) Our purpose in this discussion will be to attempt to sort out these meanings and, in the process, endeavor to advance authentic comprehension of the movements behind the word.

First let us look at the dictionary. All standard lexicons agree that the word has several different meanings which, though centering around the original significance of *cultus*, worship, its Latin source, have varying emotional and value-laden overtones that could lead to trouble if misapplied. First, it simply means worship in a more or less neutral sense, generally with reference to the worship of a particular object within a larger system,

Chapter I, "The Several Meanings of 'Cult,'" originally appeared as an article of that title by Robert S. Ellwood in *Thought*, Vol. LXI, No. 241 (June 1986), pp. 212–24. It is here reproduced, with minor editorial changes, by kind permission of *Thought*, a publication of Fordham University Press. Copyright © 1986 by Fordham University.

as in speaking of "the cult of Osiris" or "the cult of the Sacred Heart." Second, the same use can be extended to secular objects, as in "the cult of Napoleon." Third, the same meaning can be extended further to imply an excessive or unbalanced devotion or "craze" for anything, as in "the cult of disco dancing" or "the cult of success."

Then relative to religious groups, the word can mean (1) any set of people bound together by devotion to a particular sacred person, object, or ideology, and (2) any religion considered false, unorthodox, or spurious. Not seldom one of these two religious group meanings is linked up with one of the word's broader meanings, to suggest that a religion regarded as spurious is also both faddish and fanatical; or, if a more positive connotation is desired, that what some consider a cult is simply indulging a preference for a certain *cultus* or worship no less legitimate than any other.

Turning to more extensive writing by students and sociologists of religion on the sort of groups commonly designated cults, we find the same bifurcation. Some have proposed a neutral meaning for the term focused around certain sociological and psychological characteristics. Others attach to the term features they obviously expect the reader to regard negatively. We are unaware of any attempt to give the word "cult" positive significance in connection with modern religious movements, unless it be the first edition of the present book, *Religious and Spiritual Groups in Modern America*, which described the groups under consideration as cults in a sociological sense, yet displayed, we believe, a degree of empathy with their spiritual quest that went beyond mere academic open-mindedness.[1] (We would today look more critically at a few of the groups in this book, and, as will be seen, now find it difficult to use the word "cult" in any scholarly sense.)

On the neutral sociological side, J. Milton Yinger, in *Religion, Society, and the Individual,* describes the cult as a withdrawal group whose traits include small size, a search for "mystical experience," lack of strong organizational structure, charismatic leadership, a sharp break in *religious* (not social) terms with society, and concern almost wholly with the problems of individuals rather than the social order. It is, he says, a "religious mutant."[2] In this book, written before the spiritual explosion of the 1960s and the style of "cults" which devolved from it, it is clear that the author has largely in mind groups of the spiritualist, theosophical, or "New Thought" type. He unquestionably gives an accurate picture of some such entities, for there has been no lack of fairly ephemeral Spiritualist churches centered around a particular medium, or "metaphysical" societies dependent upon a single illuminator. They drew people, often of middle or upper class, who did not care to break with society as a whole, but whose inward sickness of soul led them to unconventional doctrines and a thirst for mystical experience. In Yinger's categorization the cult contrasts with the other form of withdrawal group, the sect, which represents an intense, separatist version of the dominant religion in the society. In America, predominantly Christian, examples would be the Amish or Jehovah's Witnesses. It is typically strict, legalistic in morals, close-knit, antagonistic to society, and seeking individual perfection. In the same vein, Werner Stark, in *The Sociology of Religion,* goes so far as to see in the cult "the answer to some individual woe" which does not share such characteristics of the sect as "recruitment from the lower classes and revolutionary animus," but offers a more individualized spiritual tonic appropriate to those better placed so far as the privileges of this world are concerned.[3]

G. K. Nelson, in *Spiritualism and Society*, has criticized Yinger's use of cult, pointing out that some Spiritualist institutions, for example, have survived for many decades, and that even if individual Spiritualist churches come and go, the movement as a whole has found ways of replenishing itself.[4] Indeed, one could point out that groups like the Theosophical Society or the Vedanta Societies, though often thought of in connection with the role Yinger and Stark assign the cult, have possessed fairly substantial institutional structures since the latter part of the nineteenth century. Furthermore, most sociological definitions give inadequate attention to the intellectual and experimental continuities in cults over generations. Most partake of a monistic and mentalist worldview which, though lately infused with Eastern correlates, can be traced back through Transcendentalism to Neoplatonism, and which has long served as an alternative to orthodox Judaism and Christianity in Europe and the Americas. This common basic worldview has more than theoretical significance; it helps to explain what many field observers have noted, a "floating" cult population which tends to go from one such group to another,[5] and it also helps explain the persistent appearance of such groups over centuries even as specific entities come and go.

However, while it is easy to criticize definitions like those of Yinger and Stark, particularly in light of the 1960s groups and their development, the positive aid they give must be noted. It is true that a high proportion of the young people who entered groups like the Hare Krishnas and the Unification Church, like the sixties "counter-culture" generally, were of middle- and upper-class background—a fact which had not a little to do with the immense controversy they engendered. It is true that they centered around charismatic leaders, offered above all a subjective "high," were relatively small in size, and though some advertised vague idealistic prescriptions for society as a whole were no doubt entered essentially because of personal problems or needs. What those definitions missed was that, at least for the sixties-and-after crowd, the personal problem frequently embraced a need for a tight social structure. Far from possessing a lack of strong organizational structure, these groups, as tightly-knit as any communalistic withdrawal sect, flaunted it to excess in the eyes of critics. Yinger saw trouble with succession of leadership as a further trait of the cult; while some of the newer highly organized cults have had a rocky road in this respect, a group like the Hare Krishnas has managed now to establish a second generation of leadership. Yinger has a category which he calls the "established sect," which includes groups like the Quakers which, while possessing sectarian characteristics, persevere generation after generation. As we have seen, this has really been the case with some "cults" since the last century; now, with some other examples like the Hare Krishnas and probably the Unification Church before us, perhaps (given his typologies) an "established cult" type should also be recognized.

Other definitions of cult—old and new—have placed heavier stress on such portions of the dictionary definitions as zealotry or focus on a particular person or idea. The social psychologist Hadley Cantril called it "a deviant organized action, generally rather restricted and temporary, in which the individual zealously devotes himself to some leader or ideal."[6] E. L. Quarantelli and Dennis Wenger made it "a diffuse group exhibiting inward innovative behavior that both differentiates and makes for conformity among group members and is supported by religious belief, or an ideology."[7] Andrew J. Pavlos moved toward what may be called a dynamic definition, emphasizing social dynamics within the group and between it and outside society, in pointing to three characteristics of the cult: (1) a leader who formulates group dogmas and isolates members from others who would support their former beliefs; (2) members who become dependent on the group for meeting their needs; and (3) the group identified by the community as deviant.[8] These definitions clearly put the finger on some features of modern cults to which critics and others have alluded: isolation from the larger community and particularly from data which might be disconfirmative; conformity within the group; dependence on a powerful leader; and tension between the cult and the community which is, in fact, a significant shaper of both its experience and any outside perception of it. At the same time, these definitions are idealizing insofar as any of these criteria are only imperfectly met in reality. The fact that nearly all joiners of cults later leave them voluntarily, some 75 percent within a year, indicates that any attempt on their part to establish conformity and exclude outside information meets with very limited success.[9]

Other commentators have given special heed to the heterodoxy part of the standard definitions. J. Gordon Melton and Robert L. Moore, in *The Cult Experience,* speak of a cult as "a religious group that presents a distinctly alternative pattern for doing religion and adhering to a faith perspective other than that dominant in the culture.[10] This statement has the advantage of making clear that the key variable in determining what is labelled—inevitably by outsiders—a cult is deviance from what is conventional in that society in "doing religion," a phrase which unquestionably refers not only to doctrine, but also to the practices and sociology of the group. Thus, standard Christian churches could be, and have been, looked upon in much the way "dangerous cults" are in our society in a firmly Muslim or Buddhist land.

This definition in itself, however, is incomplete insofar as it does not present the internal characteristics which have usually been associated with the word by sociologists and others. Many of these seem virtually imperative for a group in the position of adhering to a distinctly alternative religious pattern than that of its environing society, especially when the group does not have the external institutional support of, say, a mission church in India or a Vedanta Society connected to the Ramakrishna Mission in America. An emphasis on internal conformity, high level of commitment, strong authoritative and charismatic leadership, ability to induce powerful subjective experience and to solve personal problems, and legitimating linkage with an alternative occult or exotic tradition, are all likely to be necessary for such a group to counter the natural pull of the dominant tradition. For the alternative group to sustain itself, its authority and felt rewards must be potent enough to resist the pressure of family, community, and cultural ties, together with the instinctive desire most people feel for social approval. Usually this requirement entails that its leader be possessed of both appropriate credentials and highly sensed charisma, that it is effective in producing inner experiences the adherent believes are spiritually authentic and beneficial, and that it creates a closely-bonded surrogate family, community, and even culture.

Both the heterodoxy and the internal characteristics criteria are generally stated by writers on cults whose stance toward them is frankly negative. Ronald Enroth, in *The Lure of the Cults,* speaks of a cult as "a deviation from orthodoxy" and, in the eyes of this conservative Christian sociologist, that is the beginning of the other disturbing features he finds in them.[11] Another conservative Christian writer, William J. Petersen, in *Those Curious New Cults in the 80s,* says, "We think of a cult as a deviation from orthodox religion" (whether that religion is Christianity, Islam, Buddhism, or whatever) on questions central to the religion.[12] Like Melton and Moore, he therefore makes relation to the dominant religion an essential criterion. (But equating the dominant with the orthodox or authentic version of the religion is something which, at least in theory, evangelical theologians would not necessarily do.) He then proceeds to cite certain characteristics of cults which, though clearly tendentious and related to his critical position, in their own way take account of some internal features we have noted. The cult, he says, (1) has a recent founder or prophet; (2) has an authority beside the Bible; (3) is authoritarian, encouraging dependency on the part of members; (4) is separatist and secretive; (5) frequently employs a degree of deception; and (6) seems loving yet employs fear. While critics of "anticult" rhetoric have pointed out that such tactics are not unknown, in effect if not in principle, among churches and preachers of more orthodox persuasion, one does get a picture of a group marked by the sort of drives toward internal conformity and exaltation of the leader's charisma we have suggested was necessary for a deviant body. Carroll Stoner and Jo Anne Parke, in *All God's Children,* a book which though not informed by a conservative Christian animus ends up with about the same negative image of cults as those in that genre, list as among the characteristics of the cult a living leader who is the sole judge of members and has absolute authority over their lives, an exclusive social system which separates members from the outside world, and unwholesome psychological practices which induce ego-destruction and thought-control.[13]

A DEFINITION OF "CULT"

We must now proceed to the task of evolving our own definition of cult, working from current usage but attempting to resolve remaining ambiguities. We must observe at the outset that there is no "right" or "wrong" definition *per se* for a word of this sort; what we must consider is the greater or less heuristic value of definitions. That is, we must reflect on what definition (a) is most useful in pointing to a significant set of phenomena, and (b) best stimulates interest in it and indicates important areas of future study in the characteristics it isolates as salient and crucial to the definition. What way of talking about cult makes visible and clearly delimited a distinct order of religious groups, separating them from the church, the denomination, the monastery, and the rest? If, in fact, we are approaching the task phenomenologically, we seek only to give a name to what has already appeared and, so to speak, defined itself by exhibiting special features or constellations of features. The great temptation of definition, of course, is to define into existence something which is in reality much less unique as a form, in this case, of religious life than the label would suggest. This temptation has not always been resisted in the case of cults, and indeed is so intimately intertwined with the popular connotations the word has acquired as, in our view, to make that word ultimately undesirable. Cult has too often served to overisolate groups on *a priori* theological or social grounds, and then endow them with a wide range of characteristics associated in the user's mind with cults. Nonetheless, we shall proceed to use the term cult in connection with our attempt at a phenomenological definition, and then examine the question of alternative terms.

For what we need is a definition of cult which is legitimate in that it makes contact with scholarly and ordinary usage of the word, is useful in that it helps distinguish and define an important and coherent range of phenomena, and is value-neutral, usable by both empathizers with and critics of the subject, and so helps assure that they are talking about the same thing.

Not every group which falls broadly within the net of our definition will necessarily have all the characteristics of a cult we will cite; some may be missing one or another, or have other important features not cited in the general definition. Ninian Smart has spoken of "family resemblances" in the elements of religions.[14] There need not be one single feature which binds together all religious traditions within a larger set, such as the various strands of Hinduism or Protestantism. Within them one element may be linked to an element in the next group, and that to another, and common themes, like blue eyes in a family, may be reflected all up and down the line, though a family member here and there may have brown eyes but share the family nose instead. So it is with cults, or any other broad sociological category in religious life. Our definition, then, is not limited to a single variable, but embraces groups which display several, though not necessarily all, of the following characteristics.

(1) The group presents a distinct alternative to dominant patterns within the society in fundamental areas of religious life.
   (A) By definition, therefore, it is relatively small, since something else is postulated as predominant over against it.
   (B) It will be distinctly different from the dominant religious tradition in one or more of the major forms of religious expression. These forms of expression have been defined by the sociologist of religion Joachim

Wach as the theoretical, the practical, and the sociological.[15] For the present purposes we will work with this set.

(a)   The theoretical form of expression embraces fundamentally what is said: doctrine, normative "myths" or narratives which explicate the faith's worldview, and other verbal articulations of what it is about. It includes statements about the nature of Ultimate Reality or God, the origin of the cosmos and humankind, why we seem separated from Transcendence and how to get back in union with it, and religiously significant history. If the distinct difference from the predominant religion were in the area of theoretical expression, in a generally Christian society like the American we might expect to find an impersonal and monistic Ultimate Reality rather than a highly personal theistic God, separation from it due to ignorance or karma rather than Adamic sin, and other spiritual figures sharing the mediatorial role with Jesus Christ. Such an intellectual outlook is, in fact, typical of groups commonly considered cults. (We must, however, remember the family resemblance matter here: Krishna Consciousness, for example, takes karma seriously and in effect makes Krishna in his earthly avatar role the saviour, but insists at the same time he is a highly personal supreme God.)

(b)   The practical form of religious expression embraces practices, what is done: worship, rites, private prayer and meditation, pilgrimage. Here one may or may not observe distinct variation from the spiritual environment. Some older groups, like Vedanta, Theosophy, the Self-Realization Fellowship, and "New Thought" churches, emulate liberal Protestantism in their main public services insofar as they are focused on a sermon/lecture, perhaps augmented by music and scripture reading. While they may also inculcate "different" personal spiritual techniques of yoga or meditation, so far as Sunday morning or afternoon is concerned, it is as though it were realized that a novel doctrine is more likely to be received in a familiar package, that it is important to maintain symbols of continuity to complement the fascination of the exotic. Nonetheless, some newer groups, such as the Hare Krishnas, the Neo-Pagans, and various yoga and meditation movements, have dispensed with what to a younger generation perhaps seemed a rather stiff and dry format in favor of more colorful and participatory rituals. When they involve the presentation of offerings to strange gods, chanting, sacred dance, yoga postures, or group meditation they undeniably establish distinct differences from the ordinary American hour of worship.

When the practical form of expression is distinct in this way, it commonly has two characteristics: (1) It is centered on a single sure but simple practice, such as a chant (in Nichiren Shoshu), a meditation method (in Transcendental Meditation), a centered devotionalism (as to Krishna), or a ritual. (2) This practice above all produces for many definite and immediate results, in the form of alteration of consciousness, sense of power, or daily-life benefits, which effectively confirm its value. This is, of course, an important aspect of what we have already perceived as an essential quality of any sustainable new religious movement: that it must yield tangible results strong enough to counter the family, ethnic, or community pull of more conventional religion.

(c) The sociological form of expression includes a wide gamut of features pertaining to the way people relate to one another structurally and informally both within the movement and between it and the "outside." It includes nature of leadership, organization structure, "density" of relationships, and interaction with the environing community. Some characteristics under this head, like a certain degree of tension with the environment, are virtually "built in" to the fate of any alternative group. Others may not perhaps be theoretically necessary, but seem to be practical necessities for any group wishing to sustain itself as a spiritual alternative, especially in the early stages. These include strong authoritative and charismatic leadership, some internal conformity, and some separatism together with close interpersonal relations and a high level of participation on the part of members. These will be discussed among the other characteristics of cults in this list. There have been and are new religious movements without them, such as very loose and informal discussion groups centered on some book or idea, though generally these have been ephemeral and of low visibility even by cult standards. Others, such as some of those previously mentioned—Vedanta, Theosophy, Self-Realization, or the several "New Thought" churches— began with quite charismatic leadership and a fairly tightly-knit disciplic structure around the leader. But they have since passed through the classic "routinization of charisma" process in the second generation described by the sociologist Max Weber, now possessing an institutionalized, more or less professionalized type of leadership more characteristic of established churches or schools. By our particular definition, they would be small denominations or schools of spirituality so far as sociological criteria is concerned, although—bearing in mind the family resemblance matter—one might still argue for cult status on doctrinal and other grounds. The case would have to be decided on an individual movement basis.

(2) The cult, as we have already noted above, will have strong authoritative and charismatic leadership. This means the group is generally focused on one person, who is (a) the founder; (b) recipient of a special revelation or initiation, as well as special learning, upon which it is based; (c) uniquely qualified to teach or impart the special technique for spiritual experience upon which the practice of the group is centered, although he or she may delegate that authority to trained disciples; (d) uniquely entitled to call and empower disciples, being typically surrounded by a small cluster of especially privileged disciples distinct from the larger body of lay adherents and hearers; and (e) the object of a special cultus, in which symbol and practice suggest that the leader by his or her very presence, even apart from anything formally said or done, generates spiritual experience, and does so uniquely through sacramental words and deeds. In sum, the relationship of followers is more basically to the person of the charismatic figure than to a particular doctrine or practice; the latter become important because they are associated with the person and are ways of tapping the revelation and power he or she possesses innately.

(3) The cult is oriented toward inducing powerful subjective experiences and meeting personal needs. We have already noted that such an emphasis is necessary to help counter the "natural" appeal of religion grounded in family and community. Strong experiences brought about by meditation, chanting,

magical rites, initiations, and the presence of a charismatic figure give one a sense of inner identity and significance of a different character, but no less real so long as their reality is sustained, than the "placing" identity of the social order and its religious legitimations. If that placing makes one relatively inconsequential, or "status inconsistent"—in a place which does not match one's subjective sense of one's ability and potential—it may in fact be more real. Minorities, young people, women kept in conventional subordinate roles, and underemployed intellectuals not seldom find themselves in some degree of status inconsistency and consequently subject to the appeal of religious movements which put the significance of inner experience and initiation ahead of outward social role. The meeting of personal needs—assuaging psychological problems, even answering prayer for material benefits—need not be viewed as pandering to negative egocentricity; by helping bestow a wholesome sense of self-worth it can, at best, facilitate growth, though the danger of fostering dependence is always present.

(4)   The cult is separatist in that it strives to maintain distinct boundary demarcations between it and the "outside." Closely related is its tendency to require—at least of an inner core—a high degree of conformity and commitment. Boundary demarcation may be manifested in such signs as distinctive dress and diet. Even more likely are tokens closely related to the high levels of commitment and conformity—ways in which members budget time, establish friendship networks, and establish life priorities and goals. While cult adherents may range from commune members to casual droppers-in, typical of surviving groups will be at least some members who devote a high proportion of their disposable time to it, find most of their voluntary interpersonal relationships through it, and take its ideals very seriously in deciding what to do with their life. The sociologist Erving Goffman has spoken of "total institutions"—groups ranging from armies, prisons, and hospitals to many schools and religious orders (such as monasteries) which, unlike other associational connections, determine all or nearly all the segments of a member's life: dress, diet, where one lives, when one gets up and one's daily schedule, with whom one associates most of the time, and what work one does.[16] Communalist cults, such as the Hare Krishnas for many members, come close to this pattern. Even those in principle more open, with members living in separate dwellings and working "outside," may subjectively affect one's ideals in such matters as dress and recreation because they so deeply influence one's inner self-image or sense of identity. In all cultures certain types of dress, diet, recreation, or employment, the kind of furniture one has in the living room and pictures on the wall, are tacitly understood to go with certain kinds of inner self-identity or inner experience. They are all things that go into that vague but evocative word, lifestyle. So it is that Zen people are likely to carry the austerity of the zendo into their home, together with a whiff of its zest for inner liberty into their values, while Krishna and yoga people are likely to be surrounded by the brightly-colored prints and fabrics of India and enjoying its vegetarian cuisine. All such details, of course, serve to reify and demarcate the subculture of the cult.

(5)   Lastly, we must reiterate an important characteristic of such groups which has not always been taken with sufficient seriousness by sociological observers, the tendency of the cult to see itself as legitimated by a long tradition of wisdom or practice of which it is only a current manifestation. Thus the guru, as is characteristic of the East, stresses his disciplic lineage going back to the Buddha or a primordial sage. In the West, the group represents a recurrence of Hermetic or Kabbalistic teachings known to the wise of all ages. Spiritualists like to talk of theirs as "the oldest faith in the world," pointing with some

justification to its parallels with the practice of the paleolithic shaman. We have discussed elsewhere some of the historical issues behind these claims.[17] From the present phenomenological perspective, the existence of these claims giving counterweight to the immediate charisma of the leader and the practice is the important observation.

Our definition of cult—a group offering an alternative to the dominant spiritual tradition, which is small, has strong authoritative and charismatic leadership, offers powerful subjective experiences which meet personal needs, is separatist, and claims a relation to a legitimating tradition—is clearly somewhat restrictive and will not embrace all groups to which that label has been assigned. In particular, it is likely to capture alternative spiritual movements best in their first generation, and subsequently see them slip away as they, through routinization of charisma and institutionalization, become something else sociologically, even if still small and alternative. To my mind, however, that is good because the distinction between a first-generation movement and the kind of established, institutionalized bodies which, say, Theosophy or "New Thought" churches have become today, is an important one, despite our earlier mention of the possibility of an "established cult."

This definition, however elaborate and restrictive, in our view serves the crucial function which any useful and heuristic phenomenological category must serve. It isolates and significantly contours a distinct type of religious group, which can be easily perceived in the first generation of Theosophy, Mormonism, or Krishna Consciousness, and at the time of writing in movements ranging from Transcendental Meditation (especially the inner circle) to the Unification Church.

At the same time, it distinguishes the cult from other entities with which it might be confused. The cult, as we see it, is not a broad religious movement, like revivalism or even Spiritualism, with many perhaps transitory sociological reifications; one would have to consider each of the latter separately. It is not simply a teaching, however "heterodox" in the eyes of the normative tradition, unless it takes the form of a group such as we have depicted. Gnosticism, whether ancient or modern, is not a cult *per se*, although some form of it could constitute the theoretical expression of one. A group which has acquired marked routinization of charisma and institutionalization is not a cult, though (as we have seen) it may be non-normative in doctrine and practice and have had cultic beginnings. It seems to us that to put something like what institutionalized Theosophy or Divine Science have become today, a century more or less since their founding, under the same label as Krishna Consciousness or the Muktananda ashrams under their living gurus would be to mix up two quite different kinds of groups. Finally, our definition allows the customary sociological distinction between cult and sect, unless the sect is quite heterodox, for though many characteristics would obtain in both instances—separatism, relation to a legitimating tradition—the sect, as a particularly intense version of the dominant religion with withdrawal features, is usually said to possess more legalistic than charismatic authority, and to represent a spiritual alternative only in a much narrower sense than the cult.

It remains to reflect on whether, given this definition, a better word than cult can be found for its object. We have already considered the problems of stereotyping and judgmentalism that entangle the term. Some scholars have used "new religious movements" or even "new religions" (after the Japanese examples) for much these same sorts of groups, and these expressions appear to be more neutral. Both of these terms, however, may be too broad to be of optimal use. "Movement" does not necessarily suggest the sort of tight-knit, clearly-defined entity we have suggested, being indeed capable of confusion with a broad, diffuse "social movement" like a "conservative movement" or a "peace movement." "New," though not highly precise, does suggest a group in its first generation or so. But "religious" or "religion" also raises difficulties, especially over whether we are speaking of a religion which, though small, is as discrete as one of the "great religions" like Islam or Hinduism, or whether the group under question is not actually a denomination or other subdivision of one of them; many "new religions" actually are, though perhaps of Hinduism or Buddhism rather than of the dominant faith in our society.

Elsewhere we have spoken of the cult or sect type of religion, which contrasts with the conventional or "established" religion of a society, as "emergent religion."[18] It is subdivided into "expansive emergent" religion and "intensive emergent" religion, corresponding to the sociological cult and sect respectively. We feel that these terms may be as useful and heuristically helpful as any.

The usual definitions of the word *emergent* suggest several characteristics of the kind of religion under consideration. As an adjective, the word defines something arising out of a fluid which heretofore had covered or concealed it, or something suddenly appearing for no apparent reason, or as a natural or logical outcome of a situation such as rapid change, or as the result of a process of development. As a noun, "emergent" indicates something that stands out, as a single tree above the forest.

These definitions really apply well to the counterpart of dominant or established religion. New religions appear out of the fluid sea of popular religion, seemingly unexpectedly, yet actually because something previously hidden—the legitimating alternative tradition—has in them become uncovered, or as a product of evolutionary or rapid change, like a mutant. Expansive emergent religion, in contrast to the sectarian intensive form, withdraws in order to found what is, in its adherents' eyes, a more broadly based experience than that of the monochrome religion of the society. It may seek to combine elements of the dominant religion with new ideas from science, from faraway places, and from inner vision, as well as from an "underground" but legitimating past tradition. It is generally centered more on mystical experience—"expansion of consciousness"—than social or legalistic norms.

This term with its implications seems to comport well with the characteristics of cult we have outlined. But whether it be called expansive emergent religion, or by the more conventional label "cult," the important matter is to have a clear, definite, but nonstereotypical concept of what manner of group is being described.

NOTES

[1] Robert S. Ellwood, Jr., *Religious and Spiritual Groups in Modern America* (Englewood Cliffs, NJ: Prentice-Hall, Inc., 1973).

[2] J. Milton Yinger, *Religion, Society, and the Individual* (New York: Macmillan, Inc., 1957), pp. 142–55.

[3] Werner Stark, *The Sociology of Religion* (London: Routledge & Kegan Paul, 1967), vol. II, p. 313.

[4] Geoffrey K. Nelson, *Spiritualism and Society* (New York: Schocken Books, 1969), p. 220. In a more recent book, *The Scientific Study of Religion* (New York: Macmillan, Inc., 1970), pp. 279–80, J. Milton Yinger discusses Nelson's criticism of his earlier treatment of cult, accepting the latter's suggestion that some cults can be long-lasting and the seedbed of new religions, especially in the context of social anomie.

[5] See, for example, W.E. Mann, *Sect, Cult, and Church in Alberta* (Toronto: University of Toronto Press, 1955), pp. 5–8, 37–40.

[6] Hadley Cantril, "The Kingdom of Father Divine," in B. McLaughlin, ed., *Studies in Social Movements* (New York: The Free Press, 1969), p. 223.

[7] E.L. Quarantelli and Dennis Wenger, "A Voice from the 13th Century," *Urban Life and Culture*, 1 (1973), p. 384.

[8] Andrew J. Pavlos, *The Cult Experience* (Westport, CT: Greenwood Press, 1982), p. 6.

[9] See, for example, David B. Bromley and Anson D. Shupe, Jr., *Strange Gods: The Great American Cult Scare* (Boston: Beacon Press, 1981).

[10] J. Gordon Melton and Robert L. Moore, *The Cult Experience* (New York: Pilgrim Press, 1982), p. 17.

[11] Ronald Enroth, *The Lure of the Cults* (Chappaqua, NY: Christian Herald Books, 1979), p. 20.

[12] William J. Petersen, *Those Curious New Cults in the 80s* (New Canaan, CT: Keats Publishing, 1973, 1982), p. 14.

[13] Carroll Stoner and Jo Anne Parke, *All God's Children* (Radnor, PA: Chilton, 1977).

[14] Ninian Smart, *Philosophers and Religious Truth*, 2nd ed. (London: SCM Press, 1969), p. 115.

[15] Joachim Wach, *Sociology of Religion* (Chicago: University of Chicago Press, 1944), pp. 17–34.

[16] Erving Goffman, *Asylums* (Garden City, NY: Doubleday & Co., Inc., 1961).

[17] Robert S. Ellwood, Jr., *Alternative Altars: Unconventional and Eastern Spirituality in America* (Chicago: University of Chicago Press, 1979), especially Ch. 1. See also Ellwood, "The American Theosophical Synthesis," in Howard Kerr and Charles L. Crow, *The Occult in America* (Urbana: University of Illinois Press, 1983), pp. 111–34.

[18] Robert S. Ellwood, Jr., *Introducing Religion: From Inside and Outside.* 2nd ed. (Englewood Cliffs, NJ: Prentice-Hall, Inc. 1983), pp. 144–49.

2

THE HISTORY OF AN ALTERNATIVE REALITY IN THE WEST

TWO VIEWS OF REALITY

"Expansive" new religious movements are generally "new" only in their contemporary packaging. They themselves characteristically claim a long heritage, speaking of ancient wisdom or immense lineages of gurus. As we have seen, from the point of view of the outside observer as well, these assertions are not without substance, for most do, in fact, represent modern embodiments of concepts and related practices that go back centuries and millennia. Although some oversimplification is involved, it will help to think of Western civilization as possessing two basic views of reality.

The majority view is that expressed in classical Christianity and, despite the celebrated "warfare" between religion and science on certain issues, largely perpetuated in the modern scientific outlook as received and used by the ordinary modern person. For our present purposes, its most salient characteristics are the following. It emphasizes the distinction between God as Creator and the human being as created being, fallible and subject to God's will—or, in the nontheistic scientific version of the same, it emphasizes the difference between humans as thinking and feeling beings, and the vast impersonal universe in which we find ourselves and to whose natural laws we too are ultimately subject. In a related perception, it clearly distinguishes between subject and object, that is, between the thinking and knowing mind, and that which we think about and know. Knowing, therefore, is a matter of observing—empiricism—and reflecting logically on what has been observed—reason. In sum, this world view takes human beings to be each distinct centers of consciousness, separate from each other, from nature, from the universe, and from God, though with rights and duties over against each. Separatenesses prevail and with them modes of thought appropriate to understanding empirically and rationally that which is other than oneself, whether a star or another human. All this has led to the unique contributions of the West, from science and technology to democratic political institutions, as well as to certain failings.

But the West has also known an alternative view. It was developed in Platonism and Neoplatonism, enhanced at various points by contact with the East. It has informed important strands of mystical thought within Christianity and Judaism, from Dionysius the Areopagite to Eckhart and the sages of the Kabbalah. But it has most come into its own in times and places which have strained at the leash of conventional religion, whether in the "respectable" guise of Renaissance scholars or New England Transcendentalists, or as "underground" movements pertaining to magic and occultism. Most of the contemporary movements described in this book reflect some version of its basic ideology, though some articulate it in the language of traditional Western alternative worldviews and others in their Eastern counterparts.

In contrast to the majority Western outlook, the alternative view emphasizes continuity between humanity, God, and the rest of the universe. Thus, it typically talks about the divine within each of us, and sees consciousness throughout what others would view as a cosmos of lifeless matter plied by physical law. Therefore the way the mind knows itself, attains immediate awareness of itself as conscious mind, becomes, in the form of intuition and mystical experience, the supreme way of knowing God or Ultimate Reality. This does not mean that this path is antirational; to the contrary, it likes to stress that mind and nature work by understandable laws, God being more an impersonal Absolute than a personal Creator working by arbitrary will. But reason and observation can be superseded by direct Knowing, of Reality itself and of our profound interrelatedness with all that is.

The tradition further teaches that little-known laws of nature, unexplored psychic or spiritual human capacities, or superhuman hierarchies—gods, spirits, "masters"—stand between the human level and Ultimate Reality. In occult lore these hidden laws and superior beings assist the aspirant toward higher wisdom. Groups in the alternative reality tradition mediate that wisdom and power to the sincere seeker through teaching, initiations, meditation techniques, or ceremonial rites. Ancillary conceptual themes frequently accompany this hierarchical and occult-laws perception of reality, including affirmation of astrology, psychic phenomena, reincarnation, and spiritual healing. Underlying it all is a belief that the universe is fundamentally mental, that it operates more like an immense mind than a gigantic machine. Thus, most basic is sheer, infinite, impersonal consciousness; it expresses itself in both law and descending ranks of consciousness—the "Great Chain of Being"—from gods or angels to humankind and below, the whole integrated by "correspondences" or special relationships between various parts of the system. A particular planet or sign of the Zodiac may have such a particular connection with a stone, a color, or an organ of the body; such relationships may make possible astrology or magic, and on a deeper level tell us that ours is a universe of design rather than caprice, linked in all its parts by fine-strung wires of influence.

This Western alternative tradition has been present in America since colonial times, in the shape of a definite and fairly compact tradition. While it has assumed many forms, that tradition can be traced through Greek Pythagoreanism and Neoplatonism, to Hellenistic Hermeticism and Gnosticism, and to medieval Kabbalah and alchemy. In the Middle Ages this lineage, reinforced by European folk religion of pre-Christian origin, offered a covert alternative, or supplement, to orthodoxy. In the Renaissance it was revitalized by new discoveries of classical sources and by the new science which seemed initially to go well with it; it is worth remembering that modern science and occultism have common roots in the Renaissance rediscovery of ancient Greek scientist-philosophers, and in a sense that the secrets of the universe ought to yield themselves to a combination of reason and experiment, being based on laws and interrelationships that lie beneath the surface.

Even after the scientific mainstream separated itself from the alternative worldview, with astronomy supplanting astrology and chemistry alchemy, the latter continued like an underground river. It was now less concerned to maintain the cosmological worldviews of the old philosophers, with an Ptolemaic earth-centered universe and the like, than to preserve what it saw as the spiritual values of the alternative, sorely needed in the brave new world being manufactured by the new science. In the face of a scientific view of the universe which many saw becoming more and more mechanistic and "dead," those attuned to the alternative tradition wanted to reassert its underlying sense of the profound interaction of mind and matter all through the cosmos. They perceived its concept of "correspondences," its idea of man as "microcosm" or miniature of the universe reflecting on earth its true spirit/matter nature, and the allied arts such as astrology, as not outworn but crucial because they give humankind a true home in the cosmos, and make the whole cosmos humanly significant. This was contrasted with the precarious place of man in orthodox religion, subject to a capricious and judgmental God, and to the deep alienation from his universal environment man seemed to have in the new "scientific" outlook, as a puny center of consciousness and feeling in a vast and mostly empty universe moved by immense impersonal forces which cared nothing for his fate. Against this the alternative tradition, which took human consciousness to be continuous with that shaping the universe as a whole, and human experience to be aligned with subtle energies radiating through stone and star, could not but appear to some wiser and richer.

The alternative tradition was reinforced by influences from the religions of the East. Although the case has not been proven definitively, it seems likely that notions from philosophical Hinduism and Buddhism slipped into the ancient West, if only at second or third hand, to affect such mystical systems as Pythagoreanism or Neoplatonism. Some beliefs in the

Western alternative tradition often associated with the East, however, like reincarnation and the One realized through direct experience, may well have had an independent genesis in the Mediterranean world. In any event, when the West rediscovered the East in modern times, the impact on the alternative tradition was massive, so much so as almost to swamp the Western lineage. From the first translations of important Eastern texts in the eighteenth century, through the adaptation of some of their ideas— and above all their exaltation of what might be called the Eastern mystique—by thinkers like the New England Transcendentalists, obvious parallels between the two spiritual worlds vied with the fascination of the East's exoticism to draw seekers. Soon the appeal of Eastern practical methods for realization, such as yoga and Zen meditation, and the charisma of living Eastern teachers, became further magnets. Today the alternative spiritual world in America is comprised of both Western and Eastern wings, with the latter often more visible because of its greater penchant for distinctive dress, symbols, and practices. But some traditions, such as the Theosophical, have sought to integrate the two by pointing to an ancient wisdom going back before East and West were ever set asunder.

We must now proceed to examine the history of the alternative reality tradition in the West in more detail.

THE HELLENISTIC PERIOD

The exuberance of new religions in modern America has a precedent, one that has profoundly affected the shape it has taken here. Ours has not been the only period in which a struggle between the hectic pace of history, disturbing in its rapidity and ruthlessness, has thrown up a radical reaction in the form of movements dedicated to living with a different focus. In this other period, too, these movements were watered from Eastern wells or fed by shamanistic springs.

We speak of that period of Mediterranean culture known as Hellenistic. The term embraces the time from Alexander the Great to the fall of the Roman Empire. It is the culture which grew up out of the confrontation of Greek letters and philosophy with Egyptian and Near Eastern life. The sort of mystical, syncretistic, cosmopolitan culture to which this label is attached flourished in the cities of the eastern Mediterranean such as Antioch and Alexandria.

It was a time when wandering philosophers—Diogenes in his tub, Apollonius of Tyana with his magic, Neoplatonists with their gaze lost in the One Eternal, Cynics, Sceptics, Stoics, Epicureans—enlivened the markets and groves of dozens of towns with their lectures and schools. Here one might be declaiming that nothing exists, and that if it did it could not be known; another that the best life is found in the pursuit of pleasure; another that one can only submit to destiny and bear all things with equanimity; another that man's only true end is to unite with the Eternal like two concentric circles merging into one. These philosophers were their own men, and their followings often could not be called continuing religious groups in any real sense. But for some people the philosophical schools—actual or figurative—which sprang up around them or in their wake must have played the role that alternative religions play today.

The traditional gods of Olympus and Rome held little persuasion for an increasing number of these people. But philosophies of the more mystical sort, while partially compatible with their rites (Pythagoreanism and Neoplatonism), offered spiritual insights or techniques which certainly meet the test of means of ultimate transformation. In the close, almost monastic Pythagorean communities the three forms of religious expression can be found. The founder of Neoplatonism, Plotinus, seems to have been content to preside over an academic school and to keep his mystical practice private. But the later theurgic or magical Neoplatonism of Iamblichus and Proclus involved students in practice as well as doctrine. These academies are more or less the "ancient mystery schools" so much celebrated by some modern alternative religions as their authoritative precedents.

Besides the philosophers, the other vital force in Hellenistic spiritual culture was the Egyptian and Near Eastern gods. It seems that even as the native deities of the Greeks and Romans faded into inconsequence, almost any exotic import from the East had an uncanny power to fascinate and create a cult around itself. One thinks of Isis, Serapis, Cybele, Mithra, Christ. Cut loose from the ancient cultures which had nurtured them, devotion to them spread from one port to another in the free communication and open atmosphere of the new empires. No longer were they the gods or cultus of a tribe, a little people here or there. Suddenly these gods became the centers of cosmopolitan religions. Persons of different traditions freely and individually chose to undergo the initiation and plead the favors of foreign deities, often at missionary temples in their hometowns.

If the air about the philosophers was one of dignified academic reserve and private occultism, that of the Eastern religions was quite different. The devotees probably received initiation under conditions of great secrecy. Yet the general display of the cult was visible enough. For example, the priests of Isis, white-stoled, carrying bells, symbols, sacred water from the Nile, and a model of a great ship, would process their way to the shore each spring. Women in linen would scatter flowers and perfume on the way, while music of flute and pipe floated on the breeze. The mother of the stars, Isis, would be honored with tapers and torches. At the beach, the sacred ship would be consecrated with hymns and chants and litanies, and set to sail with the vows and offerings of the faithful for the succor of those on the deep.

This was a time of spiritual emptiness and fullness. Like the inside of a balloon being inflated, the spiritual sphere seemed both hollow, waiting for something to fill up the void, and expanding to embrace all things near and far. As in any vacuum, everything on the widening perimeter cluttered in toward the center to try to fill it. And much was shaken loose.

The armies of Alexander marched east through Persia and into India. Then the Seleucid and Ptolemaic Empires welded together in an uneasy combination the ways of Greece and the Orient. Finally Rome sent her armies, highways, and governors around the Mediterranean world.

The soldiers, merchants, and administrators not only went out, they also came back, making, in the process, a collection of provinces into a world. What had been the ancient faiths of integral cultures became detached *options* for the whole known world.

In our day, practices like Zen and Nichiren Shoshu have been brought to America in large part by soldiers returning from the occupation of Japan or from American military bases overseas. Likewise, some Roman legionnaires far from home became fascinated with the faiths of Isis, Mithra, or Christ. At the same time, the peoples of the far places—Jews, wandering philosophers, Greek traders, slaves, missionaries from the Nile—swarmed freely toward the centers, even as teachers of Hinduism and Buddhism today walk the streets of American cities.

This was the foreground of that lurid and luminous age. The spiritual background, the old gods of Homer and Virgil, were fading more and more into clear air and infinite starry space. It was a time of the death of the Olympian gods, not from violence or persecution, but from apathy. It was, in other words, a time of the discovery of historical time. The old was inexplicably discovered not to fit, even though only externals of human life had seemed to change—as has happened at many junctures before and after.

Hellenistic religion, then, had these characteristics: it was a reaction to the discovery of historical time, hence it saw time as the great enemy to be defeated; it was cosmopolitan, bringing together gods and rites of many places and worshipping deities without regard for place; it was individualistic, requiring each person to make an individual choice and holding out the ideal of religion centered on individual religious experience and initiation; it was a faith searching for one God, for a unity behind the many unsatisfying atoms of historical time, place, and polytheism.

The plenary power of Isis in her cult points toward what is perhaps the most profound of the spiritual drives of the age, this desire for one God. A near second, also offered by her cult, was the desire for initiation, for mystic death and rebirth. What was wished was initiation into a universal, divine state of consciousness. It was a desire to transcend both the real but fearful experience of individualism through return to the One, and the sequential atomistic particulars of history through finding them to be all aspects of the One. This one God was alike the impersonal Absolute of the philosophers, and the Lord of starry heaven of the initiates, for whom the way to union was lit by the bright torch of a savior who knew the way—an Orpheus or Osiris.

The Hellenistic cults, therefore, had many things in common with the alternative religions of our own day. Both center on ecstatic personal experience; both use syncretistic symbols. The background of both is often an ultimately impersonal universe against which all sorts of lesser spirits and saviors operate. Very often at the center of both is a charismatic personality like Apollonius of Tyana or a powerful philosopher. Apollonius was indeed a model of the exemplary type; he spoke not a word for five years, swaying the hearts and souls of men to good by his silent presence.

On the other hand, there are differences. While, like modern alternative religions, the ancient ones seized upon the terminology of the science of the day (the four elements, etc.), the modern concept of progress was lacking. Instead the mood was the opposite of that worldly optimism which pervades many new religions today. Hans Jonas has compared the psychological mood of Gnosticism to that of twentieth century existential despair.[1] For Gnostics, nothing could check the passions except the transcendent and trans-historical.

We will now look briefly at several of the most important of the Hellenistic movements. Those involving secret initiations promising salvation are often called mystery religions. This list is not exhaustive, but it is important to have some familiarity with them, since both in style and content they have influenced the whole history of Western alternative religious activity. They are what the Western world might have become spiritually had it not been for Christianity, and they are the ever-flowing fountain which feeds Christianity's and science's alternatives in every generation.

The Orphic Religion

Orphism was the first known separatist Greek religion with a founder and scripture of its own—even if mythical. Moreover, its goal is obviously ultimate transformation—blessed immortality on the other side—and it clearly had the three forms of expression. In a real sense it could be called the first known "new religion" in Europe.

Orpheus, who came from Thrace, was a fabulous singer and magician able to charm animals and even rocks and trees to follow him. After crazed jealous women had torn him apart his severed head was said to have continued to sing. He was also said to have undergone initiation in Egypt, to have conquered the world of shades, and to be able to bring his initiates into immortality. This was the main theme of the Orphic cult, whose followers believed themselves strayed citizens of a better world who, through the mystery, could be led home once again. On arrival in the other world, devotees were to say

> I am a son of earth and of starry heaven . . . By good fortune I have escaped the circle of burdensome care, and to the crown of yearning have I come with swift foot; I bury myself in the lap of the Lady who rules in Hades . . .[2]

The Religion of the Great Mother

The Magna Mater or Great Mother religion, popular across the Mediterranean, was basically Syrian though the goddess went by innumerable names—Astarte, Ishtar, Cybele, etc. She was notable for the frenzy she created among her devotees, particularly the eunuch priests.

> They danced about fanatically with a sinuous motion of legs and necks; they bent down their heads and spun round so that their hair flew out in a circle; now and then they bit their own flesh; finally, everyone took his two-edged knife and slashed his arms in various places.[3]

Here we see ultimate transformation and the three forms of

expression. The self-mutilation is evidently a way in which the devotees as individuals try to make themselves children of the Great Mother (denying their adult sexuality), and a special group is formed by those who do this.

The Religion of Isis

Isis represents the Great Mother of a thousand names in a more benign form as a protecting and rejuvenating force. Like the Roman novelist Apuleius, many in her initiation

> drew near to the confines of death . . . at the dead of night, saw the sun shining brightly . . . approached the gods above and the gods below.[4]

Here is another cult of individual salvation through an unforgettable experience of initiation, and one well furnished with richly robed celibate clergy and majestic rituals.

The Religion of Mithra

The cult of Isis brought the sacred to many in the guise of the eternal feminine, while another cult, very popular among the Roman soldiers, presented it in masculine image. This was Mithraism, the cult of the Persian sun god who made the world by sacrificing a bull, and who brought his followers into immortality through a kind of baptism with the blood of bulls. This faith has left temples from Britain to the Near East. It had a number of grades of initiation, and taught a rough code of honor and justice.

Judaism and Christianity

Of course the faiths from this period we know best today are Judaism and Christianity. The importance of their role in the ancient world is not to be minimized, even without benefit of retrospect. Perhaps as much as 10 percent of the population of the Roman Empire was Jewish, and Jews dwelt not only in Palestine but in all the major cities. Particularly at Alexandria, a Jewish intellectual life richly flavored by Platonic philosophy flourished. At the same time, Judaism with its one God and its recognition of individual moral choice had a deep appeal for many. It seemed to be an ancient tradition which, despite some very odd laws and customs, spoke to those concerns which were at the heart of the Hellenistic spiritual quest. This was a situation which led to the rise of mediating movements on the borderline between the world of the Jew and the Greek. On one level, Judaism could be made essentially a symbol system which expressed Platonism, as it was by the Alexandrian Jew, Philo.

On the level of a full religious life, Christianity provided an opportunity for non-Jews to feel "grafted into" the great Jewish tradition without having to undertake those parts of the Law which were alien to them. At the same time they could participate in a saving death-and-rebirth experience as profound as that of any Mystery. This was to prove the most powerful mix of all.

Gnosticism

Early Christianity included a set of teachings and groups known collectively as Gnosticism. Their origin remains a subject of scholarly dispute, but seems to have been a mingling of mystical Judaism with Neoplatonic and Oriental ideas; in time, if not from the start, Gnosticism also embraced Christian language by making Christ a savior. Gnostic teaching characteristically made this world of suffering the handiwork of a lesser, bumbling creator, sometimes identified with the God of the Old Testament. It is far from the sublime realm of the unknown High God in his infinite light. Human souls—or at least some human souls—are, however, sparks from that primal light entrapped in the world of matter. The means of their escape—salvation—is based on true *gnosis,* knowledge, of who they are and where they have come from, knowledge brought by Christ from the Most High. The Gnostic tradition has been treasured by modern occultists, who have frequently revived the highly allegorical interpretations of the Bible and the soul's journey through the realms of matter typical of Gnosticism, and seen the Gnostics as early exemplars of a "mystical" style of Christianity congruous with the alternative tradition.

The Magus

The ancient philosophers and mystagogues of those traditions presented a style of religious personality continuous with that of the modern alternative religions. The leaders of such groups as Pythagoreans, Hermeticists, and Neoplatonists, together with later personages such as Cagliostro and Blavatsky, offer splendid examples of the magus. This manner of spiritual personality has been isolated and examined by Eliza M. Butler.[5]

The magus is the old shaman revamped to flourish within the civilized world. The shaman, a familiar figure in primitive religion, is one who has been called by the gods, undergone an initiation, and then through trance, dance, and magical techniques is able to heal, divine the future, and communicate with gods and spirits. He or she is also often credited with the ability to fly, speak to animals, and travel to the Other World of the departed. The shaman's initiation is typically arduous, involving death and rebirth symbolism, and symbolic or actual journeying to a far place.[6]

E.R. Dodds has shown, following the Swiss scholar K. Meuli, that in the late archaic period the Greeks came into contact with peoples of Scythia, and probably also of Thrace, who possessed a central Asiatic type of shamanistic culture. From this time on, there appeared in Greece "a series of *iatromanteis,* seers, magical healers, and religious teachers, some of whom are linked in Greek tradition with the North, and all of whom exhibit shamanistic traits."[7] There was Abaris, who came riding upon an arrow as do shamanistic souls in Siberia and who banished a pestilence and taught the worship of his god. Aristeas travelled north on a fabulous journey replete with creatures from central Asiatic folklore. He was also credited with the shamanistic powers of trance, being able to appear at two places at the same time, and out-of-the-body travel. His soul could take the form of a bird and travel wherever it wished. By the time of Sophocles, who alludes to them in the *Electra*, tales like this of appearing and disappearing shamans were common. Orphism also had roots in Thrace (the region north of Greece). Dodds goes so far as to consider Pythagoras a great shaman. The Scythians and Thracians knew cannabis; the hallucinogenic drug experience may have had no small part in creating this tradition.

In any case, Dodds shows that the whole concept of the soul as separable from the body, having a separate destiny—preexistence, perhaps many lives, postexistence, the ability to leave the body, which was so important to Greek thought from Pythagoras and Plato onwards—was no more known to Homeric and archaic Hellenes than to the ancient Hebrews. For them, the only meaningful life the soul enjoyed was with and in the flesh. The separate *psyche* or soul does not appear until after Orphism, Aristeas, and the like have introduced it. The idea is clearly based on the logic of the Asiatic shaman's trance and ecstasy, with all its fateful and immeasurable impact on Plato and the whole train of Western thought and religion. The world of this thought is also the world of the shaman-in-civilization, the magus.

The magus tradition presupposes, like shamanism, not only the ultimate inseparability of valid teaching from the initiation of ecstatic experience, but also the inseparability of experience and life style for such a profoundly initiated and "different" man. In civilization, many may discourse metaphysically upon the doctrine of the soul. But when one appears who incarnates the whole kit of proofs which the shamans knew regarding the powers of the soul—initiatory experience, strange psychic abilities, extraordinary travel, mastery of spirits—he is no longer an integral part of the culture, but comes as a mysterious visitor to civilization, offering an alternative reality. This is the magus. Persons like Pythagoras, Apollonius, Iamblichus, certain medieval wizards and alchemists, Paracelsus, Saint-Germain, Cagliostro, Madame Blavatsky all are in this tradition.

While some genuine saints and mystics may have had comparable experiences, the magus is neither a saint, nor a savior, nor a prophet, nor a seer. He is a shaman-in-civilization. Like most shamans, he is part fraud, part showman, part myth, and part extraordinary ecstatic. The magus's story is always half legend, even in modern times, but the plot, like all real myths, follows a similar line.

The story of the magus will typically make contact with many of the following points—or all of them. The magus is of unusual birth and of strange and deep intellectual powers from early childhood. He travels very widely as a young man, often in Asia. He crisscrosses the world to meet sages and receive esoteric initiations. When he enters his public work, he amazes the world with fabulous magical powers, but he feels his teaching is his most important work. His teaching will be of a universe of intricate and subtle spiritual-physical forces and planes within the One, which he grasps by initiated intuition, and of a separate destiny of the soul—the "ageless wisdom." He will be able to put these forces into play in seeming miracles. The magus gathers about him both a band of disciples and invisible attendants. His disciples, however, find him puzzling, for he unpredictably appears and disappears. The magus has always about him a certain "lightness," like a shaman's. Often no one knows where he is, and he turns up unexpectedly in odd places. He has a shimmering grace and uncanny persuasive power, but unlike the saint he may not be moral or ascetic by ordinary standards; he may even be given to drink or luxury, at least sufficiently to baffle those who thought they understood him. He never, though, loses his magic or his dark, luminous wisdom. He seems not to age in the usual way, and no man knows his age. His end may be as mysterious as his life; he may finally just disappear.

The magus, with his personal mystery, is an exemplary figure, potentially the center of a cult type of group. He is a personified symbol of the "otherness" which the cultist seeks to lay hold of for himself. The magus appears like one who has been through ultimate transformation, yet is visible here. As a visible phenomenon, he may serve as focus for the three forms of expression and stimulate desire for initiation into his world.

One of the first western examples of the magus is Pythagoras (died around 495 B.C.). As a young man, he travelled to Egypt and Chaldea, then established a school at Krotona in southern Italy where he and his disciples, divided into esoteric and exoteric sections, studied philosophy and lived a life of asceticism. They were apparently vegetarian and abstained from sacrificial rites. Pythagoras was deeply influenced by Orphism (or, if E. R. Dodds is correct, it may have been as much the reverse[8]), with its teaching of a purification process by which the soul could recover its original godlike character and return to its eternal home. To the populace, he was a magician; it was said he appeared simultaneously in Italy and Sicily, and tamed a bear by whispering in its ear. Like the Orphics, he taught transmigration or the movement of the soul from one body to another life after life. The basic teaching was that the universe is a great unity which begins with the One, and unfolds in mathematical ratios comparable to those of geometrical forms and solids. Modern Theosophists have named their principal school in America Krotona, and the influence of Pythagoras is evident on almost every page of Blavatsky's work.

A later Pythagorean, Apollonius of Tyana, also exemplifies the magus. He is said to have been no ordinary infant, but an appearance of Proteus, the shape-shifting god. He followed the Pythagorean discipline scrupulously, and after Pythagorean custom, wandered for five years keeping absolute silence. He spent four years as a sort of initiation living in the temple of Asclepius at Aegae. He was said to know all languages, including those of birds and beasts. He travelled to Babylon and Susa to talk with the Magi, and thence to India, where he discoursed on philosophy with the Brahmins. Extraordinary cures and miracles were attributed to Apollonius everywhere. After triumphantly responding to interrogation in Rome by the Emperor Domitian, he is said to have suddenly vanished away from the court. He lived to a very great age, and then disappeared. Some say he walked into a temple and did not come out, others that he ascended into heaven. A cult built around Apollonius continued into the fifth century.

The Hermetic Books

Much "ancient wisdom" type of teaching and magic has gone under the name of Hermeticism. It is not clear to what degree Hermeticism was a

cult in ancient times; there are some allusions in its literature to devotions
to the sun and initiations as well as to instruction. But the name derives
from the *Book of Hermes Trismegistus,* which was composed in Alexandria in
the third or early fourth century C.E., probably on the fecund borderline
between Judaism and Hellenism, though (typically of the culture) a few
Egyptian and Christian terms are employed.

The book's prestige derives from the fact that in medieval and early
modern Europe it was universally believed to be the oldest book in the
world, dating at least back to the Deluge. This status has influenced many
moderns who have taught what they call "Hermetic science" as the oldest
accessible human wisdom. Hermeticism has been used both then and now
to embrace not only the contents of the book, but also broadly to cover an
ill-defined mass of magic, Gnostic and Neoplatonic philosophy, astrology,
theurgy, and so forth deriving from the same Alexandrian milieu, but
presented as much older.

The *Book of Hermes Trismegistus* centers around the instructions of the
thrice great Hermes (the Greek god who became, among other things,
guide of the souls of the dead and revealer of wisdom) to his son Tat (the
Egyptian god Thoth, lord of wisdom and regeneration). It begins with an
impressive initiatory experience, and continues with material on the creation of the world through personified emanations, and presentation of the
way of salvation through lofty morals and meditation.

Neoplatonism

The intellectual spine of that world was Neoplatonism, the new construction of the Platonic philosophy by Plotinus (204–270 C.E.) and his
followers. In brief, Plotinus taught that the cosmos is made of emanations
from the One, and that man's goal is to return to the One by mystical
experience through which he transcends the limitations of matter and the
intervening mental emanations—the world soul, the archetypes. One can
see the roots of a system like this in the Greek shamanistic tradition. Later
Neoplatonists like Porphyry (234–305), Iamblichus (approximately 250–
325), and Proclus (410–485) became more and more fascinated by the
practice called theurgy, the evocation of gods, who often personified various planets or points in the emanational scheme.

A basic text for them, and one indicating at least the commonly
accepted source of much of the magic, was the *Chaldean Oracles,* a turgid
prophetic text of obscure origin taken very seriously by the later Neoplatonists. It seems to have provided prescriptions for a fire and sun cult
and for theurgy. The sun, and the gods, were made into the lords of
various levels of emanation, or of segments of the cosmos, and so were
fitted into the more serious Platonic tradition. Systems like this were given
official encouragement in the days of the Emperor Julian the Apostate
(reigned 361–363), because they were considered crucial to the emperor's
attempts to save Paganism.

Dodds delineates two types of theurgy. The first was concerned with
consecrating magic statues by use of formulas, animals, plants, and miner-
als "sympathetic" to the god involved. The seven planetary gods were the

most important. The second type of theurgy was the mediumistic trance. According to Iamblichus, the most suitable people for mediums are "young and rather simple persons." The characteristics of these trances seem quite comparable to those of modern spiritualism. At times the god seems to appear in a shape formed of a luminous substance not unlike the ectoplasm of today.[9]

A third practice which might have been thought theurgy, invoking a spirit or demon visibly by incantation, perhaps into a magic triangle in the manner of the "high magic" of later ceremonial magicians, seems to have been less developed by the Neoplatonists than the use of oracular statues or spiritualism. The latter are, after all, both long-standing Hellenic traditions. There were the many magic statues of the public cults of Greece and possessed oracles like that of Delphi. All of the basic principles of the later tradition of incantational evocation were developed in the first four centuries C.E., but, though not unknown to classic Greece, largely in Egyptian, Chaldean, and Hebrew circles. The names and magic words of the tradition prove as much, as do the perennial legends of Solomon, archetype of the evocational magician, who trapped demons in jars and made them do his will. The question of the origin of modern ceremonial magic is not a simple one, however, for its practitioners work both mediumistic evocation and invocation into an exterior space or object.

The Neoplatonists and Hermeticists offered teaching and cultic activity, but their social expression is not clear. The Neoplatonists tried both to be public academic philosophers in the classic tradition—spokesmen of a wisdom compatible with the official temples and, ideally, the heritage of the total community—and at the same time custodians of very personal initiations and esoteric lore. However, only the exemplary teacher, because he leaves much unsaid, can sustain such ambivalence. But he can function only in a society which is attuned to his kind of interior spirituality. A society like the late Roman, individualized, battered by the "terror of history," threatened, haunted by the ghosts of too many dead gods, could not be reached by silent illumination so much as by a new cause which could bring it out of the past, and which was best communicated by emissary fire.

THE MIDDLE AGES

The expansive Hellenistic age, willing to try to tolerate any vagary of the spirit, did not suddenly turn into what we call the Middle Ages with the victory of Christianity in the fourth century. Nor was the spiritual life of the Ages of Faith nearly as monolithic as that term would suggest. Circles of dissent, sometimes flaring into vast movements like the Albigensianism of southern France, broke out upon the disputatious and always-changing face of Catholic Europe. The dissent often took the form of movements of the cult type, and those of the more intellectual sort were like long-lingering shadows of the very different Hellenistic world. Albigensianism, for example, had its ultimate inspiration in the Gnostic Manichaean religion.

Witchcraft

Hellenism, however, was not all that went into the medieval alternative reality tradition which countered what the dominant vision had built. The pre-Christian faiths of northern Europe had also survived. If survivals of Hellenism have produced movements of the Theosophical and occult type, so somewhere behind modern Witchcraft lies the old faith of northern Europe. It has been much twisted by its unfortunate subterranean role of opposition, and much influenced by the non-northern tradition of incantational evocation. There yet lingers within it the faint trace of another path to the world of the paleolithic shaman, and of that science of soul its practitioners call *wicca*.

Perhaps its roots lie, as Margaret Murray believed, in a Stone Age cultus of a horned god, at once the Moon and Master of Animals, the patron of a hunting people. He was celebrated at full moon, and was personified by a dancing shaman in an animal skin and deer horns, like the famous "sorcerer" painted on the walls of the cave at Dordogne, France. In some way, enough forms from this old religion survived in folk beliefs and customs to provide a frame of reference for both the persecutors and alleged practitioners of Witchcraft in the days of its persecution. Clearly some of what was then called Witchcraft derives from the Hellenic alternative reality tradition and ceremonial magic, and some from pre-Christian north European belief preserved in folkways.

The evidence concerning the nature of this tradition in the Middle Ages through the eighteenth century is very difficult to assess, coming, as most of it does, by way of the notorious witch trials and testimony extracted under torture. Remnants of the old faith survive in the home traditions of certain families in Britain to this day, as well as in certain folkways. But most of the contemporary Witchcraft circles are of independent origin, like the modern revivals of Druidism.[10]

The Kabbalah

Witchcraft was not the only medieval counter-culture. Another minority was the Jews. Judaism's most profound mystical statement of the period, and its major contribution to later alternative religions, was the Kabbalah.[11] Kabbalism is an intricate symbol system for expressing spiritual knowledge, drawn from the premise that the Hebrew Bible is also a symbol system which expresses such knowledge through allegory and the numerological and occult meanings of words and letters. The Kabbalah predicated that as man looks toward God, he faces into the infinite darkness of God's absolute self, the *En Soph,* and between this Abyss and himself, like flashes of lightning from out of a dark cloud, the seer observes a chain of ten brilliant attributes of God. These are in male-female pairs, and range from the conscious mind of God (Kether) to the Malkuth or Shekinah, the heavenly archetype of the city of man which is in a continual love affair with human society.

Clearly the system has a connection with Neoplatonism. But the Sephiroth, as the ten attributes are called, should not be regarded merely as emanations. The Sephiroth are a freer and more reversible system. On the Last Day they will be turned on their head, so that the world of humans will be raised to the top, closer to God's essence than is God's own conscious mind! The Sephiroth are ultimately coequal attributes of God which we see as a living system, portrayed as something like a diagram of a molecular structure. Many of its key ideas entered the stream of non-Jewish thought through Renaissance Christians like Pico, Paracelsus, Boehme, and Fludd who were learned in the Kabbalah.

Alchemy and Magic

Another medieval tradition which should be mentioned is alchemy, if only because it also is part of the Hellenistic wing of the alternative reality tradition, and many of its practitioners were deeply involved in Kabbalah and magic. As Jung and Eliade have shown, alchemy was by no means merely a practical science of metallurgy.[12] The serious alchemist regarded his craft as a spiritual venture, a ritual done with retort and crucible. The procedures were of two basic types: the *coniunctio*—or marriage of opposites—a statement of the quest for wholeness; and the *transmutatio*, the transmutation of base metals into higher metals. The secret of the latter was that it was not really the metal which was changed, but the alchemist himself; he was making himself the philosopher's stone. Of course, as in any mystic path, the way was beset with temptation, and one could leave aside the higher and be diverted into metallurgy and magic for wealth.

Again, there was the tradition of ceremonial magic. Its main vehicle is the group of books called *grimoires*, of late medieval and early modern Europe, which tell how to evoke and bind demons, or even planetary gods, to the magician's will, and how to perform various minor magic. The tradition uses techniques basically the same as those of the Hellenistic Greek-Egyptian magic papyri, and even Babylonian magic, but the vocabulary is full of Hebrew names, as well as Christian invocation. Perhaps the tradition derives from the fringes of the Hermetic tradition which had become the fringes of Kabbalistic Judaism and alchemistic Christianity. Legend assigns grimoires both to Solomon and Pope Honorius. In any case its continuity is with the classical world rather than with Witchcraft, although in time these two lines found their natural affinity for each other.

Together, all these lines presented an alternative vision of reality to that of orthodox Christianity for medieval man—one that was non-historical; dealt with spiritual levels or entities above man but below God; induced changed states of consciousness through contemplation or concentration on alchemical or magical rites; and declared its experiences were more real than the formal baptism and repressive social order of the dominant culture. Yet this alternative reality was a perpetuation of late Hellentisic experience, the last religious phase before Christianity. It refused to die, but has lingered as an underground alternative to the present, almost breaking through to a second victory in the Renaissance.

THE RENAISSANCE

As the Renaissance dawned, many of these traditions rose to the surface as a reaction against the medieval system. Sages like Pico took up

Neoplatonism as a counter to scholastic Aristotelianism. The Kabbalah was used by orthodox and mystical Jews alike to oppose the Aristotelianism of philosophers such as Maimonides. Neoplatonism, occultism, alchemy, astrology, and the like flourished in Europe as never before or since. The minds who took up these things were among the most independent and intelligent of the age. It was by no means a reaction into mindless superstition, but rather a plunge into the depths of the unconscious and its symbols, and into the past, in order to integrate all of man and his story in preparation for the imminent mighty leap into the modern world. For most, Neoplatonism was soon transmuted into belief in the eternality of the laws of nature upon which science is based. Alchemy became chemistry, astrology became astronomy, and finally, perhaps, Kabbalah became psychoanalysis.[13]

But teachers of the occult tradition have treasured the seminal Neoplatonism and occultism of the Renaissance for its own sake. They hold that its ideas, far from being outdated, are a deeper seed wisdom which the world is privileged to experience only once in centuries at the moments of its great turnings. It is a mental *prima materia,* a primordial half-conscious symbol-flux on the perimeters of what is graspable by man, but out of which all that is truly new and creative must come.

Renaissance occultism is a deep and complex matter; the dust that lies on its Latinate tomes is disturbed only by historians of science and religion, who trace its role in making the modern world; Jungian psychoanalysts, who see the profundity of its symbols; and esotericists, who affirm its continuing truth and worth.

For the Renaissance savants, Neoplatonism and occultism made cause against the realism and rationalism of the Aristotelian Schoolmen, who in that day seemed part of the cramped world of the passing age. The new men wanted experience in the daring, open-ended world of mystical Platonism with its use of the deepest affects and symbols, rational or not, of all planes of mind and feeling. Whether Jewish or Christian in background, they wanted to let go of the past and soar into the infinite. It was no wonder the work of such unfettered minds in both camps should influence each other.

Their cosmos offered an unbroken graded sequence descending from God to man and nature. God was not above, but as Nicholas de Cusa put it, a circle whose circumference is nowhere and whose center is everywhere. Therefore God is in man and man is in God. Moreover, man in a special way mirrors God; the mind of man is an image of the divine mind. It is able to reflect on God in nature and also on God in himself just as God knows nature and also himself. A popular concept was that of man as microcosm—a miniature reproduction of the whole cosmos, with the brain in the place of God, the various organs in the place of sun, moon, and planets, and so forth. Naturally, the external entity had correspondence or mutual influence upon its internal equivalent, and with related stones, plants, and so forth, as the theurgic Neoplatonists had taught.

Man can also influence the great cosmos. "As above, so below"—and *vice versa.* The man of wisdom need not be merely a slave to the stars and fate. Through knowledgeable manipulation of metals, elements, thoughts which are in special rapport with planets, spirits, and archetypes personifying the higher realms which control vast ranges of the cosmos, it was believed that man could, by small magical events, precipitate great results.

In the Christianized Kabbalah and occultism of the Renaissance there was almost a revival of the end of the Hellenistic period. Ideas like allegory, magic, demonology, transmigration, and Pythagorean numerology were again discussed in their ancient forms. It is not surprising that, in this Renaissance milieu, the magus enjoyed a vigorous revival. Indeed, that ideal was vigorously defended. Marsilio Ficino (1433–99), a priest, was moved to ask the question, "What has a priest to do with medicine? What again with astrology? Why should he, a Christian, interest himself in Magic and Images, and the life animating the whole of the world?"

The answer he gave, defending his own interests, drew significantly from pre-Christian precedent. The Chaldean, Persian, and Egyptian priests were also physicians as well as astronomers, serving charity as well as piety. A sound mind and body were to be maintained together by the same person—a cultured restatement of the integrative function of the shaman.

Perhaps the most striking example of the Renaissance magus is Paracelsus (1493–1541). His life was an attack on the educational "establishment" of his day—Aristotle in science and philosophy, Galen and Celsus in medicine. They were to him "so many high asses." While medicine was his field, Paracelsus (an assumed name, meaning "going beyond Celsus," the great Roman physician) seems to have had no regular degree. But, in the magus pattern, he travelled very widely, going even as far as Russia at the invitation of the Grand Duke of Moscow. There he was captured briefly by Tartars. One biographer writes of this experience, "Their primitive psychic—*shamanistic*—techniques made such a deep impression upon him that, in later years, their central principle became the kingpin of the Paracelsian teaching."[14]

Thus Paracelsus, bombastic, fiercely and principially independent, brilliant, erratic, went about learning what he could from shamans, gypsies, and workingmen as well as the wise, testing and doubting everything, teaching and practicing where he could. He made some discoveries of importance in science and medicine. He practiced alchemy according to a system of his own—he wanted to obtain the "genius" or essence of each element and metal, a personification which would incarnate its power. He wrote a famous formula for the production of a *homunculus*. He was much given to drink, but had no use for women. He always carried with him a great sword, which some said was his magician's staff, but others that he carried in its hilt laudanum, the drug made from opium, which he discovered and may have used often. He anticipated Mesmer and first used the term "magnetic" for the force by which the stars influence men and their imaginations.

Indeed, what seems to be the most interesting idea in the vast mass of medicine, alchemy, occultism, and bold independent speculation on all sorts of things Paracelsus has left is his exaltation of imagination. For him the power of thought was central, and imagination its highest ratio. He writes, as it were on behalf of all the magi:

> Perfect Imagination is the Great Arcanum. All arcana belong to Medicine. All Medicines are arcana. All arcana are volatile, without bodies: they are a chaos,

clear, pellucid, and in the power of a star . . . Man is a star. Even as he
imagines himself to be, such he is. He is what he imagines . . . Man is a sun
and a moon and a heaven filled with stars . . .
    . . . Imagination is Creative power. Medicine uses imagination strongly
fixed. Phantasy is not imagination, but the frontier of folly. He who is born in
imagination discovers the latent forces of Nature. Imagination exists in the
perfect spirit, while phantasy exists in the body without the perfect spirit.
Because Man does not imagine perfectly at all times, arts and sciences are
uncertain, though, in fact, they are certain and, by means of imagination, can
give true results. Imagination takes precedence over all. Resolute imagination
can accomplish all things.[15]

Paracelsus was far too much an independent to form any group,
though he did have awestruck students and disciples, certain of whom in
time turned against him. Yet a passage like the above might have been
articulated by a modern New Thought teacher, or for that matter by any
occultist or magician who had penetrated his art to its core.

But it was not long before his tradition, and the pattern of his life,
gave rise to the idea of arcane orders of initiates, even as the mainstream of
science was beginning to move away from affiliation with occultist and
mentalist philosophy.

THE ROSICRUCIANS

In 1614, the town of Cassel in Germany was surprised by the appearance,
from where no one knew, of a pamphlet entitled, *The Fame of the Fraternity
of the Meritorious Order of the Rosy Cross Addressed to the Learned in General and
the Governors of Europe,* usually called for short (it being written in Latin) the
Fama Fraternitatis or *Fama.* It proposed that men of learning should band
together to undertake a reformation of science comparable to that which
religion had recently undergone, and that this should be done with the
assistance of a hitherto hidden brotherhood of light—the Rosicrucians.

The old ideal of the magus is brought into play in connection with this
esotericism and modernism. The *Fama* tells of a noble German knight,
Christian Rosencreutz (Rosy Cross) who lived from 1378 to 1484, and who
as a young man had travelled to the Near East, and to Fez in Morocco,
where he had been greeted by great initiates. He was instructed by them in
all the occult sciences, including the invocation of spirits and the preparation of the elixir of life. Returning to Europe, he gathered about himself a
secret order. After Rosencreutz' death, his order continued in secret for
more than a hundred years. Then, the *Fama* relates, his hidden burial place
was discovered with the body in perfect uncorrupted condition, surrounded by certain marvelous documents and instruments all bathed in
mysterious light. This led the order to consider it was time to make itself
known; hence the appearance of the pamphlet. A year later another pamphlet, *Confession of the Rosicrucian Fraternity,* offered initiation to selected
applicants. Aspirants were to declare themselves by publishing writings so
that the mysterious brothers could get in touch with them.

But although many philosophical and alchemical treatises were written, none seemed worthy of the attention of the hidden elect, and would-be

initiates were frustrated in their efforts to obtain access to the mysteries of the East. More sober critics pointed out wild discrepancies in the documents. The *Fama* and *Confessio* soon came to be regarded by most as either hoaxes or fantasies.

Modern Rosicrucians claim that the traditional history of Rosicrucianism makes it part of a great secret order of the wise of all ages, among whose lights in the past have been Ikhnaton, Solomon, Jesus, Plato, Philo, Plotinus, the Essenes, the early Christians, the Kabbalists, Francis Bacon, and Benjamin Franklin. There is little real evidence to connect most of these with such an order. The name "Rosicrucian" and the symbols of the rose and the cross do not appear before about 1600 in connection with occultism, although they are on the arms of Martin Luther. It seems overwhelmingly unlikely that any such person as Christian Rosencreutz ever lived. Many have pointed out that his life, as well as his alleged teachings, seem to parallel those of Paracelsus in some ways.

Of course, the idea of an alchemical fraternity need not be regarded as wholly fictional. Many alchemists flourished at that time, and probably there were various gatherings and associations among them. But the Rosicrucianism of the *Fama* does seem to propose the first known modern association ostensibly devoted to the perpetuation of the alternative reality tradition we have been endeavoring to delineate. The Rosicrucian appeal was in effect to stand for that tradition against its transmutation into naturalistic science on the one hand and orthodox Christianity on the other.[16]

At least Rosicrucianism had a sort of archetypal value. Even after the initial Rosicrucian sensation died down, it left a residue in the form of a string of emulations, some equally unrealized, some of a certain substance. In England, persons like Robert Fludd (1574–1637), John Heydon (1629–?), and Thomas Vaughan (1626–66) took up the name and cause of Rosicrucianism. They flourished on the more occultist fringe of Cambridge Platonism, writing strange disquisitions on astrology, numbers, psychic arts, and the creation.

Boehme

A very influential person from this period was the German mystic Jacob Boehme (1575–1624). A simple shoemaker by trade, he took the tradition of the Neoplatonists and the Renaissance savants, especially Paracelsus, and shaped it with his Protestant Christianity and his own powerful spirit. Boehme had influence on persons as diverse as George Fox, founder of the Quakers, and Madame Blavatsky. He taught that the soul is a magic fire derived out of God's Essence, but imprisoned in darkness. Man, as microcosm, is thus a mingling of fire and darkness. The soul is in anguish so long as it is shut up in darkness, but when striving to reunite with the primal light it becomes a flame of love. The soul fire cannot die; it must either hunger, or love, eternally. Heaven and hell, thus, are always in man.

THE EIGHTEENTH CENTURY

It is in the eighteenth century that we see the first appearance of substantial sociological entities connected with the alternative reality tradition which have clear continuity with American groups today. Examples of this are Freemasonry and its more occult imitations, and the influential movements or enthusiasms connected with such persons as Swedenborg, Saint-Germain, Cagliostro, Saint-Martin, and Mesmer. If the century of the Enlightenment was the century of the triumph of sceptical reason, it was also a century of almost unprecedented success for the magus and the purveyor of mystic initiations. It has been said the age was skeptical regarding everything except occultism. In fact, the period was one of increasing polarization between several parts of man—belief and feeling, reason and fascination. In such a situation, each side must have its due turn; as each enjoys the light it may be dangerous without the restraining presence of its opposite. It was the age of Mozart's *Magic Flute,* with its light yet sympathetic treatment of Masonic and Egyptian Mystery themes, and of Weishaupt's still-controversial Order of the Illuminati, which beneath Masonic rituals and occult jargon promoted revolutionary republicanism, and was claimed by some to have had no small role in fomenting the revolution of 1789 in France.

Freemasonry

The most important of these eighteenth century phenomena for the dissemination of alternative reality ideas (and other ideas too) was Freemasonry. Eventually it became, especially in the United States, sociologically different from what it was in eighteenth century Europe. Those serious about occult ideas moved on to establish "lodges" of Theosophical, Rosicrucian, and other persuasions in the nineteenth and early twentieth centuries. But the structure, ritual, and even concept of an initiatory and degree lodge in the midst of the modern city is largely borrowed from Freemasonry.

Freemasonry was the happy combination of two strands of the early eighteenth century: the ancient English guild of working masons, and the Rosicrucianism of the seventeenth century, which had plenty of lodge theory but little functioning institutional life. All of the traditional craft guilds had rituals for the induction of members and the inculcation of moral and spiritual teaching in a language appropriate to the lore of that craft, but the guild of masons seems to have been richer in this respect than others. Its proud old guild halls appeared suitable bases on which to build something new, and yet old, in the way of ritualized wisdom of the Pythagorean-alchemical or Rosicrucian sort, well tempered with rationalistic ethics. An enigmatic hint of longstanding connection between the two strands is found in the fact that the distinguished antiquarian Elias Ashmole (1617–92) has been linked to both the Guild of Masons and the Rosicrucians.

The modern history of Freemasonry begins on June 24, 1717, when the Grand Lodge of England was inaugurated by several old guild lodges under the obvious guidance of outsiders who wished to use the old lodge halls with their fantastic rituals as vehicles for partially new teachings. The endeavor seems to have had the support of the House of Hanover, which had recently acquired the British throne, and of many of its Whig supporters. The spiritual leader of the new Masonry was a French Huguenot clergyman living in England, John Theophilus Desaguliers (1683–1744).

He was a close friend and zealous apostle of Sir Isaac Newton. The project bore the stamp of the great physicist's remarkable combination of rational science, Rosicrucian occultism, and biblical literalism.

The new Freemasonry was at base an attempt by the more responsible element of the upper classes to counteract a very real tendency toward moral and spiritual disintegration in backlash against the previous century's excessive and often sanguinary religious polemics. The Freemasonry of the craft lodge with the Rosicrucian type of lore added to it seemed an apt instrument. It taught rectitude in the most solemn manner; at the same time its ethos was not at odds with the new veneration of science and reason. It was only supportive of the discreet anticlericalism and Deism of many Enlightenment gentlemen, yet it did not disdain the British flair for ceremony which remains even in the most unpromising times. Indeed, with its unlikely but auspicious marriage of the virtues of solid British craftsmanship to an aura of the immemorial and mystic usages of oriental temples, Masonry supported both the patriotism and the yearnings of those who desired more than the flat unceremonial religion of the day.

Freemasonry spread quickly from England to the continent, as well as to America and other parts of the British world. Before long Europe was honeycombed with Masonic organizations, the most prominent of which was the famous Grand Orient of France. Its honorary Grand Master was a member of the Bourbon royal family, and its membership embraced both prominent aristocrats and eminent clergy. The liberal Joseph II of Austria (reigned 1780–90), a patron of Mozart, encouraged Masonry, as did Frederick the Great. But not all Masonic organizations were of such exalted standing. There was no unity of rite or structure among groups using that title. The name was immensely popular, and so was adopted by any sort of society with a secret handshake and pretension to ancient lore. These ranged from the Swedenborgian rite lodges, based on the teachings of the Swedish seer, to the Egyptian Masonry of the inimitable Cagliostro.

A good example of Masonic type organizations is the Order of the Illuminati, established in Bavaria in 1776 by Adam Weishaupt. It did not make much headway until a Baron von Knigge entered it in 1780. A man of powerful imagination, von Knigge had been initiated into most of the secret and Masonic orders of the day. The occult possessed a deep fascination for him. Under his leadership the Order of the Illuminati progressed rapidly among the wealthy and educated and those in positions of governmental power in Germany. It established an elaborate structure of degrees and an organization modeled on that of the Jesuits. The Order attracted progressive-minded people, and was accused of advocating political revolution. Thus the conservative, clericalist Bavarian government took steps to suppress it.

Swedenborg

Perhaps the most pivotal and influential individual figure from the eighteenth century is Emmanuel Swedenborg (1688–1772). He is the major bridge between the old medieval alchemist or Rosicrucian in his dark laboratory, and the Spiritualist seance on the American frontier or the modern Theosophical lecture. Swedenborg, a man of superb intellectual gifts, was the son of a Lutheran bishop. As a young man he found himself drawn to science. Certain of his writings in mathematics, engineering, physics, cosmology, politics, and even psychology were definitely in advance of their time. But explorations of these fields were not able to answer his deepest questings, and he began to turn more and more to philosophy.

Then, when he was about fifty-five, a remarkable series of visions began to manifest themselves to him. According to him, the spirits of the departed, and even God himself, appeared before him with perfect visual reality. Moreover, the Swedish mystic was taken on lengthy journeys through the realms of heaven and hell, which he describes with fullest detail as to housing, civic organization, economic life, and so forth. He provides us with current interviews of notables of the past, from Plato to Luther and Calvin.

Swedenborg's writing, after the onset of the revelations, was extraordinarily prolific. In addition to his descriptions of the supernatural spheres and their activities in such works as *Heaven and Hell* and *The Last Judgment*, he produced doctrinal works like *The True Christian Religion*, as well as bulky commentaries on Genesis and the Apocalypse. A survey of this literature reveals his continuity with the alternative reality tradition, even though he, like some of the Spiritualists he influenced, was at pains to keep a Christian façade.[17]

Swedenborg was more effective than anyone else in popularizing ideas that come out of the alternative reality tradition in the modern world. Even though he is not too well known today, most occult and metaphysical movements, except direct Eastern imports, are greatly indebted to him. There is a Swedenborgian church—the Church of the New Jerusalem. Swedenborg had such influence because he dealt not directly with recondite Kabbalistic puzzles, but from his concrete visions he gave answers to the sort of questions ordinary Christians would ask, such as, What is heaven like? What really goes on in hell? How do spirits live? But his method, apart from the direct visions, is Kabbalistic, as are his ultimate concepts. As Sir Isaac Newton's theological writings indicate, there was in the eighteenth century an almost Kabbalist Protestantism rife with interpretations of the words and numbers of the book of Revelation.

Swedenborg spoke of a "Lost Word," at once a primitive innocence and a Philosopher's Stone of transformation. He mentioned an arcane superancient scripture preserved in central Asia.

> The ancient Word, which existed in Asia before the Israelitish Word, is still preserved among the people of Great Tartary. In the spiritual world I have conversed with spirits and angels who came from that country. They told me they had possessed from the most ancient times and still possessed a Word; and that they performed their divine worship in accordance with this word which consisted of pure correspondences.[18]

Correspondences, as we have seen, are the Neoplatonist and Paracelsean idea of "magnetic" relationships between specific planets, stones, organs, etc., as well as allegorical interpretations of scriptural words. This idea of an ancient scripture in central Asia was also reported by Blavatsky.

In addition, Swedenborg as precursor of the modern new religions has contributed:

1. The Gnostic, Kabbalistic, and Pythagorean idea of pre- and post-existence in a spiritual state.
2. The Spiritualist idea of talk with persons on the other side.
3. A monistic idea of God.
4. A Gnostic idea of events of great importance transpiring in the invisible spiritual world known only to initiates.
5. Most significantly, the Second Coming of Christ, which Swedenborg said happened spiritually in 1757. His emphasis on this invisible consummation must be a precursor of modern "New Age" and "Aquarian Age" ideas.
6. The idea of the plurality of worlds, each with its own spirits and angels.
7. The Renaissance idea that God's consciousness is continuous with man's.

Swedenborg, with his mysterious travels to the other side, was a real magus or shaman. His rich and literalistic mysticism has been attractive to America. John Chapman, "Johnny Appleseed," was a Swedenborgian. He lived as something of an itinerant and thoroughly American Saint Francis, in love with all life here and beyond this world. As he wandered about the frontier, he left Swedenborgian literature in cabins everywhere, planting not only apples but also the Spiritualist enthusiasm of the 1850s, for Spiritualism was just a practical frontier application of the Swede's visions.

Saint-Germain

Before coming to Spiritualism, however, we must first look at a few habitués of the European courts of the *ancien régime*. The individual who called himself the Comte de Saint-Germain (approximately 1710–85) was the talk of high society in the middle of the century. He combined mystical conversation concerning ancient initiations and Masonic rites with a pleasingly flippant character. He served as a diplomat (and spy) for several monarchs. His birth and death (as he no doubt wished) are shrouded in mystery; some say he was a Portuguese Jew, but he talked knowingly of kinship with Transylvanian royalty, and above all loved to further the rumors that he had lived for millennia, and would for many more. This is the view that certain Theosophists have taken of him. They believe Saint-Germain to be one of the Masters of the Seven Rays, an adept of benign magic who lives in his ancestral palace somewhere in eastern Europe. The "I Am" movement has made him virtually its central figure. In the eighteenth century he was reputedly much involved in spreading mystical and Masonic rites.

Cagliostro

Cagliostro (died 1795) is a man of whom much more has been written, but of whom perhaps no more is known. He too appeared in the middle of the century in the courts of Europe, from England to St. Petersburg, claiming to be an alchemist, master of spirits, and healer. In coming to France, he struck up a friendship with the prominent and wealthy Cardinal de Rohan. He moved into the highest social circles. In the eighteenth century ancient Egypt was beginning to be appreciated anew as the Greeks and Romans had appreciated it—a darkly fascinating land of immemorial mystery and wisdom and occult initiations. Cagliostro admitted many people into a rite he called Egyptian Masonry, which he claimed was the oldest ceremonial in the world and was founded by Enoch. It received both men and women; Cagliostro was its "Grand Copht," his wife "Grand Mistress." Much has been written about its ridiculous pretensions, and there have been allegations of scandalous behavior and chicanery in connection with it. But probably it was actually no more than an enhancement of the magus's magnetic personality with a hodgepodge of alchemical and occult jargon.

Cagliostro seems to have been a complex personality, with strands of deep sincerity interwined with opportunism. He honestly sought to make his healing gifts available to rich and poor alike. He quietly gave much of the wealth he accumulated to charity, and strove tirelessly to spread his Masonic organization both in favorable times and in the face of adversity. Unfortunately, he was implicated with his friend de Rohan in the celebrated diamond necklace affair. Though he was acquitted, the enmity of the king and queen ruined his career. Not for the first time, malicious enemies pounced upon him. Some said, as some still do, that he was actually a certain Peter Balsamo from Sicily, a charlatan and confidence man with the assumed name of Cagliostro. Regarding his origins, Cagliostro himself told an elaborate story of his having been born of Christian parents in Arabia. He had, he said, travelled throughout the kingdoms of Asia and Africa, and in the usual way of the magus, attained to esoteric wisdom. But his end was dismal. After his fall from the light in France he unwisely went to Rome, where the Inquisition seized him, tried him for his Masonic activities, and sentenced him to the dungeon of San Leo where he perished a few years later.

Mesmer

Yet another famous eighteenth-century figure is the Austrian doctor Franz Anton Mesmer (1733–1815), who also flourished in Paris just before the Revolution. From his name derives the word *Mesmerism*, which has come to mean hypnotism. But although Mesmer was the discoverer of the hypnotic state in a form which was accessible to medical analysis and use, that was a by-product of a somewhat more occult method of healing, with an accompanying worldview, which he devised. Unquestionably Mesmer discovered anew the psychosomatic character of much illness, and the induction of altered states of consciousness in which patients were highly susceptible to suggestion aimed at healing. He believed that he had found a subtle universal substance which gives life and vitality; sickness, he considered, was due to its imbalance or loss. At first he tried to control it by magnets; later he found that it could be governed even better by techniques called "animal magnetism." They consisted of stroking, suggestion, "passes," or the moving of hands by the therapist over the patient for a prolonged time, or the famous seance-like sessions in which patients sat around a tub of dilute sulfuric acid holding iron bars in contact with it. In any case, the process was clearly capable of implying the influx of healing energies.

Later generations of practicioners were to take Mesmer's work in two directions. On the one hand, both medical hypnosis and psychoanalysis in the tradition of Sigmund Freud and his disciples owe their ultimate inspiration to Mesmer and his school. On the other, persons of more occult inclination were to make both the theory and practice of mesmerism a cornerstone of Spiritualism, Theosophy, parapsychology, and modern magic. Mesmer himself encouraged this trend, for he believed that "animal magnetism" could awaken latent capacities for extrasensory perception and understanding the secrets of the universe. Each person, he believed, has an inner sense to which all time and all places are one; dreams and clairvoyance draw from its power, but his techniques could put its use on a scientific basis. Mesmer thought that much of the experience of shamans and mystics of the past was valid, though for reasons not previously comprehended. Later, H.P. Blavatsky, founder of modern Theosophy, showed the importance of his ideas by calling Mesmerism the most important branch of magic, and indeed the true basis of what is called magical or miraculous.[19]

The Alternative Tradition Comes to the New World

In England, the Elizabethan era which lay just before the first British settlements in what is now the United States, in Virginia in 1607 and Massachusetts in 1620, was a heyday of the worldview underlying the alternative tradition as revived by the Renaissance. While not widely perceived as incompatible with Christianity, it provided its cosmological backdrop and was the basis of much science and popular belief; the worldview is finely articulated in writers of the period from Shakespeare on down. Its fundamental pillars, as we have already suggested, were Ptolemaic astronomy with its belief in the earth as the center of the universe, the "great chain of being" concept of a hierarchy of increasingly superior intelligences linking heaven and earth, and "correspondences." The last, the notion that mystical lines of force link particular elements of the universe above and below, within and without, justified such practices as astrology and alchemy. Closely allied to this worldview was the classical medicine based on "humors" and bodily "airs" possessing such linkages, the practice of ceremonial magic with its evocation of spirits, and belief in witchcraft. (It may be noted that while serious Christians, such as the Puritans, had doubts about practices like astrology considered unbiblical, they widely accepted the possibility of witchcraft since it appeared to have the sanction of the Scriptures.)

This worldview came to the New World with the more educated of the early immigrants. Its presence is symbolized by the famous Salem witch trials of the 1690s and the establishment of the Rosicrucian society in Germantown, Pennsylvania, in 1694. But through the seventeenth century that worldview had been under increasing pressure from the new science, with its fresh picture of the universe offered by Copernicus and Newton, and its new view of man sparked by such discoveries as Harvey's of the circulation of the blood. One can perceive evidence of the tension between the two worldviews in the writing of such colonial intellectuals as Jonathan Edwards, Cotton Mather, and Benjamin Franklin.

But the old picture of man and the universe receded as inexorably as a tide, so that by the end of the eighteenth century belief among the educated in such items as astrology and witchcraft had virtually vanished. However, as that old worldview declined it also fragmented, so that one held to certain tenets of the old while affirming other truths advanced by the new. Thus Benjamin Franklin, while ridiculing astrology, wrote favorably of the "great chain of being" concept with its optimistic implication that evil was only a matter of perspective. Even more important was the continuing life of what might be called the "spiritual" perspective underlying the old worldview even as certain of its manifestations dwindled: the idea that consciousness underlies the universe, that its parts are all interrelated and guided by hidden laws and relationships, and that humanity has a central place in its meaning. While very few people after 1800 believed in the old Ptolemaic astronomy, many more continued to hold that humanity, and therefore the earth on which it dwells, has a special spiritual place in the scheme of things; such ideas receded only briefly before rising once again in new forms in the nineteenth century.[20]

In America, the new forms were much influenced by Freemasonry, already discussed, symbolized by the well-known painting of Washington in Masonic garb. Deeply tinctured as it was by Enlightenment Deism and ethical rationalism, the Masonic lodge nonetheless preserved the idea of an ancient wisdom conveyed by symbols often of occult background, and of initiatory societies dedicated to its inculcation. Early in the century, Swedenborgianism and Mesmerism, their quest for transcendent reality enhanced by the fresh Romantic mood, took their place as popular enthusiasms. To that era we now turn.

SPIRITUALISM AND THE NINETEENTH CENTURY

The nineteenth century was a period of tremendous change and growth in the alternative reality tradition, just as it was in the political, industrial, and scientific life of humankind. The alternative reality tradition is not just a conservative persistence of something grounded in an obsolete age, wanting only to undo the work of history. Its dynamic cannot be fully understood if one considers it merely a negative reaction to the dominant culture of the day. The alternative reality tradition has a life of its own and its own kind of creativity which interacts with the dominant culture—not just responds to it.

Yet it is true that the dominant mood of an era calls forth, as an undertow, its opposite. Often in society the alternative reality tradition is able to fill this role, and is thereby given opportunities to surface. The religious excesses of the seventeenth century called into being that rationalistic science which finally broke up the Renaissance alliance of physical science with alchemy and occultism. But against the background of the common sense of the Enlightenment, there was an uncontained fascination with the marvelous and mysterious which appeared in the wilder side of Masonry and the careers of such men as Saint-Germain and Cagliostro.

The eighteenth century mind envisioned a clockwork music box universe in which there just might be a secret spring which, if touched, would cause delighted handclapping by making the works run backwards or set off an amazing fireworks display. But the great passion of the nineteenth century was for infinity, and hence for totality. Gothicism, romanticism, science, and revolution had shown there were more facets to human experience and potential than accounted for by the boxed-in universe of the earlier age.

At the same time, the nineteenth centry was an era of individualism, with its accompanying loneliness, and the suffering resulting from its social blindness. Finally, it was a time moved by the discovery, or rediscovery, of the East, not only as the land of spices, but as home of wonder and philosophy.

The unlimited passion for expansiveness attached itself to a variety of vehicles. Connected with the gothic past, it became Catholic romanticism or the Theosophical delight in "ancient mystery schools." In metaphysics, it expressed itself naturally in the transcendental monism of Fichte, Emerson, and Quimby, which ended in the "mind is all" idealism of New Thought of today. Attached to a future orientation, this expansiveness became utopian socialism and evolutionary optimism, which set the stage for all sorts of experimental societies and reformist causes—many with a cultist character. In politics, it became imperialism and nationalism and revolution. In science and philology, it was the quest for origins and for the comprehensive system.

Against this backdrop the claims of the alternative reality tradition were at once more serious and more precarious—more serious because their real impulse could be better understood, more precarious because there were so many rival offerings of infinities.

Yet for all that, the ordinary contemporary view of the age—an age in which, after all, poets died young while ruthless industrialists grew fat—was that it was a time of dead materialism and wingless thought. The alternative reality tradition, revamped in new dress, was able to make some appeal. Every age needs some frontier of mystery, and if the usual rites are no longer mysterious, it will discover new—or old—mysteries. In the Victorian age, wonder (the heart of the alternative reality tradition) took for some the form of passion for psychic phenomena, for ghosts and spirit communication.

Spiritualism as a definite religious movement is a product of that century. It provided a direct experience of the marvelous, in a way that goes back to archaic shamanism. The "other side" is revealed through a remarkable individual who, having been initiated, can control spirits, travel to their world, or allow spirits or ancestors to communicate. Edward

Burnet Tylor, the greatest nineteenth century anthropologist, defined the remote savage beginnings of religion as animism, a belief in souls distinct from their physical bodies or vehicles. Of course, Victorian man felt that his own scientific rationalism or ethical monotheism was entirely separate from these rude origins.

A view of the soul not greatly different from animism, and a use of psychic display reminiscent of shamanism, became popular in the drawing rooms of Victorian Europe and America. From the Court of the French Emperor to the frontier villages of the Great Plains, in Russia and Brazil, tables rose and turned, rappings sounded out occult messages, and the voices of the dear departed gone over to the "Summerland" spoke through trumpets marvelously floating in the air. The mood of the Empire parlor, with its wealth of greenery, its overstuffed chairs, its crillioned pianoforte, in which the spirit-entranced circle would gather in near-darkness, may have been different from that of the central Asian shaman with loud bells and drum and birdfeathers, shaking with trance amid his leather-clad tribesmen. But it was the same altar, and Spiritualists with some right boasted that theirs was the oldest religion in the world.

It is to what was then one of the newest nations in the world, the United States of America, that the credit must go for the reemergence of this most ancient of faiths in its modern form. Its institutional birth can be pinpointed quite precisely to the evening of March 31, 1848, in the home of John Fox at Hydesville, in upstate New York. (It had been preceded by spirit communication through rapping among the Shakers of Watervliet, New York.)

The Fox family had two daughters, Margaretta (then eleven) and Kate (then eight). Since moving into the house three months before, they had been hearing puzzling noises, mostly rappings like imitations of the recently invented Morse Code. On the night of March 31, the younger daughter, Kate, is said to have snapped her fingers at the rappings and said, "Here Mr. Splitfoot [the devil], do as I do!" She then proceeded to work out a code with the rappings. The Foxes were told that the noises were caused by the spirit of a peddler who had been murdered in the house four or five years before. A skeleton which seemed to confirm the story was allegedly found in 1904 after a cellar wall collapsed.

In 1848, the story of the Hydesville occurrence was an immediate sensation. A circle began meeting in the Fox home to discuss and experience the phenomena. Committees of ministers and others from nearby Rochester investigated it and disputed their results amidst great publicity. An enthusiasm for spirit manifestations spread rapidly. Circles met everywhere to reproduce, if possible, the remarkable events. Lecturers and publications followed. Soon not only rappings but voice mediumship from the spirit world, table tilting, and other such phenomena were reported. The Fox sisters aided the growth of the Spiritualist movement by their traveling, lectures, and demonstrations. The speed with which Spiritualism grew, however, indicates the nation must in some way have been in remarkable readiness for such a breakthrough; it was like a field dry and ready for the torch.

Prominent supporters of Spiritualism included Horace Greeley,

James Fenimore Cooper, W. C. Bryant, Governor Talmadge of Michigan, and, by 1857, Abraham Lincoln. In the early 1850s six or seven Spiritualist newspapers and magazines were published, and sensational stories in the secular press also whipped the enthusiasm to greater and greater heights. In 1857 it was reported the majority of the inhabitants of Cleveland and the Western Reserve section of Ohio were Spiritualists. In many places the regular churches were forced to close; Spiritualist meetings were packed.

One of the most significant aspects of the spiritually restless early nineteenth century in America was the establishment of many utopian communities, whether based on socialist or religious principles. It was not long after 1848 that a number of such communities appeared with Spiritualist connections. Sometimes, as in the case of the Mountain Cove community in Virginia, the whole enterprise was directed by the spirits (in this case such exalted biblical figures as St. Paul, St. John, and Daniel) through the medium. Both the Rappite and Owenite communities in New Harmony, Indiana, ended amid an effusion of psychic phenomena.

Brook Farm, Hopedale, and Ceresco were well-known utopian communities which developed Spiritualist practices after their founding. These three had been established before 1848, but they experienced spirit manifestations after the enthusiasm began, submitted to important guidance from the spirits (in the case of Hopedale, from the shade of the founder, Adin Ballon, after his death in 1852), and did much to help advance Spiritualism. Other Spiritualist communities, like Harmony Springs, Mountain Cove, and Kiantone, through bizarre excesses of free love, crank teaching, and flagrant claims, brought discredit to the movement.

In America Spiritualism suffered wild fluctuations in its support. At times it received spectacular accolades, at times vehement ridicule. But the ridicule grew stronger. The enthusiasm of the fifties proved a passing fad. The movement was hurt by a series of exposures of fraudulent mediums, by the follies of the fringe, and by the opposition of the churches and important segments of the academic world. Finally, the passions of the Civil War swallowed up all other national emotions.[21]

While many fell away after 1860, a remnant carried on Spiritualism, and it was to enjoy later moments of comparative fame, especially in the period between the two World Wars. Moreover, the seed of the movement was carried in the fifties from America to Europe, where it experienced less meteoric but more stable success.

Why did Spiritualism emerge when and where it did? The upstate New York territory in which it started has been called the "Burnt-Over Country." It was a region that had experienced a surfeit of revivals during the first decades of the century. After these had exhausted the potential for evangelical Christian conversion, other alternatives moved in to fill the void. But the revivals had also helped pave the way, for the phenomena they had manifested such as speaking in strange, rapturous ways, made the trance process in mediumship less unfamiliar.

On the other hand, the frontier experience also worked in favor of unorthodoxy. The frontiersman was an individualist, cut off from his roots. He believed he was creating a new and far better civilization out of the wilderness. At the same time, hardship and death were his constant companions. Both his individualism and his nearness to death cemented the appeal of Spiritualism. He would phrase spiritual issues in terms of "Have those I loved survived physical death *as individuals* with whom I can communicate? Will I so survive? Can this be proven in ways concrete enough to convince a hardheaded, practical American who still desperately wants to believe?" The fact that the teaching was new and denounced as unorthodox would have only enhanced its appeal for many frontier Americans. The freedom to form new churches allowed by the religious liberty of the American nation, the institutional flux and lack of any long-established churches on the frontier, and the idea of a new age with new ways being born, all combined to permit Spiritualism to find ready expression in all three of the forms of expression, and Spiritualist churches to spring up rapidly.

Certain intellectual influences also paved the way such as Swedenborgianism, which people like John Chapman had spread through the frontier. A generation was already familiar with the idea of investigating the lives of those who had gone beyond. The "animal magnetism" of Mesmer had made the phenomena of trance and clairvoyance familiar.

All these influences are evident in the career of Andrew Jackson Davis (1826–1910), the "Poughkeepsie Seer" who became the most important American Spiritualist writer. With little formal education, Davis was put into trance by a Poughkeepsie tailor who had heard a series of lectures on "animal magnetism." Davis became a professional clairvoyant. In 1844 he said that he had fallen into a trance while alone and conversed with Galen and Swedenborg.

Later he gave a series of trance lectures which were published in 1847, just before the Fox sisters' experience, as *The Principles of Nature, Her Divine Revelations, and Voice to Mankind*. Fundamentally Swedenborgian, this work presented an evolutionary view of nature. It held, moreover, that the earth is surrounded by a series of spiritual planes. The soul naturally gravitates to its own level, and remains on that plane until it is ready to evolve to the next higher; the progress is always upward, whether fast or slow. In social thought, Davis, like many early Spiritualists, was a radical. He predicted a new utopian dispensation preceded by a social revolution.

The other most important Spiritualist philosopher was the Frenchman Hyppolyte Léon Denizard Rivail (1803–69), who wrote under the name of Allan Kardec in the 1860s. He differed from Davis in holding to reincarnation, which could occur periodically as decisive events in the career of the soul until it reached a very high level. To this day there is a large and influential Kardecist church in Brazil. The argument over reincarnation has been a major issue among Spiritualists ever since.

The idealism of a system like Davis's carries into occult dimensions the Transcendentalism of Emerson. The belief that consciousness is fundamental to existence, creates its own world, and is continuous with an evolving world spirit is of course a steady component of the alternative reality tradition. It rolls like a great river through the fields of early nineteenth century philosophy. Later the river was dammed by a new realism and scientific positivism, but dribbling streams continued to trickle on.

Finally, proximity to the shamanism and spiritism of the American

Indians may have influenced the movement. Descriptions of the evocation of spirit guides by the Native American shamans had been published early in the century by pioneer ethnologists like Henry Rowe Schoolcraft. The popularity of the Indian guide theme in later Spiritualism suggests a half-conscious tribute to those who were the first American Spiritualists, and who, despite the frontier wars, have always been much respected by their white imitators. In nineteenth century Spiritualism there was a great enthusiasm for the "Shawnee Prophet" (1768–1837), brother of Chief Tecumseh, who became a legendary seer.

There is also the influence of the European occult tradition. Masonry, Witchcraft, and Rosicrucianism had all been imported to America. The Salem witch trials of 1692 and the Anti-Masonic Party of the mid-century bear them ungrateful witness. But essentially Spiritualism is a folk, home-centered movement. It was not founded by a single magus and does not boast mighty initiations or proud lodges. It is what becomes of the occult tradition when processed through the minds of a literalistic Swede and an American original like Davis, and then potently mixed with the wild, open society of the frontier with its direct exposure to an archaic shamanistic people, its enthusiasm, and its hope of building a new order.

THEOSOPHY

The return of the magus is the theme of the next great nineteenth century movement, Theosophy. This is a movement which has behind it one of the most memorable of those who have played the role of magus, Helena Petrovna Blavatsky.

Helena Blavatsky, or H.P.B. as her friends and followers affectionately call her, was a lady of great mystery and complexity. She was clearly composed of several personalities, all of them extreme. Whether she is considered a fraud and confidence artist, or a sage of sages, or a compulsive liar, or a rare psychic and intimate of supernormal entities—whatever she was, or if she was all of them together, she was that to an unrivalled degree. Furthermore, she was laden with the exotic aura of a lady of Russian aristocratic background. She seemed an exile from a world of monarchical splendor. Moreover, she told tales of long intervening years of fabulous travel and initiations by members of a secret occult order in Greece, Egypt, and Tibet. The "Masters" and the Order were not unlike those portrayed in the then popular novels of Bulwar-Lytton such as *Zanoni*. H.P.B. had eyes of a singularly opaque, yet piercing, hypnotic quality, as though she penetrated everything while revealing nothing of herself except sheer, burning psychic power. Nor could any equal her public work, whether in mysterious phenomena produced, in fascination of conversation, in mass of pages written expounding the philosophy of the "ancient wisdom," or in travel and fame.

The real H.P.B. was born in Russia in 1831 and died in London in 1891. Her family was of high nobility. As a child she was unusual—headstrong, secretive, imaginative. She would hide in strange places reading myths and legends for hours while her family searched desperately. She would tell her brothers and sisters marvelous tales of the fossils and animals in the manor's zoological museum, describing not only the animal's immediate life, but also its previous incarnations.

She was a quite an uncontrollable child—at once obstinate, of a terrifying temper, and fanciful and mystical. She was married at the age of sixteen to N. V. Blavatsky, Vice-Governor of Erivan and a man in his forties. Less than a year before she had plunged her leg into scalding water rather than attend a fancy ball at a Viceroy's. She later said that at that time if any young man had dared to speak to her of love, she would have shot him like a dog who bit her, and on another occasion said, "I wouldn't be a slave to God Himself, let alone man." It seems her sudden and surprising decision to contract the marriage was but another example of her strong-headed contrariness, and was apparently in response to taunts that no man would want such a strange and graceless young lady. Also marriage at least made her independent of her family. In any event, the marriage did not last long. Whether the ill-matched couple remained together less than three weeks, as H.P.B. asserted, or longer as others have said, she managed to flee her older husband and her native country very soon. Apparently she was supplied with some funds by her family.

In 1851 she was in London with her father, and here she says she first viewed her "Master," a striking turbaned man of the East. During the later Russian period, she amazed her family and social circle with remarkable displays of psychic and magical powers. H.P.B. then virtually disappeared from sight for some twenty years, with the exception of 1858–64 which she spent again in Russia with her family and, it seems, in part with N. V. Blavatsky.

As for the balance of years, if we take her word for it, H.P.B. ranged widely and wildly over the world, contacting shamans and masters of arcane lore in places as far apart as Egypt, Mexico, Canada, and inner Asia, always seeking her ultimate goal, Tibet. She finally achieved it, spending 1864–67 there undergoing initiations with her Masters. Thus she fulfilled the archetype of the magus—remarkable birth and childhood, wide travel, esoteric initiation, enigmatic personality, supernormal powers.

She came to America in 1874 and met a successful agricultural scientist and lawyer who was also keenly interested in investigation of Spiritualist phenomena, Henry Steel Olcott. The mysterious Russian lady and the American man of affairs became inseparable. Together they were founders of the Theosophical Society in 1875. With the help of the Masters, and of Olcott, H.P.B. wrote her first book, *Isis Unveiled*, published in 1877.

The Theosophical Society was founded to discuss ideas regarding ancient lore, supernatural phenomena, and the expansion of human powers of mind and spirit. Its nucleus was a group which had gathered in H.P.B.'s apartment to hear a lecture putting forth curious Egyptological speculations. The group included a Unitarian minister and General Doubleday, the inventor of baseball, but seems to have been composed mostly of persons of the artistic and literary sort, probably rather Bohemian.

Olcott's fascinating *Old Diary Leaves* vividly recalls the New York days.

The room where H.P.B. held commerce with her Masters, wrote *Isis Unveiled,* and entertained Olcott and others with psychic "phenomena," was heavy with smoke from incense and her imported cigarettes. Olcott and H.P.B. held legendary parties replete with thrillingly serious discussions of the occult lore, or else put on uproarious charades which might spoof Theosophy first of all. The fantastic apartment in New York was the center of something at once dangerously avant-garde—the first cremation in America was under Theosophical auspices—and full of whispers of ancient caves and tombs. Above all there was the presence of H.P.B., defiant of society, talking in exotic accent of mysteries far outside its purview. There was the aura of her Spiritualist antecedents—the arcane books and pictures in the room with its bizarre decorations, one wall plastered by a jungle scene made of colored leaves. There was the independence of the principals regarding social convention. It is not surprising that the early Theosophists quickly won a notoriety like that of the "hippies" in the 1960s.

The New York period ended in 1878, when Madame Blavatsky and Colonel Olcott sailed to India. That land, and beyond it enigmatic Tibet, had become the magnet of their spiritual adventure, surpassing Egypt, the Kabbalah, and the old Rosicrucians. Those Western sources had been the major inspirations of *Isis Unveiled,* which does not make much mention of reincarnation. But the author had been talking increasingly of India and Eastern Masters. By the time she and Olcott arrived they were heady with the classic quest of the westerner for spiritual light from the East. Olcott wrote that upon landing in Bombay

> the first thing I did on touching land was to stoop down and kiss the granite step; my instinctive act of pooja! For here we were at last on sacred soil; our past forgotten, our perilous and disagreeable sea-voyage gone out of mind, the agony of long deferred hopes replaced by the thrilling joy of presence in the land of the Rishis, the cradle country of religions, the dwelling place of the Masters, the home of our dusky brothers and sisters, with whom to live and die was all we could desire.[22]

Eventually a Theosophical headquarters was established at Adyar in Madras, India. The society spread throughout Europe and America. The respect Theosophists showed for the indigenous religions of Asia played a role leading to cultural revival, national self-consciousness, and finally the independence movements of the present century which should not be underestimated. For his work in promoting Buddhism, Colonel Olcott is regarded as a major national hero in Sri Lanka (Ceylon) he has been portrayed on a beautiful commemorative stamp of that nation.

The history of the Theosophical Society was never smooth, however. In the early 1880s, certain Theosophists, particularly A. P. Sinnett, had been receiving letters signed by one of the Masters. He would find them in unexpected places—tucked in the inner fold of a napkin, or among the papers on his desk or in a special "shrine room." When Blavatsky returned to Europe in 1884, a Mr. and Mrs. Coulomb, who had been left in charge of the Adyar buildings, charged that they had been given instructions by H.P.B. to produce the letters fraudulently. The matter was investigated by the Society for Psychical Research, together with other of H.P.B.'s "phenomena," and the ensuing report, though still disputed, did much damage to the Theosophists.[23]

After the death of Blavatsky, the American society broke with the Adyar headquarters. The lady who became head of the American society, Katherine Tingley, established a remarkable Theosophical utopia at Point Loma, in San Diego, California which survived over forty years. The Adyar society, which soon recovered its ground to embrace most American Theosophists, was dominated during the first three decades of the twentieth century by Annie Besant and C. W. Leadbeater. During their time the concept of the Masters was refined into a schematic hierarchy. A young Indian boy, Krishnamurti, was advanced as likely to become the World Teacher for this era. This caused considerable excitement until he renounced the claim in 1929.

Theosophy was successful in the middle and upper classes of American society before the First World War and in the 1920s. It was a time when after-dinner lectures were popular, and the magnetic personalities, both European and Indian, who represented Theosophy provided sensational and thought-provoking presentations.[24]

Theosophy occupies a central place in the history of new spiritual movements, for the writings of Blavatsky and some of her followers have had a great influence outside of her organization. They represent an interesting and significant attempt to interpret the alternative reality tradition. The notion of hidden Masters, far ahead of the rest of mankind in spiritual evolution and secret holders of earth's destiny, is not new in that tradition. It had been suggested by theurgic Neoplatonism, Rosicrucian lore, and earlier in the nineteenth century by the Polish philosopher Hoene Wronski, the French writer on magic Eliphas Levi, and Bulwar-Lytton the novelist.

But the Theosophists developed the "Masters" idea more fully than anyone else, and, connecting it with similar Eastern ideas such as the role of the transcendent Rishis in Hinduism and the Bodhisattvas in Buddhism, made it a foundation of a world view. In her greatest book, *The Secret Doctrine* (1888), Blavatsky brings together planetary and individual initiation. Both move from the consciousness of the atom to planes far beyond our scan—animals, man, and the Masters are on a great ladder. This makes initiation, expanding one's consciousness to move from one rung to a higher one, central. It suggests what we may call a psychological view of the nature of reality in contrast to a mechanical or even biological one. Matter is, with spirit, an original production of the One and is not rejected. But areas of experience, planets, the solar system, all have behind them high minds who control them. It is perhaps a bold way of saying that the most adequate way to describe reality is to say its expressions are expressions of chains of consciousness—the minds of individual men are like embodied archetypes, fantasies, memories, or ideas in the vaster mind of the planet, and in turn parts of the mind of the solar system, and on up. The "White Lodge" Masters are intermediate figures who prepare themselves and others for planetary and cosmic initiations.

In a cosmos like this, the important thing is to move from one level of consciousness to another—from an animal's to man's, a man's to a Master's, and Master's to a planet's or a solar system's. This would mean being able to include things within one's awareness which were not included before. The great moments of a mind are when new connections are seen, like a gestalt, and are emotionally and subjectively realized. These would correspond to the great moments of initiation into a "higher plane" with a wider scope of activity or understanding so celebrated by Theosophists.

NEW THOUGHT

Belief in the supreme reality and power of mind is fundamental to another late nineteenth century development, New Thought. It is not so much a church in itself as a type of teaching which has influenced a number of groups. Certain churches, like the Church of Religious Science, Church of Divine Science, and Unity, are based on its tenets. But a vast variety of what is called "metaphysical," or even "positive thinking," derives from this tradition and its major writers—Phineas Quimby, Ralph Waldo Trine, Horatio Dresser, Thomas Troward, and Ernest Holmes.

New Thought is a modern Western adaptation of the assumption that mind is fundamental and causative. This means that the real cause of every event is an internal, nonmaterial idea. Like Theosophy it holds the inner reality of the universe to be mind and idea. It does not point to Masters as the minds which make things happen, but to the mental potential of every individual. New Thought teachers have always striven to show how, in very practical ways, thoughts of health, wholeness, and success can create their corresponding material realities. If mind is the ground of the physical world, then changing one's thoughts ought to change the physical world. Even if one concentrates on particular objects, for example a needed sum of money, this act will draw corresponding physical realities into being. New Thought has always put special emphasis on healing—both of mind and body. It has generally taken a style similar to that of liberal Protestantism and has thus emphasized verbal expression and forming congregations. Its atmosphere is optimistic, theologically liberal, extravertive, generally nonradical in life style and social opinion.

The remote roots of New Thought may lie in Hegel and Emerson—German idealism and New England transcendentalism—but the real originator of the movement is Phineas P. Quimby (1802–66). J. Stillson Judah has shown that there are large areas of agreement between Quimby and the Spiritualist Andrew Jackson Davis, which in turn shows how pervasive the influence of Swedenborg has been.[25] Both agreed that God (pure mind or spirit) is wisdom and man's real nature. But while Davis, like Blavatsky, was interested in world evolution and life after death, Quimby was concerned with healing. Disease, he taught, has its roots in mind. Behind every illness is an erroneous idea. It is the false idea that matter has a reality and power of its own that cause disease. Actually matter comes into being at the behest of God, and God, as wisdom, continuous with one's own wisdom, knows it to be nothing but a thought. To regard matter as a possible source of discomfort is the result of ignorance.

Quimby, functioning as a hypnotist, healed Mary Baker Eddy of serious ailments by the power of mind, or so she believed. She later discovered Christian Science, based on the belief that the mind of God is all. New Thought teachers have, however, developed independent positions.

Despite its American pragmatism and its relative success, it is interesting to observe what New Thought has in common with movements like Theosophy and Spiritualism. All three have been much more open than the major churches to feminine leadership and have had women as important founder figures. Perhaps the spirit of these movements is closer than the Western norm to the feminine psyche, too, and perhaps the whole alternative reality tradition is really a more psychologically feminine view of the cosmos than the obviously masculine values which exist in the dominant culture—or have until recently.

Like Spiritualism and Theosophy—and the whole tradition—New Thought too has shared the basic presupposition that the mind is capable of transcending all limitations the world seems to place around it, because mind is ultimately sovereign, or is all that is. Mind can enjoy communication with those who have seemed to die; mind can expand through initiations to embrace the cosmos; mind can create by its own direct force all desirable conditions of life.

EASTERN IMPORTS

Fundamentally, the sovereignty of mind has always been the position of the alternative reality tradition. But it has seen several changes in methods of communication of this principle. It was changes of this sort which overtook it as it went into the twentieth century. Two important things happened: it was reinforced, if not almost swallowed up, by the direct importation of Eastern religions; and it later found verbal communication giving way in large part to nonverbal communication, as it moved into the world of meditation and experience-oriented spirituality. It is as though it finally wanted to express the mind's independence of everything, even words.

The introduction of oriental religion in explicit institutional form into America can be dated from the World Parliament of Religions held in Chicago in 1893. One memorable address was that of a man from India, Swami Vivekananda, a disciple of the great Hindu saint, Ramakrishna. Vivekanada had been a brilliant student and had received a Western scientific education, but, finding it did not answer his deepest needs, had turned to the ancient spiritual path of his native land as exemplified in his God-realized master. Then he had sought—a radical notion in those colonialist days—to bring the spirituality of the East to the West, in exchange for the technological and political sophistication and the Christianity Europe was confidently exporting to Asia. He brought it in the form of Vedanta philosophy. This is the most important school of Hindu thought, and he no doubt rightly considered it Hinduism's most universal form, more applicable to man at large than particular devotional deities or yoga techniques. Vedanta holds that the only reality is Brahman, the Absolute One, realized in profound meditation. The phenomenal world is *maya*, illusions of mistaken identity, or *lila*, the games the One plays with itself, which are all that is seen by a person in a state of ignorance.

The mission of Vivekananda inspired the establishment of Vedanta Societies dedicated to the study of this teaching in the major cities of Europe and America. Usually the spiritual leader was a *swami* from India of the Ramakrishna Order. Typically he interprets his message in such a way as to minimize discontinuity with the spiritual traditions of the West. There is a service with address at the usual hour on Sunday morning, and may be emphasis on passages in the Bible congenial to Vedanta. The Vedanta Society has generally attracted the most intellectual of those westerners who have been persuaded by the wisdom of the East; persons such as the novelists Aldous Huxley and Christopher Isherwood have been among its adherents.

Two other major speakers at the Parliament of Religions were Buddhist, and both were to have a significant impact on the fortunes of their faith in the West. One, Soyen Shaku, a Japanese Zen monk, was the teacher of several monks who came to America in the early years of the twentieth century to begin formal Zen centers in this country, building on contacts Soyen had made through the Parliament; another student of his, the layman D. T. Suzuki, did more than anyone else to popularize Zen abroad through lectures and an almost endless stream of books and articles. The other, Anagarika Dharmapala of Ceylon (now Sri Lanka), had worked closely with H.S. Olcott of Theosophy in endeavoring to revitalize Buddhism and interpret it to the modern world; the Maha Bodhi Society, which he established to those ends in 1891, helped stimulate western Buddhism in Europe particularly.[26]

Other Eastern groups and teachers followed these teachers. In the 1920s another missionary from India appeared in America. He was called Paramahansa (the title of a supreme yoga master) Yogananda, and he was the founder of the Self-Realization Fellowship. His dramatic *Autobiography of a Yogi* is well known. The Self-Realization Fellowship, now large and successful, also retains definite elements of syncretism.

THE SIXTIES AND AFTER

Each generation of new religious movements in America has had a distinctive character. The Spiritualism of the 1840s and 1850s possessed a freewheeling frontier quality, and was associated with both the sentimentality and the high-spirited optimism of the age. Turn-of-the-century groups, like the Theosophy and New Thought of that day, tended to emphasize heavy reading and formal lectures and services structurally inspired by liberal Protestantism. During the years between the World Wars, the 1920s and 30s, new shoots from these older roots emerged which often focused on colorful personalities embodying certain aspects of the alternative tradition. There was Krishnamurti, Swami Yogananda of the Self-Realization Fellowship, the Ballards of the "I Am" movement, not to mention William Dudley Pelley, whose notorious "Silver Shirts" in the 1930s combined anti-Semitic, Fascist-style political activity with a worldview in the spiritualist and esoteric tradition.*

The postwar years, the late 1940s and the 1950s, are widely remembered as the heyday of the "mainstream" denominations, above all in the burgeoning suburbs. But scattered evidence also tells of a more deeply mystical vein of spirituality lying just beneath the surface of that decade and a half. Popular books included Thomas Merton's *The Seven Storey Mountain*, the tale of the author's conversion to Roman Catholicism and subsequent entry into a Trappist monastery; he was later to become a highly sensitive interpreter of dialogue between Eastern and Western religion. There was also a vogue for Aldous Huxley's *The Perennial Philosophy*, and later his *The Doors of Perception*, a seminal work for the next decade's fascination with the idea that psychedelic drugs can induce mystical experience. Zen Buddhism received quite a bit of attention, both because of its popularity among the so-called "Beats," as celebrated in a semi-autobiographical novel like Jack Kerouac's *The Dharma Bums*, and from more straightforward presentations in books like Alan Watts's *The Way of Zen* and the many lectures and publications of D.T. Suzuki, supreme apostle of Zen to the West.

Although older groups—what Martin Marty has called "the occult establishment"—continued quietly to promote Spiritualism, Theosophy, or Vedanta in the 1950s, little of the new Zen or other mysticisms then took institutionalized shape.[27] Its enthusiasts, like Kerouac's youthful Zen heroes, held too strongly to the virtues of spiritual spontaneity and formless faith for that. It was as though a deep trench was being quietly dug, from out of which the next generation would go "over the top" to astound the world with fresh, iridescent spiritual causes and highly visible groups to go with them.

That generation came of age in the turbulent 1960s, a decade racked by riots, assassinations, bitter conflict over civil rights and the Vietnam War, and the first stirrings of environmentalism and feminism in their late twentieth century forms. For all its blood and turmoil, it was an exciting time to be alive, and above all to be young. Key words of the decade were "alienation," "love generation," "generation gap," "counter culture," and "Aquarian Age." What all these suggest is a new idealistic generation who felt themselves to be profoundly different from those who had gone before, particularly their parents and teachers.

Demographically they were special, in the sense that these were the

---

*It should be emphasized that this political posture is not at all characteristic of American groups in the alternative spiritual tradition, whatever the case elsewhere; most have supported democratic values in society as a whole at least as well as other religious groups of their time and place, and indeed, like Spiritualism in the 1840s and 1850s, have sometimes particularly attracted people of "progressive" views or experimented with utopian communalism. A minority of "alternative" spokesmen have employed the sort of "patriotic" rhetoric associated with the extreme—though not necessarily racist or fascist—right.

come-of-age children of the postwar "Baby Boom," born in large part to the veterans of the Second World War. But these youths themselves were innocent of the Depression and War years, knowing only the relative affluence of the fifties. There were more of them than of any other age—in July 1967, in the very heart of the "Summer of Love" which was in a real sense the apex of sixties' spirituality, the U.S. Census Bureau estimated that there were nearly eighteen million people 15 to 19 years old, and only eleven million in the 30 to 34 age bracket.

Not all of those teenagers or their slightly older brothers and sisters, of course, were caught up in what was distinctive about the era. Some were fighting in Vietnam, others were interested only in a "straight" education and career. But it was those who wanted something else who naturally attracted attention, and they were apparent enough, starting with their long hair and beads.

Many of them had first been awakened to concern for a different kind of society by the passions of the civil rights movement, and by the charisma and then the traumatic murder of John F. Kennedy in 1963. They hated the bureaucracy of the educational system in which they were enmeshed, and they did not want to shoot people in Vietnam. Yet the sixties spirit embraced much more than such social attitudes, especially as one moves along the spectrum from its political to its spiritual side. It harbored a special mystique, a special feeling about human nature and human experience of the infinite that was to lead to much use of expressions like "expansion of awareness" and "the ultimate high," and would lead to movements like Transcendental Meditation and Krishna Consciousness. A good many ingredients went into the mix: an interest in Native American culture, in the East, in communal lifestyles, in living close to nature, in sexual freedom, in revolution, in mysticism and meditation. But its ultimate roots may have lain beyond any of these themes.

Opinions vary as to what they were. Some say that rock music, especially as personified by the lyrics and style of groups like the Beatles and the Grateful Dead, really ignited the counter culture and remained its profoundest bond. This is where Charles Perry, in *The Haight-Ashbury: A History,* starts, though he ends with a good discussion of the motifs of self-discovery, exploration of psychic "wild territory," and semiconscious fear of the "straight" world.[28] Another famous participant/commentator, Timothy Leary, in his reminiscent *Flashbacks,* remained true to his convictions at the time that the heart and soul of the new consciousness was the psychedelic drug experience. Drugs, he believed, enable one to "drop out" of "the system" and "turn on" to deeper and better realities; much of the strange and vivid poster art associated with the counter culture reflected the psychedelic vision.[29] Theodore Roszak, in his celebrated *The Making of a Counter Culture,* saw antitechnology as its deep theme. The new people, he asserted, were rising up in resistance to the regimentation and dehumanization they perceived would be the end product of a world of standard brands, multinational corporations, and computer printouts.[30]

Walter Truett Anderson, in his engaging history of the Esalen center on California's Big Sur coast, *The Upstart Spring: Esalen and the American*

Awakening, stresses the importance of the "human potentials" movement of which Esalen was the Vatican for the new freedom and new consciousness celebrated in the sixties.[31] But Peter Clecak, in *America's Quest for the Ideal Self: Dissent and Fulfillment in the 60s and 70s*, counters the stylish view that the sixties were a decade of hope and spiritual buoyance after which the "me decade" of the seventies presented only sterility and pessimism; he views the continuities of the two periods as more important than the contrasts, perceiving both as parts of an "uncompleted chapter in American civilization."[32] This perspective is to some extent supported by the persistence, indeed flourishing, of the sixties' new religious movements in the seventies. Several, such as Transcendental Meditation and the Divine Light Mission, reached their apex of numbers and influence in that decade. In the seventies the sixties' groups usually had developed a tighter institutional structure which preserved the "best" of the sixties' often helter-skelter quest for community and spiritual experience while striving to contain the earlier decade's tendency to slide all too easily into personal and communal chaos, as Steven Tipton has shown in a study of three such groups in the seventies, *Getting Saved from the Sixties*.[33]

The most pervasive theme of the sixties—and if you wish, of the seventies—was probably that of exploration, especially the exploration of consciousness and what it could potentially mean to be a conscious, feeling human being, whether as a sixties trailblazer or on a seventies guided tour. This quest could express itself in the exploration of alternative social roles, symbolized by dress and lifestyle, in political paradigms or in ways of relating to nature, God, and the Infinite. Certainly these openings could be— and were—triggered by drugs, yet they were also susceptible to symbol and ritual, and to meditation, because these also seemingly could alter the focal length of consciousness. Occult systems such as astrology, tarot cards, or palmistry were also significant not only in themselves but because they suggested the presence of invisible forces or realities awaiting exploration by inward, consciousness-oriented means. Fascination with fantasy was another aspect of the new culture. Works like J. R. R. Tolkien's *The Lord of the Rings* were immensely popular, as were groups like the Society for Creative Anachronism, which delighted in the dress and artifacts of periods from the Medieval to the Edwardian. The mood was aptly called "Neo-romanticism"—like the nineteenth century romantics, they exalted the roles of imagination and ecstasy as ways of *knowing* and *being* in contexts far larger than the one-dimensional here and now.

Unquestionably, some of the explorers were in just for a few thrills or were unstable individuals who found the new frontiers more than they could handle. Those either burned out or found their way back to the "straight" world. There were also those who, confronting the gods and demons of the new consciousness, turned to the power of Jesus as presented by Christian Fundamentalism. These were the people of the "Jesus Movement" much discussed in the early 1970s.

But some found in the new experiences, whether drug-induced or simply conveyed by the counter culture's art, fantasy, and "love," a vision neither false nor wholly matched in conventional American religion. They sought ways to perpetuate the vision. One important way was through new religious movements emerging out of the sixties, or revitalized by them. As we have seen, new religious movements generally center on subjective experience powerful enough to counter the claims of conventional religion or society, and offer simple, sure keys to realizing it which, to some people at least, work well enough to support their ongoing practice. The leader as a charismatic figure is also an important key. All this was crucial to the sixties' movements, noted for their colorful "gurus" and their conspicuous practices like meditating or chanting. Many of them were also characterized by a vivid, dramatic quality which answered the new culture's love of spectacle and multimedia sensibility, and by authoritarian, communalistic ways of life much denigrated by critics of "cults" but which had roots in the new generation's hunger for love, family, and new and better forms of human society.

Important examples presented in this book which display most if not all of these features include the Krishna movement of Swami Bhaktivedanta, with its dreamlike altars and vigorous dancing and chanting; the Maharishi Mahesh Yogi's Transcendental Meditation Movement, which attracted spectacular media attention in the sixties through the brief involvement of the Beatles; Nichiren Shoshu, a form of Japanese Buddhism which grew dramatically in America in the late sixties and offers a simple chanting practice; and the Unification Church of the Rev. Sun Myung Moon. Although they had a few precursors, for all practical purposes Neo-Paganism and Witchcraft also first took organized shape in modern America in the sixties; far more diffuse than the preceding groups, their piebald diversity clearly responded to the Neo-romantic's love of nature and wonder.

If the sixties had been the time of the original dream, the seventies were as we have seen a time for consolidation and institutionalization. Several of the movements, such as Nichiren Shoshu, Transcendental Meditation, and the Divine Light Mission, grew considerably in the early seventies despite the decline of the counter culture as a whole. But by the end of the decade nearly all were stable or declining numerically. At the same time, they maintained a committed core of leaders and devotees and were typically concerned to integrate themselves into the American religious mainstream.

It was also during the 1970s that controversy about "cults" reached its modern height. Several "anticult" organizations, composed largely of parents of young people who had entered such movements, appeared to charge them with misrepresentation, "brainwashing," and other chicanery. In some instances members of the groups were abducted to be "deprogrammed" out of their belief. Many sensational stories and programs, most of them hostile, appeared about "cults" during the decade.

By the 1980s, however, despite continuing reverbations the controversy had begun to subside. As the groups themselves matured in both attitude and average age of members, they could less viably be seen even by critics as "preying on youth"; at the same time, some of the groups, stymied by legal problems and internal tensions, were no longer confronting the world with their earlier confidence. Finally, as the sixties with its counter culture receded more and more into history, its particular style, fossilized in these groups, inevitably became less in touch with the spiritual quest of new generations. In the late 1980s, the sixties groups seemed unlikely to grow vigorously again. But some established alternative groups such as Theosophy seemed to be increasing modestly, activities connected to feminist spirituality attracted attention, and there were rumors that Satanism was on the rise deep underground.

NOTES

[1]Hans Jonas, *The Gnostic Religion* (2nd ed., rev.) (Boston: Beacon Press, 1963), pp. 320–40.

[2]Frederick C. Grant, ed., *Hellenistic Religions* (New York: The Liberal Arts Press, 1953), p. 108–9. Hymns from two Orphic gold plates are combined here.

[3]Grant, *Hellenistic Religions*, p. 121. The passage is from Apuleius, *Metamorphoses*, VIII, 27.

[4]Grant, *Hellenistic Religions*, p. 142. The passage is from Apuleius, *Metamorphoses*, XI, 23.

[5]Eliza M. Butler, *The Myth of the Magus* (New York: The Macmillan Company, Publishers, 1948).

[6]See Mircea Eliade, *Shamanism, Archaic Techniques of Ecstasy*, trans. Willard R. Trask, Bollingen Series LXXVI (Copyright © by Princeton University Press, 1964)

[7]E. R. Dodds, *The Greeks and the Irrational* (Berkeley: University of California Press, 1951) pp. 140–41.

[8]Dodds, *Greeks and the Irrational*, pp. 143–44.

[9]Dodds, *Greeks and the Irrational*, pp. 283–311.

[10]Margaret Murray, *The God of the Witches* (New York: Anchor Books, Doubleday & Company, Inc., 1960). First published 1933. For a more recent treatment of the controversies over the origins of modern Witchcraft that is readable, sympathetic yet balanced, see Margot Adler, *Drawing Down the Moon* (New York: Viking Press, 1979), especially Chapter 4.

[11]See Gershom G. Scholem, *Major Trends in Jewish Mysticism* (New York: Schocken Books, Inc., 1967), and by the same author, *On the Kabbalah and its Symbolism* (New York: Schocken Books, Inc., 1969).

[12]See *The Collected Works of C. G. Jung* (Princeton: Princeton University Press), Vol. 12, *Psychology and Alchemy* (1968), Vol. 13, *Alchemical Studies* (1968), Vol. 14, *Mysterium Coniunctionis* (1963): and Mircea Eliade, *The Forge and the Crucible* (New York: Harper & Row, Publishers, 1962).

[13]See David Bakan, *Sigmund Freud and the Jewish Mystical Tradition* (New York: Schocken Books, Inc., 1965).

[14]John Hargrave, *The Life and Soul of Paracelsus* (London: Victor Gollancz, Ltd., 1951), p. 72. Italics in original.

[15]Hargrave, *Life and Soul of Paracelsus*, p. 102.

[16]The Rosicrucians have, however, always insisted upon their Christianity, and more than other such groups, have sought to employ Christian verbal and graphic symbols, giving them their own interpretation.

[17]A curious book exists, obviously by a writer steeped in the Theosophy of Blavatsky and A. P. Sinnett, endeavoring to show that Swedenborg was actually a Buddhist (at least, in the sense that Sinnett used the term in his *Esoteric Buddhism*, a partisan of the "ancient wisdom"). It is Philangi Dasa, *Swedenborg the Buddhist* (Los Angeles: The Buddhistic Swedenborgian Brotherhood, 1887).

[18]Emmanuel Swedenborg, *The True Christian Religion* (London: Everyman's Library, 1936), p. 335.

[19]An accessible work on Mesmer, with good bibliography, is Vincent Buranelli, *The Wizard from Vienna* (New York: Coward, McCann and Geoghegan, 1975). On Mesmerism in America see Robert C. Fuller, *Mesmerism and the American Cure of Souls* (Philadelphia: University of Pennsylvania Press, 1982).

[20]See Herbert Leventhal, *In the Shadow of the Enlightenment: Occultism and Renaissance Science in Eighteenth-Century America* (New York: New York University Press, 1976).

[21]Geoffrey K. Nelson, *Spiritualism and Society* (New York: Schocken Books, Inc., 1969), see Chapter 4. Slater Brown, *The Heyday of Spiritualism* (New York: Hawthorne Books, Inc., 1970).

[22]Henry Steel Olcott, *Old Diary Leaves, Second Series, 1878–83* (Madras: Theosophical Publishing House, 1900, 1954), pp. 13–14.

[23]*Proceedings of the Society for Psychical Research* (London: 1884) Vol. III, part ix. For the Theosophical response, see Adlai E. Waterman, *Obituary: The "Hodgson Report" on Madame Blavatsky* (Madras: Theosophical Publishing House, 1963). Certainly some of the accusations made against Blavatsky, such as that she may have been a Russian agent, are dubious. On the other hand, it seems likely that, as even some Theosophists are able to concede, the answer to the mystery of the Mahatma Letters lies somewhere in the fabulously complex personality of H.P.B.

[24]A fascinating picture of the world of the early Theosophists is given by Mrs. Rosa Praed, herself a Theosophist, in her novel, *The Brother of the Shadow*. The incident which inspired it is related in her biography by Colin Roderick, *In Mortal Bondage: The Strange Life of Rosa Praed* (Sidney, Australia: Angus and Robertson, 1948), pp. 125–33. In 1885 a rumor spread through the esotericist set that a Dugpa, a "black magician," was abroad in London. A certain *chela*, named Mohini—a Hindu follower of H.P.B. living in London and much in demand for after-dinner lectures—explained at lunch with Mrs. Praed that this was true, and that he could be known by his red cap, which by occult law he had to wear. His goal was the satisfaction of sensuous desire, and could create by diabolical means passions contrary to the purity of heart required of adepts; they must therefore be in special devotion to the good. The same biography contains another episode typical of the Theosophical mood, a vision of a deva or nature spirit (pp. 177–91).

[25]J. Stillson Judah, *The History and Philosophy of the Metaphysical Movements in America* (Philadelphia: Westminister Press, 1967), pp. 149–54.

[26]An excellent study of oriental spiritual influence to the end of the nineteenth century is Carl T. Jackson, *The Oriental Religions and American Thought: Nineteenth-Century Explorations* (Westport, CT: Greenwood Press, 1981).

[27]Martin Marty, "The Occult Establishment," *Social Research* 37 (1970), pp. 212–30.

[28]Charles Perry, *The Haight-Ashbury: A History* (New York: Random House, Inc., 1984). The Haight-Ashbury district of San Francisco was a center of the "hippie" counter culture in the late 1960s. Perry, as an associate editor of the popular music and culture periodical *Rolling Stone*, was able to write of events there as both observer and participant.

[29]Timothy Leary, *Flashbacks: An Autobiography* (Los Angeles: J.P. Tarcher, 1983).

[30]Theodore Roszak, *The Making of a Counter Culture* (Garden City, NY: Doubleday & Co, Inc., 1969).

[31]Walter Truett Anderson, *The Upstart Spring: Esalen and the American Awakening* (Reading, MA: Addison-Wesley Publishing Co., Inc., 1983).

[32]Peter Clecak, *America's Quest for the Ideal Self: Dissent and Fulfillment in the 60s and 70s* (New York: Oxford University Press, 1983), p. 6.

[33]Steven M. Tipton, *Getting Saved from the Sixties* (Berkeley: University of California Press, 1982).

3

NEW VESSELS FOR THE ANCIENT WISDOM:
Groups in the Theosophical and Rosicrucian Tradition

Out of respect for their venerable place in the tradition we are exploring, we will begin with Theosophical and Rosicrucian groups. At first glance they may not seem to represent that tradition in its fullness. The magus and the mentalist philosophy are certainly evident, but it may seem there is more talk about initiation into states of expanded consciousness than experience of it. The mood may seem intellectual, or at best liturgical rather than spiritually active like yoga camps or Zen meditation halls. It must be kept in mind that the tradition is defined as much by *fascination with the possibility of entering* ecstatic and cosmic states of consciousness as by techniques. The era in which these groups took modern shape was one dominated by verbal communication and deferred reward presuppositions. If the realization of ecstasy beyond words, study, and waiting was not anticipated until after many years or many lifetimes, it was still the object.

Each of the groups we are studying is best understood through the portal of one of the three forms of religious expression. For Theosophy, it is certainly the verbal, both myth and doctrine. It is through the word, more than ritual or social interaction, that most Theosophists are drawn toward the transcendent. Though the other forms exist, especially in the Full Moon Meditation Groups, the Liberal Catholic Church, and "I Am," they pale beside the vast richness of Theosophical lore and wisdom. To understand Theosophy one must understand this wisdom's fascination, its ability to warm those to whom it appeals to a certain inner ecstasy here and now, and its focus on the ultimate wonder of cosmic harmony and consummation.

Some of the groups treated in this chapter consider themselves Christian, but most make central the "ancient wisdom" contained in many cultures and faiths, and speak of Christianity as a symbolic expression of it suitable for our culture. A few might consider the Christian expression of it final, but even so interpret it in a way most mainstream Christians would probably regard as unusual, but characteristic of the alternative reality tradition.

Around Theosophical institutions one always has a rich sense of the tradition's past. There is now a calm after the storms of excitement and schism, gorgeous hope and grim disappointment, of Theosophy's first decades. The staid gray photographs of Helena Blavatsky, Annie Besant, and C.W. Leadbeater on the walls call to mind, for the informed, flamboyant personalities and colorful incidents now locked behind a wall of years. In back of these figures is a lineage of books, teachers, and temples stretching up the centuries.

Inland from Ventura lies the small California town of Ojai, famous in Theosophical as well as regional history. Here in the 1920s Annie Besant and Krishnamurti sometimes summered, and here is situated Krotona, a major Theosophical school. Toward the front of the Krotona complex of buildings is a library with high shelves reached by ladders, and spotless polished reading tables.

A first-time visitor to the library can see one of the main lecture halls, a striking room. Around the walls are a set of "mystical" paintings, ghostly representations in pastel blues and silvers of lakes, mountains, and faces. One feels in the presence of a reality not yet quite solidified, or else so far beyond the physical as to leave only a shimmering trace behind.

A director of Krotona has said that materialism, the equation of the physical with the totality, is the fundamental error, the error which Theosophy must combat. It is not necessary, he said, to accept any one of the traditional teachings of the Theosophical Society. But one can recognize that their purpose is to open up a world in which matter is an expression of mind rather than the other way around. He believed that to read the Theosophical classics is like listening to great music; one is carried, as on waves, to where one's own mind and imagination seize new intuitions unconstricted by conventional horizons.

The rejection of materialism, though not of natural law, is a key to the understanding of the many varieties of Theosophical experience. The world-wide movement has never counted more than twenty or thirty thousand members. But it has produced an array of religious forms, from the liturgical to the messianic, though it generally falls back in the end upon the lecture hall and verbal expression.

Theosophy really has two sides. First, there is what amounts to a cult of the marvelous, a delight in wondrous psychic phenomena, and of apparitions of the Masters. Second, there is a vast and deep mentalist philosophy squarely in the alternative reality tradition. Both are egregiously represented in the life and work of H.P. Blavatsky. Both have in common a rejection of the ordinary presuppositions of materialism. The two sides are appropriately linked together, for the same tradition which sees mind as the basis of all is also rooted in that shamanistic ecstasy which sees the spirit as separable from the body. The mentalist and the marvelous in Theosophy may both seem off-base to the empiricist, but they are not really inconsistent. Nor, if our hypothesis of an alternative reality tradition is correct, is Theosophy's boast of representing the "ancient wisdom" empty. That wisdom is the knowledge of mental powers and supernormal entities and strange initiations which the old shaman knew.

These two sides are also evident in the development of the concept of the Masters, those great mediating figures who represent individuals much more highly evolved than the ordinary person. They live both in East and West and are heirs to the wisdom of Egypt, India, and other ancient cultures. Just as they unite East and West in the mind of the Theosophist, so the Masters are one unifying experience in Theosophy itself. Their appearance and the individual's contact with them is a marvel—their message is deep wisdom.

In the last chapter, the journey was described which Helena Petrovna Blavatsky and Colonel Olcott made to India in 1878–79 after the publication of *Isis Unveiled*.[1] The impressive advent of the occultist pair in the mysterious East is a watershed in Theosophical history, and, in a certain sense, in the history of East-West relations. Once in India contacts with the Masters, especially those of the Himalayan lodge, naturally multiplied. Through psychic contact with them, H.P.B. was seemingly able to work miracles. Most important, epistles (the famous Mahatma Letters) from the Masters explaining important points of Theosophical doctrine were given to members and prospective members. Sometimes they came by ordinary post, but often they materialized in enigmatic ways. Soon, as a sort of routine correspondence, they were "precipitated" regularly in response to queries in the "Shrine Room" of the Theosophical headquarters in Adyar.[2]

Allegations of fraud in the production of the letters in 1884, instigated it seems by Christian missionaries, led to investigation by the Society for Psychical Research whose still controverted conclusions were critical of Blavatsky. Afterwards, a near split between H.P.B., who had returned to Europe, and Olcott occurred over the establishment of an Esoteric Section of the Society to supervise its study of arcane doctrine. Despite all this, Blavatsky managed to publish her major work, *The Secret Doctrine*, in 1888.[3]

After the death of H.P.B. in 1891, a schism occurred between the American lodges, under the leadership of William Q. Judge, and those in most of the rest of the world which followed Olcott's presidency from Adyar. Disputes arose over further letters from the Masters, this time supposedly produced by Judge, and other matters. The division took place in 1895. Subsequently each of these leaders was succeeded by a remarkable woman. Katherine Tingley took the place of Judge in America shortly after his death in 1896. Annie Besant followed Olcott in 1907.

New manifestations shaped the character of each of these branches of Theosophy. In 1899 Mrs. Tingley established a great utopian Theosophical community at Point Loma, in San Diego. After summoning the leading spirits of her tradition of Theosophy to Point Loma, she dissolved the other lodges in her association, leaving the field to Annie Besant and Adyar. The Point Loma community, complete with heroic architecture, schools, notable musical and dramatic groups, and model agricultural programs, survived until 1942.

Adyar Theosophy, under Mrs. Besant and C. W. Leadbeater, took a more speculative direction. Leadbeater, who possessed remarkable clairvoyance or imagination and a facile pen, described in pleasant detail the lives of the Masters, and the past existences of many living Theosophists in Atlantis and the ancient world. Charges of homosexuality brought adverse attention to Leadbeater, yet he still exercised a powerful influence on Adyar Theosophy in the first three decades of this century. His writings emphasized, besides the lives of the Masters and the apocryphal past, occult initiations. Persons who were to be initiated to new levels were believed to be taken out of the body to the abodes of the Masters, usually at night, where remarkable gifts would be imparted.

Feeling a need for a liturgical and sacramental expression of Theosophy, Leadbeater, a former Anglican priest, entered the Liberal Catholic Church. This body, established in 1916 by the Theosophist James Ingall Wedgwood, employed a liturgy similar to that of the Roman Catholic or Anglican mass. But an interpretation was given of ceremonial worship, especially in Leadbeater's writings, based on Theosophical concepts of the meaning of the life of Christ and the nature of man's relations with the divine.

Finally, Leadbeater and Mrs. Besant came to believe, on the basis of Leadbeater's psychic reading, that a certain young Indian boy, Jiddu Krishnamurti, was destined to be the next vehicle of the World Teacher, the Christ. The boy was brought up by devoted Theosophists with care worthy of a crown prince. But in 1929, when he was expected to enter fully into his mission, the young Krishnamurti instead caused Theosophy to suffer yet another shock by renouncing any special claims and totally disaffiliating himself from any organized movement. He subsequently became a notable lecturer and writer, advocating his philosophy of life lived wholly in immediacy.

In 1912 the Adyar lodge opened a school and community under the name Krotona in the Hollywood Hill. It moved to Ojai in the twenties. While it was in Hollywood, an Englishwoman, Alice Bailey, joined the community and began to produce writings purporting to come from one of the Masters. Not all Theosophists, however, accepted her claims, and after certain personality conflicts, Mrs. Bailey left Krotona to become the leader of her own movement. Never an organized institution, it has been held together by the Alice Bailey books and correspondence courses based on their teachings issued by the Arcane School and the School of Esoteric Studies, both in New York. It adherents are characterized by the practice of meditating together at every full moon. The movement offers standard speculative Theosophy, but has become more eschatological in orientation. The full moon meditations are considered to create channels for force which will aid in the return of the Christ or World Teacher.

This and the other devolutions from Theosophy fall into two general classes. On the one hand, there are what might be called the Western groups, which reject the alleged extravagance and orientalism of evolved Theosophy, in favor of a serious emphasis on its metaphysics and especially its recovery of the Gnostic and Hermetic heritage. These groups feel that the love of India and its mysteries which grew up after *Isis Unveiled* was unfortunate for a Western group. In this category there are several Neo-Gnostic and Neo-Rosicrucian groups. The Anthroposophy of Rudolf Steiner is also in this category. On the other hand, there are what may be termed "new revelation" Theosophical schisms, generally based on new revelations from the Masters not accepted by the main traditions. In this set would be Alice Bailey's groups, "I Am," and in a sense Max Heindel's Rosicrucianism.

The fountainhead text for all these developments is still Blavatsky's *The Secret Doctrine*. This massive and remarkable work is a description of the genesis of the solar system by emanation from the One, in accordance with tremendous cosmic cycles of divine rest and activity, and of the evolution of man through several worlds and races. The whole is allegedly based on very ancient but hidden learning, communicated to the author by the Masters. The book ends with an elaborate display of the cryptic expression of these teachings in ancient symbolism.[4]

The Secret Doctrine is a book not easily forgotten, even by those who despise it or who, like many outside the Theosophical orbit, find it almost impossible to read. As the modern classic of occultism, it represents a certain pinnacle, either of profundity or absurdity. To understand what it has to offer, one must learn how to read it. *The Secret Doctrine* is not a text book, but is like an ocean with waves and currents and eddies and whirl-pools and quiet caves. It calls for suspending one's normal mode of conceptual progress until one has discovered where the tides and techniques of this new medium will carry him. Water is, to man, a distorting element, and probably whatever he sees in it will not be seen as it really is. The ecstatic surges in his body as he rides the swells will not be forgotten after he has found his feet once again on the sand. Like riding the waves, or like listening to great music, this book wafts one to where he can perceive reality in new configurations that unite the subjective and the objective. It does not so much convey specific fact as arrange science, myth, philosophy, and poetic narrative in peculiar combinations which can generate remarkable experiences—or so it has been with Theosophists.

The very terminology of *The Secret Doctrine* is exciting, for it unites names and concepts from many systems, East and West. Any system appearing venerable enough to be regarded as a legitimate custodian of primordial vision is taken into account in the synthesis which sets forth the contours of that range of perception. But it seems that while Eastern terms, especially Sanskrit, are most favored, the actual concepts still are more of the Hellenistic heritage than anything else (except the notion of karma), particularly the Kabbalah, Manichaeanism, and Proclus.

As one grows into the world of *The Secret Doctrine*, one understands more and more that it presents a psychological model of the cosmos. The more its vision is comprehended and interiorized, the more the reader shares the workings of universal consciousness. Levels of Theosophical initiation take in wider and wider sweeps of the thought processes of the cosmic mind. Each level—man, Master, world—is more subtly attuned than those below to the whole scale of vibrations. As a person evolves, he is at once more invisible to lower levels—more a part of the background—and more powerful, sharing in the strength of that background. This is the mode of being described for the Masters.

The fully developed Hierarchy of spiritual rulers was not worked out until the second generation of Theosophy. A little surprisingly, it seems to have been first presented in Alice Bailey's earliest book, *Initiation Human and Solar* (1922), but was quickly expounded by C. W. Leadbeater in *The Masters and the Path* (1925), and then by Annie Besant and others. Most of the leading figures in the Hierarchy and their interrelationships had, of course, been given by H.P.B., A. P. Sinnett, and Olcott, but the full pattern had yet to be schematized.[5]

The developed Hierarchy found a place for adepts of all national lines, symbolizing thereby the syncretism. The personal "God" is the Solar Logos, ruler of the solar system. At the terrestial summit is Sanat Kumara, Lord of the World, the supreme guide of earthly evolution of mind who came from Venus some eighteen million years ago. He resides in Shamballa, a mysterious paradise in the Gobi desert. Under him the Buddha is spiritual head and the goal of interior development. There is under the Buddha the Bodhisattva, or future Buddha, and under Sanat Kumara the Manu, the archetypal man and future world Lord.

On the next plane we find the earthly expression of the Seven Rays, seven lines of activity emanating from above, governing seven broad areas encompassing the spectrum of terrestial life. Each is governed by a Master. The Masters of the first and second, respectively, are directly under Sanat Kumara and the Buddha. The other five are under a sort of Prime Minister called the Mahachohan. The First Ray, of rulership and the founding of nations and of analysis and science, is thus under the governance of the Lord of the World. Its Master is Morya, a special guide of H.P.B.

The Second Ray, of wisdom (in the sense of *prajna*, that direct intuitive nonverbal understanding necessary to enlightenment), is ruled by the Buddha, and its Master is Kuthumi (or Koot Hoomi). He was also a special companion of Madame Blavatsky, and is familiar to readers of the Mahatma Letters.

The Third Ray is that of service to mankind and also of astrology. The common meeting-point of these two is the idea of right timing, of skill-in-means in the matter of human service involving above all a subtle and precise penetration of the humanistic meanings of time. The illuminati of this Ray grasp the deep but inescapable organic unity of the tides of human affairs with the forces and periodicities of the cosmos as a whole, which is the profoundest meaning of astrology. Its Master is called the Venetian.

The Fourth Ray, of harmony and beauty, is under the Master Serapis, of vaguely Alexandrian-Egyptian background.

The Fifth Ray is guided by the Master Hilarion. He was once the Neoplatonist Iamblichus. More recently he produced (apparently through automatic writing) two Theosophical classics by Mabel Collins, *Light on the*

Path and the fictional *Idyll of the White Lotus,* and also a story or two published by H.P.B. But despite this literary excursus, Hilarion is particularly concerned with exact science, though he includes in his science laws and forces little known to conventional savants. He may be considered the paragon alchemist.

The Sixth Ray is that of devotional religion and is epitomized by the Master Jesus. He was next incarnate as Apollonius of Tyana, then as the medieval Hindu theologian of *bhakti* or devotion, Ramanuja.

The Seventh Ray is that of one of the favorite Theosophical heroes, and the special patron of the "I Am" movement, the Master Rakoczy, also called the Comte de Saint-Germain, identified with the famous eighteenth century courtier and elegant mystagogue. He has an impressive list of previous appearances, however, having been Francis Bacon, Lord Verulam, Robertus the Monk, Hunyadi, Janos, Christian Rosencreuz, Roger Bacon, Proclus, and St. Alban. His is the realm of mysteries and ceremony and of European politics. "I Am" makes him the patron of America, a land which has a particular vocation in this age. They tell of his appearing in visions to Washington and Lincoln, and helping to write the American Constitution.

The general schema of the Rays is subtle and majestic. The Logos, which is the fundamental constituent of our world as an expression of the Solar Logos, boasts three aspects: Lordship, the First Ray of Sanat Kumara and his lieutenant Morya; Wisdom, the Second Ray of the Buddha and his lieutenant Kuthumi; and the variegated third aspect of the Mahachohan and his five under-Masters which can be summed up as activity. The seven rays, like the colors of a spectrum, play over the world.

But wisdom and rulership have special roles as goals beyond goals. The highest historically incarnate initiate is the Buddha. His successor, the Bodhisattva, has already appeared twice, in Krishna and Christ, and will soon appear again—the driving idea, of course, behind the Krishnamurti and Full Moon Meditation Groups movements.

These notions, so deeply stirring to persons of a certain temperament, have inspired a variety of expressions. In general, whether in the Liberal Catholic high mass or Theosophical meditation, the object has been to open lines of force to the great figures of the Hierarchy to make it easier for their benign influence to penetrate the world. But, by and large, Theosophy has been more concerned, at least collectively, with exposition and spontaneous experience of the Masters than with corporate work; the lectures and books, verbal expression, have been most conspicuous.

Social expression, therefore, has in Theosophy been most lastingly oriented around verbal expression. The many ventures centered about ritual—Co-Masonry, the Liberal Catholic Church, and others—have, like the utopian experiments at Point Loma, not seemed as adequate to the task of Theosophy today as the lecture hall and study group. However, the Full Moon Meditation Groups of Alice Bailey lineage have continued to prosper quietly, and some Gnostic and "I Am" groups have had substantial ritual expression.

The importance of Theosophy in modern history should not be

underestimated. Not only have the writings of Blavatsky and others inspired several generations of occultists, but the movement had a remarkable role in the restoration to the colonial peoples of nineteenth century Asia their own spiritual heritage. We have mentioned Olcott's work in Ceylon. Gandhi was first given an English copy of the *Bhagavad Gita*, the Hindu scripture which became virtually his bible, in London by a Theosophist. No European was more effective in advancing Indian education, unity, and independence than Annie Besant, who led in the establishing of the Home Rule League in 1916, and whose support greatly strengthened the Congress Party during the First World War. She was, in fact, briefly imprisoned by her own countrymen for her activities on behalf of home rule for India.

In the West, Theosophy's most important cultural impact was doubtless in the "Irish Renaissance." Writers like W. B. Yeats and "A.E." (George Russell) were sometime members of the Theosophical Society and deeply affected by its vision. In the hands of such persons as these, Theosophy was a vehicle for a deeply visionary presentation of the alternative reality tradition, the ancient wisdom, to the modern world. Perhaps its essence, and the flavor of its inward and initiatory way back, was never caught more movingly than in the poetry of "A.E.," a writer and economic activist who treasured Blavatsky's *The Secret Doctrine* above all other books. Here is one of his verses:

Ancient

The sky is cold as pearl
Over a milk-white land.
The snow seems older than Time
Though it fell through a dreaming and
Will vanish itself as a dream
At the dimmest touch of a hand.
Out of a timeless world
Shadows fall upon Time,
From a beauty older than earth
A ladder the soul may climb.
I climb by the phantom stair
To a whiteness older than Time.[6]

THE THEOSOPHICAL SOCIETY IN AMERICA

American Theosophy today is comprised of three groups—the Theosophical Society, the descendent of the Point Loma community and the Judge-Tingley tradition; the United Lodge of Theosophists, founded in 1909 by Robert Crosbie, essentially representing the stance of those who were disenchanted with Mrs. Tingley's experiment, but who also resisted the claims to universal legitimacy of the Adyar leadership; and the Theosophical Society in America, which is the United States branch of the world organization headquartered at Adyar.

The first, the Theosophical Society, now has little sociological or cultic expression. Informal meetings are held, but the main link is an attractive inspirational magazine, *Sunrise,* published at the headquarters in Altadena, California. The Headquarters also issues correspondence courses, and sees as one of its main missions the maintenance of a fine library of some 20,000 volumes in theosophy, religion and philosophy. Leadership in this Theosophical Society, in the tradition of Judge and Tingley, is emergent rather than formally elective.

The United Lodge of Theosophists, on the other hand, represents a conservative interpretation of Theosophy. It holds close to the writings of Blavatsky and Judge, rejecting even Olcott's undue humanizing of the great lady in *Old Diary Leaves.* The group's scattering of lodges and discussion groups, headquartered in Los Angeles, maintain a highly austere and intellectual Theosophy.

Undoubtedly most active Theosophists today belong to the Theosophical Society in America. In 1987 the Society reported 5,414 members. Lodges or study groups may be found in most cities. Growth seems to be greatest not in places like New York and California, but in parts of the country such as the south central states where most groups in the alternative reality tradition have not penetrated, but into which Theosophy has long been able to send lecturers. American headquarters are at Olcott House in Wheaton, Illinois. Here also is the Theosophical Publishing House. The Krotona school in Ojai and five summer camps in different parts of the country are also part of the Society.

The typical Theosophical lodge is an older, somewhat plain building with pictures on the walls. It will have a fairly large lending library and bookstore. On the stage in front may be a podium and a table with a vase of flowers or even potted palms. A Theosophical symbol, such as a serpent-entwined tau cross, may be hung behind the podium. Lectures are likely to be on one of the major Theosophical books, karma, reincarnation, an aspect of astrology, psychic phenomena, meditation, or an oriental work such as the *Bhagavad Gita* or *I Ching.* Difficult matters such as the Masters and the several stages of evolution of the world and its races seem to be giving way to more general topics in orientalism and spiritual philosophy. The developed view of the world hierarchy of Besant and Leadbeater is often seen as a general symbol of spiritual evolution. To a great extent, Theosophical lodges seem to play the role of forums where speculative spiritual ideas can be freely presented by all sorts of speakers. Among lecturers who definitely represent Theosophy, some find most appealing the sense of security and self-reliance given by confidence in the law of karma, some love to dwell on the colorful history of Theosophy, and some emphasize such antimaterialistic concepts as the Solar Logos. There is little current talk of contacts with Masters. Particularly in more staid parts of the nation, this function doubtless meets a felt need. Each lodge is democratically self-governed, and the national organization operates on the federal principle.

In some places young people have been brought into Theosophy through general interest in the occult. But the typical Theosophist is middle-aged, white, and middle-class, although Spanish-speaking lodges flourish in the U.S. as well as in Latin America.

The sometimes controversial inner circle of Theosophy, the Esoteric Section, still continues its work, headquartered in Ojai. Its members, who must have been Theosophists three years to be admitted, do not partake of tobacco, alcohol, or meat. They practice a definite secret meditation method to attune them with the Hierarchy. They also follow a study regimen, and in larger places meet periodically.

The Theosophical Society in America, then, is a group teaching that there is a "secret doctrine," knowledge known to a few but which could be known widely, which explains why things are as they are and how one can evolve beyond his present state. These teachings are mainly presented verbally. The Society is oriented more to knowledge than to mystical or yogic practice; it is a body of occult intellectual activists. Even in India, and rather more in America, it draws people who are Western in temperament but Eastern, or Gnostic, in spiritual sympathies, and who sense themselves called out to set their feet to the endless path.

Reading Selection: Theosophy

We have chosen two selections to represent the central tradition of Theosophy, one from H. P. Blavatsky's *The Secret Doctrine,* to indicate its philosophical wing, and one from C. W. Leadbeater's *The Masters and the Path,* to illustrate the marvelous and hierophanic experiences which have attended those living in this tradition. *The Secret Doctrine* is certainly the book considered most authoritative by most Theosophists. The lines below summarize concisely the basic points of Theosophical teaching which are elaborated in the rest of the book. The passage from Leadbeater in a sense takes up where the Blavatsky quotations end, for the Masters, appearing and helping the Theosophical Society, are of course beings in the transhuman states of evolution suggested by her words.

The Secret Doctrine establishes three fundamental propositions:

(a) An Omnipresent, Eternal, Boundless, and Immutable PRINCIPLE on which all speculation is impossible, since it transcends the power of human conception and could only be dwarfed by any human expression or similitude. It is beyond the range and reach of thought—in the words of the Mandukya Upanishad, "unthinkable and unspeakable."

(b) The Eternity of the Universe *in toto* as a boundless plane; periodically the playground of numberless Universes incessantly manifesting and disappearing, called the manifesting stars, and the sparks of Eternity. The Eternity of the Pilgrim [the "Pilgrim" is the Monad or immortal principle in each individual] is like a wink of the Eye of Self-Existence. The appearance and disappearance of Worlds is like a regular tidal ebb of flux and reflux.

This second assertion of the Secret Doctrine is the absolute universality of that law of periodicity, of flux and reflux, ebb and flow, which physical science has observed and recorded in all departments of nature. An alternation such as that of Day and Night, Life and Death, Sleeping and

Waking, is a fact so common, so perfectly universal and without exception, that it is easy to comprehend that in it we see one of the absolutely fundamental Laws of the Universe.

Moreover, the Secret Doctrine teaches:

(c) The fundamental identity of all Souls with the Universal Over-Soul, the latter being itself an aspect of the Unknown Root; and the obligatory pilgrimage for every Soul—and spark of the former—through the Cycle of Incarnation (or "Necessity") in accordance with Cyclic and Karmic law, during the whole term. In other words, no purely spiritual Buddhi (Divine Soul) can have an independent (conscious) existence before the spark which issued from the pure Essence of the Universal Sixth Principle—or the OVER-SOUL—has (a) passed through every elemental form of the phenomenal world of that Manvantara, and (b) acquired individuality, first by natural impulse, and then by self-induced and self-devised efforts (checked by its Karma), thus ascending through all the degrees of intelligence, from the lowest to the highest Manas, from mineral and plant, up to the holiest archangel (Dhyani-Buddha).

> H. P. BLAVATSKY, *An Abridgement of The Secret Doctrine*, Elizabeth Preston and Christmas Humphreys, eds. (Wheaton, Illinois: Theosophical Publishing House, 1967), pp. 10–13. Quotation marks and references to other parts of *The Secret Doctrine* omitted.

I myself can report two occasions on which I have met a Master, both of us being in the physical vehicle. One of Them was the Adept to whom the name of Jupiter was assigned in the book, *The Lives of Alcyone,* who greatly assisted in the writing of portions of Madame Blavatsky's famous work *Isis Unveiled,* when that was being done in Philadelphia and New York. When I was living at Adyar, He was so kind as to request my revered teacher, Swami T. Subba Row, to bring me to call upon Him. Obeying His summons we journeyed to His house, and were most graciously received by Him. After a long conversation of the deepest interest, we had the honour of dining with Him, Brahmin though He be, and spent the night and part of the next day under his roof. In that case it will be admitted that there could be no question of illusion. The other Adept whom I had the privilege of encountering physically was the Master the Comte de St. Germain, called sometimes the Prince Rakoczy. I met Him under quite ordinary circumstances (without any previous appointment, and as though by chance) walking down the Corso in Rome, dressed just as any Italian gentleman might be. He took me up into the gardens on the Pincian Hill, and we sat for more than an hour talking about the Society and its work; or perhaps I should rather say that He spoke and I listened, although when He asked questions I answered.

Other members of the Brotherhood I have seen under varying circumstances. My first encounter with one of them was in a hotel in Cairo; I was on my way out to India with Madame Blavatsky and some others, and we stayed in that city for a time. We all used to gather in Madame

Blavatsky's room for work, and I was sitting on the floor, cutting out and arranging for her a quantity of newspaper articles which she wanted. She sat at a table close by; indeed my left arm was actually touching her dress. The door of the room was in full sight, and it certainly did not open; but quite suddenly, without any preparation, there was a man standing almost between me and Madame Blavatsky, within touch of both of us. It gave me a great start, and I jumped up in some confusion; Madame Blavatsky was much amused and said: "If you do not know enough not to be startled at such a trifle as that, you will not get far in this occult work." I was introduced to the visitor, who was not then an Adept, but an Arhat, which is one grade below that state; he has since become the Master Djwal Kul.

Some months after that the Master Morya came to us one day, looking exactly as though in a physical body; He walked through the room where I was in order to communicate with Madame Blavatsky, who was in her bedroom inside. That was the first time I had seen Him plainly and clearly, for I had not then developed my latent senses sufficiently to remember what I saw in the subtle body. I saw the Master Kuthumi under similar conditions on the roof of our Headquarters at Adyar; He was stepping over a balustrade as though He had just materialized from the empty air on the other side of it. I have also many times seen the Master Djwal Kul on that roof in the same way.

> C. W. LEADBEATER, *The Masters and the Path* (Adyar, Madras, India: The Theosophical Publishing House, 1925, 1965), pp. 8–9.

THE FULL MOON MEDITATION GROUPS

Alice Bailey (1880–1949), the founder of a devolution of Theosophy, had a varied and eventful life. Born, like Annie Besant and other of the strong women of occultism, of an upper class English family, she was an ill-adjusted and headstrong child. When she was fifteen, she saw a vision of a man in a turban whom she later believed was her Master. But as a young woman, she was for a time fervently evangelical, working with a mission to preach hellfire sermons to British troops in India during the First World War. Again like Annie Besant, she was briefly and unhappily married to an Anglican clergyman, and came to Theosophy after the emotional ordeal of marital breakup. In Alice Bailey's case, this happened in America, where she had come with her husband. Soon she was working as manager of the vegetarian cafeteria of the Theosophical school at Krotona in Hollywood.

One afternoon as she was walking in the hills surrounding the community, she felt she was being contacted by a Master called "The Tibetan" who wished her to serve as his amanuensis. She produced a long series of books. This development, and her charges that the Theosophical Society was controlled by members of the Esoteric Section, led to her withdrawal with her fiancé, Foster Bailey. In 1923 they established the Arcane School in New York, and out of it have emanated the teachings which mark the distinctive set of groups now under consideration.[7]

It was in the Second World War period that the peculiarly eschatological quality these groups acquired first became apparent— especially in Mrs. Bailey's *The Reappearance of the Christ*. We are told that because of the tremendous exigencies of the day, the spiritual yearnings of humankind are raised to such a pitch that the coming of the Christ principle, whether in an individual or a new age of illumination, is being brought closer. The work of meditation groups was to encourage this advent by setting up spiritual currents. This is done by repeating prayerfully a Great Invocation, in conjunction with visualization of the funnelling down of the power of the Hierarchy.

The atmosphere of groups in the Full Moon Meditation tradition is a little different from that of continuing Theosophists. The Full Moon groups have made an impact in certain idealistic circles. There is much talk of the United Nations, and international understanding and cooperation, perhaps epitomized by a recording one member has of Eleanor Roosevelt reciting the Great Invocation. The groups have also acquired a certain tincture of avant-garde art and music. Festivals and meditation group meetings are likely to be enlivened with modern dance performances and futuristic concerts, as well as by Wagner, favored by an older generation of occultists.

One of the authors attended a series of Full Moon Meditation Group meetings in a large home in Los Angeles. The group consisted of some twenty persons, mostly elderly. Inside, a pale blue-green fireplace bore small white statues of the Virgin Mary on either end of the mantle. In the center of the room, a square white column had upon it a living flame surrounded by greens—reminiscent of old Druidic or Brahmanical rites. The lady of the house, a tall, statuesque woman, presided over the ceremonies. She opened one meeting by telling of the fact that they met every full moon and at equinoxes and solstices. These are times when special spiritual energies are available from the Hierarchy. The group listened to music of Bach, Mahler, and Wagner.

The next event was modern dance by a pupil of Ruth St. Denis, a famous teacher of choreography, who had been a member of this group until her death. To the music of the "Ave Maria," the dancer interpreted the figure of the Blessed Virgin. Candles held by each member of the group were lit from the central fire in a simple ritual. An elderly lady gave an address. Since it was the full moon of Leo, she talked on its message in simple, rational terms, including the main esoteric concepts. Finally, the meeting concluded, after long preparation, with a slow and solemn recitation of the Great Invocation Alice Bailey received as the most effective means of strengthening the Hierarchy:

> From the point of Light within the Mind of God
> Let light stream forth into the minds of men.
> Let LIGHT descend on Earth.
>
> From the point of Love within the Heart of God
> Let Love stream forth into the hearts of men.
> May CHRIST return to Earth.

From the centre where the Will of God is known
Let Purpose guide the little wills of men—
   The PURPOSE which the Masters know and serve.

From the centre which we call the race of men
Let the Plan of Love and Light work out
   And may it seal the door where evil dwells.

Let Light and Love and Power
Restore the Plan on Earth.

The great occasion of the Meditation Groups is the annual Wesak Festival, held in late spring in the full moon of Taurus every year. The legend of this occasion, based on a vision of Alice Bailey, tells us that on this day the Buddha, the Christ, and the Masters gather in a certain valley in the Himalayas, and that the union of meditation with theirs is of special power. Typically, all the meditation groups of a wide area will gather together to unite in silence, to hear an address, and to appreciate modern music and dance. The festivals are typically done with great taste and beauty.

There is no central organization of Full Moon Meditation Groups, although the two correspondence schools, the Arcane School and the School of Esoteric Studies, the periodical *The Beacon,* and the informal publicity organization in Ojai, Meditation Groups for the New Age, serve as unifying forces.

In this school, we see a movement grown out of Theosophy which has acquired its own flavor. There is a show of modernity and rationality and scientism, together with a new myth blending the eschatological hope of the 1940s kind of liberalism and One World idealism, a continuing covert excitement in the old marvel at revelations of the Masters, plus an affirmation, stronger than in other Theosophy groups, of the communicative power of the new aesthetic. It had some difficulty as well as some success in finding its place in the spiritual climate of the sixties and seventies. But it remains an attractive expression of Theosophy.

Reading Selection: Full Moon Meditation Groups

This is a passage from one of the books published under the name of Alice A. Bailey, but believed to have been given to her by "The Tibetan." The passage summarizes what has come to be the central focus of these groups—spiritual preparation for the return of the Christ principle. The Hierarchy of Masters is striving to prepare mankind for this great event, but the lines of psychic force which can prepare a way for his return need also to be strengthened by human desire, invocation, and mediation. Thoughts have a life of their own; to know how to form them rightly to make vessels for this next step of spiritual evolution is a skill. Training in this task, and the exercise of it, is the work of the meditation groups.

This new invocative work will be the keynote of the coming world religion and will fall into two parts. There will be the invocative work of the masses of the people, everywhere, trained by the spiritually minded people of the world (working in the churches whenever possible under an enlightened clergy) to accept the fact of the approaching spiritual energies, focused through Christ and His spiritual Hierarchy, and trained also to voice their demand for light, liberation and understanding. There will also be the skilled work of invocation as practised by those who have trained their minds through right meditation, who know the potency of formulas, mantrams and invocations and who work consciously. They will increasingly use certain great formulas of words which will later be given to the race, just as the Lord's Prayer was given by the Christ, and as the New Invocation has been given out for use at this time by the Hierarchy.

This new religious science for which prayer, meditation and ritual have prepared humanity, will train its people to present—at stated periods throughout the year—the voiced demand of the people of the world for relationship with God and for a closer spiritual relation to each other. This work, when rightly carried forward, will evoke response from the waiting Hierarchy and from its Head, the Christ. Through this response, the belief of the masses will gradually be changed into the conviction of the knowers. In this way, the mass of men will be transformed and spiritualised, and the two great divine centres of energy of groups—the Hierarchy and Humanity itself—will begin to work in complete at-one-ment and unity. Then the Kingdom of God will indeed and in truth be functioning on earth.

ALICE A. BAILEY, *The Reappearance of the Christ* (New York: Lucis Publishing Company, 1948, 1962), pp. 152–53.

ANTHROPOSOPHY

Rudolf Steiner (1861–1925) was born of Austrian Catholic parents. Fascinated by the type of mind which could combine scientific insight with romantic and mystical vision, he early attained some distinction as editor of Goethe's scientific work. A youthful bent for occultism led him into Theosophy. He served as head of the German section of the Theosophical Society from 1902 to 1909.

But Steiner was uneasy with Theosophy's orientalism and its emphasis on marvelous occurrences. He felt that stress should be placed on the scientific study of the spiritual world and man's initiations into it, and he also felt that Christ was an even greater symbol of its reality than any Eastern Master. In 1912 he founded a new group, originally intended as a fellowship within Theosophy, but soon for all practical purposes independent—the Anthroposophical Society (from the Greek *anthropos,* "man," and *sophia,* "wisdom").

The new Anthroposophical Society retained, with some technical differences, Theosophy's view of the spiritual basis of reality, the subtle constitution of man, reincarnation, and the possibility of initiatory experiences which expand consciousness of the spiritual realm. Steiner taught that man had originally shared the spiritual consciousness of the cosmos, its fundamental reality. Matter is real, but is derivative from spirit. The mind of man has two parts, like the Hindu *jiva* and *atman,* one which can know and the other, the Absolute, which is the ultimate that can be known and is within as well as without. Man's present knowledge is only a vestige of primordial cognition. He has, however, a latent capacity for horizonless vision, and there are certain disciplines by which it can be recovered. Steiner did not reduce the process to mere techniques, however; the initiatory openings may come through study, music, art, and the informed use of imagination. The matter can be objectively and usefully understood to some degree, and Steiner saw his work as the organization of a science of initiation. Such categories as the Theosophical "law of seven," which saw levels of mind, stages of cosmic evolution, grades of Masters, planets, etc., as arranged in septets, were important to him.

Partly through the work of a former Evangelical pastor, Friedrich Rittelmeyer (1872–1938), Anthroposophy came to have a definite Christian bias. Jesus Christ is the one avatar, the one fully initiated person in human history, the one who has full supersensory perception. The story of his life, death, and resurrection is interpreted as a mystery drama of initiation.

Steiner and Rittelmeyer formed the Christian Community as a worship-centered expression of Anthroposophy. The Society and the church are not necessarily identical in either membership or governance, but are closely affiliated in spirit.

Meetings of the Anthroposophical Society are mainly of the lecture and study type. Topics include not only matters from the revered works of Rudolf Steiner, but a great variety of other subjects, for that is in keeping with the founder's vast range of concerns. He himself contributed to education, agriculture, architecture, political thought, and, at least as to philosophic theory, science and medicine. He designed the Goetheanum, or headquarters of the Society, in Dornach, Switzerland; he wrote plays and contributed to the theory of organic farming. Anthroposophists are likely to be interested in architecture, art, and music (especially the operas of Richard Wagner), in the education of retarded children, in organic agriculture—in any matter like these which is related to understanding man's spiritual nature and the evolution of spirit through initiatory openings. Anthroposophists have made real contributions in many of these fields.

The worship of the Christian Community Church is basically on the Protestant model, but the clergy are called "priests" and the central act of worship is the Eucharist or Holy Communion. The rite is seen as a contact with Christ, the fully developed man, which opens one to what he was, true man. It is called the Act of the Consecration of Man.

In harmony with its emphasis on education, Anthroposophy has established well-regarded private schools called Waldorf Schools. They have stressed the value of art and drama in creative education, and make use of eurhythmic exercises.

At the present time, Anthroposophy seems to attract a certain number of people of all ages, perhaps due in part to its educational work. Despite the practical emphasis on verbal communication, artists, dancers, and musicians find in it an integrative philosophy which makes what they do more meaningful. There is a rather charming flavor of cultural central Europe about it—one might even say a Weimar Republic style of aesthetic intellectualism and mystical idealism. One meets many persons of Germanic descent. But Anthroposophy has deeply impressed many persons in other cultural areas, such as the distinguished British linguistic philosopher Owen Barfield. Perhaps Anthroposophy could be called a "demythologized Theosophy," for it keeps the metaphysics and adventure of initiation of Theosophy without the elements which personify cosmic mysteries and make them into narratives.

Reading Selection: Anthroposophy

The world of Anthroposophical literature, beginning with the books of Rudolf Steiner himself, is vast and weighty. It is not easy to isolate any few paragraphs which do justice to the whole of the concept. Perhaps these from an article in an Anthroposophical journal suggest the tone, and something of the content, as well as any. We see a typical continual reference to the seminal ideas of Steiner, as well as an exemplification of several of his fundamental principles. Steiner was above all concerned with the unification of the scientific and spiritual world views. He held that matter and spirit were both equally real. To him this was no lip service platitude, but a firm operating axiom to be applied in every sort of investigation and to every decision of life. *Spirit* meant the idea, consciousness, and unitive factors. Ideas are absolutely real entities, independent of the particular thinker, and constitute a whole real world to be explored by initiatory experiences. This world can be known just as the physical world is known by the scientist. Finally, both worlds can be wholly known together at once with all the factors of their interaction. This is the final goal, manifested in the Christ. But along the way, say Anthroposophists, even an imperfect awareness of these things opens up great new dimensions in the understanding of aesthetics, education, and physical matter, and new possibilities in fields like agriculture and healing.

Everything in nature is built upon logical, mathematical, numerical principles and laws which were in existence in the mind of the Creator even before nature existed. The *idea*, the blueprint, the architectural plan of things to come must exist prior to physical manifestation. At best, man can discover the principles according to which nature operates. "To recognize nature means to re-create it in one's mind," said Schelling. These principles belong in the realm of *idea*, not however as abstract thought or speculation but within a realm of reality which is accessible to observation and logic. With this background in mind, a different concept of that which we call "life" arises.

Considering life as a phenomenon in the Goethean sense, we cannot be satisfied to seek the seat of life in matter alone. It is true that matter is necessary to make life manifest, visible, to show things which grow. How often do we hear the question: what is the "substance" which carries life? Is it oxygen, protein, enzymes, ribonucleic acid, ATP, or what? No single substance is life; it is the concerted interaction of many or all substances, organized for "definite purpose and performance," which makes life. No chemist will ever discover "life," for his concern is substance, matter. He learns about the "body" of life. In order to analyze, he has to destroy life and operate with its corpse.

Comes the biologist and physiologist and points out the functional relationship, the directional or organizing factor. One would wish the biologist would grow wings and accept life as an independent agency, force, principle or energy. It is here that the difficulty of the modern scientist lies. He is fascinated by the performance of physical energies—warmth, electricity, magnetism, mechanical energy—which are convertible, one into another, obeying the laws of thermodynamics. He studies the spectrum of light with its different energy displays. He has the electron, the atom, the proton and neutron and many other smaller and smaller particles already known and more particles still to come. He uses the electron microscope to look deeper into the minute structures of the cells—the nuclei, the mitochondria, the helical structure of genetic material, etc., etc. All these are parts of life but not life itself. These are the tools with which life operates.

The manifold differentiations and specializations have brought about the desire for integration, grouping together, in order that one might see the interrelationship. Toward the middle of the present century, science made many strides in the direction of this integration. It even now begins to rediscover the truth of that fundamental concept so important to Goethe—"the whole is more than the sum of its parts." The whole of life, its totality, is more than all the knowledge about the "body" of life, that is, its physical manifestation.

The breakthrough in the conceptual realm was made by Rudolf Steiner. His theory of cognition, his teachings with regard to the etheric, formative forces have shown the path.

EHRENFRIED E. PFEIFFER, "A New Concept of Life: An Alternative to an Atomized World," *Journal for Anthroposophy*, No. 6 (Autumn 1967), published by the Anthroposophical Society in America, New York, N.Y. 10016, pp. 3–4.

ROSICRUCIANISM

We have seen that the title Rosicrucian has a long-standing history in the alternative reality tradition. In the seventeenth century, Rosicrucianism became almost synonymous with this tradition. Today, however, the name is chiefly identified in the popular mind with the specific teachings of two organizations, both founded, at least outwardly, in this century, though drawing from the remoter past. A few other groups also claim the title, and there has been no small acrimony among them as to legitimacy of its use.

The two most substantial groups of Rosicrucians are the Rosicrucian Fellowship, with its international headquarters at Mt. Ecclesia, Oceanside,

California, and the Ancient and Mystical Order Rosae Crucis in San Jose, California. The latter is the best-known group. It has engaged in a widespread advertising campaign for a number of years.

The older of the two groups, and the one most influenced by Theosophy, is, however the Rosicrucian Fellowship, founded in 1907 by Max Grashoff, who used the pen name Max Heindel. Born in Germany in 1865, Heindel came to America in 1895 and to Los Angeles in 1903. There he became active in Theosophy, serving as vice-president of the local lodge from 1904 to 1905. Thereafter, he worked as a Theosophical lecturer.

He claimed that while he was in Europe in 1907 a marvelous being, whom he later learned was an elder brother in the occult Rosicrucian Order, appeared to him and offered him help. After several more visits, in which he was tested, Heindel reported he was taken by the brother to a temple of the Rose Cross near the border between Germany and Bohemia. Here he spent about a month receiving personal instruction by the elder brothers. This initiatory experience is considered by the group as its real founding. Heindel wrote what he had learned in his basic book, *Rosicrucian Cosmo-Conception.*[8] By 1910, the book had been published and Heindel had established several Fellowship Centers. Later, it was imparted to him that he was to establish a temple, which he did at Mt. Ecclesia. Heindel died in 1919.

The basic doctrine of the Rosicrucian Fellowship is common to Theosophy—world evolution, reincarnation, secret initiation, invisible helpers, and elder brothers. But the atmosphere is all Western, and there is special emphasis on healing and on astrology; the initiatory symbolism of the latter is much elaborated. One who is admitted into the Fellowship must give up tobacco, liquor, and meat.

The few Rosicrucian Fellowship churches have something of an old-fashioned Protestant atmosphere. Over the altar hang curtains, opened only when worship begins, unveiling a rose-covered cross. The service will have the usual hymns and scripture, but the prayer will be more in the New Thought style of sending out "good vibrations" than of intercession. There is generally no minister; members conduct the service themselves. At times there are lecturers from Oceanside. It appears that this group is attracting few younger persons at the present time.

The other Rosicrucian group, the AMORC, as it is usually abbreviated, is far larger. It claims not to be a "religion," but a "worldwide fraternal organization" on the Masonic model which teaches a philosophy and practices designed to enable the individual to use ordinarily latent faculties for the sake of improving his abilities and leading a more satisfying life. The Order has a temple and conducts ceremonies of a lodge type, as do branch lodges on a smaller scale. In its literature, the Order states as its "traditional history" that it is descended from an ancient Egyptian mystery school whose first Master was the Pharoah Akhnaton, and that a great number of the most enlightened minds of history have been counted among its members. In some periods, however, it has been less visible than in others. The present cycle of visible work was begun in 1915 by H. Spencer Lewis (1883–1939), a New York advertising man.

Its place as a voice in the alternative reality tradition is evident from the fact that the literature of Rosicrucianism speaks of the golden secret, which is that man has two natures, a "duality of self." Besides the physical body, there is a "greater inner self." This secret is the key to the Rosicrucian understanding of the question of death and the development of psychic powers, including the projection of consciousness out of the body. These techniques and the philosophy which goes with them are obtained in lessons sent out from the headquarters in San Jose, which the individual may study at home or with a local lodge.

The headquarters in San Jose, Rosicrucian Park, reflect the magnitude of the activity. Covering an entire city block, it contains not only modern, computerized offices for the extensive mailing activities of the Order, but a fine Egyptological museum and a science museum, reflecting two interests which the Order clearly hopes to unify, and a large temple and auditorium. These have all become a major tourist attraction.

The AMORC is much larger, and more geared to a popular audience, than most other groups in this book. This fact has to some extent shaped the character of its message. The similarity of the structure, ritual, and some of the terminology to Freemasonry has no doubt aided in its acceptance in America, where Masonry is very "establishment." The insistence that AMORC is not a religion has unquestionably helped many who would feel reluctant to reject their traditional church to accept the Order's teaching and membership—and the alternative reality tradition. In part, for this reason, AMORC has played a special role in shaping the culture of modern America.

Reading Selection: Rosicrucianism

The following passage is from an attractive introductory booklet issued to prospective members by the Ancient and Mystical Order Rosae Crucis (AMORC). It makes clear the basic teachings: a dualistic view of mind and body, the possibility of greatly developing the powers of mind, the conviction that wisdom regarding this has been acquired by ancient secret brotherhoods and is now available through the Order. It emphasizes the belief that this particular wisdom—all that the Order is concerned with—is not tied to religion.

You have often had the experience of an *intuitive impression,* a hunch or idea that was most enlightening but seemed to come from nowhere. Do you know that intuition can provide an answer for almost every question, a solution to many predicaments in which you find yourself? Do you know that it can aid you in keeping the affairs of your life in order? Do you further know that this *intuitive knowledge* is part of a universal cosmic intelligence which pervades the entire universe and every cell of your being and that you can command it to serve you—that you can draw upon it as you will? While millions of men and women rely solely upon their brains and the training which is given to them through education, those who know the esoteric wisdom wait for no hunches. They do not rely solely upon their outer minds but are able to draw upon the vast resources they possess and which also exist in the cosmic forces around them.

Psychologists today say that man uses only a fraction of the inherent power with which he is imbued as a human being. The secret brotherhoods have known for centuries how to command and use much more of this power to round out and enjoy an enriched life. Hundreds of the so-called mysteries are understandable and workable laws of the universe to those who master this esoteric (inner) knowledge.

"Why," you may ask, "is not this knowledge generally and widely disseminated to mankind today? Why, if such illuminating truths exist and are available to man, is he deprived of them?" We have shown what occurred in ancient times when the attempt was made to teach man these simple truths. They were often suppressed. Even today, such knowledge cannot be taught to everyone. To those who are sincere in bettering their own lives and advancing humanity, such knowledge becomes a power for good. On the other hand, in the hands of the selfish and the bigoted, the same knowledge might become a factor for misuse and further persecution of the ignorant and the helpless. But today, as we have said, it has survived because of the careful guardianship of the brotherhood mystery schools and societies.

The oldest of these *humanitarian societies,* worldwide in extent and *not a religion,* is the Rosicrucians. It offers you this knowledge, as old as time, for the fullness of life, free of any religious intolerance or political or other prejudices or biases.

THE MASTERY OF LIFE (San Jose, California: Supreme Grand Lodge of The Ancient and Mystical Order Rosae Crucis, 1965), pp. 13–14.

MODERN GNOSTICISM

The greatest problem which early Christianity had to face was not persecutors without, but diversity of opinion within. The main challenge was the collection of schools known as Gnosticism. Gnostics accepted the special meaning of Jesus Christ, but their interpretation of him, and of things in general, was far closer than that of normative Christianity to the alternative reality tradition.

Details of different Gnostic systems varied.[9] But they had in common a world view shaped by Hellenism and Neoplatonism, as well as by esoteric Judaism, Zoroastrianism, and the ancient heritages of Egypt and Mesopotamia. The Gnostic sought, out of the symbol systems of all these strains together with Christianity, to construct a picture in which he could find his identity. His quest was, in the words of one ancient writer, "to seek myself and know who I was, and who and in what manner I now am, that I may again become that which I was." In the midst of the destruction of cultures and the appalling brutality of the Roman world, there were those who needed above all to know who they were. They felt they were isolated individuals with some kind of wholly valuable essence within, lost and strayed into a callous and meaningless world for which they were never made.

Stephan Hoeller, the Los Angeles leader of a modern Gnostic group, states that what is most important about Gnosticism to him is that it presents an "intrapsychic" deity. God in all his complexities is found within the self as well as without. It is perhaps the first religion, at least in the West, which is wholly nontribal and centered upon the discovery of infinity within the psyche of the single individual. Society and history are alike irrelevant to this discovery, which leads out of them as out of realms of evil.

In Gnosticism, then, the soul of the individual was seen as a spark of the divine which had fallen an inexpressible distance from the world of light. Usually a mythological interpretation of the fall is provided, employing spatial metaphors for psychological realities which are actually, according to modern Gnostics, subjective. (The thought of C. G. Jung, who was quite sympathetic to Gnosticism, is much employed.) The spark in man is viewed as alien in this world of time and matter. Like a fish out of its element, it undergoes great suffering in such an uncongenial environment. Jesus Christ is an envoy from the worlds of light, from far above the God of the Old Testament (who was sometimes regarded as a false god, a part of the fallen sphere). Jesus draws to himself those lost fragments of the light who are able to see in him a beacon lit in their true home.

Mythical narrative language is always a necessary part of the expression of ultimate things. Our problem is that while we incurably want to know the most that can be known, what things are in their widest dimension, who we were and who we are and who we can become, all our experiences are limited to particulars. We do not experience Pleasure and Pain, but this pleasure and that pain, this excellent meal or that toothache, as C. S. Lewis once pointed out. We can, however, tell stories in such a way that particular joys and pains and events seem to explain what is always true. The Gnostics devised complicated stories of how the lower aeons, or transcendent spheres of light, fell through ignorance and desire, and in the end produced this world of space and time in which sparks of light were trapped, and of how the escape could be made through Christ. But the Gnostic was looking for radical reversal, for experience of a wholly other state of consciousness. This state should be immediately available since it is predicated by the ground of one's being, the divine snared within, and not upon historical processes. The Gnostic mood was antihistorical, since the route to salvation via kings, battles, laws, and eventually a Last Day was associated with the enslaving God of the Old Testament still honored by other Christians. For Gnostics, it was rather a matter of a vertical ascent *now* by means of a new and total state of consciousness bestowed by right *gnosis*—knowledge that is not so much factual as total insight, intuitive understanding, called *epignosis*, or recognition. The experience is brought down to an intrapsychic process triggered by certain symbols such as Christ.

The complex theological issues cannot be discussed here. Basically, Gnosticism appeals to a feeling that the anguish of one's alienated state, and the pathetic suffering of the world, are beyond help under the conditions of the world, or even of space and time. One is then susceptible to teachers who say, "What you have heard is the outer shell, but there is within a deeper, more immediate mystery of why you suffer in this harsh world, and how to escape from it. You are not meant for this world at all; forget it, prepare to return to your eternal home far above in the arena of light."

There are those in this age who have made the same Gnostic appeal. One is the Gnostic Society, headquartered in Los Angeles. It grew out of the Order of the Pleroma, founded by an Australian-born Gnostic teacher, Ronald Powell, who called himself Richard, Duc de Palatine. He had been a Theosophist and priest of the Liberal Catholic Church in Australia. In the early 1950s he went to Europe and, after associating with certain tiny Gnostic sects which had functioned there for some years, established the Order of the Pleroma in England together with an ecclesiastical expression of it, the Pre-Nicene Catholic Church. In 1959 he appointed the Hungarian-born Theosophist, Stephan Hoeller, a man of considerable esoteric learning, to begin its work in America.

In the early 1970s Hoeller separated his work from de Palatine's. It is now called the Gnostic Society and its church, of which Hoeller is bishop, is the Ecclesia Gnostica. The Society's work consists largely of lectures on Gnosticism and such related topics as the mystical meaning of Christianity, alchemy and kabbalism, or Jungian theory, interspersed with delightful social events. The church celebrates the Holy Eucharist every Sunday and Holy Day. Its lavish liturgy employs vestments and ceremonies reminiscent of the Roman Catholic or Anglican mass, but the language is dilated with Gnostic terminology. Scripture readings may well be from the Pistis Sophia or the Gospel of Thomas, ancient Gnostic texts. A prayer toward the beginning starts with characteristic Gnostic flourish:

> Give ear unto us, O Indwelling One, while we sing Thy praises, Thou Mystery before all Uncontainables and Impassables, Who did shine forth in Thy Mystery, in order that the Mystery that is from the beginning should be completed in us . . .

Reading Selection: Modern Gnosticism

The following passage was written especially for this book by Stephen Hoeller, leader of the Ecclesia Gnostica and The Sophia Gnostic Center in Los Angeles.

AN OUTLINE OF GNOSTICISM*

Gnosticism may first of all be defined simply as *mystical religion*. By this we do not mean that occult phenomena and psychism ought to take the place of traditional religious practices, or that purely negative conceptions of Divinity, vague reasoning, or a distaste for practical action should con-

---

*As taught in such modern Gnostic movements as the Gnostic Society, The Brotherhood of the Pleroma, The Pre-Nicene Catholic Church, The Church of the Gnosis, and others.

stitute the essence of religious life. None of these things are the essence of mystical religion but its aberrations.

Gnosticism in the above noted sense is as old as humanity itself. Gnosis means knowledge, as distinguished from mere belief, or blind faith based on hearsay. The Gnostics of all ages and faiths have asserted that man is capable of first-hand knowledge regarding the essential nature of things human and divine, and that the attainment of such direct, immediate and absolute knowledge is the greatest hope and promise of our earthly existence. Statements advancing this proposition can be found in all religions and religious philosophies, from the Upanishads to the wisdom of ancient Egypt, and from the Gathas of Zarathustra to the mystery-cults of Greece and Rome. In a more restricted sense the Gnostic movement of the first Christian Centuries includes the teachings of Basilides (*c.* 130 A.D.), Valentinus (*c.* 150 A.D.), Marcion, Ptolemaeus, Cerinthus, Menander, Saturninus, Bardesanes, but there exists much justification for including Apollonius of Tyana, Simon Magus, Clement of Alexandria, and the church father Origen into the illustrious company of the Gnostic teachers. Many students feel that St. Paul the Apostle could be justly included in this company, for his Gnostic orientation is evident in many of his epistles, perhaps most clearly in First Corinthians 2:7, where he says: "But we speak the wisdom of God in a mystery, the hidden wisdom [Gnosis] which none of the rules of this aion knew." Some of the most important points of Gnostic teaching are as follows:

At the root-base of all consciousness there is a transcendental field, named Pleroma or fullness, from which emerge more limited fields of consciousness in series, each with properties revealing the original Principle. This fullness may perhaps be envisioned as identical with the basis of psychic energy resident within the Collective Unconscious discovered by C. G. Jung, and the objective and purpose of the efforts of the Gnostic is to establish an effective, conscious contact with this ultimate Source of all Power and Life, which resides constantly at the very back of our consciousness, and is therefore always available. This unobstructed contact can be established only when the dominion of the rulers (demiurgoi, archons) is broken, that is, when man is no longer subject to the attachments and fascinations of the lower worlds of sense perceptions, emotions, and analytical reason, but having transcended the latter, has put on the "vesture of light" and thus has accomplished what modern analytical psychology calls total integration, and the mystics of the first Christian centuries called "the divine Gnosis."

This process of integration, or growth, in the Gnosis is attained by the double method of (1) esoteric sacramental ritualism, and (2) the allegorical interpretation of the biblical scriptures through the proper recognition of their spiritual and psychological symbolism. It is interesting to note that the two remnants of this double method are still to be found in the exoteric orientation of the Catholic and Protestant churches, which are still the exponents respectively of sacramentalism and of an interest in the Bible. Thus in a certain sense Gnosticism supplies the missing link between Catholicism and Protestantism by explaining the sacramental rituals not as mere magic performed in memory of historical events, but as the externalization of internal psychic alchemy, and on the other hand by regarding the Bible not as history but as mythology of the most sublime and valuable kind. To the Gnostic myth is truer than history, for it depicts the eternally recurring story of man's soul, its vicissitudes and its ultimate triumph over the external world.

The Gnostic believes that Divinity is resident in every man, and that the mission of great teachers, such as Christ, is to facilitate the emergence of the innate Divinity of all humans. Most Gnostics believe in some form of reembodiment and they hold that although life in the body on earth must of necessity appear as a limitation and a calamity to the soul, it is a self-imposed limitation, a calamity voluntarily entered into for a definite purpose, namely the overcoming of the world and the transforming of all creatures and things into the essence of light. In order to properly explain the nature and purpose of man's life on earth the modern Gnostics distinguish between the *lesser self* (Personality) and the *true self* (Divine Soul) of man. The former perishes after every earth life while the latter endures. In the Gnostic system we find the statement that the temporal personality survives the death of the body, but not indefinitely. After the passage of some time, the emotions and intellect of man, which survived the passage of his body, also undergo a form of death, and then the true self or soul begins to form a new personality for the purpose of a new incarnation. The Gnostic is aware of and studies the manifold environmental forces and influences which are involved in the formation of his personality in the shaping of his earthly destiny. Hence at least a rudimentary knowledge of astrology and of some of the other occult arts are considered useful tools for the Gnostic while he still finds himself in incarnation and in the physical universe.

Essentially, however, Gnosticism ancient and modern is *mystical* as well as *psychological religion,* i.e., a view of the religious effort wherein God, the Commandments, the Angelic and Demonic powers, and just about every aspect of religious doctrine are considered to be interior to man. No wonder that such great students of psychology as the late Dr. C. G. Jung have given abundant evidence of their interest in and admiration for Gnosticism. Indeed to all well-informed modern Gnostics, Jung must appear as one of the major apostles of their ancient faith in contemporary guise.

The great student of Gnosticism, G.R.S. Mead, wrote, "The Gnostic strives for the knowledge of God, the science of realities, the Gnosis of the things that are; wisdom is his goal, the holy things of life his study." To this most eloquent and true statement we may add that unlike the believer, who remains content with secondhand knowledge derived from the testimony of others, the Gnostic fervently desires to become a knower of the ultimate realities of authentic being. He follows no one, save the eternal light within his own heart; he trusts no other Savior except the saving power resident within his soul. Thus, in the words of the Gospel of Phillip, the Gnostic becomes not only a Christian, but a Christ.

STEPHAN A. HOELLER

THE "I AM" ACTIVITY

A number of persons have claimed contact with Masters and with ancient and esoteric orders offering a message to the world. The most dramatic movement of this type is "I AM." Few religious activities have had such a meteoric rise and apparent fall as the "I AM" Activity. At its apex in the late 1930s, it must have represented the greatest popular diffusion Theosophical concepts ever attained. Its leaders, the Ballard family, could fill large auditoriums with fervent followers. Now the movement, while still in existence with some 300 centers worldwide, is less in the news.

The founder was Guy Ballard (1878–1939). Born in Kansas, Ballard had long been interested in occultism, and had studied teachings of the Theosophical sort in libraries in Chicago and Los Angeles. By profession he was engaged in mining exploration and promotion. In 1930, while he was working near Mt. Shasta in northern California, he had his initiatory contact with the hidden world.

Deep in the woods, Ballard reports in his first book, *Unveiled Mysteries*,[10] he encountered a beautiful, godlike figure who gave him a marvelous drink and introduced himself as the Master Saint Germain. Using Ballard as example and messenger, the adept first of all wanted to restore to humankind the truths of reembodiment. He showed Ballard many of his former lives, which he had shared with his wife Edna (Lotus) and their son Donald, in fabulous ancient civilizations. In the course of these tours, the Master painstakingly imparted information about karma, the inner reality of the divine (the "Mighty I AM Presence"), occult world history, and the creative power of thought. The writing is very smooth and simple. One cannot but admire the effectiveness with which Ballard presented in a truly popular and American manner the basic teaching and sense of wonder which underlies Theosophy. The author employed fast-paced interspersing of fantastic events with philosophical discourse phrased in homespun and highly visual language.

Apart from the general Theosophical worldview, the "I AM" teachings have certain distinctive characteristics, all of which no doubt contributed, along with the readability of the books, to its remarkable spread. One trait is the American setting and nationalistic overtones. The Masters are found not in faraway Egypt or Tibet, but in the then romantic American West—Mt. Shasta, the Grand Tetons, and Yellowstone. The Masters became known to Wyoming ranchers, Colorado miners, and Arizona prospectors. Moreover, it is said that humanity began in America, and that this is the seventh and last cycle of history, under the Lord of the Seventh Ray, Saint Germain. As the history of this epoch began in America, so will it end there. This nation will be the vessel of light to bring the world into new and paradisal times. While there were and are rightist overtones to the movement's attitude toward America, in large part it can be seen simply as thorough indigenization of the Theosophical experience.

The "I AM" Activity makes rich use of color. The rays of the Masters, the spiritual characteristics of people are all given vivid color adjectives. The "I AM" bookshops and centers are bright with color diagrams and lights. Ballard's writing is packed with color words. Fascinated by mines and gold, Ballard loved to depict the Masters' retreats as underground, reminiscent of the halls of fairy tale dwarves. One leader in the movement has confirmed that color is very important because of the vibratory action of each color. Everything is energy and electrons, and energy manifests in different qualities through various colors. Sound—talking—is also energy, but can be largely destructive, and has done much to get humanity into the trouble which surrounds us. "I AM" students believe that surrounding oneself with harmonious colors can greatly assist in bringing forth constructive activity.

The three Ballards travelled in the 1930s as "Accredited Messengers" of the Masters lecturing about these revelations. Sometimes further messages from the Ascended Masters were produced in public or private, especially from Saint Germain or the Master Jesus. The basic teaching is that the "Mighty I AM Presence" is God-in-action, and is immediately available. With typical concreteness, it is said that one's "individualized Presence" is a pure reservoir of energy. Power can be drawn from it at will. Mediatory between the "I AM Presence" and humans are a host of Ascended Masters, such as Saint Germain and Jesus. At one time all were human beings who, through purifying their lives, became able to transcend the physical world.

Ascension is the goal of human life. The karma-made aura about a person reflects his deeds and desires. Ordinarily the aura is both dark and light, and when its darkness reaches a point where the person can no longer be of much service, or make much progress, he dies physically to begin another life. But, through purification of thought and feeling, the causal body may become fully luminous, and acting like a magnet, draws the individual into the Ascension. The person ascends to join the Ascended Masters and share their unconditioned state of Joy and Freedom. However, in 1938 a dispensation was given that persons who had devoted themselves so much to the movement that they had not given all they might to personal purification could upon normal death ascend from the after-death state without reembodiment.

The "I AM" Activity believes manifestation of constructive activities can be brought forth through one's acknowledgment and use of the power of qualification and visualization through music, contemplation, and Decrees. A Decree is an Affirmation or prayer, used only for constructive purposes. All that is destructive comes from human beings. Records of past karmic debts can be consumed by the use of the "Violet Consuming Flame," which is like the grace of the New Testament, and through the use of this "Sacred Fire" humankind can be liberated from the toils of what has gone before.

From 1937 to 1940, we are now told, the "I AM" Activity worked publicly in order to establish a group of devoted followers numbering over one million. The decline of the movement began with the death of Guy Ballard on December 29, 1939. Despite the claim of Edna Ballard that he had become an Ascended Master, the fact that physical death rather than evident ascension had taken place was too much for some believers. The following year a sensational trial of the leaders of the movement ensued, brought on by disgruntled members of Ballard's personal staff, accusing the Ballards of obtaining money under fraudulent pretenses. The indictment was later voided by the Supreme Court in a 1944 landmark decision on religious liberty. Justice Douglas, in stating the prevailing opinion, asserted, "Men may believe what they cannot prove. They may not be put to the proof of their religious doctrines or beliefs." The case was finally dismissed in 1946.

The "I AM" Activity is still alive today and in the 1980s is experiencing new growth. It has temples, reading rooms, and radio programs in a number of cities. It was directed by Edna Ballard until her death in 1971, and today is governed by a board of directors. Mr. and Mrs. Gerald Craig are the "Appointed Messengers," and Mt. Shasta is a major center.

In the summer of 1970 one of the authors visited Mt. Shasta and talked with a pleasant lady who had been a member of the "I AM" for many years. She lived on the spotless grounds of the Saint Germain Foundation. In an ampitheater on these grounds every summer the "I AM" Activity of the Saint Germain Foundation stages a pageant on the life of the "Beloved Master Jesus." The crucifixion is left out of this version, for the ascension is what is believed to be important. The Saint Germain Foundation also owns the large Shasta Springs resort near the town of Mt. Shasta, where youth and adult conclaves are held every summer. Services are held every evening in a sanctuary on their property. The pageant is done by the young people, and attracts thousands of visitors to that area annually.

The story of relations between the "I AM" Activity and the community of Mt. Shasta is rather interesting. When the "I AM" Activity began to establish work at their sacred mountain in the 1940s, there was considerable local antagonism. The "I AM" Movement was accused of weird and fantastic practices, and slander followed its members. In 1948 Mrs. Ballard was a special guest of the Mt. Shasta Chamber of Commerce. She explained the "I AM" Activity, stressing the work for a better world and saying their beliefs were based on the Bible.

Full acceptance did not come until 1955, however, when the general public was first invited to attend the pageant on the life of Christ. Three thousand came and were awed. The play culminated in an ascension of Christ by means of an elevator cleverly concealed in a pine tree. Then Mrs. Ballard solemnly bore an American flag to the device and had the flag wafted aloft as a symbol of the ascension of America as a nation. The next day seventeen local business concerns purchased a full-page ad in the *Mt. Shasta Herald* thanking the "I AM" Movement for the invitation to the pageant and warmly praising the group. The pageant is now held every summer to the mutual benefit of the religion and the tourism-based economy of the town.

Reading Selection: The "I AM" Activity

This passage, described as delivered orally by the Ascended Master Saint Germain in the home of Guy and Edna Ballard in 1932, is characteristic of the teaching of the

Ascended Masters, which is the foundation of the "I AM" Activity. Note the emphasis on the power of affirmation reminiscent of "New Thought" or positive thinking, combined with the special aura of wonder and magic lent by the role of Ascended Masters and the vivid "I AM" imagery.

INVOCATION: Thou Infinite All-Pervading Presence—Thou Mighty Master within each human form! we acknowledge and accept Thy Full Presence manifest within these forms, and within the human form of every individual that God has sent forth. We give praise and thanks that at last, we have become aware of this Mighty Presence to Whom we can turn and recognize the Fulness of God's Activity, the "I AM" of all things.

GREETINGS: to you all.

The Discourse

When Jesus said: "I AM the resurrection and the Life," he gave forth one of the mightiest utterances that can well be expressed.

When he said, "I AM," He did not refer to the outer expression, but He did refer to *The Mighty Master Presence—God Within,* because he repeatedly said: "I of my self can do nothing, it is the Father within—the 'I AM'—that doeth the works."

Again Jesus said: "I AM the Way, the Life, and the Truth," giving recognition to the One and Only Power—*God in Action within him.*

Again he said: "I AM the 'Light' that lighteth every man that cometh into the world," prefacing every statement of vital importance with the words—"I AM."

Contemplating "I AM," as *anything* and *everything* you wish to be, is one of the mightiest means of loosing the Inner God Power, Love, Wisdom, and Truth, and setting It into action in the outer experience.

Again, let us refer to His mighty utterance, perhaps one of the greatest ever spoken into the outer expression: "I AM the open door, which no man can shut." Do you not see how very vital this is, when you come to review understandingly, these Mighty Statements?

When you recognize and accept fully, "I AM," as the *Mighty Presence of God in you—in action,* you will have taken one of the greatest steps to liberation.

Now mark you, in the utterance of the Truth that, "I AM the open door which no man can shut," if you can but realize it, you have the key that allows you to step through the veil of flesh, carrying with you all consciousness, that you have generated or accumulated, which is imperfect, and there transmute it, or in other words, raise it into that Perfection into which you have stepped. . . .

If one *feels* critical, inquisitive, or out of harmony toward a person, condition, place, or thing, it is a sure signal that the outer-self is acting, and the right attitude is to correct it immediately. Everyone, especially students, must realize, that they have only one thing to do and that is to feel, see, and be Perfection in their own world.

This is so very important is the reason I am stressing it so much at this time, because as students begin to experience unusual manifestation through their efforts, there is always that presence at first, which will say to the individual: "I AM able to use the Law better than the other person." This you know, without my saying it, is a mistake.

One cannot long use the statement "I AM" even intellectually, until he begins to feel a deeper and deeper conviction that: "I AM all things." Think often, what these marvelous two words mean, and *always couple with the use of these two words the statement that: "When I say, 'I AM,' I AM setting in motion the Limitless Power of God in whatever I couple the expression 'I AM' with."* In the Scriptural statement: "Before Abraham, was 'I AM.'" Abraham represents the outer expression of Life and "I AM" represents the Principle of Life, which was expressing through Abraham. Thus, was the Perfection of Life, before any manifestation ever occurred, and thus is Life without beginning and without end.

My beloved students! my heart rejoices exceedingly in the nearness with which some of you are feeling the conviction of this Majestic Presence, "I AM," which you are. Do your utmost to feel calmly, serenely, and if you cannot see it otherwise, shut your eyes and see Perfection everywhere. More and more there will come to you proof of the marvelous Presence of this Truth. You will hear, feel, see, and experience that marvel of all marvels which as children you have lived in,—miracles performed.

There have been written for your benefit, descriptions and explanations of the use of this "Mighty I AM Presence." You, who hold fast to the Truth will come into the three-fold action, seeing, hearing, and experiencing these so-called miracles, miracles until you understand their operation, and then majestic simple truths, which you may forever apply, when once understood.

With all my centuries of experience, I cannot help but say to you as encouragement, that my heart leaps with joy at the nearness with which some of you are grasping the Scepter of Dominion. Go forward, my brave ones. Do not hesitate. Grasp your Scepter of Dominion! Raise it! for: *"I AM the Scepter, the Quenchless Flame, the Dazzling Light, the Perfection, which you once knew."* Come! let me hold you in my strong embrace, that where there have been so long two, there will only be one, "I AM."

Discourse II, from Vol. III, *"I AM" Discourses*, Oct. 6, 1932.
Reprinted by permission of The Saint Germain Foundation

THE CHURCH UNIVERSAL AND TRIUMPHANT

A movement which has attracted considerable attention in the 1970s and 1980s is the Church Universal and Triumphant. Its fundamental motif is an acceptance of progressive revelation from the Ascended Masters of the Great White Brotherhood through their anointed Messengers Mark and Elizabeth Clare Prophet.

The Ascended Masters, in the view of this church, have sponsored various movements over the centuries, such as the mystery schools of Pythagoras, the Essenes, Camelot, and Theosophy, as well as the "I AM" Activity. However, the Church Universal and Triumphant stresses that it is distinct from "I AM." The Ascended Masters, it teaches, have an ongoing message, with a certain continuity, but each new dispensation of truth and enlightenment is released for the culture, consciousness, and milieu of the day.

Sociologically, Church Universal and Triumphant is distinguished by its members' great respect for the mantle and mission of the Messengers and by a close-knit circle of disciples who have formed a new-age Community of the Holy Spirit. Committed members of the group, called Keepers of the Flame, undertake a demanding regimen of spiritual study and service, both at the headquarters in Malibu, California, and in Church teaching centers and study groups throughout the world.

In 1958, the movement was inaugurated as The Summit Lighthouse by Mark L. Prophet under the direction of the Ascended Master El Morya. Three years later, while delivering the Ascended Masters' teachings in Boston, Mark Prophet met Elizabeth Clare Wulf (1940–), who was studying political science at Boston University. Elizabeth became a devotee of the Ascended Masters and was tutored in their teachings by Mark Prophet and El Morya. Several years later, Mark and Elizabeth were married and both carried on the work of the Great White Brotherhood.

The Summit Lighthouse was first located in Washington, D.C., then in Colorado Springs, Colorado. In 1969, it moved to California, first to Santa Barbara, then to a former college campus in Pasadena, and finally, in 1978, to a beautiful site in the Malibu hills, renamed "Camelot." In the mid-1980s, plans were under discussion to move to the Church's 30,000-acre Royal Teton Ranch in Montana.

Mark L. Prophet died in 1973 at the age of fifty-four, like Guy Ballard leaving his movement at a comparatively early age in the hands of a vigorous and capable widow. According to Church teachings, Prophet ascended immediately and as the Ascended Master Lanello continues to provide guidance and inspiration to his students. In 1974, Mrs. Prophet and a board of directors incorporated as the Church Universal and Triumphant, and The Summit Lighthouse became the publishing arm of the Church.

The movement has attracted considerable media attention and the inevitable controversy centering around the Church's religious concepts, its communal practices, and its successful growth.

The Church emphasizes karma, reincarnation, and the "I AM THAT I AM" as the spark of divinity within the heart. Its members accept the hierarchy of Ascended Masters, those immortals who stand far in advance of ordinary human beings and who continue to guide the spiritual growth of earth's evolutions. The Church stresses that they are "ascended," that is, spiritualized and no longer dependent on a physical body. These Masters include Jesus Christ, Gautama Buddha, Saint Germain, and other saints and sages from both East and West who are known in the scriptures as "the saints robed in white."

Spiritual practices include the delivery of dictations from the Ascended Masters to the Messengers and the practice of the science of the spoken Word—the recitation of prayers, decrees, and mantras. The Messengers preach from the Old Testament and the New Testament and from Eastern scriptures, basing their teaching on biblical and scriptural authority as well as the dictations of the Ascended Masters.

The teachings contain themes commonly associated with the conservative movement, such as support of the family unit, opposition to abortion ("the murder of God"), the upholding of the four sacred freedoms, and the exaltation of the spiritual mission of America.

Church Universal and Triumphant teaching centers and study groups are currently located in major cities in the United States and around the world.

Reading Selection: The Church Universal and Triumphant

The following passage, from a booklet introducing the Keepers of the Flame, the organization of committed inner-circle members of the Church Universal and Triumphant, suggests many of its dominant themes. Notice that it begins with Theosophical themes, refers to Christian beliefs, and emphasizes the role of Mark L. Prophet in our day as embodied representative of the Great White Brotherhood of Ascended Masters, a calling answered by other great men of faith in the past.

A MESSAGE TO ALL WHO WOULD KEEP
THE FLAME OF LIFE

The Coming of the Ancient of Days

Long ago the Ancient of Days came to Earth from Venus to keep the flame of life, that you and I might live and one day know the self as God. His name was Sanat Kumara. He was one of the Seven Holy Kumaras who focus the light of the seven rays on behalf of the evolutions of the planet Venus.

When cosmic councils had determined that no further opportunity should be given humanity—so great their departure from cosmic law, their desecration of the flame—Sanat Kumara raised his hand and offered his heart to serve the souls of mankind until the few and eventually the many would respond to keep the flame of life. Granted the dispensation by solar lords, Sanat Kumara came with many volunteers who vowed to support him in his mission as Keeper of the Flame. He established his focus on an island in the Gobi Sea, now the Gobi Desert. And there at Shamballa he remained to tend the sacred fires until some among mankind would rise from the low estate to which they had descended by their ignorance (ignoring) of the law of the flame.

Through adoration and invocation, Sanat Kumara and his band of devotees magnified the trinity of cosmic consciousness which in the original creation the Lord God had placed as the flame of life within his sons and daughters. They worshiped God as Lawgiver, as Father Principle, as will and power in the first aspect of the flame, the blue. They sent forth praise to the Christos as the eternal Son, the wisdom of the law embodied as the teacher, incarnate as the Word, in the second aspect, the yellow. They ministered unto love as Holy Spirit, as fires of creativity, individuality, and the cloven tongues, twin flames of the Comforter, in the third aspect, the pink. And they sought to quicken the action of all three in mankind by awakening the soul's inherent devotion to the Mother—the fiery core, the energy of purity that ignites the trinity in the hearts of mankind.

The Flame That Burns within Your Heart

The flame that burns within your heart is the spark of God, the potential of your divinity. It is the gift of life of the Creator to the creation. "For God so loved the world, that he gave his only begotten Son. . . ." This son, the eternal Christos, is the flame—the trinity of God's energy focused as power, wisdom, and love—that he gave to every son and daughter. Truly it is the light which lighteth every man and woman that cometh into the world. This is the individualization of the God flame whereby the Word is made flesh and whereby we behold the glory of the Lord of All. The flame that burns within your heart is the fiery core of cosmic consciousness. It is your link to reality, to being, and to life eternal. The flame comes forth from the heart of God, the I AM Presence. It is your identification mark as a son or daughter of God. It is the anointing of the Real Self of all who choose to keep it in his name.

To Be a Keeper of the Flame

Your threefold flame is, in fact, God. It is life and truth and love. It is a sacred fire kindled on heaven's altars. It is a spiritual fire not native to the material plane. Anchored in time and space, burning on the altar of the heart for the salvation of the soul, this flame, in order to be retained, must be acknowledged and adored. Through prayer and meditation, it must be expanded to magnify the Lord on earth as in heaven. This is to increase God Self-awareness in oneself and in all mankind; for the flame is consciousness, intelligence, intuition, love, understanding, and will. All attributes of real being come forth from the flame, for the flame is the Word, the Logos, without whom was not any thing made that was made.

To be a keeper of the flame is to live to preserve the sacredness of life in all. When men cease to be their brother's keeper, they cease to keep the flame. The consequence for the total disregard for the sacredness of life is total cataclysm—of body, mind, soul. On such acts continents have sunk, worlds have been destroyed. In this day and age men and women dare not ask, as did Cain, "Am I my brother's keeper?" But rather, when given the opportunity to account for life, "How can I keep the flame of life for a planet and a people?" Jesus and Gautama and the avatars and saints of the ages, overcoming the curse of Cain, have one and all laid down their lives for their friends. They are the true keepers of the flame. They have held the torch and passed it from hand to hand, heart to heart, through the ages, that you and I might take it again to master life's sacred energies and one day take our place with the immortals.

The Great White Brotherhood

The immortals are those who have kept the flame and then become one with the flame in the ritual of the ascension. This is the same flaming presence of God that appeared to Moses out of a bush, that Zarathustra adored, the same flame ("a chariot of fire") into which Elijah ascended and which as "a cloud" received Jesus from Bethany's hill. All who have merged with the flame through obedience to the inner law of being, through the sacrifice of the lesser self unto the Greater Self, have taken their place among the hosts of the Lord. Because they have mastered time and space and "ascended" (stepped up their vibration) to the fiery core of cosmic consciousness, they are called ascended masters. They are keeping the flame for mankind. Their fraternity is the Great White Brotherhood.

Dedicated to the salvation of all mankind through the major religions of the world, the members of this brotherhood are marked by the white light, the eternal Logos into whose presence they have ascended. Regardless of race, creed, religion, or national origin, the children of God can walk the same path of initiation which they have walked, can ascend into the Presence of the living God and become a part of their band.

The Keepers of the Flame Fraternity
Founded by Saint Germain

Down through the ages, members of the Great White Brotherhood have come forth to sponsor uplift movements and to assist mankind in every aspect of his evolution. Great artists, inventors, scientists, statesmen, and religious leaders have been sponsored by various members of hierarchy as they formed the avant-garde of achievement in their field.

In this century, Saint Germain, one of the foremost sponsors of man-kind—founder of America and master of the Aquarian dispensation—stepped forth once again to sponsor an outer activity of the Great White Brotherhood. In the early 1960s he contacted his embodied representative the Messenger Mark L. Prophet and founded the Keepers of the Flame Fraternity in memory of the Ancient of Days and his first pupil, Prince Siddhartha. Marking the way of Maitreya and Jesus, Confucius and Mohammed, and all who responded to the light and the call of Sanat Kumara, he dedicated his organization to the rekindling of the light of freedom in the souls of all mankind.

THE LIBERAL CATHOLIC CHURCH

The interior of the typical Liberal Catholic Church looks very much like that of a Roman Catholic or high Anglican church quite untouched by any recent liturgical reforms. The altar will be against the back wall of the sanctuary, ornamented with six candlesticks, cross, and frontal. The only unusual item is a picture of Jesus directly over the cross on the altar. The celebration of high mass in the Liberal Catholic Church too reminds the visitor of an ornate, traditional Roman Catholic or Anglo-Catholic rite. Numerous clergy and acolytes in resplendent copes and chasubles and surplices, swinging censers which cloud the church with fragrant incense, enter in procession. Moving with the slowness of ancient ritual, they approach the altar chanting and genuflecting.

The words of the rite are in English, generally reminiscent of the Episcopal or Roman Catholic rite, but with certain variations, some in the direction of Gnostic interpretations of Christianity. The confession does not suggest that "we are miserable sinners," but rather that "often we forget the glory of our heritage and wander from the path which leads to righteousness." After the consecration of the elements of bread and wine for the Communion, all stand to sing "O Come, All Ye Faithful."

It is in the sermon that the traditional Christian may be most surprised, however. He may hear of an impersonal Absolute beyond the conceptualized personal God, of the appearance of Masters and the deceased in etheric bodies, of "esoteric" interpretations of Christianity in which the festivals of the Christian year and events in the life of Christ are symbols of occult realities far older and more far-reaching than the short span since the first century A.D.

The Liberal Catholic Church is a body founded by Theosophists; many of its members are also Theosophists. While priding itself on allowing complete freedom of belief, it generally interprets Christianity along Theosophical lines. It was founded by James Ingall Wedgwood in London in 1916. Wedgwood was a former Anglican theological student who had left Anglicanism to become a Theosophist. But the real intellectual leader of the new ecclesiastical expression of Theosophy was a former Anglican priest, C. W. Leadbeater. His book, *The Science of the Sacraments,* is the standard Liberal Catholic theological work.

Why did a Theosophist like Leadbeater, who had for so long repudiated ritualism and distinctively Christian concepts, suddenly and enthusiastically support this seemingly unlikely new movement? Leadbeater was a man of remarkable psychic vision who, at least according to his descriptions, saw many things beyond ordinary visibility—Masters, angels, devas, auras, the colored shapes assumed by various thoughts and moods and emotions above the person's head, and lines of psychic force. One Sunday he happened to attend mass in an obscure Sicilian Catholic Church, and was amazed to observe powerful waves of prayerful feeling rolling from the peasant congregation to the altar, and splendid light descending from above onto the priest and altar and consecrated bread and wine. The experience suggested a new view of the rite. It combined word, gesture, and thought to funnel and focus the transcendent energies which the Masters know and serve to make them accessible to humans. A basic premise of Theosophy was the existence of such invisible mental energy; here was a way it could be tapped. To do so through a rite modeled on the mass did not, in Leadbeater's view, require acceptance of the orthodox concept of the uniqueness of Christ. The Liberal Catholic liturgy could be seen as a Western counterpart to the Vedic sacrifices of India, which can also be interpreted Theosophically.

The Liberal Catholic Church, then, is an institution designed to put into operation these forces, and to teach the esoteric interpretation of Christianity—within freedom—in the context of its Catholic rather than Protestant tradition. That is to say, it puts nonverbal ceremonial as well as verbal communication at its center.

The most fundamental idea is that of "Thought-forms." Leadbeater and Annie Besant wrote a book of that title with paintings illustrating what Leadbeater saw around the forms of persons in various spiritual states; these can be modified by ritual, prayer, and sacrament. Thought and form create a single whole and enhance each other. The ritual builds up a geometric form which contains power, as do the vestments, gestures, and meditations. Even the incense is full of elves, delightful beings entrapped in it, who help to distribute its grace, and angels come to bathe in the light radiating from the Host.

It is a concept of worship and the sacraments suggesting a programmed impartation of grace. But the notion of the relation of matter and thought, and of the power of thought, is certainly different from that of either ordinary materialism or ordinary Christianity.

Unfortunately, like Theosophy itself, Liberal Catholicism has suffered from personality problems and divisions. By the late 1980s, however, some schisms had been healed and the majority of Liberal Catholics nationwide were in the 4,000-member Liberal Catholic Church, Province of the United States of America, though a few smaller bodies exist. This province is in communion with the worldwide Liberal Catholic Church.

It does not appear that the Liberal Catholic Church is growing rapidly in numbers or influence today. But in its basic work of creating out of the mass a psychic cathedral of powerful invisible forces lies an enduring charm and beauty. Many priests have private altars in their homes and say mass alone daily, for the work of creating good psychic forces, while strengthened by the presence of a congregation, is not dependent upon its presence.

Reading Selection: The Liberal Catholic Church

The passage given below from C. W. Leadbeater's *Science of the Sacraments* concerning the meaning of the consecration of the Host, or round flat wafer of bread, in the Roman Catholic and Liberal Catholic mass illustrates the nature of his beliefs, and those generally of the Liberal Catholic Church, about this sacrament. To him, the celebration of the mass is really the creation of a psychic structure, by thought and act, through which certain supernal spiritual forces can flow. Reflecting the Theosophical concept of God, these spiritual forces are essentially impersonal (unlike the Roman Catholic view) though splendid, and one can "plug into" them in a rather objective way, though of course a deep sense of morality and reverence is important.

To understand the true relation between the physical matter of the Host and its counterparts requires the sight of other and higher dimensions of space. So in a sense we are only describing a diagram when we say that the Angel of the Presence brushes aside a bundle of wires or lines running up from the wafer to the Deity, but there is no other way of making the process thinkable to those who cannot see in the inner worlds. If we try to analyse the thing we shall find it rather complicated, because every atom has always its connection with the Deity. Truly the divine life is everywhere, as I have already said, but through the act of consecration, a special manifestation of it flashes out in the matter of the Host, welling up from the very heart of the Christ, so that it becomes in that moment a veritable epiphany of Him. It is then that the Host glows with unearthly radiance, as befits the most precious gift of God to man.

It was this glow which first brought to my notice the possibility of studying clairvoyantly the hidden side of the eucharistic Service. It may perhaps help the reader to realize the actuality and the material nature of the phenomenon if I reproduce here an account (written soon afterwards) of the first occasion on which I had the opportunity of observing it.

> My attention was first called to this matter by watching the effect produced by the celebration of the Mass in a Roman Catholic church in a little village in Sicily. Those who know that most beautiful of islands will understand that one does not meet with the Roman Catholic Church there in its most intellectual form, and neither the Priest nor the people could be described as especially highly developed; yet the quite ordinary celebration of the Mass was a magnificent display of the application of occult force.
>
> At the moment of consecration the Host glowed with the most dazzling brightness; it became in fact a veritable sun to the eye of the clairvoyant, and as the Priest lifted it above the heads of the people I noticed that two distinct varieties of spiritual force poured forth from it, which might perhaps be taken as roughly corresponding to the light of the sun and the streamers of his corona. The first (let us call it Force A) rayed out impartially in all directions upon the people in the church; indeed, it penetrated the walls of the church as though they were not there, and influenced a considerable section of the surrounding country.
>
> THE RT. REV. C. W. LEADBEATER, *The Science of the Sacraments*
> (Adyar, Madras, India: Theosophical Publishing House, 1929),
> pp. 232–34. Quotation in the last two paragraphs originally from
> C. W. LEADBEATER, *The Hidden Side of Things*, Vol. I, pp. 232–
> 34.

NOTES

[1] Helena Petrovna Blavatsky: *Isis Unveiled: A Master-Key to the Mysteries of Ancient and Modern Science and Theology* (New York: T. W. Bouton, 1877). Since republished several times by others. Unlike later Theosophy, this book shows limited influence of Eastern thought, not even generally affirming physical reincarnation, but retaining successive planes in the world of spirit akin to those of A. J. Davis.

[2] The phenomenon of the letters is presented in A. P. Sinnett, *The Occult World* (London: Theosophical Publishing House, reprinted 1969). Many of the letters are published in A. T. Barker, ed., *The Mahatma Letters to A. P. Sinnett* (London: Rider and Co., 1933).

[3] For the controversy see Chapter Two, note 21. In this connection, it must be remembered that Madame Blavatsky was a magus, that is to say, a "shaman in civilization." William

Howells has this to say about the shaman (and much the same could be said about many spiritualist mediums):

The shamans know, of course, that their tricks are impositions, but at the same time everyone who has studied them agrees that they really believe in their power to deal with spirits. Here is a point, about the end justifying the means, which is germane to this and to all conscious augmenting of religious illusion. The shaman's main purport is an honest one and he believes in it, and does not consider it incongruous if his powers give him the right to hoodwink his followers in minor technical matters.

The Heathens: Primitive Man and his Religions (New York: American Museum of Natural History, published by arrangement with Doubleday & Company, Inc., 1962), pp. 132–33.

H.P.B. undoubtedly did believe in the Masters, and that she was receiving dictation from them as she went into the various states of altered consciousness which came so easily to her and in which she did so much of her writing. But it may not have always been clear to others that, as she herself recognized, letters ostensibly by a Master's own hand could actually be written by a *chela* or disciple in that hand. How H.P.B. reconciled in her own mind—whichever that was—the many things done by the many personalities who appeared to use her is a mystery. See Mary K. Neff, *Personal Memoirs of H. P. Blavatsky* (Wheaton, Illinois: Theosophical Publishing House, 1937, 1967), pp. 151–53.

[4]*The Secret Doctrine* begins with a commentary on a cosmogonic poem called "The Stanzas of Dzyan," which H.P.B. says was originally written in a very ancient language called Senzar, and preserved by Masters in central Asian caves. Nonetheless, various scholars have detected familiar motifs in the poem. René Guénon, *Le théosophisme: histoire d'un pseudo-religion* (Paris: Éditions Traditionnelles, 1965), p. 97. says the Dzyan seems to be based on fragments of the Tibetan Kanjur and Tanjur published in 1836 as the twentieth volume of the *Asiatic Researches* of Alexandre Csoma de Körös, the distinguished pioneer Orientalist, in Calcutta. But the renowned scholar of Jewish mysticism, Gersham Scholem, in *Major Trends in Jewish Mysticism* (New York: Schocken Books, Inc. 1961), Note 2 to Lecture VI, p. 398, expresses the opinion that the mysterious *Book Dzyan* owes much to a Jewish Zoharic Kabbalistic writing, the *Sifra Di-Tseniutha*. A Latin translation of this medieval work appears in Knorr von Rosenroth's *Kabbala Denudata* (1677–84), from which H.P.B. drew heavily.

To some Dzyan suggests the Sanskrit *dhyana* (meditation; cf. Chinese *Ch'an*, Japanese *Zen*, which are transliterations); but to Scholem it suggests Di-Tsen.

[5]The influence of Edward Bulwer-Lytton (Lord Lytton; 1803–73), *Zanoni* (Boston: Little, Brown, and Co., 1932), and other of his novels as well, on H.P.B., A. P. Sinnett, and others for the concept of the Masters should be appreciated. This romantic tale of a mysterious Italian gentleman of indefinitely great wealth and age, yet continuing youth, who resided for some years in the interior of India, who was equally at ease with all languages, who talked of occult initiations and of the lore of the Chaldeans, Magi, Platonists, and the like, and who turned out to be a survivor of the Rosicrucian fraternity, is mentioned by H.P.B. Sinnett even castigates Lytton for "having learned so much as he certainly did, [being] content to use up his information merely as an ornament of fiction." The jibe is not entirely pointless for it is well known that Lytton did take magic and occultism seriously and was much influenced by Eliphas Levi. In any case, Lytton's books so powerfully affected the imagination of certain persons of his day, in reviving the ancient and Eastern figure of the magus, that they became part of that small class of fiction which creates fervent and invincible belief in the veracity of its world. In the novel, Zanoni, disciple of the Rosicrucian Mejnour, gave up the occult for the sake of human love when a choice was necessary—quite the opposite of the choice of H.P.B. and others of the leading early Theosophists. See, on Lytton and H.P.B., Sten Bodvar Liljegren, *Bulwer-Lytton's Novels and Isis Unveiled* (Cambridge: Harvard University Press, 1957).

[6]"A.E." (George Russell), *Voices of the Stones* (London: The Macmillan Company, Publishers, 1925), p. 21. Reprinted by kind permission of Mr. Diarmuid Russell.

[7]The fullest independent summary of the life and teaching of Alice Bailey is found in J. Stillson Judah, *The History and Philosophy of the Metaphysical Movements in America* (Philadelphia: Westminster Press, 1967), pp. 119–33.

[8]Max Heindel, *Rosicrucian Cosmo-Conception* (Oceanside, Calif.: Rosicrucian Fellowship, 1937).

[9]See Hans Jonas, *The Gnostic Religion* (Boston: Beacon Press, Inc., 1958, 1963); Robert M. Grant, *Gnosticism and Early Christianity* (New York: Harper & Row, Publishers, 1966); and, for Gnostic texts, R.M. Grant, *Gnosticism* (New York: Harper & Row, Publishers, 1961).

[10]*Unveiled Mysteries* was written under the pen name Godfré Ray King (Chicago: The Saint-Germain Press, 1934).

4

THE DESCENT OF THE MIGHTY ONES:
Spiritualism and UFO Groups

Spiritualists are those for whom the most meaningful religious experience is communication with the spirits of the departed—spirits either of loved ones, or of great and noble figures on "the other side." UFO (Unidentified Flying Objects) groups are centered around the "flying saucers" which have been staples of journalism and discussion since 1947. Invariably, these groups believe that many, at least, of these astounding vehicles bear envoys from a superior and benevolent civilization from another world who have come to warn and aid us in our folly.

What do these two have in common? First, as with many other groups, they have a conviction that against the backdrop of an ultimately monistic and impersonal universe range powerful and generally invisible friends superior to man and to what we would consider natural. But among Spiritualists and UFO people, these mighty ones do not have the *recherché* atmosphere of the Theosophical masters with their overtones of the cryptic past and the exotic Orient.

Rather, save in the case of the Aetherius Society which has obviously been influenced by Theosophy, Spiritualism and the UFO groups fundamentally reflect a new and direct discovery of symbols of mediation in the fabric of American life. The wise ones come as American Indians, Spirit Doctors, departed relatives, or from a futuristic technology. Both types of groups employ the same manner of communication: vision and marvelous journeys, trance speaking and writing, seance circles, and telepathy. The close interaction between Spiritualism and UFO groups is not surprising, for one finds there is much exchange of persons between them.

At a meeting of a UFO group, Understanding, Inc., attended by one of the authors the speaker was an individual who claimed to be Chief Standing Horse, a full-blooded American Indian, despite his blue eyes and pale features. He was a "contactee" whose story related trips to Mars, Venus, Orean, and Clarion (the last two being planets unknown to science but described by several UFO groups).

The story had elements in common with many shamanistic and UFO accounts. He originally made contact with "saucerian" friends through three mysterious men who called on him in Oklahoma during a Spiritualist convention. He met a beautiful initiatory female aboard the ship to which they took him. One spaceship on which he rode was shaped like a giant Indian arrow. He displayed a strange piece of metal as evidence of his story. His forte was a very folksy humor and sentimentality which oddly changed the milieu of saucerism from pseudoscience to an atmosphere more akin to that of certain southern churches. It turned out, in fact, that the Chief was pastor of a Spiritualist church. (One is reminded of the Indian Guide theme so prominent in Spiritualism.) He ended by saying that he had subsequently made spiritualist contact with some of the other-worldly friends he met in his marvelous journeys. His wife reported also that departed persons from earth have been located on the paradisal planet Orean, along with the beautiful initiatory lady and other acquaintances from his space voyage.

In the writings of Spiritualism and UFO cults alike, the Ultimate will be spoken of in such rather abstract terms as "Infinite Intelligence," "Great Oversoul of All," "Great Guiding Force," and so forth. But the spirit inter-mediaries, and space brothers, will be addressed in terms of intimate, though respectful, fellowship: "Help us, O Angel Loved Ones . . ." "thrice blessed are these Saviors of a whole planetary race."

Companionship with these intermediaries has typically a par-ticularism, delightful naîveté, and casualness toward rational structure which, together with the shamanistic overtones in technique, makes the phenomena best approached through folk religion categories. Indeed, it could perhaps be argued that Spiritualism is an original religious creation from what may be the closest approach there has been to a genuine folk culture in America—the frontier. (The UFO cults would then be a typical folk revitalization movement, akin to Cargo Cults elsewhere, of this tradi-tion.) Of course, there is in Spiritualism an absence of long folk tradition and an almost absurd lack of significant scale in comparison to the popular religion, for example, of Bolivia or Brazil.

Yet there are interesting parallels. The folk religion of Latin Amer-ican peasants is local and particular. Devotion is not to a saint in general, but to his manifestation in a particular shrine, and vows to the saint are finite, explicit, and on behalf of specific favors. God becomes virtually a *deus otiosus,* a vague and impersonal absolute behind the colorful and par-ticular cultus of the saints, their glittering shrines, festivals, and pro-cessions. In Bolivia, the Virgin of Copacabana is popularly thought to be different from the Virgin of Cotoca; people make a particular commitment to an individual saintly patron.

But in a broader sense, they are all the same. There is no real difference in function, related to the historical characteristics of each, between the Blessed Virgin, the Saint Benedict, or the Saint Anthony of Latin American folk piety. Gibbon remarked once that for the common people all the religions of the Hellenistic world were equally true. Perhaps this has always been the case with the "common people," insofar as their religion is folk religion. Within the confines of this system, change means only change in form—a new patron, a new shrine, a new but equivalent devotional practice. Change is not propelled by rational construction or by historical process, but by new hierophany; it may be called "innovation by miracle."

There are significant parallels between pilgrimage myths—in particular, myths of origin of pilgrimages of the apparitional type—and UFO "contactee" stories. Apparitional pilgrimages are those which have come into existence on the basis of a report of an apparition or vision, most commonly of the Virgin. They include such popular places of pilgrimage as Guadalupe in Mexico, Knock in Ireland, and Lourdes in southern France. Typically the place of pilgrimage was established by an account of the appearance of the Virgin to a simple person (a shepherd or young girl, for example). The Virgin communicates to this unlikely person a warning of dire events to come, coupled with the possibility of deliverance if the warning is heeded and ways are changed. The recipient is told to communicate the message to others, often beginning with the ecclesiastical officials. With little or no "proof" the recipient attempts to carry out his or her mission but is initially met with skepticism, especially by church officials. At length the common people begin to hear and believe, and to make their way as pilgrims to the place where the apparition occurred. The folk nature of such pilgrimages is evident from the beginning, and persists. Ecclesiastical approval usually comes only after the pilgrimage has in fact been established by popular acceptance.

The contactee narrative tends to follow a formula, with variations. It is related that beings from another planet, often described as more or less utopian, have made contact with an ordinary and unsuspecting human being accidentally or by design. These extraterrestrials communicate with the human, perhaps by telepathy, take him aboard their spacecraft and perhaps take him for a ride. The technology of the spacecraft and of space travel is explained. He also learns of the superior civilization from which the visitors have come, often from an old man and/or a beautiful woman. He receives also a prediction of dire events soon to occur on earth because of the failure of humans and their civilization (atomic testing, wars, inequalities, etc.). Life on other planets is said to be affected by the activities of earthlings (e.g., radiation from atomic testing). The contactee is given a mission. Its success is crucial, for it will allow earthlings to avert catastrophe and to live in peace and plenty. The contactee initiates a campaign, giving lectures and writing books, in order to get the message across, although he is certain to be greeted with skepticism and ridicule, for he has little or no proof of his encounter with "saucerians."

It is no doubt understandable that in Latin America, especially in Brazil, Spiritualism and UFO enthusiams have had great modern success. But in the same way, Spiritualism in America evokes a world of individual helpers and particularized miracle. Despite the fact that a large number of

American Spiritualists are of Roman Catholic background, the frontier Protestantism which lies behind it has precluded the building of great pilgrimage shrines for its supernormal allies.

But the helpers are there. In a Spiritualist church in Indiana, the woman minister and her assistants (also mostly women; like other forms of folk religion, Spiritualism has strong matriarchal overtones) went about the congregation telling every person present individually of the guardianship of his particular "spirit band."

Life histories in the religion are constructed of marvelous events. A Spiritualist minister received, he said, his call as a child with a series of seizures during which strange untoward voices spoke through him. His parents were deeply concerned, but finally an elderly Spiritualist minister recognized them as spirit voices. When the subject realized this, the voices resolved themselves into four aides on the "other side," who have ever since been this medium's "controls." This happened on a farm in Illinois in this century; it might have been the call of a paleolithic shaman.

Communication with intermediaries is mainly by subjective means, although one may be initiated into contact with them by an event which seems concrete and objective. It is like the shaman's initiatory experience, followed by his relatively quiet and steady communication with the spirit band he has subdued. But though the initiatory event was private, the public manifestation of the sacred will display its fruits—regular communication with the other world in trance.

The UFO group, unless it is itself also Spiritualist, has less emphasis on the production of phenomena in the meeting. There will, in fact, perhaps be no formal worship, only a lecture style account by the contactee of his experience. The UFO circle may represent modernization in the sense that the reinterpretation of the Spiritualist tenet in the terminology of "technological myth" has led to an ostensibly more secular organization. But the group certainly lives in the aura of UFOs as bearers of mystery and transcendence. Accounts of sightings are eagerly exchanged. Many persons believe themselves to be in telepathic communication with the saucer's occupants. They receive not only messages of world importance, but also guidance from extraterrestrial friends in personal problems.

In some cases, individual contactees have delivered trance messages from UFOs in a manner virtually identical to the trance-preaching of Spiritualism. Another device has been the "circle," in which each individual in a small group adds something to a message the group believes it is collectively receiving from another world. Basically, however, UFOism is even more centered than Spiritualism upon the charismatic, shamanistic individual. Its greatest events are focused upon them and are principally opportunities for these contactees to tell their story.

The several UFO contactee movements form a distinctive clique of their own. Though they are rather remote from the externalia of the counter culture generation or the sensitivity awareness enthusiasts, they do not live in the world of the older Spiritualists either. For them, lectures, books, verbal communication, and conceptual thought are still normative, yet UFO "cults" could only have come after science and technology had crossed the mental horizon decisively. The power of myth has not been lost in nonverbal immediacy. The power of the present world has not given way to the attractiveness of the past as the locus of mythical reality. The UFO religious movement peaked about 1960. This moment seems to coincide with the final stages of uncritical popular acceptance of science and technology as the primary bearers of meaning in the secular world, and of the whole acceptance of mythical scenarios in the religious before the later reversal in favor of social orientation or nonconceptual sensory and mystical immediacy. The present UFO movements are a perpetuation of that point through their amalgamation of technological and mythical visions among their now aging members.

Most of the major contactees (George Adamski, George van Tassel, Truman Bethurum, Daniel Fry, Orfeo Angelucci, and Howard Menger) told their stories during the fifties.[1] Many are now deceased. Few of them actually established groups, succeeding rather as lecturers and writers who reached an audience. Their activities coincided with the post-World War II period of the Cold War and fear of "the Bomb." More recently, as space flight has become an actuality interest has declined in its mythical aspects and hence of UFO "cults," although there are still reported sightings of UFOs, and UFO motifs in new religious groups (for example, the group initiated by the prophecies of "Bo and Peep" in the mid-seventies).

C. G. Jung, in his important treatment of the psychic meaning of the phenomenon written about 1960, *Flying Saucers: A Modern Myth of Things Seen in the Sky,* calls attention to the appearance in the cultic type of literature of "technological angels" who come carried by these vehicles. He wrote:

> We have here a golden opportunity of seeing how a legend is formed, and how in a difficult and dark time for humanity a miraculous tale grows up of an attempted intervention by extra-terrestrial "heavenly" powers—and this at the very time when human fantasy is seriously considering the possibility of space travel and of visiting or even invading other planets.[2]

Jung did not emphasize the character of the contemporary myth-forming so much as the archetypal nature of the UFO form itself—the disc-shaped object in the sky. He felt that it typified the mandala, the circular symbol of psychic wholeness. In a characteristic way, he illustrated from the dreams of modern persons, from art ancient and modern, and from myth, the recurrence of this symbol. Some saucer enthusiasts have also ransacked ancient literature to produce previous cases of celestial disc apparitions. However, they also generally stress that the present contacts are connected with the "New Age," and hence are of a different and eschatological nature.

Despite the fact that certain ancient parallels, like Ezekiel's wheels and the *vimana* of the Mahabharata, may occur, we should stress the paradox of continuing religious content and new symbol. This is what is implied by Jung's saying they are *"technological* angels." Virtually all the other new religions, however futuristic they may claim to be, keep a metaphysical frame of reference, or make contact with quasi-spiritual beings, like the Theosophical Hierarchy. These contacts could have been talked of thousands of years ago as well as today. But the precise form of revelation which animates the saucer movements could have only emerged in the context of modern astronomical and technological awareness. It is a religious by-product of science, not to mention science fiction. These groups are of no less interest than the Cargo Cults, for like them they represent an almost entire transference to modern vehicles of a traditional religious scenario and cast. It is the ancient story of angelic and savior beings from an (or the) other world who communicate with elect persons and transfer marvelous powers and esoteric knowledge, and thereafter usher in a paradisical age. But in the UFO groups, the myth and cast are as modern as the flight of NASA spacecraft, though not secular.

THE SPIRITUALIST CHURCHES

This section will not attempt to sort out the denominational history of Spiritualism. This has been done, at least sufficiently to indicate the fluidity of the situation and the kinds of issues and personality clashes that have caused division.[3] The basic points of contention have been controversy over the introduction of reincarnation and other Theosophical principles, and whether or not Spiritualists are Christian. Andrew Jackson Davis, the major Spiritualist thinker, accepted neither reincarnation nor Christianity, but his spiritual progeny have found themselves pulled by the Christian environment and the Theosophical domination of the intellectual life of the occult world.

But excessive attention could be given the denominational forms of Spiritualism. If, of the three forms of religious expression, the social may be given first consideration in Spiritualism, it is not because the organization of Spiritualist churches or denominations is important, but because of their actual social structure as gatherings around an initiated, charismatic leader.

Forms have a strange symbolic value for Spiritualists, but there seems to be a marked dichotomy between theory and practice. Perhaps because they are unequivocally in the nineteenth century tradition, Spiritualists generally have a highly elaborate constitution both on the local and denominational levels, and are constantly tinkering with it. They are careful to incorporate as a religious body. Of course, to some extent this protects them from laws against fortune-telling. Yet at the same time, there is a sense of unreality about the formal structure. Most groups are very small, probably the majority of attenders are not members, and attendance is often quite fluid and overlapping. Spiritualist churches appear and disappear, and change names and denominations, with remarkable alacrity. Denominations are little more than paper organizations issuing certificates of ordination, manuals, and periodicals. In recent years this process of flux and fragmentation seems to have accelerated. The reason is, of course, that in reality Spiritualist churches are merely the followings of particular mediums, who even buy and sell church buildings. Each gathers his or her own congregation. If the medium retires or moves away, the church is not likely to continue under the same name, and perhaps not under the same denominational affiliation with the National Spiritualist Association, the Universal Church of the Master, or some other of the score or more groups.

Training of Spiritualist ministers is spotty. Some denominations offer schooling in connection with summer camps, or by correspondence, but standards are rarely rigidly enforced. Of course, these features of loose organization, personality-centered churches, and little training are "bad" only if the pattern of the major Christian denominations is taken as a standard. But this may be like comparing the amoeba and the whale. Spiritualism may represent a different, and in some ways more persistent, type of religious experience which of its own nature does not require the same orientation to denominational social expression or ministerial initiation by verbal education.

Doubtless because it has the oldest continuing tradition of all the groups we are examining, the Spiritualist church may strike the visitor as having a conservative if not "dated" atmosphere. Something in it remains of the 1850s. Yet beside the old Americana is a sense of doing a daring thing which puts its practitioners at odds with their background. The ethos is lower-middle class theological liberalism. The typical Spiritualist church offers a strange combination of pietistic hymns and decor and very broad doctrine: there is no hell, truth is in all religions, man is judged by his deeds, the "New Thought" concept of the value of thinking positive, creative thoughts. It offers an excellent example of the history of religions theorem that cultic form in religion usually changes much more slowly than verbal expression.

But rather than continue with general discussion, perhaps it would be more interesting to describe a typical Spiritualist church. One of the authors visited one in a run-down, inner-city section of Los Angeles. This church was at the time a branch of the United Church of the Master. Characteristically it was in the process of revising its constitution to set itself up as the flagship of a new denomination, to be called United Christ Church. In an inordinate number of cases, Spiritualist churches visited have been in this process.

The typical Spiritualist church is designed like a traditional Protestant church, with pulpit, altar holding open Bible, and stained glass windows, but with a perhaps garish maximum of such accoutrements as flowers, candles, cloth altar hangings, and sentimental pictures of the Master. There is an odd resemblence in taste to the cluttered Victorian parlor. This was true of the church visited. It was a store-front building, and had the conventional altar and portrait of Jesus. But the difference lay in the fact that behind the altar were crudely painted symbols of the major religions of the world.

The service opened with hymns, led by a short, stocky lady minister. She was of quite advanced years, but obviously strong, determined, and keen-witted, a typical Spiritualist priestess-matriarch who guides a band of children of all ages both in this world and that of spirit, and who makes up for what she lacks in formal education with the ageless psychic intuition of the village wise-woman. The hymns were of a sentimental type, such as "Blessed Assurance," and "In the Garden."

The congregation was mixed; there were blacks, whites, and Hispanics, young and old, but the leadership was mostly white. All were clearly lower-middle class, dressed in neat, simple clothes. None, not even the young people, showed other than docile external conformity to the norms of the respectable, industrious workingman. If there was rebellion, it was clearly spiritual, for this was no working class Catholic parish or evangelical temple.

The principal minister was a youngish, handsome man with close-cropped black hair and a short-sleeved gray clerical shirt. The elderly lady minister took a seat in the sanctuary and smiled benignly; the young man was obviously her protégé. He spoke an invocation and a word of welcome. He said that the church draws from the scriptures of all faiths. The lesson that morning was read from the *Aquarian Gospel of Jesus Christ.* This book, written by Levi H. Dowling allegedly through "tuning in" to the "akashic records" which Theosophists and others believe carry a permanent imprint of all past events in the atmosphere, contains supposed events in the life of Christ not found in the ordinary New Testament, including a journey to India. This book is very frequently read as scripture in Spiritualist churches. The passage read described Jesus talking in Benares with brahmans.[4]

The reading was followed by a short, simple, attractive sermon on knowing God everywhere. After another hymn, announcements were given: a Tuesday evening message-only service, a Thursday evening healing service. The announcements were typical. Spiritualists like a week-night service at which they can concentrate on what to them is most exciting—receiving messages from the spirit world. Healing by prayer and laying on of hands is also important in most Spiritualist churches; it is part of the atmosphere of warm, comforting psychic force and charismatic power the faith produces. The new denomination, United Christ Church, was then discussed. Over two hundred ministers, it was said, had expressed interest in it. Emphasis was placed on the fact that the new denomination would be run by ministers only; there would be no lay boards. In this connection, of course, it must be kept in mind that few Spiritualist ministers are full-time professionals and that many members of the congregation in any church have mediumistic gifts, are accounted ministers, and bear impressive ordination certificates.

Next came the part to which everyone was obviously looking forward, the spirit messages. Typically, the minister-medium takes a seat facing the congregation, and goes into light trance, often with a few jerking, spasmodic motions. Then, with the help of one of his "controls," who will speak through him in altered voice, he will give a general message and deliver individual messages to members of the congregation. Individuals are told about the future of their health, family relations, travel, and job. Pastoral advice and encouragement is intermixed with the message, and assurance given of spirit guardianship.

In many cases, other mediums or ministers in the congregation—those who have taken "medium development classes"—get up to give either individual or general messages.

Then the young minister gave a remarkable account of a trip he had taken the past week—allegedly in the body—by Air Force jet to Washington, where he had been asked to give a seance and service for the President and his family in the White House. This fantastic narration was given with perfect calm and control, convincing manner, and great elaboration of detail.

Most Spiritualist churches do not vary greatly from this pattern. A few decades ago more use was made of devices such as the trumpet through which the spirit spoke, production of ectoplasm in which the spirit takes shape, and the like. These performances may still be seen at Spiritualist camps such as Lily Dale in New York and Chesterfield in Indiana.

The Spiritualist Science Church in Durham, North Carolina, meets Sunday evenings. The minister, a large white lady, appears to know the intimate details of the lives of her parishioners. During the week she practices as an "advisor," using cards (including tarot), and, it appears, some psychotherapeutic techniques. She has occasionally been accused of fortune-telling but has not been found guilty. Most of those present for the Sunday evening meetings have been her clients. About a third are black. About half indicate that they regularly attend other churches on Sunday mornings. In style and format the religious service is like that of many small Southern churches. The sermon, however—on every occasion at which one of the authors was present—was on death and the land of the dead, with much emphasis on the wisdom the dead have acquired in their after-life existence.

Following the regular service a seance is held in a room apart. The number of participants is limited to about a dozen; invitations are sought both by those associated with the church and by newcomers. One of the authors was allowed to be present on two occasions. The group was seated in the usual circle in semi-darkness. The minister invited all present to direct their thoughts to their deceased loved ones. She gradually entered a trance, and at a certain point began to speak softly and somewhat strangely. Her voice became louder and more distinct. It appeared that she was engaged in a conversation with someone unseen by the others. The unseen visitor was her guide Sarah, a woman who died in childbirth in the eighteenth century. Though it was actually the minister who spoke both sides of the dialogue, the two voices sounded quite different. For a time Sarah gave what might be called the news of the day in the spirit world. Now and again another guide, Tom, tried to enter the dialogue but was rebuffed by the minister. His comments were half-comical, half-threatening. After Tom departed Sarah began to relay messages from spirit friends and relatives of some of those present, most containing advice about their circumstances and problems. They were given to understand that things would turn out well for them if they followed the spirit guidance. The level of credulity and trust increased as the seance moved towards its end some forty-five minutes after it began. Members of the group departed quietly rather than talking among themselves of what had transpired.

The doctrine of Spiritualism, as summarized in the *Spiritualist Manual* of the National Spiritualist Association, affirms belief in "Infinite Intelligence," nature as its expression, individual continuity after death, communication with the "so-called dead" proven by Spiritualism, and moral responsibility.[5] The tone is perhaps what is of most interest. The language tends to be abstract, and omits any reference to Christ or the authority of the Christian scriptures. It would be possible to affirm these principles, as did Andrew Jackson Davis, and reject the name Christian, though many Spiritualists will state that Spiritualism is taught in the Bible. Belief in the "planes" proposed by Davis, based on Swedenborg, is widespread. The reference to scientific proof of communication with the departed indicates that Spiritualism, like UFOism, can perhaps be seen under the guise of "technological myth"; a shamanism rationalized and justified by modern physical research.

Most important, though, is the experience of mental expansion towards infinity and ultimate transformation through the phenomena of communication. Spiritualist experience suggests an "unobstructed universe." Mind—spirit—overcomes the conditionedness of space, time, and body. The hierophany of mediumistic miracle suggests a cosmos less drab and confining and hopeless than it seems. Spiritualism provides a church for people, like the young minister who related the marvelous journey to Washington, of uncircumscribed mind. Its mentalist orientation suggests, finally, that one can construct one's self, life history, and world from that which emerges out of psychic phenomena and the images and personalities from the unconscious. This audacious proposition, radically dangerous or liberating as one wishes, is really the premise of the whole alternative reality tradition.

Reading Selection: Spiritualism

The following passages from a Spiritualist textbook illustrate the religion's mentalist tone, and the high value given the ideas of progress and education.

Invisible communicators have often made the point in their explanations of the Etheric that the after-life is mental, but then they sometimes add slyly, "But so is your world!" This is profoundly true. The only difference between the earth plane and the higher spheres is *vibrational frequency of consciousness.* This difference, of course, is of very great importance, and is very real to those experiencing it.

The lower planes or spheres of the Etheric World are relatively low in vibration and tend to harmonize easily with the consciousness of earth. As one ascends in the hierarchy or graded levels of the spheres the vibrations become progressively higher, and a more refined consciousness is required for attunement.

B. J. Fitzgerald, *A New Text of Spiritual Philosophy and Religion* (Los Angeles: De Vorss & Co., 1954), p. 38.

The reader inevitably asks the question at this point, just what are the dwellers in the Etheric doing? . . . Just as our earthly life centers largely about the physical body and its insistent needs, so does spiritual life center about the growth of mind and soul. Life in the spheres is basically *educative* and devoted to the unfoldment and elevation of consciousness . . . It may surprise some to know that in the Etheric are wonderful schools, conservatories of music, academies of the arts, of all beauties and refinements. There are marvelous libraries and books, truly heavenly music.

Most strugglers in the vales of earth fail to obtain adequate expression in realms of creativeness, beauty and culture. The harsh struggle to maintain the body does not permit sustained cultural activity. In the Etheric the situation is much changed.

FITZGERALD, *A New Text of Spiritual Philosophy and Religion*, pp. 46–47.

UNDERSTANDING, INC.

Most UFO contactees did not establish ongoing groups but, rather, attracted audiences by their lectures and books. An exception was George van Tassell who in 1953 published a book entitled *I Rode in a Flying Saucer*, in which he told the story of his initiatory experience with UFOs. Van Tassell was an enterprising UFO enthusiast who succeeded in making the small, private Giant Rock Airport, of which he was proprietor, near Yucca Valley, California, the base for the Giant Rock Space Convention. He claimed that Giant Rock is a "natural cone of receptivity" for saucers and telepathic communication. Giant Rock became the annual gathering place for other contactees and UFO followers. The Ministry of Universal Wisdom, established by van Tassell, was one of the most explicitly religious of the UFO groups. Van Tassell also began to build an Integratron—an instrument for recharging and rejuvenating the human body—following plans given him by an extraterrestrial visitor, Solgonda. The Integratron was not yet complete when he died in 1978. The group he organized no longer exists.

Understanding, Inc. (recently reincorporated in Arizona as World Understanding, Inc.) was founded about the same time (1955), and continues to exist. It is the creation of Daniel Fry, an early contactee who wrote *White Sands Incident* in 1954. He was an employee of the White Sands Proving Ground near Las Cruces, New Mexico. On July 4 of that year he missed a bus going into town for the holiday and took a solitary walk on the desert in the evening. He was met by a UFO in which he was given a ride to New York and back in half an hour. In the course of the journey he was given messages from Alan, his invisible mentor. These included homilies on true science, the importance of understanding, and information that the saucer people are the remnant of a past supercivilization on earth which destroyed itself through wars. Only three shiploads of persons managed to escape death or biological degeneration through radiation by flying to Mars. They returned to warn their earth kin. (It is interesting to note that a number of contactees presume the saucer people to be not alien but separated and highly perfected earthlings, or at least some sort of mysterious kin.)

Less specifically religious than van Tassell's creation, Understanding, Inc. is quite eclectic. While it encourages piety toward the Creator, it emphasizes a wide range of esoteric themes and techniques, including the great pyramid, occult knowledge, mental telepathy, and hypnosis. Its great ambition, however, is to discover and extend a worldwide "area of mutual agreement" among all races and creeds regarding "spiritual science" and human behavior in order that they may live in harmony and be better prepared psychologically and sociologically for the space age. "Understanding," according to Fry, is the means to its realization. By it earthlings may avoid the fate of their ancestors. To this end Fry has distributed numerous copies of "The Area of Mutual Agreement," a statement of his basic position and project, to world leaders and lesser lights.

Earlier, Understanding, Inc. had its headquarters in Tonopah, Arizona, then the residence of Fry. On fifty-five acres of desert was situated the International Cultural Center. He then moved to Alamogordo, New Mexico. At the beginning of the 1980s the group was in serious decline as Fry was unable to give sufficient attention to it because of the long illness and death of his wife. He subsequently remarried. The new Mrs. Fry joined him in promoting the activities of (World) Understanding, Inc.

About sixty "units" of the organization currently exist in the United States and abroad, some more active than others. One of the authors attended an anniversary meeting of a local unit (Understanding Unit 15, Inglewood, California). The speaker for the occasion was Daniel Fry himself. A stocky, rich-voiced, articulate man, he gave the image of the science entrepreneur rather than the religionist. He did not discuss his initiatory experience, but rather talked knowingly of Washington and universities and UFO and rocket research, indicating that saucer enthusiasts are only ahead of their times. He showed a movie on the history of flight. Then, moving into scientific eschatology, he projected a human future—now enjoyed by the saucer people—in which humans freed from the face of planets, will live generation after generation on great self-sustaining ships in space, swinging as whim directs from one world to another.

Reading Selection: Understanding, Inc.

Here are the contents of a mailing announcing the program of a coming meeting of a branch of Understanding, Inc. Most articles in the organization's periodical deal with world peace, inspirational topics, and relatively unsensational reports from newspapers of UFO sightings. But UFO contacts and telepathic communication with beings from other worlds are probably what kindles greatest enthusiasm among members. Notice how, typically, the communications in this broadsheet pull together favorite themes of esotericism, such as the great pyramid, piety toward the Creator, and a feeling of wonder that such ordinary people as those in the organization are made privy to secrets unknown to the wise of our world.

THE INGLEWOOD UNIT OF UNDERSTANDING PRESENTS
"VOICE FROM OTHER PLANETS"

This coming Saturday, March 22, 1969 at 8:00 P.M., the Inglewood Unit 15 of Understanding will present another program of special tape recordings of "VOICES FROM OTHER PLANETS". . . .

On this occasion four tapes will be played, all narrated by Beings from other planets. These are:
1. *"INTERPLANETARY SPACECRAFT."* The message on this tape tells of the different types, sizes, shapes, and speed of the spacecraft used in interplanetary travel. Mention will also be made of two most unusual spacecraft used only on rare occasions and then only under circumstances of the utmost importance.
2. *"A GALACTIC TOUR."* This tape takes us on a journey far removed from our solar system and out into that area of space known as our Galaxy. Several of the brightest stars are visited: Alpha Centauri, Beta Centauri, Aldebaran, Betelgeuse and Procyon where the wonders of our Creator's handiwork and the cultures and technologies of his people are touched upon. Most astounding.
3. *"THE GREAT PYRAMID."* The message on this tape takes us back into the far distant past and tells when, why, and how our great Pyramid was constructed. Furthermore, it unveils in part the mystery of the great Pyramid.
4. *"MASAR."* The message on this tape deals with the planet Mars. It tells of many facets of Martian life, education and cultural developments.

PLAN NOW to come and bring your entire family and friends to hear the voices of these Beings and their messages for, truly, this is "THE PROGRAM UNIQUE portraying events and revealing information that may affect the lives of all people, even YOU."

The public is cordially invited. Tape recorders too. Admission is by donation.

AMALGAMATED FLYING SAUCER CLUBS OF AMERICA

Gabriel Green is one of the most attractive figures of the saucer world. He is head of the Amalgamated Flying Saucer Clubs of America (AFSCA). Not a major contactee himself, Mr. Green has, through his periodicals, conventions, lectures, saucerian paraphernalia, wide friendships, and integrative reflection, served as a focal point. He has also been politically active. In 1960 he ran for president, withdrawing finally in favor of John F. Kennedy. In 1972 he ran for U. S. Senator in the Democratic primary on an ultraliberal antibomb platform. In 1972 he also was the presidential candidate of the Universal Party and had plans for a 1988 campaign.

These political efforts seem to have been the results of promptings from saucer contacts, although this is not mentioned in the campaign literature. The contacts, he says, were from the planet Clarion. They first reached him through the mediumship of other saucer enthusiasts, or even by telephone. Then the extraterrestrial persons appeared at his home, keeping appointments made by these contacts. One, named Rentan, was only four feet tall, but otherwise was indistinguishable from earthly humans by sight. The stage of meeting these visitors physically, he says, seems to pass with all contactees. It is a kind of initiation or preliminary in the adventure. After rapport has been achieved by such gross means, telepathy takes over.

Green moved to Yucca Valley, California, mentioned earlier as a traditional gathering place for UFO enthusiasts. There he busied himself with editing, lecturing, and selling pins, books, bumper stickers ("Flying Saucers are Real—the Air Force Doesn't Exist"), and other curiosities, including saucer photographs and tapes of communications with extraterrestrials.

In 1956 he organized the Los Angeles Interplanetary Study Group, which sponsored contactee speakers. When their messages were presented on tape, music was often played beforehand on the same tape to set a mood. Green claims that on one of the first occasions the music continued even after the tape was turned off—only one of many signs.

Green has been both a critic and a defender of contactees. He has criticized the claim of some to the absolute truth of their own messages as well as instances of unethical behavior and desire for financial gain. At the same time, he affirms that most of them have had genuine contacts and are sincerely dedicated to spreading the message. He argues that the ability to receive contacts requires certain psychic and telepathic gifts, and that this ability does not necessarily accord with intellectual or moral stature. Moreover, the extraterrestrials are said to seek out ordinary persons because those established in the academic or financial or political worlds would find contact too threatening and would be quick to reject a commission.

All in all, Green is an articulate spokesman for the UFO contactee point of view. He responds to the suggestion that UFO contactee experiences have much in common with Spiritualism by observing that saucer communication is concerned with world problems rather than contacting departed loved ones. He points out that most of the contactees bring essentially the same message of reform from the saucer people. The extraterrestrials see us as savages, but they are trying to help us, within the limits of respect for our freedom, to develop sufficiently to enter their universe.

The AFSCA periodicals have emphasized economic reform and world unity from the beginning, in terms of "Universal Economics" and "the United World." By the former is meant a nonmoney economy based on responsibility and sincerity in producer and consumer. It is an economy developed by space people and is the basis of the prosperity and absence of economic competition in their worlds. The latter ("the United World") refers to a theocratic world government based upon universal laws and spiritual principles. Green has characterized it as "Christ-oriented."

Later statements by Green have appeared to be more Christocentric than before, with frequent allusions to elements of traditional Christian mythology, especially as regards the return of Christ. Also, the "Forces of Darkness" are contrasted with the "Light Forces." If the latter can gain the upper hand, he says, the Doomsday will be cancelled and God's Kingdom will begin to appear. Further, the way will have been prepared for the public reappearance of Christ. ". . . the end result will be," he has written, "a new beginning, a New Order of the Ages, as the 'Golden Eagle' leads us into the Promised Land of Heaven on Earth, the establishment of the Great Golden Millennium Age of Mankind, and at long last, a reuniting with our space brothers and sisters from the stars."

Green has supported his activities in part by conducting sessions on "past life regression," "higher self attunement," and "distant viewing." By the first is meant the use of a technique, which he claims to have received from an extraterrestrial, by which one can enter an altered state of awareness and get in touch with happenings in past lives. The second refers to the experience of telepathic contact with one's own higher self (and, as well, with Space People, Ascended Masters, deceased loved ones, and historical personalities). By "distant vision" is meant the projection of consciousness to other times and places, including other worlds as well as the "Inner Earth." None of these interests and techniques is, of course, unique to Green or UFO enthusiasts.

Reading Selection: Amalgamated Flying Saucer Clubs of America

The following paragraphs are from a one-page informational flyer issued by the Amalgamated Flying Saucer Clubs of America. They were written by Gabriel Green. We can here see clearly his combination of utopian social idealism and open acceptance of the claims of UFO contactees.

The appearance of Flying Saucers in our skies is fast becoming common knowledge, but it is not as well known that hundreds of people have not only seen them, but have actually ridden in these craft and personally met their occupants. These "contactees" discovered that the pilots and other crew members of these interplanetary spaceships were *not* grotesque beings, but were, instead, highly intelligent, friendly men and women from civilizations evolved far in advance of our own.

To the Earth people they contacted, the Space People told of their advanced sciences and of their relatively Utopian way ·of life. To our planet, in the throes of social and political upheaval and teetering on the brink of self-annihilation by nuclear warfare, they had come, they said, to show us the way out of our crisis and the solutions to our problems. It is this information and knowledge that the Amalgamated Flying Saucer Clubs of America, a nonprofit organization, has endeavored to bring to public attention since its inception in January 1959, and which is published in our magazine *Flying Saucers International.*

The scientific and technical knowledge to be gained from the Space People is a wealth of beneficial information which could transform this world from its present chaotic state into a utopian-like society, far beyond today's most optimistic concepts. Some of the many amazing benefits of the knowledge already received from the Space People, or promised by them if we will welcome them in a friendly manner, are: elimination of disease, poverty, and smog; solving of the problem of automation and unemployment; a way to finance all public works projects and aid to other countries without taxation; an extended life span; a greater measure of personal freedom, economic security, and abundance; and for many living today, personal journeys to other planets beyond the stars.

With the aid of our Space Brothers, the Flying Saucer movement is rapidly growing into a dynamic worldwide social reform movement, dedicated to the mental, physical, spiritual, and economic emancipation of man. This new Space Age ideology to champion the dignity and rights of man, to free him from economic bondage, and to liberate him from the confines of regimentation, limitation, and want, will render impotent those antiquated, totalitarian philosophies based upon force and coercion. This will create a true Brotherhood of Man on Earth through the application of the philosophy of love, through service to others.

> GABRIEL GREEN, "A Letter from AFSCA's President," in
> Amalgamated Flying Saucer Clubs of America mailing, undated,
> early 1960s.

THE AETHERIUS SOCIETY

If most of the movements and contactees discussed so far are broadly eschatological, the Aetherius Society represents the apocalyptic wing of the movement. Perhaps significantly, it has by far the tightest organization, and the most explicitly religious structure. To present it in a few paragraphs is a difficult task, for its writings are oceanic and its concepts and undertakings elaborate. It has moved away from a grounding in saucer phenomena to direct psychic communication with etheric beings and to "metaphysics," although its inception is certainly tied to saucer stimuli and it originally made much of observations by members and others to establish the authenticity of life on other planets and the visits of extraterrestrials to Earth.

The Aetherius movement began with revelations received by George King in London, England, in May 1954. King, who had long studied and practiced occultism and yoga and allegedly could go easily into samadhic trance, was and is the focal point of the society. An audible voice told him, "Prepare yourself, you are to become the voice of the Interplanetary Parliament." Eight days later he was visited by a mysterious Indian who instructed him in advanced yogic practices by which he was able to enter into telepathic rapport with a Venusian known as Aetherius. Early the following year he was named by Master Aetherius the "Primary Terrestrial Mental Channel." Thereafter King began delivering, in trance, wisdom and instruction from Aetherius and other Masters such as Jesus and a Chinese saint, Goo-Ling. These Masters appear to be identical to the "Great White Lodge" of Theosophy, but saucers are regarded as the bearers of these beings or of their emissaries as well as of "magnetic" or spiritual power which is to be appropriated and radiated to the world. Thus at certain times, called "Spiritual Pushes" or "Magnetization Periods," a large interplanetary spacecraft in orbit around the Earth, referred to as Satellite No. 3, radiates Spiritual Power to all groups and individuals on Earth who are performing unselfish service and will use the Spiritual Power for the benefit of humankind. This radiation enhances by a factor of 3000 times all such unselfish actions.

Originally something of a sensation in England, King spoke out of trance in a dramatic manner on television and radio. A small but dedicated group gathered around him in London to carry out the Cosmic instructions, and the Aetherius Society was founded in 1956. Several years later (1959) he moved to Los Angeles, claiming to have been instructed to do so by the Cosmic Masters.

One of the early and very interesting endeavors of the Aetherius Society was Operation Starlight, to give it its typically military title. Under instructions from Master Aetherius, George King went to Holdstone Down in England, where he met physically the Master Jesus on July 23, 1958. During this meeting the Master Jesus sent an initial charge of Spiritual Energy into the mountain itself, thus making it the first "Holy Mountain" or "New Age Power Center" to be charged during Operation Starlight. Subsequently, eighteen other mountains were similarly charged by the Cosmic Masters. These are places of pilgrimage by members, for the power of unselfish prayers said on these mountains is believed to be greatly intensified by the power now resident in them.

Between July 1963 and November 1964, the Society performed Operation Bluewater in conjunction with the Cosmic Masters. The wrong thoughts and actions of humans throughout the ages have erected barriers around Earth that repulsed certain cosmic energies needed by Mother Earth (who is a mighty living being, Terra) for her continued development. Using specialized instruments designed by George King, spiritual energies beamed down by the Cosmic Masters were directed into a psychic center of Earth off the coast of California, bringing about the needed balance (and preventing a massive earthquake that would have caused the inundation of the West Coast by the Pacific Ocean).

On July 8, 1964 (the greatest Holy Day of the Society) George King received telepathically from the Master Mars Sector VI a report of the Initiation of Earth, while it was being performed under the latter's guidance. Streams of mighty divine initiating energies were directed into the heart of Terra. These energies are now held within the body of the compassionate Mother Earth for gradual controlled release by the Aetherius Society through Operation Earth Light.

In 1965 and 1966 George King was again the channel for a series of transmissions. This time the Master Aetherius described, as they were occurring, sorties by three interplanetary Adepts now living on Earth in physical bodies, into the lower astral realms of Earth, in order to evict from these realms an alien android from another galaxy who had been hidden in the "hells" for thousands of years. Had this not been done, says the

Aetherius Society, this fiendish android, with power beyond human comprehension, would have annihilated or taken over every other being on Earth.

From March 1966 to March 1967, George King received a series of transmissions describing, as it occurred, an intergalactic conflict called "The Battle in Gotha," in terms anticipating "Star Wars" scenarios.

The Society teaches that the present time is a period of crisis as Earth prepares to enter the New Age (the Aquarian Age), but the weight of negative karma, especially that which engendered recent wars, has instead given reign to certain "evil magicians" who are striving to enslave humankind. They inhabit the "lower astral realms" and are of demonical power. In the past they gave power to such men as Nero and Hitler; now their power is all the greater. They can weave ghastly mental illusions as well as employ hideous bacteriological and atomic warfare. Humankind unaided could not hope to withstand them, and they would shortly render earth a literal hell. However, from October 1967 to February 1969, George King received a series of transmissions from Master Aetherius who described, as they occurred, the sorties by six interplanetary Adepts into the hells of Earth where, in a titanic struggle on behalf of humankind, they battled the forces of darkness for the freedom and life of the masses on Earth. In the final sortie of February 24, 1969, these Adepts brought the "Prince of Light from the Spiritual Hierarchy," Lord Babaji, into direct battle with the dark evil power known as "Satan" or the "devil" who was defeated and transmuted, and put back into the reincarnation cycle. This was Operation Karmalight. Though not all the evil entities were transmuted, the most fiendish of them was thwarted in his plan to enslave earthlings.

According to the Society's teaching, it was humankind, with its greed and hatred, its wars and tyrannies, and its refusal to follow the laws of God, that created the hells and gave the evil magicians their demonical power, culminating in the diabolical power of Satan. Earthlings are completely helpless against the might of evil they have unwillingly helped to create and were it not for the intervention of the glorious Adepts from other planets, they would have suffered a fate worse than death and their evolution would have been held up for centuries. The great Adepts sacrificially and courageously entered the realms of deep danger on their behalf. The Master Jesus in one of his Transmissions acknowledged the Adepts' actions as being greater than his own earlier saving action on Earth and lauded their heroism.

The Society places emphasis on decision. The continual theme is "this is the hour." The New Age may come only through strenuous combat, and fantastic times of trial will attend its birth. It is humans who allow evil, and they must cooperate in its eradication, even though the Saviors do what humans cannot. The world is finally awaiting the next great Avatar to Earth, but he can only come when karma is moving towards good balance.

One has the feeling of witnessing a mythologization of the modern experience in the conclusion of Operation Karmalight. The story was that up to now Satan, the "Black Magician," and his cohorts in the "Lower Astral Realm" have controlled most of humankind's actions. Now this power is shattered and broken, and there is a vacuum of force into which light can be poured. For a month after February 24 the energy transmitters of the Society put force into the hole, it was said, but now it is up to humankind. The astral and karmic forces are churning, and millions could turn into the way of evolution. The dark pressure is off, but where we go from here is up to us. Cannot the "Lower Astral Realm" stand for the unconscious, and "casting light into it" after its central power is broken—though lieutenants of Satan are still around, able to cause wars and other trouble—speak of the experience of "mankind come of age"?

Following the success of Operation Karmalight by the Adepts in 1969, the Society continued its vital missions on behalf of earthlings and Terra by resuming an Operation begun in 1966 called "Operation Sunbeam." The Aetherius Society evidenced an ecological concern in its realization that humans have plundered and damaged the surface of the planet (the body of Terra) that has given them a home, food, and the essential environment in which to gain experience, without ever giving heartfelt prayers of thankfulness. The consequences have been that karma has become "unbalanced" and that Mother Earth has not received the streams of harmonious spiritual energy such prayers would afford. The imbalance has resulted in devastating catastrophes and pestilence throughout the world as well as the weakening of Terra. Operation Sunbeam was devised to help alleviate these repercussions as much as possible. George King invented an apparatus enabling the spiritual energies stored in the Holy Mountains during Operation Starlight to be collected and discharged into psychic centers of Terra and her subtle nerve membranes which exist in the body of the planet. By this means a token repayment of humankind's almost infinite debt to Earth was made and the karmic balance was partially restored, softening the blow of humans' negative karma.

In 1973 yet another Operation was initiated: Operation Prayer Power. Members of the Society generated power by the recitation of mantram and prayers, which subsequently was directed into "Spiritual Power Batteries" designed by George King. (The prayers included some received from Master Jesus during a series of transmissions much earlier [1958] called "The Twelve Blessings.") By this means great quantities of spiritual energy can be accumulated over time, later to be discharged in a great flood of spiritual power, as has been done on crucial occasions in various parts of the world since 1973 with miraculous results, according to the Society.

More recently (beginning in 1981), George King undertook the Saturn Mission (not "Operation" this time) at the command of the Lords of Saturn, comprising the spiritual hierarchy of this solar system. A Spiritual Power Battery was charged by highly-elevated Masters and taken to a psychic center of Earth where the energies within the battery were drawn out and intermingled with the magnetic flow of natural energies radiating from that center. The effect of this controlled release, we are told, was to stabilize the Devic Kingdom, alleviate catastrophe, and help the cause of peace throughout the world. George King was more specific about the results. He said in 1982: "For every minute of Spiritual energy discharged during The Saturn Mission, 250 people are saved from either death or mutilation. Each Sub-Phase of the Mission consists of 120 minutes discharge; thirty thousand (30,000) people are saved during each Sub-Phase. Three Sub-Phases constitute one Phase of The Saturn Mission; ninety thousand (90,000) are saved during each completed Phase!"[6] The Aetherius Society claims that on the basis of its records of "natural" disasters since 1981 there has been a miraculous drop in the percentage of casualties. Somewhat more specifically, it is claimed that by May 1985, one million persons had been thus saved.

Also in recent years the Aetherius Society has intensified its involvement in spiritual healing, whether by contact or absent healing techniques, and has trained a corps of such healers. It has also established a College of Spiritual Sciences in London and has undertaken to establish a similar institution in Los Angeles.

The Aetherius Society is headquartered in an attractive stucco building complex in the heart of Hollywood. One enters through a commodious bookstore full of the group's periodicals, books of George King, and tapes, which include some of the transmissions delivered by Cosmic Masters. Some members are usually in attendance and others are on call for special operations. George King lives in a small apartment on the premises and is greatly venerated by the faithful. The tapes containing his transmissions from the Cosmic Masters are carefully stored in vaults for posterity. The most important (except for the highly sacred, classified ones) find their way into the many books published over the years. From the beginning of the Aetherius Society George King has had a monopoly on revelation for his followers as "primary terrestrial mental channel," the sole communicator with the Cosmic Masters. More recently he appears to have acquired more than an instrumental role and status, joining the company of the Masters as one of them.

Healing ministrations are available at the headquarters, as are general lectures in which George King has presented a basically Theosophical view of such matters as life after death and the Masters.

To the right of the bookstore is a simple but tasteful hall with a seating capacity of perhaps fifty. The strains of sacred music come from a speaker, and incense is in the air. The ornamentation suggests the syncretism of the group. Over the rostrum is a conventional colored picture of Jesus, on the front of the rostrum the Sanskrit letters for Om, to its right on the wall a quotation from Goo-Ling. Around the wall are pictures of members in the mountains and at sea on various Operations.

A visit to a Sunday morning service found about thirty worshippers present. Somewhat surprisingly, all were very conservatively dressed, and a good portion were elderly persons. The service included such oriental practices as reciting the mantram "Om mani padme hum" and meditation, reading lengthy dictations from the Masters including Jesus, delivered through George King, and old-fashioned Protestant elements such as a sermon and the singing of evangelical hymns. There was a typical excited fervor combined with military precision. The Aetherius Society, despite a rather more relaxed and "churchly" atmosphere in the worship service, sees itself as an army engaged in an apocalyptic battle at the end of the age, all unknown to the mass of bemused people of the world, whose salvation is now being wrought by spiritual struggles far beyond their comprehension.

Reading Selection: The Aetherius Society

These lines are from a broadsheet issued by the Aetherius Society announcing regular sessions of Operation Prayer Power, which take place at the American head-quarters in Los Angeles, the Society's branch in Detroit, the European headquarters in London, and the Northern headquarters in Barnsley, South Yorkshire, England. The broadsheet is issued to all members and sympathizers of the Society and urges them to take part in this Cosmic Mission.

OPERATION PRAYER POWER is being used directly by the Cosmic Masters as a vitally important way to send out Spiritual Energy to mankind. During every Spiritual Push, the energy which you can help to put into an OPERATION PRAYER POWER Battery by your Prayers and Mantra will be broadcast to mankind under the strict supervision of one of the greatest Cosmic Manipulators ever known in the history of this or any other Planet in the Solar System, Mars Sector 6.

As a Member, Associate Member or Sympathizer, you are hereby invited to take an active part in this wonderful, uplifting, Divine Mission.

This is one of the great honors ever extended to you in your present life.

Up to now, Aetherius Society Members and Sympathizers have charged many Batteries in OPERATION PRAYER POWER and these have been discharged to the world in cases of dire emergency. If you read our Newsletters you will see the modern miracles which Prayer energy has brought about.

We have been commissioned by the Cosmic Masters to charge as many OPERATION PRAYER POWER Batteries as possible throughout The Aetherius Society. Some of these Batteries will be used as working Batteries so that your Prayer energy can be discharged under the direction of the Cosmic Masters in order to benefit mankind. The other Batteries will be charged to their fullest extent and kept as Divine emergency tools, which can be used in cases of great stress in the world, such as earthquakes, tornados, disease waves, or wherever the discharge is requested by the Cosmic Hierarchy.

As it takes about *1200 Prayer hours to charge each Battery,* you can see that we have a gigantic task in front of us.

A job which is absolutely essential for your brothers and sisters. A vital Mission which we have been entrusted with, *and have been specially chosen to perform out of every other New Age organization on Earth.*

This choice has been made by the Cosmic Masters in deference to the outstanding abilities and ingenuity of our Spiritual Leader, His Eminence Sir George King.

He was the Master who formulated the idea called OPERATION PRAYER POWER and invented all the equipment necessary to see it through.

This invention represents to Metaphysics what the wheel represents to physics.

It is the greatest breakthrough in Metaphysical history!

Your Prayer energy used correctly in OPERATION PRAYER POWER can help to change the world for the better.

The Spiritual Energies you invoke by your Holy Prayers and Ancient Mantras are put into a specially devised physical container and preserved until needed. Then, on demand, this charged container, or Battery, is connected to a machine called a Spiritual Energy Radiator. This apparatus brings about a total discharge of all the Spiritual Energy put into each Battery. This Spiritual Energy is then manipulated by Higher Forces to whatever part of the world it is needed most in conjunction with the Divine Law of Karma.

When you consider that each Battery holds about 1200 Prayer hours of Spiritual Energy and ALL this vital power can be released in about 100 minutes, it is obvious that a massive concentration of energy is brought about. *A ratio of 700 to 1 is not unusual!*

This is the great occult secret behind the miraculous OPERATION PRAYER POWER.

As you are hereby invited to take part in this magnificent Cosmic Mission to help mankind in a more potent way than help given in other directions, it is surely your duty to come forward and do so.

BROADSHEET, The Aetherius Society American Headquarters, 1985

NOTES

[1]See Bryant and Helen Reeves, *Flying Saucer Pilgrimage* (Amherst, WI.: Amherst Press, 1957), pp. 95–98. This book, although far from scholarly, is a fascinating introduction to the major contactees and their activities. See also George Adamski and Desmond Leslie, *Flying Saucers Have Landed* (New York: British Book Center, 1953); George Adamski, *Inside the Flying Saucers* (New York: Abeland-Schuman, Ltd., 1955); Truman Bethurum, *Aboard a Flying Saucer* (Los Angeles: Devorss and Company, 1954); George Van Tassell, *I Rode in a Flying Saucer* (Los Angeles: New Age Publishing Co., 1953); Daniel Fry, *The White Sands Incident* (Los Angeles: New Age Publishing Co., 1964, and Louisville: Best Books, 1966) and his *Alan's Message to Men of Earth* (Los Angeles: New Age Publishing Co., 1965).

[2]Carl G. Jung, *Flying Saucers: A Modern Myth of Things Seen in the Sky* (New York: Harcourt Brace Jovanovitch, Inc. [Signet Books], 1969), p. 27.

[3]See Charles S. Braden, *These Also Believe: A Study of Modern American Cults and Minority Religious Movements* (New York: The Macmillan Company, Publishers, 1949), pp. 319–57; and J. Stillson Judah, *The History and Philosophy of the Metaphysical Movement in America* (Philadelphia: Westminster Press, 1967), pp. 50–91, for summaries to date of publication of these books.

[4]Edgar T. Goodspeed, *Modern Apocrypha* (Boston: Beacon Press, Inc., 1956) gives a useful account of the story of this and other modern "scriptures" used by Spiritualists and eso-tericists.

5The major points of the "Declaration of Principles" adopted by the National Spiritualist Association, 1899 and 1909, are as follows:

1. We believe in Infinite Intelligence.
2. We believe that the phenomena of Nature, both physical and spiritual, are the expression of Infinite Intelligence.
3. We affirm that a correct understanding of such expression and living in accordance therewith constitute true religion.
4. We affirm that the existence and personal identity of the individual continue after the change called death.
5. We affirm that communication with the so-called dead is a fact, scientifically proven by the phenomena of Spiritualism.
6. We believe that the highest morality is contained in the Golden Rule, "Whatsoever ye would that others should do unto you, do ye also unto them."
7. We affirm the moral responsibility of the individual, and that he makes his own happiness or unhappiness as he obeys or disobeys Nature's physical and spiritual laws.
8. We affirm that the doorway to reformation is never closed against any human soul, here or hereafter.

Spiritualist Manual (Washington, D.C.: National Spiritualist Association, 1944), pp. 22–23.
6Aetherius Society Broadsheet.

5

THE CRYSTAL WITHIN:
Initiatory Groups

In certain Australian tribes, it is believed that the shaman has had his internal organs removed as a part of his excruciating and regenerating initiatory ordeal, and that they have been replaced by organs of crystal or quartz. The ordinary person has only soft, corruptible viscera, but the shaman is transformed; he holds within himself the hard, geometric, quasi-eternal luster of miraculous crystal. These deep-concealed splendors give the initiated shaman vision, awareness, and knowledge of the mysterious currents which run in the worlds of spirit and destiny.

Comparably, the goal of occultists and initiates today is a new self of crystalline lucidity, permanence, and luminosity. The groups they belong to believe it is possible for human beings to enjoy states as different from the present condition as rock is from flesh, and much better able to withstand the vicissitudes of the world. They believe these states can be attained by employing laws and forces in nature and psychology which are hidden from the uninitiated mind, and therefore may be called *occult*. Actually these laws and forces are not mysterious, but knowable and almost mathematically precise, working as normally and predictably as gravitation. It is not so much by fervor that one attains the goal, but by knowledge, technical skill, and persistence. The goal, however, is more than knowledge. It is the shaman's goal: crystal, lucid vision, mobility on all levels of being, power and invincibility.

Michael H. Murphy, Director of the Esalen Institute, has said we need a Western *sadhana*. In India, a *sadhana* is a spiritual path, in the sense of a concrete and specific program for the use of meditation techniques, physical activities, and ritual under the direction of a master. If one practices a *sadhana* undertaken faithfully, whether it be yoga, devotion to a particular god, or Buddhist contemplation, it should lead to radical but predictable changes in the individual's mental and spiritual state. All cultures except our own, says Murphy, have within them traditional *sadhanas* for those who wish them: the way of the shaman, the holy man, the adept, or even of the householder who, as many do in some societies, embarks upon a carefully plotted spiritual regimen with an interior goal in mind. But the emphasis in Western religion upon freedom, God's sovereign grace, and the primary importance of ethical obligation to others has resulted in a corresponding disparagement of calculated individual spiritual attainment. That is why our culture as a whole lacks this element which older cultures have. It is easy to disparage these paths and those who undertake them as "selfish." But Murphy believes that the neurotic materialism of our culture is due to a lack of real personal spiritual goals and a failure to release the potential in humanity which such paths unlock.

Of course there has been no shortage of attempts to present *sadhanas* to the West. Western psychoanalytic procedures, and even more some newer techniques emerging out of the humanistic psychology movement, are rightly considered by Murphy to be steps toward the development of a *sadhana* deeply rooted in the nature of the Western psyche. They are, however, outside the scope of the present survey. Other groups, to be considered later, present *sadhanas* imported intact from the East with the contention that there is no real reason why westerners cannot utilize them. The Theosophical and Neo-Pagan groups represent in part attempts to recover *sadhanas* believed buried in the Western tradition, but half-forgotten. However, in practice they are more ritual or educational than initiatory "mystery schools."

The occult groups now under consideration are in a special class because they represent modern Western endeavors to articulate a precise *sadhana,* and their major concern is to initiate people into it and lead them through its convolutions. They may owe some debts to the remote past or to the East, but they are not mere reconstructions of the ways of a magus of antiquity. Rather, they all have behind them a Western and modern individual of the magus type. The magi who founded them have walked the hard streets of our modern European and American cities; they have travelled in automobiles and spoken on telephones, even if in their hearts they were shamans or wizards. They are people like Paul Francis Case of the Adytum Temple, or L. Ron Hubbard of Scientology, or G. Gurdjieff. Enigmatic, independent men in the midst of our steel and concrete, they have baffled or infuriated many, but have drawn followers with a promise of making them new men, with powers far beyond those of others.

GURDJIEFF GROUPS

An excellent example of the modern, Western magus is Georges Ivanovitch Gurdjieff (1872–1949). He has probably influenced Western esotericism more than any other modern figure except Helena Blavatsky. Gurdjieff was born in the Caucasus region of Russia of Russian, Greek, and Armenian ancestry. His early life is even more obscure than that of Helena Blavatsky, but like her he claimed to have travelled widely in central Asia and there to have met representatives of a Hidden Brotherhood (probably Sufi) which preserved an occult tradition. The teaching concerned opening up higher levels of consciousness than that attained by the average person; the vehicle was to be what were called "Fourth Way Schools," which were not for the fakir, or yogi, or monk, but for the person in the midst of ordinary life.

Gurdjieff's theories became widely known through his greatest disciple, P. D. Ouspensky (1878–1947), who met him in Moscow in 1915 and later came with him to western Europe. Ouspensky had the mind of a philosopher, however, and it may be questionable whether his classroom lecture tone fully represents the master. Gurdjieff was a magus, and his own approach had about it the lightness, the puzzlement, and the indirectness of his kind. At his famous "Institute for the Harmonious Development of Man" in Fontainebleau, France, his disciples found stringent manual labor alternated with lavish banquets and classes in Eastern dance (of which he was a master) interpreted by dialogue worthy of a Zen *roshi.* His writings, such as *All and Everything,* are not metaphysical exposition, but fantastic allegorical satire striving to awaken man to the futility of trying to improve his unhappy condition simply by changing his external environment without changing himself.

Gurdjieff was a small, dark man with a huge Nietzschean moustache. He was perhaps nondescript save for the marvelous piercing black eyes which impressed all who met him. His manner ranged from radiant expansiveness to mysterious remoteness, but seemed never unintentional. Of him Olga de Hartmann wrote:

> Mr. Gurdjieff was an unknown person, a mystery. Nobody knew about his teaching, nobody knew his origin or why he appeared in Moscow and St. Petersburg. But whoever came in contact with him wished to follow him . . . He was a magus, and he presented a new way to the world . . .[1]

Everyone who writes about Gurdjieff and his teaching seems compelled to give prominence to the recitation of how he came to meet the great man, how his life was transfixed and transformed by the meeting. No one particularly writes about Gurdjieff who has not had this experience; no one who had it and can write refrains.

Thomas de Hartmann, one of his most faithful disciples, tells of his first meeting with Gurdjieff during the First World War. De Hartmann was an aristocrat, an officer, and a promising composer. But Gurdjieff had required that they meet in a disreputable Petrograd cafe at which de Hartmann did not want to be seen. Gurdjieff and a companion appeared in Caucasian black coats, bushy moustaches and dirty cuffs. Then de Hartmann noticed Gurdjieff's eyes:

> By this time I realized that the eyes of Mr. Gurdjieff were of unusual depth and penetration. The word "beautiful" would hardly be appropriate, but I

will say that until that moment I had never seen such eyes nor felt such a look.[2]

They said little, but after leaving, de Hartmann reports he was long silent, and that after the meeting

> my life became a sort of fairy tale. From early childhood I had read fairy tales and their meaning stayed with me always. To go forward, and never forget the real aim, to overcome obstacles, to hope for help from unknown sources if one's aspiration were a true one. . . . The wish to be with Mr. Gurdjieff now became the only reality.[3]

Another devoted disciple, P. D. Ouspensky, also first met Gurdjieff in a cafe during the First World War through a friend. He describes the impression this way:

> I remember this meeting very well. We arrived at a small cafe in a noisy though not central street. I saw a man of an oriental type, no longer young, with a black moustache and piercing eyes, who astonished me first of all because he seemed to be disguised and completely out of keeping with the place and its atmosphere. . . . [He] in a black overcoat with a velvet collar and a black bowler hat, produced the strange, unexpected, and almost alarming impression of a man poorly disguised, the sight of whom embarrasses you because you see he is not what he pretends to be and yet you have to speak and behave as though you did not see it.[4]

Yet such is the trickster quality of the magus. Soon enough de Hartmann, Ouspensky, and many others were caught up in his web. All else became for them unreal, and what was real were the discussions they had with Gurdjieff about awakening higher planes of consciousness, and the calisthenic exercises Gurdjieff taught them which expressed the teaching. When the Russian Revolution came shortly after these meetings, a small band accompanied Gurdjieff in exile, first to Tiflis, then to Constantinople for about a year, then to Berlin. Finally in 1922 the emigré group arrived in Fontainebleau.

There Gurdjieff and his group bought a manor, the Château du Prieuré, where it was at last possible to establish the Institute on a proper scale. The life at the Institute was demanding, particularly when one considers the aristocratic background of many of its members. Married persons could belong; otherwise it was virtually monastic. Residents at the Prieuré included Russians, Frenchmen, Britishers, and the New Zealand novelist Katherine Mansfield, who died there. A bell at six woke everyone, breakfast was coffee and bread, and members went straight to work. Save for a simple lunch, outside work continued until darkness. Then they would dress for the evening meal, which on occasion would be a banquet in the grand style. After supper, at eight o'clock, Gurdjieff would sometimes speak, and the "Sacred Gymnastics" would take place. In his management of the center, Gurdjieff would very often play the role of a cruel and unreasonable despot; he would order a project begun, and then abandoned, or shout harshly at people for stupidity, or demand work be done at top speed. At other times he would explain the reasons for these episodes.

In 1923 the entourage presented their "Sacred Gymnastics" with music arranged by de Hartmann in Paris, and in 1924 in the United States. These events sparked widespread interest in what Gurdjieff was doing. After his return from America, Gurdjieff suffered an automobile accident (he was said to be a terrible driver) from which he was slow to recover. However, this gave him time to write. He began *Meetings With Remarkable Men* and *All and Everything,* his two books.

Gurdjieff felt that pupils should remain with him only for a limited period of time, and then go back into the world. Some could not break the spell of his fascination, and failed to go; upon them he made more and more intolerable demands. He made life so intolerable for Ouspensky that he was forced to leave in 1924. Finally, by the early thirties, very few were left, and in 1933 the Prieuré was sold. Gurdjieff continued to travel, and groups based on his principles were organized by former students of the Prieuré around the world. Gurdjieff died in 1949.

There are today groups studying the teachings of Gurdjieff in the major cities of Europe and America, some under the leadership of persons from his succession. They maintain as did Gurdjieff that humanity is not now living at full potential, but is asleep. To evolve to greater awareness requires work. (Gurdjieff's way is often spoken of simply as "the work.") In a real sense this awakening is "against nature," for the organism can function as it is and does not need to evolve. Yet there is a capacity for more if one can set his will to it. Certain little-known laws can help. The universe is made of vibrations, and one can jump from one level to another. These jumps can be induced by the experiences of Gurdjieff's music, dance, and labor.

Gurdjieff groups try to continue this program of active improvement. The groups feel there should be alteration between public and private work. Some are now very quiet and even secretive. Visitors are usually not invited to group meetings. Enquirers are encouraged first to read a book like Gurdjieff's *All and Everything.* If one emerges from that task aflame with enthusiasm, he or she may be considered a serious candidate. Meetings consist mainly of living room discussions, but from time to time the group devotes weekends to the practice of labor and calesthenics in the Gurdjieff manner. Members tend to be upper class professional people; musicians are especially attracted to the movement, perhaps because of the influence of de Hartmann, and because of the great use of musical metaphors.

There is no central organization in Gurdjieff groups, but the name and tradition is potent. Teachers and groups, some independent and some in a succession going back to the Fontainebleau school, spring up continually. As often happens in such traditions, disciples disagree as to what the Master taught. In one group, members were asked to practice daily yoga-type exercises, maintain awareness of themselves as a center of consciousness, and try to experience a variety of kinds of temperament by deliberately experimenting with walking and talking like an opposite personality type. At some meetings, costumes would be used. On other occasions the individual would be asked to stand nude alone in front of a mirror for fifteen minutes a day. A diary of one's high and low points, omissions, and experiences would be kept. The purpose of all these activities is to make the individual much more aware of himself, and to attain the experience of opposites and hence of wholeness on one level. From this platform one can climb to higher consciousness in the midst of life.

Undoubtedly the most serious and important group in America is The Gurdjieff Foundation of New York, which keeps in touch with the major Gurdjieff groups abroad. Founded in 1953, the New York Foundation owns a building on 63rd Street containing meeting rooms, dance studio, library, workshops, and music room. Some 500 people are involved in activities such as a class for academic studies of initiatory traditions and music, dance, and work projects which are intended, in the Gurdjieff tradition, to create a combined mental-emotional-physical experience leading to progress in coordinating one's thinking, emotional, and moving centers, thus leading to an awakening from sleep. A comparable Gurdjieff Foundation was started in San Francisco in 1955. Gurdjieff put considerable emphasis, as we have seen, on the importance of group experience for his kind of teaching, and on its applicability to life in the modern world. The Foundations try to preserve these emphases, as do the other Gurdjieff groups.

Reading Selection: Gurdjieff

Gurdjieff intended *All and Everything* to be the name of a series of three books. The first is generally called *All and Everything,* with the subtitle, *An Objectively Impartial Criticism of the Life of Man, or Beelzebub's Tales to his Grandson.* The second book is *Meetings with Remarkable Men.* The third never appeared. Parleying to fantastic extremes of complexity, wit, and subtlety the oriental gift for veiling philosophic acumen in fancy and parable, in the first book Gurdjieff describes with whimsical satire the follies of human life in the form of an account by a visitor, Beelzebub, from another planet. The book was published only after his death, for although Gurdjieff first wrote it in the late twenties, the author preferred to keep it in manuscript form for reading aloud to his followers. His intent was to bring the hearer, or reader, gently and with laughter to the hard conclusion that nothing man does on the level of changing his environment—the horizontal level, as it were—can improve his state of inner dissatisfaction. Only changing the level of his consciousness can do this. In a note at the end of the book, "From the Author," Gurdjieff hints at his solution.

The expression which has reached us from ancient times, "the first liberation of man," refers to just this possibility of crossing from the stream which is predestined to disappear into the nether regions into the stream which empties itself into the vast spaces of the boundless ocean.

To cross into the other stream is not so easy—merely to wish and you cross. For this, it is first of all necessary consciously to crystallize in yourself data for engendering in your common presences a constant unquenchable impulse of desire for such a crossing, and then, afterwards, a long corresponding preparation.

For this crossing it is necessary first of all to renounce all that seems to you "blessings"—but which are, in reality, automatically and slavishly acquired habits—present in this stream of life.

In other words, it is necessary to become dead to what has become for you your ordinary life.

It is just this death that is spoken of in all religions.

It is defined in the saying which has reached us from remote antiquity, "Without death no resurrection," that is to say, "If you do not die you will not be resurrected."

The death referred to is not the death of the body, since for such a death there is no need of resurrection.

For if there is a soul, and moreover, an immortal soul, it can dispense with a resurrection of the body.

Nor is the necessity of resurrection our appearance before the awful Judgment of the Lord God, as we have been taught by the Fathers of the Church.

No! Even Jesus Christ and all the other prophets sent from Above spoke of the death which might occur even during life, that is to say, of the death of that "Tyrant" from whom proceeds our slavery in this life and solely form the liberation from which depends the first chief liberation of man.

> G. GURDJIEFF, *All and Everything* (New York: Harcourt Brace
> Jovanovitch, Inc., 1950), pp. 1232–33.

SCIENTOLOGY

Few of the organizations we are dealing with have attracted as much enthusiasm or controversy as Scientology. It has been accused of many things. Its members, on the other hand, with joyful, contagious fervor claim that Scientology can give "total freedom." Those who have reached the state of "Clear" make statements like:

> There is no name to describe the way I feel. At last I am at cause. I am Clear—
> I can do anything I want to do. I feel like a child with a new life—everything is
> so wonderful and beautiful.
>   Clear is Clear!
>   It's unlike anything I could have imagined. The colors, the clarity, the
> brightness of everything is beyond belief. Everything is so new, I feel new
> born. I am filled with the wonder of everything.[5]

An organization which can produce, by any means, such moving statements as these must have something remarkable in its life—and some remarkable personality behind it. On first impression, one may wonder just where to look for the marvel. The usual pictures of the founder, L. Ron Hubbard (1911–1986), which hang in every Scientology building, do not suggest at first glance what the man was—a contemporary magus and master in a class with Blavatsky or Gurdjieff, if not greater. The face is fairly ordinary save for tiny, sharp eyes embedded in kindly crinkles. But from out of the mind behind those intense blue eyes has grown an initiatory procedure of fantastic complexity and effectiveness, a technique which challenges orthodox psychology, and a worldwide organization. Those few Scientologists who had the privilege of meeting "Ron" himself describe the experience in ecstatic terms.

The churches and centers of Scientology have about them something of the atmosphere of a regimental office in the modern bureaucratic army, with its abbreviations, neologisms, routing charts, chain of command, its air of intricate and mystifying efficiency. Behind much of this is the stream of tapes, books, bulletins, and directives which came from L. Ron Hubbard. The experience of Scientology seems essentially two-pronged. On the one hand, there is the sense of enthusiasm, confidence, and camaraderie which derives from being part of an aggressive, close organization, together with the feel of modernity and certainty which technical language and organizational polish communicate. On the other hand, the product is not a new brand of soap or the services of a government department, but an experience described in language which reminds one of the shaman's flight, and a philosophy in which dimensions, indeed universes, rise and fall with the shifting of consciousness.

These sides are represented respectively in the outer and inner life of Hubbard. He was born in Tilden, Nebraska. His father was an officer in the Navy. Hubbard grew up on his grandfather's Montana ranch, though he accompanied his father on tours of duty in the Far East. He graduated from high school in Washington, D.C., then studied at George Washington University, leaving in the early thirties. He participated in three ethnological expeditions to Central America, did some pioneer flying and became an accomplished sailor. The range of his interests was matched by his boundless energy. His main vocation, however, came to be film writing and science fiction; he had published in *Astounding Science Fiction* by 1938. He was remarkably prolific. He returned to science-fiction writing before his death with the publication of *Battlefield Earth: A Saga of the Year 3000* and several other novels. Certain of his stories suggest in embryo that imaginative and futuristic idealism which is expressed in developed Scientology. There is the idea that living men can be trapped in a writer's fantasy, or the idea that the whole cosmos may be the fantasy of a single organism living in it. In later Scientological thought, we find that all sense of individual alienation, and all universes, stem from turbulence in theta or thought, which in its pure form, as "static," is without motion or dimension and the ground of the universes. Keen perception can dissolve these enslaving veils; only that which is not directly observed tends to persist.

The life of L. Ron Hubbard displayed several motifs of the magus archetype: an out-of-the-ordinary childhood, wide travel, and a spirit-is-all and power-of-imagination worldview. He appeared to fulfill the same pattern during the war years. Hubbard was a Naval officer. He said it is a matter of medical record that he was twice officially pronounced dead during that time—the shaman's initiation. He was once dead for eight minutes during an operation, and during this time he received a vital message to impart.[6]

After the war, Hubbard resumed writing. By the end of the forties, however, he had taken up with another intense concern. In 1950 L. Ron Hubbard published his most famous book, *Dianetics* in which he claimed that "the hidden source of all psycho-somatic ills and human aberrations has been discovered and skills have been developed for their invariable cure."[7] It was an immediate sensation, rating articles in the mass media and much discussion. The ideas of this book are the basis of Scientology.

Hubbard taught that there are two parts to the mind, the analytic and the reactive. They correspond roughly but not exactly to the psychoanalytic conscious and unconscious. Experiences of shock cause "engrams" or sensory impressions of the event to be recorded in the reactive mind. These records produce mental and psychosomatic troubles until they are dislodged. Dianetics effected dislodgment of engrams by "dianetic reverie"—a patient would talk with an "auditor" until the engrams were released through reenactment of the event. Unlike in Freud's psychoanalytical theory an individual's difficulty was not necessarily rooted in events in postnatal life. Many engrams, it seems, were produced prenatally in the womb, often by attempted abortion. When the process was completed, the patient would be what was called "Clear." (The present use of this term in Scientology connotes a higher state of spiritual development than the Dianetic "Clear.")

Hubbard established a Hubbard Dianetic Research Foundation in Elizabeth, New Jersey. Differences involving the direction of research in the organization centering around the matter of past lives and the immortal spiritual nature of man, together with legal problems, led him to move the Foundation to Los Angeles, to Witchita, and finally to Phoenix. There Scientology was founded in 1952 as the Hubbard Association of Scientologists. Scientology differs from the original Dianetics in several respects: the myth of the thetans, reincarnation, a new and higher goal, and the use of the E-meter. According to the myth, in the beginning were the thetans— eternal, omnipotent, omniscient beings—who became bored with their static immortality. In order to make things more interesting they began to play games, which included creating various kinds of curious worlds. Ultimately, they became so engrossed in their games that they forgot they were just playing and gradually attributed reality to what they had created out of MEST (matter, energy, space, and time). Indeed, they became hopelessly ensnared in the material universe, forgetting their true nature as immortal, omnipotent thetans. (The myth reminds one of ancient gnostic myths in which beings of divine origin become trapped in the material, historical world, lose knowledge of their true origin, nature, and destiny, and need the liberating *gnosis* that restores them to their proper destiny.) The revelation that L. Ron Hubbard brought is that we are all thetans, the individual consciousness that has the capacity to separate from the body and mind and to create MEST (the phenomenal world). Thetans reincarnate in a seemingly endless series of lives, acquiring engrams in every one of them. Thus the scale of the human problem is greatly enlarged. No longer does one has to deal only with the engrams (including prenatal) of a single lifetime. One has to "clear" the whole course of one's transmigratory lives. To be Clear is to understand more fully how one is a spiritual being or a thetan, and thereby to gain control over one's mind and physical environment.

The E-meter, the indicator used in liberating the thetan, has been used frequently—though not exclusively—as a "confessional aid" since the early fifties. It is an electrical device which measures the resistance of an object to electric current. In processing the procedures undergone in becoming Clear, the E-meter is employed to indicate areas of reaction, that is, of tension, in a person's response to verbal and other stimuli so that he can explore that area of resistance. The "preclear" holds a metal can attached to the dial of the machine in each hand as he is asked questions by the "auditor," with concentration, of course, on dealing with troublesome areas. The response is measured on the dial. The electric charge is very slight, but in Scientological experience this measurement is related to uncovering areas of emotional stress and marking one's elimination of them so that he can "go Clear" and find "total freedom."

In 1954, Hubbard established the Founding Church of Scientology in Washington, D.C. Since then, the symbolism of the movement has become increasingly ecclesiastical, though participation in this side of it is optional. Ministers of the Church of Scientology frequently wear clerical collars and pectoral crosses. There are informal Sunday services and a liturgical manual for occasional offices such as weddings and funerals.

In 1959 Hubbard moved to England, where he started the Hubbard College of Scientology at Saint Hill, in Sussex. From 1964 until his death in 1986 he was usually out of public view, living at times aboard a ship in the Mediterranean, surrounded by an elite body called the Sea Org (for "organization"). Scientology has been through many parliamentary and legal battles in Britain, the United States, and Australia, and some of them continue. Scientologists have frequently had strongly adversarial relationships with their critics, the psychiatric profession, and agencies of the federal government, including the Food and Drug Administration and the IRS.[8]

The next stage in Scientology after becoming Clear is to become an "Operating Thetan," or OT. The OT is independent of time and place and all the toils of MEST. "Out of the body" experiences are common among them, to judge from accounts of OTs. One says:

> To be stably exterior to my body as I am now is the fulfillment of one of my oldest and most favorite dreams. I can extend myself at will, permeating the substance of the physical universe. I can sense, touch, taste, and see things without using my body. I can really know. . . .

Another:

> There were times when my auditing room seemed to dissolve and I found myself being and perceiving in a completely different location. Once I found

myself on a beach. I could see and hear the waves of the ocean and smell the salty spray. Another time I visited a castle and was intrigued to find that it was electrically lighted. I continue to have such experiences at quiet times when I am not distracted by the demands of life.

I know who I am in or out of a body. . . .9

Such experiences certainly suggest the perpetuation of shamanistic motifs and the alternative reality tradition. So does the intensely initiatory character of Scientology. Its whole reason for being is to pass candidates through its "tech"—the grades, self-discoveries, and break-throughs which culminate in such states of consciousness as these. The monetary cost is not slight; few individuals are likely to reach Clear without the expenditure of thousands of dollars, and there are the OT stages beyond Clear. Money is said to be refunded to those who are dissatisfied, however, and the whole process is supposed to be at once challenging and delightful, like a game. "If it's not fun, it's not Scientology," is a common saying. With its certified staff, its magus, and its strongly in-group feeling, Scientology is not unlike an ancient wisdom school with a totally twentieth century vocabulary and environment.

Here is a description of a "Clear Night," a weekly event at the "Celebrity Center" of Scientology in Los Angeles. The Celebrity Center had the atmosphere of a small night club, complete with uniformed doorman, hinting at entry into a world of glamor which some of those attracted to Scientology have perhaps never known. Inside there was an auditorium and, against one wall, a nonalcoholic bar. The atmosphere was very friendly, warm, and outgoing. It was evident that the world of Scientology was, for those in it, happy, secure, and virtually a family. There was no admission charge, but attractive girls behind desks by the door made sure they got the names and addresses of non-Scientologists who came to Clear Night. They would be made members of the "I Want to Go Clear Club" and would receive weekly mailings thereafter.

The program began with banjo and guitar music of professional quality. Then a high-ranking member of the Sea Org—an older, balding man with a winning smile—announced amid wild cheers that Ron had just released a new grade: Class VII OT, the highest so far, in which the thetan becomes even more free of the body, mind, and MEST. He indicated it is precise, "closely audited," yet he could only describe its effects with ecstatic "wows," "gollies," and pauses. He also said seventy-five new auditors would be hired at good pay. Then an official just back from Ron's ship told about a new "power processing" route which will give auditors especially the effectiveness they need to help their preclears.

The dual role of Ron, the Founder, as chief teacher and charismatic initiator through the "tech" was vividly apparent. The veneration of Scientologists for this man, who so adeptly combined efficiency, paternalism, and a hieratic remoteness, was evident; and he once spoke of himself in virtually messianic terms, talking of his wearing "the boots of responsibility for this universe."

Clear Night proceeded with the remarkable testimonies of those who had just made Clear or one of the OT grades. One young lady who had become Clear mentioned the song, "Someone Else is Singing my Song," and said, "Now I know what my song is." A man who had achieved OT III commented that he no longer had stage fright. Most impressively, a legal secretary who had achieved OT VII, the highest mark to date, said that as one goes through the grades it's like a big thetan hand was reaching down to help. She said that now she is in a MEST body, but is really independent of it; she is really in a thetan universe, looking in and controlling the MEST one. She read from a Buddhist scripture and from an article about the coming Buddha Maitreya. This suggested an interesting eschatological interpretation of the thetan experience. She said the thetan is like Maitreya—in the world, but no longer reactive to it. This would mean that like a bodhisattva, the thetan is free of karma but remains in the world out of compassion, and is able to operate solely on that level. Typified by this attractive statement, recent Scientological literature has used far more sympatheticaly than before the art and scriptures of Buddhism and other Eastern religions, with which it obviously has much in common metaphysically despite totally different (and, Scientologists would say, much more effective) terminology and techniques.

Like most successful new and initiatory religions, Scientology is a meritocracy in which appointment to office comes down from higher levels in the organization. Attention is always paid to maintaining integrity of teaching and example among officers and members. It has developed work in the rehabilitation of prisoners and institutionalized drug users, while continuing Ron Hubbard's old feud with professional psychiatry.

Scientology has also given considerable attention to the spiritual needs of artists, musicians, and theatrical people. The Celebrity Center in Los Angeles, and similar centers in other cities, house not only Clear Nights, but amateur and professional drama and music performances. There are studios available for painting and sculpture, and continual art shows. At any time of day, the attractive building is full of young people happy and busy with creativity. The freedom in creativity of the artist is said to be a part of the total freedom Scientology releases, and the power of its artists the first fruits of what it will bring the world.

Most of the people in Scientology are young adults. Since, for many people, it involves a heavy commitment both of time and money, it may immediately become the most important thing in life; social life and intellectual life revolve around it. But unlike traditional psycho-therapy, Scientology also provides a vital, sustaining, creative "family" during the time of this commitment and after. When one considers that, in investing in Scientology, one is acquiring almost a total life—friends, entertainment, and avocation—the very high cost, whether one agrees philosophically with Scientology or not, is seen in a new perspective. Of course, many persons who take auditing do so only as a part-time matter and without this degree of life reorientation. On the other hand, some, after Clear, enter professional work for Scientology, partly to pay for their own further auditing, partly no doubt because the organization has become very central to them, and because producing results and conviction in others is reinforcing to their own experience. It remains to be seen what course this vigorous and controversial movement will take after the passing of its founder, L. Ron Hubbard.

Reading Selection: Scientology

The literature of Scientology, most of it from L. Ron Hubbard's hand, is vast. The following passage, however, sums up some of its basic assumptions, and appropriately culminates in a breathtaking suggestion of the Scientological goal. The idealistic and monistic philosophy is evident; the flat and technical diction is typical of the original sources, in contrast to the ecstatic testimonies of Clears.

Scientology as a science is composed of many axioms (self-evident truths, as in geometry). There are some fifty-eight of these axioms in addition to the two hundred more axioms of Dianetics which preceded the Scientology axioms.

The first axiom of Scientology is:

Axiom 1. Life is basically a static. (Definition: A life static has no mass, no motion, no wave-length, no location in space or in time. It has the ability to postulate and to perceive.)

Definition: In Scientology, the word "postulate" means to cause a thinkingness or consideration. It is a specially applied word and is defined as causative thinkingness.

Axiom 2. The static is capable of considerations, postulates and opinions.

Axiom 3. Space, energy, objects, form and time are the result of considerations made and/or agreed upon or not by the static, and are perceived solely because the static considers that it can perceive them.

Axiom 4. Space is a viewpoint of dimension. (Space is caused by looking out from a point. The only actuality of space is the agreed upon consideration that one perceives through something, and this we call space.)

Axiom 5. Energy consists of postulated particles in space. (One considers that energy exists and that he can perceive energy. One also considers that energy behaves according to certain agreed upon laws. These assumptions or considerations are the totality of energy.)

Axiom 6. Objects consist of grouped particles and solids.

Axiom 7. Time is basically a postulate that space and particles will persist. (The rate of their persistence is what we measure with clocks and the motion of heavenly bodies.)

Axiom 8. The apparency of time is the change of position of particles in space.

Axiom 9. Change is the primary manifestation of time.

Axiom 10. The highest purpose in the universe is the creation of an effect. . . .

It is as though one had entered into an honorable bargain with fellow beings to hold these things in common. Once this is done, or once such a "contract" or agreement exists, one has the fundamentals of a universe. Specialized considerations based on the above make one or another kind of universe.

[Hubbard then says that there are three classes of universes: the agreed upon or physical universe, one's own universe, and the other person's universe, in which an individual may become entrapped, as for example, a son in his father's.]

We must, however, assume, because it is so evident, that an individual only gets into traps and circumstances he intends to get into. Certain it is that, having gotten into such a position, he may be unwilling to remain in it, but a trap is always preceded by one's own choice of entrance. We must assume a very wide freedom of choice on the part of a thetan, since it is almost impossible to conceive how a thetan could get himself trapped even though he consented to it. By actual demonstration a thetan goes through walls, barriers, vanishes space, appears anywhere at will and does other remarkable things. It must be, then, that an individual can be trapped only when he considers that he is trapped. In view of the fact that the totality of existence is based upon his own considerations, we find that the limitations he has must have been invited by himself, otherwise they could not be eradicated by the individual under processing, since the only one who is present with the preclear is the Auditor, and past associates of the preclear, while not present, do desensitize, under auditing, in the preclear's mind. Therefore it must have been the preclear who kept them there. The preclear by processing can resolve all of his difficulties without going and finding other persons or consulting other universes. Thus the totality of entrapment, aberration, even injury, torture, insanity and other distasteful items are basically considerations a thetan is making and holding right now in present time. This must be the case since time itself is a postulate or consideration on his own part.

L. RON HUBBARD, *Scientology: The Fundamentals of Thought.*
Copyright © 1956 by L. Ron Hubbard. (Edinburgh: The
Publications Organization Worldwide, 1968), pp. 75–80.

BUILDERS OF THE ADYTUM

The Builders of the Adytum is a small but interesting group which is representative of those who, without going the way of Witchcraft or Neo-Paganism, seek to focus their spiritual life upon the Hermetic and Kabbalistic tradition. Rather than starting anew, with new terminology, like the Gurdjieff and Scientological groups, the BOTA, as it is commonly called, has remained conservative in language and symbol. Its temple is brilliant with beautiful luminous paintings of the Tarot cards around the walls, and the altar is rich with the black and white pillars of Solomon and the Kabbalistic Tree. But this group is in the tradition of the modern return of the magus.

Its real founder was Paul Foster Case (1884–1954). When young, Case had been a magician especially interested in playing cards. At sixteen, he was asked by someone where playing cards came from. Not knowing, he began research. His investigations led him to the Tarot, and thence to the Kabbalah and Hermeticism. About 1910, he was initiated into the Order of the Golden Dawn in New York. This was the famous esoteric and magical society which, based in London, at one time numbered among its members such writers as W. B. Yeats, Algernon Blackwood, Arthur Machen, A. E. Waite, and the notorious Aleister Crowley, who was expelled. Six months after his initiation, the U.S. head of the Order died. Case succeeded him. But his youth and the fact that he had published (before his initiation) two articles on the Tarot allegedly revealing secrets of the Order led to dissension, and Case resigned. In 1920 he founded the Builders of the Adytum (a Greek word meaning inner temple or sanctuary) in New York. He believed that he had been led in this, as he was in his studies, by a "Master of Wisdom," like the Theosophical masters, who spoke to him in a gentle, reasonable voice, instructing or guiding him to particular pages of books. In 1933 he moved the BOTA to Los Angeles.

His calling, he believed, was nothing less than to synthesize and present to the modern world a body of knowledge comprised of the teachings of "Ageless Wisdom" for which the ancient Mystery Schools had been primary repositories. It is now most effectively taught, however, through the "language" of Kabbalism and the Tarot cards, in which the esoteric meanings of the Hebrew alphabet are prominent. All of these interweave to form an unbroken "tapestry of Light" which, though stranded of many traditions, in the end witnesses to a single truth or Reality: the divinity of the Cosmos of which humans are an integral part. Case effectively carried out this destiny through books, lectures, and correspondence courses.

After his death he was succeeded by Ann Davies, a vivid and charismatic woman who enacted the ritualistic worship of the BOTA with a dramatic flair, and did much to enhance its popular appeal.

Since her death in 1975, leadership has fallen on a panel of some six ministers, both men and women. The work continues much as before. What is perhaps most distinctive about the Builders of the Adytum is the use of ritual. Although the basic structure of the service is more Protestant than Catholic or—despite the extensive use of Hebrew elements—Jewish, it does involve a degree of communal work—chanting, singing, raising hands. Much is made of the importance of ritual. Ann Davies used to say that the world itself is the ritual of God, down to the atoms and electrons. All of life is ritual; without it one would have no evolution because there would be no reorganization. Consciousness in everything is the creator, but it works through ritual. There is also instruction in the service. At one service in 1986, the preacher, a black man, spoke simply and very effectively on the relation of knowledge and wisdom, referring from time to time to a vividly colored chart of the Kabbalistic "Tree of Life" in the sanctuary.

Membership at the Los Angeles headquarters church is not large, but remarkably well-distributed as to race, age, and sex. The greatest growth of the movement is in correspondence courses and study groups around the world. Long established in New Zealand, it is now taking hold in Colombia, France, and Spain, as well as centers in the U.S. Some members are active. only for a time, seemingly with a need to touch the "tapestry of Light" before turning to other concerns, others regard its study as a life work, while a few become stewards of the tradition.

Reading Selection: Builders of the Adytum

The following passage by Ann Davies appeared in an issue of the *Adytum News-Notes,* a periodical of the Builders of Adytum. It was written, we are told, in response to many requests. Here Ann Davies in her direct, vivacious, and far-reaching manner, tells about an initiatory experience of her own, and also reveals something of the difference between the Western and Eastern mystical traditions.

At age 27, having spent several years in concentrated occult study and research, coupled with strenuous self-analysis, I realized that I was now well prepared to undertake *formal* meditation. I had already developed considerable facility in watching my thoughts, emotions and actions from the vantage point of the observer, though I had no teacher (so I thought!). I had carefully mapped my course that I might be protected from falling into the traps of, or being snared by, self-delusion or illusion.

I was going to settle for nothing but REALITY . . . *whatever that Reality might be!* IS THERE A GOD? I had to know the answer to this question as desperately as a drowning man gasps for air.

I had a light lunch on the date I set for my first formal meditation. I then cleansed the apartment thoroughly, holding in mind that this was a symbolic cleansing of my environment. At dinnertime instead of eating, I took a bath, concentrating on washing away (symbolically) all patterns of false knowledge. I spent the next two hours analyzing the Quest that had brought me thus far. Realizing that this, my first formal meditation, was just a beginning, I reminded myself that I would probably have to meditate daily for years . . . or a lifetime . . . in order to receive an answer to my question . . . if there *was* an answer!

I donned a loose robe, turned off all the light except for the night light in the hallway, and sat down in a comfortable chair. I started to breathe deeply, rhythmically, slowly. I instructed myself to let go of all tensions as the deep, rhythmic breathing continued. I then placed my full and concentrated attention about a foot above my head as I literally hurled my question upward to that point.

. . . *IS THERE A GOD?*

IS THERE A GOD? The quivering, all-consuming question! Every fibre of my being . . . every inbreath . . . every outbreath . . . everything meaningful . . . my entire past . . . my entire future . . . all this energy, and more was gathered together by my mind and heart into the question of questions! Unwaveringly I held my question as the one and only point of concentrated attention. Nothing was permitted to impinge or disrupt. No other thought was permitted to intrude. NOTHING ELSE MATTERED!

The vibration continued up, and when it reached my meditative point I became Beginningless-Endless Consciousness. Never a time I was not. I was pure Consciousness with nothing to be conscious of . . . except I AM. Neither birth nor death . . . neither Person nor persons. Never a time I could not BE, because WAS and WILL BE were eternally I AM. I was Cosmic Consciousness. I was Samadhi. I was Foreverness. Ecstatic but serene.

Did I receive an answer to my meditative question? The answer is, of course, "Yes!" I achieved Samadhi at my first formal meditation. That which Eastern Swamis and Gurus yearn for through a life time of disciplines. That which Eastern Occultism considers the GOAL! But I knew better! I knew that this was just a beginning. I knew that Cosmic Consciousness could even be a trap. An invitation to rest in the Ultimate, thereby giving up further evolution in the delusion that the Ultimate had been attained. I therefore *BEGAN* my researches into Consciousness at the point where others have mistakenly thought they had achieved the final liberation.

I was out to discover *WHY* evolution existed with all its pain, separateness, etc. I was out to discover how individualism occurred and what was its destiny. I was out to prove or disprove Reincarnation, Personal survival, etc.

Now that I knew *GOD IS*, I had Eternity in which to research the rest of the Mysteries.

ANN DAVIES, "My Mystical Universe, Part XII," *Adytum News-Notes*, (1967), pp. 1–3.

NOTES

[1]Thomas de Hartmann, *Our Life with Mr. Gurdjieff* (New York: Cooper Square Publishers, Inc., 1964), p. xiii.

[2]de Hartmann, *Our Life with Mr. Gurdjieff*, p. 5.

[3]de Hartmann, *Our Life with Mr. Gurdjieff*, p. 6.

[4]P. D. Ouspensky, *In Search of the Miraculous* (New York: Harcourt Brace Jovanovitch, Inc., 1949), p. 7.

[5]Advanced Organization of the Church of Scientology of California, *Advanced Success Stories*, 1970. Single sheet publication.

[6]Biographical data is largely based on "L. Ron Hubbard," *Scientology: The Field Staff Magazine*, I, No. 1 (© 1968), p. 7.

[7]L. Ron Hubbard, *Dianetics: the Modern Science of Mental Health* (Los Angeles: American St. Hill Organization, 1950), p. ix.

[8]Roy Wallis, "Societal Reaction to Scientology," in *Sectarianism*, ed. Roy Wallis (New York: John Wiley & Sons, 1975).

[9]Advanced Organization, *Advanced Success Stories*.

6

THE EDENIC BOWER:
Neo-Paganism

In Pasadena, California, on the second floor of an old Victorian house, there is an Egyptian temple. Around the walls of the room are bright life-size paintings of some of the oldest known gods of humankind, gods long dead but now alive again—Isis, Osiris, hawk-headed Horus, wise ibis-headed Thoth, Hathor, Sekhmet. At the center of the room is a magic circle, and in the middle of it an altar on which rests an ankh and other implements of ritual magic. A black mirror is set against one wall. In it the ancient gods of the Nile are called up visibly. They are not dead, this group, the Church of the Eternal Source, believes, though it is long since they have been worshipped. What they represent is still real in our minds (in the same sense as the Jungian archetypes), and in the Mind beyond our minds. They can be called back. As one Neo-Pagan put it, "The ancient gods are not dead, but they think we are."

The diverse people in tiny groups who make up Neo-Paganism in America have in common that they believe something in us died with the death of the ancient gods. They are not, many of them, virulently anti-Christian. But besides our conventional American world, they have another homeland too. One of the devotees of ancient Egypt said, "The Egypt of the pharoahs and the gods is like a state, a country, to which we belong." They may be patrons of ancient Egyptian or Greek religion, or Druidism, or Wicca (Witchcraft), ceremonial magic, or even Satanism. They are partisans of some Western religious tradition other than Judaism or Christianity.

The "other country" is a land of a different feeling for the relation of humanity to nature, to the passions, to the imagination. If they are polytheistic, it is in terms of Paul Tillich's statement that polytheism is not a matter of quantity but of quality. It is a way of affirming as religiously valid the subtle, shimmering changes of color, mood, and force in nature and the psyche. One is not subordinate to another, but they are different, and nature and man (the two are deeply continuous) are cooperations of different forces within a pluralistic universe.

At the Egyptian temple, it was said that the real meaning of ancient Egyptian religion is that the gods represent many paths to the goal of the central religious experience which defies words and images. The gods represent the different desires and goals of life (one prays to a god of wisdom for wisdom, to a god of love for love). All of them can be brought, not into an absolute unity, but into a balanced pattern, like Jung's mandalas, which represent totality. The members of this group strongly rejected any suggestion that their view of the cosmos was one of pluralistic chaos; they instead brought out quaternary diagrams of the relationships of the Egyptian gods showing their interaction with the four seasons, directions, and so forth. They also indicated that they always represented the balancing of male and female. These two principles are coequal in Egypt. If the masculine may seem to have a slight edge (the primacy of the sun and of pharaoh), that is because the feminine, Isis, is by nature more reticent and concealed, but is no less powerful. The Egyptian temple group is not an exception to the theorem that the new religions are monistic; the mandalic symbols of totality suggested the monistic mind at work.

The unifying theme among the diverse traditions represented in this chapter is the ecology of one's relation to nature and to the various parts of one's self. As Neo-Pagans understand it, the Judaeo-Christian tradition teaches that the human intellectual will is to have domination over the world, and over the unruly lesser parts of the human psyche, just as it, in turn, is to be subordinate to the One God and his will. The Neo-Pagans hold that, on the contrary, we must find a niche in the world, neither high nor low, where we cooperate with nature and its deep forces on a basis of reverence and exchange. Of the parts of man, the imagination should be first among equals, for man's true glory is not in what he commands, but in what he sees. What wonders he sees of nature and of himself he leaves untouched, save to glorify and celebrate them.

What Neo-Pagans seek is a new cosmic religion oriented to the tides not of history but of nature—the four directions, the seasons, the path of the sun—and of the timeless configurations of the psyche. They seek not that morality which comes of imposing the will on the reluctant flesh, nor the mystical trance which is the fruit of asceticism, but the expansiveness of spirit which comes of allowing nature and rite to lower the gates confining the civilized imagination. For them, this is the spirit called up by the names "pagan" and "polytheism." These words do not suggest for them, as they still do for others, images of unbridled orgies and grotesque idols reeking with the blood of sacrifice. Rather they suggest a romantic, living, and changing world continuous with human fancy and feeling instead of one dead and subdued; a religion of atmosphere instead of faith; a cosmos, in a word, constructed by the imagination (considered the surest guide to what is in the heart of things) instead of by the analytic intellect or bare faith, which seeks only the outer husks.

When respected and indeed deliberately heightened, imagination is a faculty not only of fantasy but also of tremendous power. It can make the emotions feel the gods within things, and the eyes see them, and divine forces go out into the world to sow love, or prophesy, or fear. Evocation, calling up the gods from within the self, is true magic. Magical evocation is propelled by unleashing the forces touched by one's childhood wonder at sunsets, fairy tales, and dreams, forces too much pent up in the modern adult. These are the powers called "anagogic" by Jung, a great favorite of almost all in the modern alternative reality tradition.

These Neo-Pagan groups have in common a particular emphasis on the second of the three forms of religious expression, the "practical"—rite, gesture, ceremonial act. It is through corporate "work" that the magical cosmos is evoked; it is "made" by ritual actions that demarcate and celebrate it, and by acts done as if it were present.

The essence of each group discussed in this book, like each of the great world religions, is best approached through one of the three Wachian forms of expression, even though all three are found in every group. In Theosophy it is verbal expression which gives the easiest avenue for initial understanding. With most of the Neo-Pagan groups, it certainly is the second, cultus and ritual. The teaching is often pale in comparison with the fascination with the rites, both for members and observers. Despite the necessity of a group for the performance of the rites, the composition and persistence of particular groups is often unstable.

By looking at the rites, it is possible to grasp what is being done. A secondary world is created in a special time and place, one far different from the outside world—though it may be, as with all sacred times and places, intended to manifest the hidden archetypes and realities behind the outer shadows. A magic circle is drawn, the sacred is separated from the profane. Within the circle the implements of ceremonial magic—wand, sword, cup, and pentacle—reign with power. Or an old Druidic festival is celebrated with flowers and dance. By these gestures a world is perceived in which anagogy and wonder write their own history. When this is seen, one may ask about the other forms of expression:—*what* people are doing this, and *how* they explain themselves.

These groups pride themselves on being in the Western tradition. Much is made of differences between Eastern and Western psychology. It is said that yogic and meditation techniques of the East are not suitable for the average westerner. Rather, the methods involving imagination and magical operations are a truly Western method of achieving the same ultimate goal, and are the methods most people in the West should be using.

The Neo-Pagan groups have a close relationship with the occult and initiatory groups. Whether they call themselves witches, magicians, or something else, the Kabbalah, Tarot cards, astrology, and the Gurdjieffian idea of opening up a new level of consciousness comprise the intellectual framework. The main difference is that the Neo-Pagan groups may use formal rite, often quite elaborate, in place of more purely psychological or intellectual exercise, and recently have become more and more concerned with human relationship with nature, and with the exfoliation of mythologies. But they also treasure the Western alternative reality tradition. They typically hold that the Kabbalah, magic, and the rest of it originated in ancient Egypt (though the Kabbalah was later superficially Hebraicized) in the "ancient mystery schools." Egypt and its progeny thus make up an eternally valid realm of the spirit, not less capable of reality and power today than ever.

The roots of modern Neo-Paganism lie in romanticism. The romantic's exaltation of feeling and imagination as ways to move out of the prison-house of William Blake's "number, weight, and measure" has obvious affinity with the magician's more systematic use of the same forces. A key figure in the application of romantic feeling to magic was the French ex-seminarian Alphonse Louis Constant (1810–75), who wrote under the name Eliphas Levi. While remaining a Roman Catholic, Constant claimed also to be an occult initiate. He wrote books, elegant in style and daring in speculation but often suspect as to scholarship, on the history and theory of the Kabbalah and magic. He pressed home the concept of the supremacy of imagination, the eye of the soul by which the magician gains power over the primal matter—inert until awakened by its life-bearing touch—and hence is able to do what he will. Another well-known French occultist, and the founder of an order, was Gerard Encausse (1865–1916), who wrote under the name Papus.

In Britain, certain Masons realized that this world was rightly theirs as well, though the average lodge was scarcely concerned with real magic. In 1888 a group of Master Masons organized the Order of the Golden Dawn, by far the most famous of the many esoteric groups which sprang up in the late nineteenth century. A number of well-known names were connected with it, or the Stella Matutina (a reformed and more Christian version), including writers like W. B. Yeats, Algernon Blackwood, Arthur Machen, and Charles Williams. The Golden Dawn's principal leader was S. L. Mac-Gregor Mathers (1854–1917), brother-in-law of the philosopher Henri Bergson. Mathers claimed occult contact with three Secret Chiefs in Paris who belonged to a mysterious inner order guiding the Work. The Golden Dawn offered a series of degrees of initiation. Each had its own rituals. To attain each degree, the candidate had to prove he had acquired competence in magical works, such as invocation, evocation, crystal-reading, making symbolic talismans, and astrology. An "Egyptian mass" invoking Isis was performed in Mathers's home, which was appointed like an Egyptian temple. Mathers translated and edited the works of Abramelin the Mage (1362–1460?), which offer a clarity and practicality rare among the grimoires.[1] The Order's institutional life was never smooth, and came to an end after the First World War. But it shaped the thinking of a number of persons who have since been very influential in occult and magical circles.

The most important figure influenced by its activities was Aleister Crowley (1875–1947), notorious magician and writer of a number of books on magic, or "magick" as he insisted on spelling it. His personality has fascinated biographers and imitators.[2] Flamboyant, gifted, poet, given to exaggeration, heroin addict, widely travelled, he played the role of magus with rather too much self-dramatization. Yet he made the idea of "magick" an exciting game and motif for a style of life in which his motto, "Do what you will shall be the whole of the Law," was the theme (meaning, of course, "Let magic give you the power to do what you will"). Recently his books have been enjoying a revival. Expelled from the Golden Dawn, Crowley founded his own order, A. A. (*Argentinum Astrum*). In 1912 he became head in Britain of a German group called O.T.O. (*Ordo Templarum Orientalis*) founded in 1895 by Karl Kellner. This group, which still survives in German and Crowleyite wings, practiced sex magic and used some Eastern as well as Western terms.

The Neo-Pagan movement breaks down into two broad categories: the magical groups, deeply influenced by the model of the Order of the Golden Dawn, the O.T.O., and Crowley; and the nature-oriented groups. The former are the more antiquarian; they love to discuss editions of old grimoires, and the complicated histories of groups and lineages. They delight in precise and fussy ritualism, though the object is the evocation of an intense emotional power which can, it is said, produce levitation and the apparition of gods and demons.

The pagan nature-oriented groups are more purely romantic; they prefer woodsy settings to incense and altars; they dance and plant trees. They are deeply influenced by Robert Graves, especially his *White Goddess*. They are less concerned with evocation than celebration of the goddesses they know are already there. The mood is spontaneous rather than precise, though the rite may be as beautiful and complex as a country dance.

The feeling is well articulated by one of the most acute protagonists of modern Wicca or Witchcraft, the woman who writes under the name Starhawk.

> People often ask me if I *believe* in the Goddess. I reply, "Do you believe in rocks?" It is extremely difficult for most Westerners to grasp the concept of a manifest deity. The phrase "believe *in*" itself implies that we cannot *know* the Goddess, that She is somehow intangible, incomprehensible. But we do not *believe* in rocks—we may see them, touch them, dig them out of our gardens, or stop small children from throwing them at each other. We know them; we connect with them. In the Craft, we do not *believe* in the Goddess—we connect with Her; through the moon, the stars, the ocean, the earth, through trees, animals, through other human beings, through ourselves. She is here. She is within us all. She is the full circle: earth, air, fire, water, and essence—body, mind, spirit, emotions, change.[3]

Wicca itself is in the middle between ritual magic and nature-oriented Neo-Paganism. It is profoundly aligned to the cycles of nature, especially those of the Moon and the seasons. Typically, Wicca covens or groups worship a Horned God and a Triple Goddess (Maiden, Mother, and Crone). In their version of ancient agricultural and fertility mythology, the Horned God is born each year at the winter solstice, becomes the Goddess's lover in the spring, and dies at Halloween, as the Goddess becomes the Crone of winter.

At the same time, its rites may include real efforts at the evocation of the God and Goddess in the appropriate form. Intense and dynamic dance and chant may be employed, along with gestures reminiscent of ceremonial magic such as wielding a sword to "raise energy" and invoke the deity, generally in the person of the high priest and priestess. Spells and blessings may also be enacted.

American Wicca, with possibly forty or fifty covens at any given time, is divided into several different traditions. They have mainly to do with the style of ritual. "Gardnerian" covens, in the lineage of those founded by Gerald Gardner,[4] generally employ highly energetic chanting and dancing in the nude. "Traditional" covens used clothed and slower paced rites supposed to be derived directly from the "Old Religion" through an underground transmission; homey implements, bones, herbs, and stones take the place of the elegant equipment of the mage as aids to the transformation of consciousness and the evocation of the Old Ones, the gods of Wicca. On the other hand, "Alexandrian" Witchcraft, founded by Alexander Sanders in England, augments the Wicca heritage with the familiar Kabbalist-occultist line of astrology, ceremonial magic, and cognate lore.

In all of this, it is significant that some religionists, and some independent writers and psychics, now want to call themselves witches. The word has a tortured heritage among us.

It evokes at once fantasy images from fairy tales and Walt Disney movies, the all too true horrors of the great witch persecutions of early modern Europe and the Salem witch trials, and biblical prohibitions. Modern witches cling to the name nonetheless, at once seeming to relish its provocative character and taking pains to explain that witches are not what most people think. On a deeper level, no doubt many have been drawn to the Craft, as they like to call it, just because they have long experienced themselves as spiritual "outsiders," and so identify with a lineage of women who, though often despised, found wisdom and power beyond the margins of established religion and society. Witches were the only liberated women in the Middle Ages, they like to say, for they were women with a potency they gathered in their own way, apart from the male-dominated church, state, or family.

Satanism is also a special case. Satanists may be fewer in number than publicity would suggest. But there are those in America who consider themselves worshippers of Satan. Satanism's apparatus is like that of ceremonial magic—though with its own symbols and rites—and its beliefs have contact with nature orientation. Satan is held by some Satanists to be not the "enemy" but the life-force, and so cannot be other than a good to be affirmed. But there is a special psychological convolution in the mind of the Satanist which sets him apart, or rather by which he sets himself apart. His "good" must be precisely that which commonly represents what is most evil. In a peculiar manner he binds himself to the world of the majority culture as Neo-Pagans do not. Strictly, his use of a Judaeo-Christian name for his "deity" perhaps excludes him from the category Neo-Pagan.

In practice, however, Satanists inhabit the same spiritual under-ground as the others; people in all the groups in this chapter tend to know each other, and some move from one orientation to another, and borrow techniques from one another—though we hasten to add that those who are not Satanists regard Satanism as rather silly, and are careful never to iden-tify themselves with it or its usages. Satanism must be distinguished from modern Witchcraft and ceremonial magic.

The Neo-Pagans experiment with ways of creating through action, through performed gestures of rite and festival, or imagination, a second-ary world which in time becomes, as it is meant to, the participant's primary world. They seek to restore a proper balance between masculine and femi-nine symbolization of the sacred. They seek to recover a sense of wonder and respect as religious feelings towards nature in all its moods and toward the human body and psyche. Thus they want to find a new totality, perhaps in reaction to a schizophrenic culture. They look for it in a new cosmic religion that vehemently rejects the religious value of history, while it radi-cally affirms the religious value of raising the level of consciousness through stimulation of the imagination by ritually creating a suggestive and sacred milieu.

In the 1970s and 1980s several trends become increasingly important to American Neo-Paganism. The first was its growing interconnection with the burgeoning feminist movement. Rising interest in "feminist spir-ituality" in American society as a whole suddenly offered this tiny circle a stunning opportunity to make an impact on the historical course of religion. At the same time, in the eyes of some, it presented temptations to sidetrack modern Paganism into "political" or sexist diversions.

In the 1970s, many persons concerned about the equality of the sexes found that they could no longer truly accept a God referred to exclusively by such titles as Father and Lord, and by the pronoun He. Names have power, and these names seemed to relegate women and the feminine psyche to spiritual subordination. For some, even moves to give women equal opportunity, including ordination, in mainline churches were not enough so long as the language and imagery of worship remained firmly masculine. Books appeared like Mary Daly's *Beyond God the Father,* Naomi Goldberg's *The Changing of the Gods,* and the anthology *Womanspirit Rising,* edited by Carol P. Christ and Judith Plaskow, containing Starhawk's essay "Witchcraft and Women's Culture" and Christ's "Why Women Need the Goddess." Many women found themselves responding deeply to the clear message of such works.

For some, intellectual response was sufficient. Others were content to work for changes in attitude and the language of worship within the major denominations. For a small but significant number, however, nothing less than actual worship of the Goddess was sufficient, worship replete with song and dance and the ceremonial exploration of women's mysteries, as well as spelling out the long-forgotten sacred meaning of women's lives. These seekers made connection with the Wicca and Neo-Pagan movement.

The covens they established, unlike earlier ones in which the Horned God and the Goddess were coequal, often focused on the Goddess and feminine sacrality alone, though without necessarily denying the other side. They were commonly called Dianic. Some were composed chiefly of lesbians, but many more were simply women—and sometimes men—who felt a need to explore the feminine sacred world by itself for a while. Not a few of these groups were likewise perceived as identified with "radical" perspectives on such issues as ecology, peace, and opposition to nuclear power. By the mid-1980s, however, the sharp edge seemed to have worn off their involvement in feminism and the other issues in political and social terms; women's and other Wicca were still advancing, but with inclination toward a quieter exploration of its rich spiritual dimensions.

A second important Neo-Pagan trend was toward Native American religion, especially its traditions of healing and shamanism. Several groups, under leaders claiming initiation as American shamans or medicine men, are exploring the meaning for Americans of non-native descent of the sweat lodge, the vision quest, the way of the warrior and the shaman, and traditional Native American healing arts.

Paralleling the emergence of feminist and Native American trends in the Neo-Paganism of the 1980s has been a countervailing trend toward seeking a unified Pagan vision for our day. "Revivalist" Neo-Pagan groups, those endeavoring to revive a specific Pagan past, whether Egyptian, Greek, or Norse, seem in decline. Their explorations were useful, but increasingly those inclined to the Pagan way appear to realize that one cannot simply go back to the past; the call now is for a religion of Earth, nature, the seasons, the masculine and feminine alike, and the shamanistic adventure in the contemporary idiom. Groups therefore are becoming more experimental and spontaneous in their worship, and common ground underlying Goddess and Pagan lore around the world is being sought. Harley Swiftdeer, a leader in the Native American religion movement, has travelled to Africa to share perspectives with African medicine men.

Groups in the Neo-Pagan tradition are numerous and present a continually shifting spectrum; it is still a movement in flux and formation, though increasingly gives evidence it will survive and make a solid contribution to American spiritual life. Something of the rich panorama of paths it offers can be perceived in the second volume of Gordon Melton's *Encyclopedia of American Religions*. For our purposes, however, it seems better to present a portrait in some fullness of only a few groups, as typical as any sample can be of what American Paganism is like today. The first is Feraferia. While nearly dormant in the 1980s, except for the practice of the founder himself, it has been immensely influential conceptually, and in our minds reflects the romantic, polytheistic, nature-oriented style of Neo-Pagan vision more profoundly than any other group.

FERAFERIA

A sprinkling of groups around the country have attempted to revive specific religions long believed dead, or to create new religions in the ancient spirit. The British Druids who perform rites from time to time at Stonehenge are fairly well known. In 1963 the Reformed Druids of North America was founded at Carleton College in Minnesota. At first it was mainly a joke. Undergraduates could avoid the compulsory chapel attendance requirement if they expressed a religious preference other than Protestant Christianity and practiced it. But the movement spread to several other campuses, and it is said that even after the chapel attendance regulation was repealed the following year, the Druidic rites continued, for some had found the ancient ceremonies in oak groves, celebrating the passing seasons—Beltane, Samhain, and so forth—to be more meaningful than they had at first supposed.

An even more serious movement of the Neo-Pagan type is Feraferia. It merits careful study for several reasons. Feraferia represents the role of leader, history, teaching, rite, and sociology characteristic of Neo-Paganism. Significantly, Feraferia emphasizes rite, and uses a highly mythic language in its verbal expression. But the ritual expression is the glory of the group; it has shown a remarkable ability to create a sacred cosmos in and out of which individuals may move.

The founder of Feraferia is Frederick M. Adams. He incorporated Feraferia on August 2, 1967, but this action was only the culmination of a long string of preparatory events. Adams was raised in the Altadena area north of Los Angeles. As a youth he spent great amounts of time exploring the mountains in the region and getting to know nature intimately. In his college years, he studied Greek and Celtic folklore, and read the works of Jung, Carl Kerenyi, Mircea Eliade, Robert Graves, J. J. Bachofen, and Henry Bailey Stevens.[5] All of these writers, and others of the same type, influenced him profoundly.

Adams states that in the spring of 1956, while walking across the campus of Los Angeles City College (where he had been studying fine arts and anthropology), a sudden illuminative experience struck him. He was seized by a sense of the "mysterium tremendum" in feminine form. He suddenly realized that "the feminine is a priori." The experience was not quite visual, yet it was a real confrontation with a presence outside himself. He was dazed, and walked about confusedly for some minutes, muttering "This is it . . . She is it." The reading and meditating he had been doing in an inchoate, unresolved way all fell into place. From then on Adams devoted himself wholly—apart from the necessities of life—to the service of the feminine sacred.

He first tried this vocation between 1957 and 1959 by living in a multifamily commune in the Sierra Madre with a group interested in the same ideals. Seasonal festivals were held in an outdoor temple to the "Maiden Goddess of Wildness." In the name is foreshadowed two major themes of Feraferia, the pedomorphic or child-form representation of the goddess, and the equation of wilderness with sacred ground. A publication called *Hesperian Life* was issued, celebrating the concept of a return to a paradisical horticultural society. Stevens, a major guide to this group, believed the garden of the Hesperides was a mythical representation of that ideal. The communal group made some use of psychedelic drugs (then legal), recording all their experiences in a journal. After 1959 Adams withdrew from the community to write and travel. He visited the principal sites of Paganism in Europe and made contact with Neo-Pagan groups in Britain.

The name Feraferia ("nature celebration") came to the founder in 1967 as an intuition. By similar inspiration he received the group's symbol, the "stang," a trident with sun and crescent moon superimposed. The banner was unfurled for the first time on the vernal equinox of 1967 at a great "love-in" in the Los Angeles Elysian Park. The concept of Feraferia was now virtually complete.

Feraferia holds that religious life should be a part of sensitive interaction with nature and one's own erotic awareness. Any mysticism, or dualism, or false monism which divorces the real from the natural, or the particular, or the erotic is wrong, for man with earth, sky, and sea are one huge biome, or living organism. One is whole only insofar as he recognizes this unity and lives to celebrate it. The symbol of the whole earth biome is Kore, the divine maiden of the Greeks.

The feminine is for Adams and Feraferia a more fundamental archetype for the whole than the masculine, though paradoxically they are also equal. The nature of the masculine is to penetrate, separate, and analyze; that of the feminine is to include, to underlie, to unite. Therefore without impairing the essence of either, the feminine—the Kore—is the mythical, living, personal name for the unity of all things. Much is said of the harm man has done to himself and to nature by the exaltation of the masculine archetype, good in itself, to a supreme place.

Kore is all aspects of the feminine, for they are all one in supplying the ground of union. Kore is alike mother and daughter, Demeter and Persephone. She is reborn every year and goes every year through all stages of femininity. The Feraferia calendar, based on Robert Graves's "Tree Calendar," is a celebration of her progress—her birth with the divine lord Kouros in early spring, her emergence from childhood, her nuptials, her retiring beneath the earth in winter.

However, the supreme archetypal form of Kore, Frederick Adams maintains, is not the "Great Mother" but the pubescent maiden, for the heart of nature is not merely nourishing and life-bearing, but also erotic, flirtatious, arousing passion.

> To inform the dawning Eco-Psychic Age of Aquarius, wherein celebration will determine subsistence, a long repressed image of divinity is reemerging: the Merry Maiden, Madimi, Rima, Alice in Wonderland, Princess Ozma, Julia, Lolita, Candy, Zazie of the Metro, Brigette, Barbarella, and Wendy—a grotesque and incongruous assembly at first sight—are all early harbingers of the Heavenly Nymphet. She alone may negotiate free interaction between the other three anthropomorphic divinities of the Holy Family. These are the Great Mother, Who dominated the Old and New Stone Ages; the Great Father, Who initiated the Early Patriarchal Era; and the Son, Who crystalized the megalopolitan mentality of the Late Patriarchal Era. It is the Dainty Daughter of the Silver Crescent Who will transmute the saturate works of Father and Son to wholeness in the Maternal Ground of Existence, without sacrificing the valid achievements of masculine articulation. And She accomplishes this without a crippling imposition of parental or heroic authority images. How delightful to behold Her tease and tickle Father and Son into respectably natural, Life-affirming pagan Gods again.

The character of the KORE SOTEIRA, or Holy Maiden Savioress, is hard to delineate precisely because it portends the para-rational and permits incommensurables to interfuse without violence at last. The Antic Covenant of the Magic Maiden is radically permissive.[6]

A visitor to Frederick Adams's home is made immediately aware that this is no ordinary suburban house. The front porch is full of signs and symbols from out of the past—wreaths, crossed sticks, painted stones. In the backyard trees have been planted and given names. There is a henge— a circle of forked sticks oriented to the pole star and the rising sun. The group has a larger henge in the mountains to the north. Within the house are shrines to sun and moon, and a shrine room whose floor is a large wheel on which the passing days and seasons and motions of the planets are marked with stones. Here, the important news is not what comes in the paper, but what nature is doing.

Permissive polytheism is quite consistent with the cultus of the Magic Maiden. Its whole mood favors an openness to the coequal spirituality of each particular of time and place. The now voluminous writings of Frederick Adams in his monthly periodical, *Korythalia,* frequently evoke this feeling. He disparages one-pointedness, whether of heroism or of asceticism or intellectualism. Celebrate rather the unique beauty of each season, weather, tree, mountain, and mood—under the aegis of the imagination this sensitivity is best expressed by polytheism.

A glance at a Feraferia rite makes this evident. Consider the spring seasonal festival, Beltane.[7] At the beginning, nude male and female participants form separate files and face the gates of henge. The leader, holding a torch, faces west and chants:

Moon Door, Moon Door, Door of Alder, bound with Willow, open now, revealing night, and fiery stars, and silver moon, and demiurgic dark.

Then, facing east:

Sun Door, Sun Door, Oaken Door, bedecked with holly, open now, revealing day, and azure airs, and golden sun, and archetypal light.

The participants then one by one enter the circle of unhewn treetrunks, with the care one shows toward a sacred place. They make a slow circle clockwise within it, and gather at the east end. The upright there is made an altar. Incense is lit on it. All raise arms in invocation, and the leader calls:

Antheides and the Great Fays of the East, Dawn, and Spring, join us now in the Faerie Ring between Worlds. Through the portal between Moon and Sun, return into your Earth Abodes from the far Faerieland of Stars.

Other prayers and invocations are offered, such as:

Oh Holy Maiden of the kindling quick of merging mist and mazing echo: The Innocent Bounty of the trees bares your Faerie Flesh and Wildness, Wonder,

Magic, Mirth, and Love. . . . Your beauty seals our bridal with all Life. The dance of your green pulse unfolds all bodies from earth's fragrant form. Evoe Kore!"

Within the ring the group structure dissolves somewhat. Members sing, dance, or meditate individually. About half an hour later they re-form to leave. They circle clockwise again, embrace mildly, and depart. The gates of the Other World are once more solemnly closed.

Another popular rite is a tree planting ceremony, which can be performed any time.

The rites of initiation into Feraferia are designed to give the novice an experience of identification with nature and with Kore. The rite takes place at the henge. First, the gods and goddesses of the twenty-two biomes of earth and the astronomical bodies are called to the vicinity of the circle. They are then invoked to its center, where they combine to form mystically the body of the Magic Maiden. The initiate then associates the parts of his own body with the corresponding ecosystem of nature through the image of Kore's body. He uses sounds and words which capture the energy of each part. There is then ecstatic dancing; one may, if moved to, take a pledge to Kore.

The purpose of Feraferia clearly is to recover an ecstatic vision of wholeness and unity which utterly respects the reality of the particular. It brings together not only man and nature, but man and each seasonal and geographical particular of nature, and also man and each style of consciousness—masculine and feminine, analytic and dream, vision and fantasy. Feraferia art, often quite beautiful, is generally surrealistic, reflecting the sacred worlds of dream and fantasy.

The membership of Feraferia is mostly middle-aged. Typically, Feraferians are people who have been involved in movements like pacifism, ecology, and utopianism. In Feraferia they seem to find adequate religious expression of what have long been their spiritual concerns. Contrary to what one might expect, Feraferia is not just a product of the "sixties'" culture—its roots go back before it, and it outlasted its peak. But parallels and mutual influence with the larger spiritual quest of the sixties exist.

The vision of Feraferia is predominantly Frederick Adams's and most of the writing, devising of rituals, and art has been his. The group has little structure except as a circle around a charismatic leader. His vision is so personal and intricate that it does not communicate itself easily. Some have been through Feraferia and have left to explore other forms of Neo-Paganism. The role of the symbol-maker is often thankless and ambivalent. Only time can tell whether Adams is in anticipatory touch with emerging changes in the collective psyche.

Feraferia sees itself as a precursor of a future culture in which the feminine archetype in Magic Maiden form will recover religious centrality, and in which humankind will recover a sense of ecological reverence. The new culture will be in part something new—Feraferians prefer to talk less of return to the past than of "transformation."

Some aspects of ancient paganism they do not wish to emulate. The new Magic Maiden personification of the feminine sacred will not desire the cruel sacrifices or somber dedication of the older loving/devouring Mother. The concept of the primal horticultural paradise is recognized to be something of a valuable myth. There has been talk among some Feraferians of the establishment of a paradisal community which would probably be horticultural, vegetarian, and in all ways—work, play, celebration— live close to nature and its shifting moods, preserving trees, wildness, and all things intact. Feraferians believe that now society must move in something like this direction, or perish. They see themselves as the advance guard of a future culture very different from the present. Their real task is to aid this evolution through providing symbols and stimulation.

Reading Selection: Feraferia

To appreciate fully the spirit of Feraferia, one must have some experience of participation in its life. Next best is reading the monthly magazine, *Korythalia*. This magazine is not simply a chronicle of meetings and events—it is an immersion in another world. There are ecstatic comments on books, mountains, music, and pagan theology, mostly written by Frederick Adams. For every month there is a lunar calendar, providing for each day a wide series of correspondences, ranging from stages of dress or undress of Ishtar to types of terrain which fit the mood of the day. Here is a passage on polytheism, one more systematic than much of Adams's writing:

There are five modalities of polytheistic manifestation:

A. The great Pantheistic-Panerotic Goddess, the Lady Breath of Wildness, the Queen Tree of Stars and All Worlds. One of Her condensed vowel names is AWIYA. Ultimately She allows every unique being to share Her ontological priority.

B. Her two children, the Divine Lovers, who establish the passionate polarity of creation. They are KORE and KOUROS, acknowledging the precedence of KORE. As Maiden Savioress, she enshrines the essence of childlike delicacy, lyrical sacredness, romantic and spritely spirituality. She guarantees transcendence for every unique Presence. Finally, she is the true Muse of the dawning Faerie Age of Aquarius.

C. The seven Gods and Goddesses of the major World Biomes, or Archetypal Landscapes, who link with Sun, Moon, and the five visible Planets through the days of the Sacred Week.

D. Indwelling tutelary Spirits of specific Nature regions, features, forms, and forces. With the help of pagan Celebrants, these may quicken Holy Earth into fully conscious LAND-SKY-LOVE-BODIES.

E. Freely roving Faerie Bands of Ancestral Spirits promoting the growth potencies of the Biosphere while awaiting reincarnation.

The natural fountainhead of human endeavor is not reasonable utility but extravagant mythopoeia. The myths and dreams of Paradise, common to all peoples, predict future actualities for this Planet. Trans-cultural images of the glowing orchard of innocent love constellate from the Collective Unconscious an evolutional FIAT of Cosmos. Feraferia will found Sanctuaries in accordance with the universal specifications of Paradise . . . These Sanctuaries are intended to replace trash heap cities as normative environs for human community. From these centers, men, women, and children will find their true pagan vocation in seasonal celebration and service to the surrounding Wilderness region, and thus help generate Faerieland.

> FREDERICK C. ADAMS, "Oracles of the Faerie Faith," *Korythalia* I, 6 (1970) p. 2.

WICCA: THE MOON BIRCH GROVE

The women of the coven began arriving at the home of the High Priestess about 7:30 on the eve of the fall equinox. Each brought with her candles and offerings of such foods as fruits, breads, and cheeses. For an hour or so they milled about greeting one another, preparing food, and assembling the implements of the Craft. When everyone had arrived, carpools were formed and the group went to a nearby studio where the sabbat of the equinox would be celebrated. All were burdened with mounds of food, flowers, candles, tambourines, and such ritual objects as swords, knives, wands, and chalices.

A small table was set up in the center of the studio room; it was soon bedecked with flowers, candles, and images of goddesses. The food was tastefully arranged beneath and about this altar, giving the chamber a festive air.

The women formed a circle round the altar. Each in turn introduced herself and spoke of what she hoped from the evening's rites. The High Priestess and several others talked of the significance of the fall equinox: as the days grow shorter, we think of withdrawing into the depths of the Earth our Mother, or into the depths of ourselves. Everyone held hands and began softly humming and chanting to "raise energy."

Then the circle was formally cast. Four women stood at the four compass points; a ritual sword was passed from one to the other. As each of the four "corners" received the implement, the entire circle turned toward her, and holding the sword she invoked the goddess of that direction. When the sword returned to the East, the circle was pronounced closed.

Next commenced a portion of the rite directly connected with autumn and the fall equinox. Each woman was handed a seed to plant in a small flowerpot; the seed was said to symbolize a part of herself the woman wished to nourish over the winter so that it might bloom the next spring. Then each woman was led to the side of the altar, where she lay down and was covered by a veil. As she lay there as though dead, another whispered in her ear the ancient myth of Demeter and Persephone. The Grove uses an early version of the myth, told in Charlene Spretnak's *Lost Goddesses of Early Greece,* in which Kore or Persephone was not abducted by Hades but chose to go to the Underworld to become Queen of the Dead. There, she comforted and guided the spirits of the departed on their journeys to other realms. But her mother, the Earth-Mother Demeter, still mourned the loss of her daughter, as mothers mourn a daughter leaving home to become her own person separate from her. She wandered the world looking and weeping for her while vegetation withered and died, finally descending into the Earth to become reunited with the beautiful young goddess. Their reunion was joyous in the realization that they are separate but also one. To share in this myth, then, is to die mystically to separateness that after a season in the depths of one's psyche to learn inner wisdom one might be reborn united with one's source. As individual women received the myth, spiritually going to the Underworld and returning united with the Mother, the rest of the circle continued to hum or sing softly.

When the myth-giving was over, the High Priestess sang a song. Then the assembly danced in a circle slowly. Next each woman went to the altar and lit a candle, stating a request for which she was lighting it. After each the group, now falling into a mood of good-natured joking and laughing, shouted "Blessed Be" or, three times, "As we will it, so shall it be." The spellwork, as it was called, was done for purposes ranging from an end to the arms race to personal career goals.

The last part of the formal ritual was begun when the High Priestess filled the chalice with wine as a libation to the Goddess. The vessel was passed around the circle, each woman taking a sip and sprinkling the altar with a bit of the beverage. The circle was dismantled as it had been built, the sword going around to the four corners in the opposite direction from before and the goddesses of the four directions being bid farewell. Then everyone sat down to attack the feast spread around the altar. Before taking food or drink oneself, each gave a bite and a sip to another, saying respectively "May you never hunger" and "May you never thirst." Then they broke into small parties, eating and chatting like any set of friends about jobs, acquaintances, travel plans, and the like.[8]

This is a characteristic ritual celebration of the Moon Birch Grove, a Dianic or feminist Wicca group meeting in the Los Angeles area. (Technically, it is not a coven since covens are restricted to thirteen or fewer members and this group does not wish to so restrict itself; hence the term "grove," a more loosely-constituted group of witches. Popularly, however, it is spoken of as a coven.)

Moon Birch Grove is a descendant of the Susan B. Anthony Coven #1, founded in Los Angeles by the strongly feminist Wiccan called Z Budapest in 1971. After she subsequently moved to the San Francisco area, taking the name with her, the Los Angeles group was reorganized as the Moon Birch Grove in December 1980. Its High Priestess, called Rhiannon, had been a student of Budapest. The group's character has perhaps changed somewhat since Budapest's time. Most members continue to feel strongly about liberal and feminist political causes, and rituals have been done on behalf of the Equal Rights Amendment and nuclear disarmament, and against patriarchy, child abuse, and nuclear power. Yet, while recognizing that it is important to allow oneself to feel and express anger and hurt at oppression, and to work politically and spiritually against it, the present spectrum of the group's concerns are well summed up in its own self-description:

> Moon Birch Grove is a Dianic Circle that celebrates women's mysteries and our planet's seasonal cycles. We are dedicated to World Peace and to countering human abuse and atrocity. We integrate contemporary feminist political activism and ritual magick to protect Mother Earth and all Her children.

The group is Dianic, which means that it is restricted to women (save for a few public activities) and worships feminine spiritual power—the Goddess in her many aspects and manifestations—virtually exclusively; though it does not deny the divine masculine, its adherents feel a need in themselves to explore the feminine side of the sacred. Many have come to this need through negative experience with normative Judaism and Christianity; one leading member said that she was a conservative Christian until she read passages in the Bible like Leviticus 27:3–7, which suggests that the value of a woman is little more than half that of a man.

In contrast to a patriarchal, male-oriented God, they worship the Goddess to whom things feminine are sacred, and who is not up in the sky, but is the "swirls of energy," the life-force that animates the universe and all that lives within it. She is not apart from the world; she *is* the world. Most witches reject any idea of heaven and hell, preferring some sort of reincarnational or pantheistic return-to-nature belief concerning the afterlife. This world, in effect, is all there is, but that is enough when it is seen not as merely dead or subject to the caprice of a despotic deity, but as alive with the love, life, and magic of the Goddess.

Being women of keen intellect and excellent education, many feminist witches are aware of the philosophical problems of "exactly what do you mean" raised by such an identification of Goddess and world. But they refuse to be pushed into saying either that such talk is "only" symbol or metaphor, or on the other hand to reduce it to abstract metaphysics. To them, such thinking is tied up with patriarchy's use of "dualisms" like spirit and matter, or of hierarchy as in saying God has dominion over man, man over woman and nature. Such thought divides to rule and kills with analysis and abstraction. For those in Dianic Wicca, the Goddess is not a theory or a rationalized belief but an experience, a way of relating to the universe which they have found profoundly liberating for themselves as women.

Some other Neo-Pagans accuse Dianic worshippers of the Goddess of merely substituting a monotheism of the divine feminine for the patriarchal God the Father, forsaking the polytheistic richness and the counterbalance of the god and goddess in "mixed" Wicca. Dianics retort that polytheistic texture is maintained in the numerous goddesses, such as those invoked in the four directions and in seasonal themes. They say that the divine male principle is not denied, since the Goddess includes it and so gives birth to both male and female from her body. But the focus of worship is solely women's mysteries. Dianics strongly believe that, inasmuch as women have too long been given no claim to divinity in most Western and Eastern religion, the need now is to concentrate on the exploration of spirituality within feminine language and experience.

A significant feature of feminist spirituality lore is discussion of an era of matriarchal social order and goddess worship that preceded the "patriarchal revolution" at the dawn of history, when father gods usurped power in heaven and men subordinated women on earth.*

Our earlier account gave a picture of what Dianic Wicca sabbats are like. In the Moon Birch Grove, sabbats are held at the quarters—that is, the equinoxes and solstices which begin the four seasons—at the "cross-quarters," a day midway between one quarter day and the next, and on a smaller scale at every full and new moon. The quarter sabbats like the one described, highly attuned to the spiritual meaning and energy of that season, are open to all sincere women who wish to attend; the cross-quarter and other sabbats are restricted to initiated members or personally invited guests. Only a very few public occasions, such as a Hiroshima Day rite against nuclear war offered one year, are open to men as well as women.

The basic purpose of sabbat worship is said to be "raising energy"— the life force which infuses one with a sense of love, joy, power, and nearness to the Goddess within and without. The "energy" is kept up by the singing and chanting throughout the rite, and circulates through the circle of hand-holding women. Yet the rite also is a vehicle for providing sacred models for one's life through the year and throughout the pilgrimage from birth to death, as we saw in the use of the Persephone myth. In particular, Moon Birch endeavors to make holy through attitude and observances aspects of a woman's life regarded as neutral if not downright polluting in the standard-brand religions: menarch, menstruation, birth-giving, lactation.

As we have seen, the spirit of Moon Birch worship can often be more light and merry than solemn. The trend is toward hanging loose to set liturgical forms, and allowing a playfully creative and intuitive spirit to supplement the regular in worship. If someone feels moved to add a word or a ceremony as it proceeds, fine. As with Neo-Pagans generally, interest in reviving something past is giving way to innovating something new that is true both to the eternal pagan spirit and to contemporary American life.

At the time of writing, Moon Birch Grove had some twenty initiates and a "core group" of eight women. It is thus not large, though as many as seventy have come to open circles, and all indications are that it is part of a growing interest in feminist spirituality. Most members are college graduates; by profession they include a psychological counselor, an artist, a librarian, a massage therapist and writer, an instrument maker, musicians, and a legal secretary. In this group all are aged roughly between eighteen and thirty-five, and represent a variety of ethnic and cultural backgrounds.

The Wiccan journey, like that of Columbus, began as a voyage to an ancient land and has turned into an argosy of discovery instead. Whether humans have ever before known the separate sacredness of male and

---

*Some archaeological and mythological evidence supports this, ranging from the prevalence of goddess figures in Europe from the Neolithic era before the ancient civilizations to the removal from center stage in many mythic cycles of the primordial Earth Mother, Gaia of the Greeks, in favor of celestial kings and warriors and even saviours. The issue is, however, much argued by scholars, and many religious feminists are willing to accept primal goddess-worship as perhaps itself a mythic idealization, but one that, like all good myths, can be very life-giving and religiously true.

female, or of the swinging seasons and the gathered coven with its rising energy, in quite the same way, perhaps no one can now say. But Wiccans in our day seem to have found something that is bound to stay with us, and one way or another will have an effect on the religion of the future.

NATIVE AMERICAN SPIRITUALITY REVIVED: THE DREAMWEAVERS

It really got moving in the spring of 1982. Then, under the sponsorship of the Ojai Foundation, a California center for modern spirituality, Harley Swiftdeer led a multiracial pilgrimage to traditional Native American holy places and power centers in the Southwest. The journey ended but the pilgrimage did not; many participants and their friends had been caught up in a new dream: recover for all peoples of whatever race the nearly-lost spiritual lore of America's first and longest inhabitants, who doubtless knew—and know—its spiritual contours better than anyone else. Find once again the wonder of the shaman's vision quest, the initiatory power of the sweat lodge, the healing power of native herbs and crystals, the gods released by dance and chant.

They continued working under Harley Swiftdeer. Swiftdeer, of mixed Cherokee and Irish descent, states that he had a powerful spiritual experience in a helicopter during the Vietnam War which turned his attention toward spiritual things. He studied for many years under the legendary "Grandfather" Tom Wilson, a Navaho shaman and sometime President of the Native American Church*; he is rumored to have been one inspiration of Carlos Castaneda's celebrated "Don Juan" books. Swiftdeer established the Deer Lodge, a group of people interested in the serious exploration of the Native spiritual path; the Dreamweavers is a semi-independent teaching unit of the Deer Lodge.

The revival had other roots as well, of course. Midcentury books on shamanism and myth like those of Mircea Eliade and Joseph Campbell had helped reawaken the beat of the medicine drum. The sixties and seventies vogue for nature and ecology had prepared the way for the fresh discovery of hierophany in stone, tree, and sun, and the "consciousness expanding" trip of the same decades for the vision quest. For that matter, as we have seen, an interest in Native shamanism has been a longstanding theme of alternative religion in America (especially Spiritualism) going back at least to the days of the "Shawnee Prophet." So far as the contemporary meeting of Native and immigrant America is concerned, it is said, though apparently this cannot be verified, that in August 1980 the Sweet Medicine Council, an assembly of medicine men recognized by more than one tribe, determined that the time had come to open their spiritual teachings to non-Indians, for their preservation and for the benefit of the world; it is also said that the "Grandmothers," elderly women both in this world and in

---

*The Native American Church is a religious organization combining Christian and Native American features with a sizable following among Natives; it is known for its legally-recognized sacramental use of peyote.

spirit who share custodial power over the sacred lore, concurred in this decision. (On the other hand, it must be noted that Harley Swiftdeer and others teaching Native American spirituality to non-Indians have suffered much abuse and even violence from some tribesmen who believe they have no right to do this.)

Several teachers have been part of the revival. Besides Swiftdeer, there is Sun Bear and Lame Deer and their groups. The anthropologist Michael Harner, an authority on South American shamanism, has become an important instructor in its practice. We shall, however, concentrate on the Dreamweavers as an example of the movement.

The Dreamweavers are headquartered in a semirural private home located above a deep canyon high in the mountains overlooking the Los Angeles basin. It is the residence of Brigit and Kathleen, two Roadwomen or teachers of the Native spiritual path. Upon entering this home, one is immediately struck by evidence of a remarkable, even magical, ambience. The main room is full of crystals of all sizes and structures, the colorful designs of native art, kachinas and heavy Mayan faces, together with the wizards and winged horses of Western lore. The emphasis is on light and color; clear and colored glass hangings are everywhere, casting their rainbows over these collected revenants of a thousand dreams. Light sifts also over a rich assortment of books, including titles on color, on ancient Druids and Egyptians, on magical erudition and the *Star Wars* movies, as well as on Native Americana.

In this enchanted atmosphere, one learns about the teaching and practice of the Dreamweavers. Teaching is almost subsumed in practice, for the Dreamweavers' trail is walked through the inexpressible awakenings wrought by experience far more than ideas. Yet certain themes emerge. Grandmother Earth is alive and we are her children. Like rebellious adolescents who think they know more than their parents, we have strained at the bonds linking us to her; for the sake of our own authentic growth we need to get back in right harmony with her, and in so doing with our own true nature as beings capable of deep memory and divine vision. The rhetoric of the movement is full of language suggestive of this perspective: the use of life, parental expressions for nature, idealizing human activity as a dance. Nature itself holds the energies we require to get into proper relationship with Earth. The Sun is male energy, the Moon female; these can be tapped and balanced. Crystals, "the brain cells of Grandmother Earth," have remarkable healing and spiritual properties when employed with wisdom. But the movement stresses that, while the trail it pursues can awaken psychic powers, these are not ends in themselves and must be explored with caution.

Reincarnation is an important concept in the Dreamweavers. We have, they say, danced in other temples in past lifetimes; its practices can arouse the "memory circles" where that recall is stored, whether from ancient Egypt or the primordial woods in which the Druids sang their spells. There have, in fact, been eight great Circles, or major religions, in human life, each divided into twelve tribes. At the present, with the Earth passing through a great crisis, the time has come for them to draw together and exchange wisdom, with emphasis on the primal shamanistic lore which underlies and unifies all on the deepest level. To this end Harley Swiftdeer has, for example, travelled to Africa to share medicine-secrets with the shamans of that ancient continent, discovering that their world and that of the Native American enjoy much convergence. A "Rainbow Festival," bringing together religionists of many backgrounds holding in common a special interest in the way of the wizard and the shaman, was convened in Switzerland in the summer of 1985.

Dreamweavers practice centers around a trail of initiatory ordeals. The vision quest entails fourteen of these, including the "Night in the Mountain of Fear," spending a night alone in a medicine circle in the mountains; dancing for three days and three nights around a tree chanting; the "Hole in the Ground," when one spends one day in a shallow grave lightly covered with earth; and the sweat lodge experience, when one fasts amid heat and steam, partaking only of the sacred pipe, until vision of one's Guardian Spirit is vouchsafed.

The Dreamweavers also do healing rites, for giving away is as important as gaining. The afflicted person is placed in the middle of a healing circle, comprised of eight dancers holding mirrors to contain the energy, while in the center the "doctor" works chiefly with herbs and crystals.

Besides the healing and initiatory pathwork, the Dreamweavers conduct open workshops on such topics as crystals. The groups consist of some twenty-five apprentices, who may become teachers (Roadwomen) when the path is completed. The majority are college-educated professional people, averaging thirty-five years of age. Many previously had been on such other paths as the Wiccan or the Buddhist. They seem finally to have been drawn away from that which is exotic, whether European or Asian, toward a yearning to explore that which is primordially American. The group is predominantly women, but seems gradually to be becoming more balanced.

Native American spirituality can weave dreams of glowing color and intricate balance, but it is also second to none as a hard path testing to the extreme one's powers of psychic and even physical endurance when it is fully undertaken. But one senses that, in our "advanced" safety-netted and pushbutton society, some are drawn to it just for that reason. They want to be tested, and to know what the wise knew in a day when nature was pure but human life demanded the warrior's strength, the hunter's patience, and the sacred dancer's balance, and each person finally had to meet his or her dreams and gods alone. As an Eskimo shaman said to the Danish explorer Rasmussen: "All true wisdom is only found far from men, out in the great solitude, and it can be acquired only through suffering. Privations and suffering are the only things that can open a man's mind to that which is hidden from others."

CEREMONIAL MAGIC: THE OTA, ORDO TEMPLI ASTARTES

In the spring of 1970 one of the authors attended a meeting of a number of the leading ceremonial magicians, Satanists, and witches in the Los Angeles area. The meeting was held in an apartment in Hollywood, dark save for red and black lamps. Against one wall was a slowly spinning hypnotic disc. In the gloom about twenty people sat talking in low, vibrant voices; conversing on magic amid such an atmosphere was part of the self-image which shaped the life of each.

Yet it was also a question of image which had brought them together. It was shortly after the Tate murder case, the movie *Rosemary's Baby*, and certain sensational magazine articles about the occult. These people were concerned for the public relations image of their craft. However, it was not easy to arrive at any common plan of action, though the discussion was fascinating to an outsider. Witches, magicians, and Satanists did not wish to be identified with one another. More important, there were two kinds of attitudes toward public relations (both often apparent in the same person). First was a feeling of wanting the public to understand that they were kind, harmless folk who had their own religion, an ancient one with much to be said for it, and that the popular notion that they were people who perform vile rites and work evil was base calumny worthy of the witch hunt days. Secondly there was a feeling of rejoicing in being known as a great wizard, or even Satanist, and loving the glamor of dark mystery and strange arcane rites which clusters around them. The legend which goes before the mighty sorcerer is, in fact, a part of his technique for attaining the real purpose of magic, some argued, the opening up of new levels of consciousness. It is like Gurdjieff's enigmas, or Crowley's exaggeration; it shakes loose the ordinary footings of the mind.

This led to a second discussion on what really happens in invocation. The central act of ceremonial magic is the calling up of a god, generally one of the pagan gods of Egypt, Babylon, or Greece, or one of the "demons" of vaguely Alexandrian or Hebrew derivation mentioned in the old grimoires. Those present who were involved with ceremonial magic debated what actually occurs. Some said that they truly see a figure, however vague and shadowy, appear in the magic triangle at the heart of the rite. Others argued, with some sophistication, that the real invocation is an evocation. It is a calling up of the veiled wisdom and splendor of the unconscious; the intense emotion and suggestive setting of the rite enable gods to surface. As one put it, "I don't know whether the god is objectively outside myself or is a part of myself, but it doesn't matter because in any case he teaches me things I didn't know before."

The meaning of this remark became clearer several months later. In the fall of 1970, campuses in the Los Angeles area were blanketed with a flyer which read:

THE OTA PRESENTS AN OPEN CLASS IN THE ART OF . . . MAGICK

. . . THE 'GREAT WORK' OF THE HERMETIC PHILOSOPHERS, THE SECRETS OF SOLOMON, AGRIPPA, CROWLEY—THE AUTHENTIC TECHNIQUES AND ANCIENT RITUALS THAT OPENED THE FORBIDDEN DOOR TO IMMORTALITY!

MAGICK is not to be confused with witchcraft (wicca) and has nothing whatsoever to do with satanism. However, real MAGICK is not for the timid soul or the prude. The student of MAGICK is concerned with *eternal* truths and values.

Operations in certain spheres require courage and total personal commitment. You do not have to be a recondite occult scholar to learn THE ART. In fact, the less misinformation you have assimilated the better . . . The Magickal student's greatest asset is his or her *imagination* . . .

At the bottom of the sheet phone numbers were given. The leader of the OTA turned out to be one of the magicians at the previous meeting, although the OTA in its present form is a new body. The founder has been in the practice of magic for some twenty years, and has a marvelous collection of the requisite books and equipment.

The meetings were held in private homes, but the atmosphere was unmistakable. An ornate cloth was laid over a square altar on one side, and on it lay the traditional four implements—sword, wand, cup, and pentacle. A collection of the principal books was evident behind the altar: Regardie's edition of the rituals of the Golden Dawn, Mathers's translation of Abramelin the Mage, the Goetia, the Legemeton, Barrett's *Magus,* and the like. The members of the Order were clad in long, hooded, monkish robes.

A student presented a talk on history. It was given out, rightly or wrongly, that this tradition originated in ancient Egypt in the priestly "mystery schools," was encapsulated in the Kabbalah, and is in fact the source of much of Eastern yoga, Buddhism, and so forth. It has been perpetuated in the Western esoteric tradition running down through the Golden Dawn and (in part) Crowley to the present Order.

Of greater interest was the informal discussion of the actual practice of magical operations by a group like this. As stated, they center around the evocation of a "demon"—really a pagan god, like Apollo or Astarte. As in Neoplatonic theurgy, they are invoked in a "receiver," an individual of the same sex as the deity. The group does not claim the powers of "high magic" visibly and externally to manifest the deity. The "receiver" has about the same function as a Spiritualist medium, although this term is not used. There can be either a "contact" or a "possession" evocation, depending on whether the presence of the Other is merely felt, as a force of tremendous emotional weight, or totally occupies the subject.

The presence is called up through manipulation of the implements with strong, massive gestures, and above all uttering the Words of Command for that deity in the old grimoires. The air is one of robes, fervor, incense, and the altar surrounded by the magic circle. Admittedly, on occasions the evocation fails, and may be repeated over and over. When it comes, though, the feeling is unmistakable. The "receiver" shakes and becomes transformed with the visage of the god. Then, the deity must be dismissed, or serious psychic effects will follow.

The rite is, the OTA founder stated, in a sense an evocation of madness as the world understands it. Yet it also gives wisdom and an assurance of immortality, a feeling of anagogic wonder, a knowledge of the power of will to create a world. One also hears of the conjuration of the power of visible levitation and lesser magic.

Even though ceremonial magicians will use one of the grimoires as a guide, the details of the rite may vary from one magician to another, for the purpose is to produce an effect which is basically psychological, and different practitioners may find different procedures best suited to the individual personality. Yet there are three basic steps.

First, the magician purifies himself by fasting, continence, and breaking the ordinary pattern of his life, as preparation for producing the altered state of consciousness to be evoked in the ritual. He takes elaborate steps to prepare the implements. He may perform quiet routine rites to the four directions or to consecrate the tools.

Second, he robes himself and stands in the circle, behind the altar, and holds the wand and sword. Smoke from incense and burning herbs swirls around him. He begins an incantation to call up the spirit he has determined to summon. If there is a receiver, he or she stands beside him; other members of the circle present are at hand. He speaks in a tone of command, uttering the words in a rhythmic, hypnotic voice, over and over. Thus his inner energies are raised to a fever pitch. As one magician put it, he is deliberately inducing a "temporary insanity." In this atmosphere, surrounded by the fumes of the burning herbs and the intense engagement of psychic fervor, the spirit is believed to appear—the "receiver" trembles and beholds the god in a crystal or dark mirror set up in the triangle.

Third, after the invocation or evocation, it is necessary to dismiss the spirit. This is believed just as important as summoning it, for a spirit who remains after the rite can cause no small amount of harm.[9]

In the mid-1980s the Ordo Templi Astartes was flourishing as one of the most active ceremonial magic groups in the country. Its magical temple was now equipped with a cyclorama of the Zodiac thirty-six feet in diameter to aid in initiations taking candidates through the constellations and the inner gods they unlock. The group put somewhat less emphasis, in fact, on the classical evocational magic and more on opening inner psychic centers correlated with the Kabbalistic tree of life, and on transformations attained through a variety of innovative and ingenious rituals—one includes lying on one's back and allowing oneself to be drawn into a flickering dark mirror illumined by candlelight suspended above. The OTA speaks of "building your own religion and making it work for you"—a statement which well reflects the creative, eclectic spirit presently gathering force in this group and much of the Neo-Pagan movement. It has fifteen or so active members, largely young professional people, together with about the same number of additional occasional participants.

Reading Selection: The OTA

Here follows an account of a magical evocation performed by the OTA.

On May 6, 1977, the author attended an evocation of Astarte, the ancient Canaanite goddess of love, performed by the Ordo Templi Astartes. The rite exemplified how the intensive ritual work in a close-knit group can arouse psychic energy leading to strong ecstatic or religious experience.

group can arouse psychic energy leading to strong ecstatic or religious experience.

This affiliation of eight or ten persons generally does an hour or so of yoga asanas (postures) and pranayama (breathing exercises) before a magical operation in order to get into a light transic state. They then stare at jewels of the right color according to laws of correspondence for the deity to be evoked, in order to reach a calm and one-pointed state of mind. They next sit around a table bearing bright zodiacal and planetary signs and a candle of the proper hue. Holding hands, they engage in breathing exercises and spirtually absorb the rays of the candle, passing the power around by squeezing hands. Then, robed, they stand and silently enter the magical temple.

Initial entry into this fane of wizardry is an overwhelming experience. On the floor was a large pentacle, or five-pointed star, laid in a circle. Just outside it were a wide mirror on a low stand and a desk uplifting a large ritual book. The many diagrams and esoteric ornaments were painted in brilliant luminiscent colors that glowed in the ultraviolet light.

The group first lit candles in the four cardinal directions. They chanted together a creedlike affirmation, which emphasized that magical evocation is done by power of will. The human will, they believe, can make itself sovereign over all entities cosmic and intrapsychic, for it expresses the divine essence of human beings. An invocation of the spiritual powers, more reverent in tone, was also said. After the initiates walked around the pentacle seven times chanting, they took their places.

The principal parts in the rite were those of the Receiver and Operator. The Receiver, a woman (since the deity was female), stood before the mirror with a candle in each hand. In her, it was believed, the goddess would manifest her personality and power. Also a glimpse might be caught of the passing glory in the mirror.

The Operator or Magus stood within the circle facing the Receiver. His function, supported by the concentrated energies of the entire group, was by the force of his will and his magical words to summon up Astarte into the woman's body and the mirror. Thus, he repeated over and over an invocation of Astarte in a chanting tone, his voice full of concentrated power. The emphasis was on his *command* to the ancient goddess in the name of Elohim (God).

Breaking the mood, he quietly asked the Receiver if Astarte was now there. She said in a low voice, "One more time." The Magus called out the invocation once more. The Receiver shook; the candles moved, making dim patterns in the mirror. Then suddenly the Receiver laughed, a lilting, sexual, musical laugh quite different from the woman's ordinary tone. At this point I myself felt a surge of tremendous tingling excitement.

The Operator addressed the now present goddess. I was introduced. Astarte said, through the lips of the Receiver, "I already know Robert Ellwood." She was asked petitions by others who came up to face her and touched her shoulder to receive power.

Someone inquired if she had an oracle—a divine message for the group or anyone in it. She said she would give one later to the right person, as it was private. To petitions she gave short answers, such as "You always have my blessing."

Finally the Magus asked the Receiver, "Is she still there?" The answer was yes, the goddess-presence was still strong, but she was leaving soon. Then followed a solemn dismissal of the visitant, an apology to her for the trouble, and a short rite of banishing, for which everyone knelt, as the Magus swung a sword to the four quarters.

Away from the temple, a critique succeeded the ritual. The Order keeps a magical log of all operations. Members of the group now submitted information for it from this experience. That was done in a generally critical, yet humorous and bantering tone. They joked even about the gods and the rituals—someone called Aphrodite "a flip goddess"—and recalled amusing incidents from other rites. It was very much like the "in group" jocularity of any religion, often found especially among seminarians. The members of the Order at this point gave an impression of being immensely alive, enjoying life, keyed up, and outgoing. The rite itself, the potent atmosphere of the temple and the transitory presence of divinity, had clearly induced a residual euphoria.

The Magus, also head of the Order, first asked about visual experience. No one had seen anything apart from the contact change in the personality of the Receiver, except for one person who saw a flashing glimpse of a woman other than the Receiver in the mirror. The Receiver delivered two or three messages she had gotten from the goddess but had felt it inappropriate to speak in the temple itself. For example, one member was told that she cried too much. The recipient of this admonition claimed she cried very little, but someone else commented that maybe it was not meant literally, that perhaps she cried too much internally.

From this discussion, and also from the asides in the temple itself, it was evident that the consciousness of members of the magical Order operated on two levels at the same time. On one hand, they were caught up in the presence of divinity; or the other, they, even the Operator and Receiver, maintained a critical distance from what was happening, being self-aware manipulators and observers of the performance. Yet the mystical experience was certainly real, however produced and interpreted. I myself have very, very seldom known such a powerful and unanticipated change of consciousness or bolt of ecstatic energy passing through me as I did at the climax of this rite.

From ROBERT S. ELLWOOD, JR., *Mysticism and Religion* (Englewood Cliffs, NJ: Prentice-Hall, Inc., 1980), pp. 136–38. Reprinted by permission.

SATANISM

One of the participants in the discussion about the public image of Witchcraft and magic was a leader of a Satanist group called The Brotherhood of the Ram. This individual was also the proprietor of a night club. The club had one wall covered with satanic symbols—inverted cross, inverted star with the two points up, ram's head—and was obviously the scene of after-hours rituals. Adherents of this group must sign a "pact" and seal it with their own blood—a pledge to renounce all other devotion, and adore Satan alone, to renounce "chrism baptism" and follow the way of joy and pleasure with Satan now and forever.

However, the traditional Satanic act of worship, the "black mass," appears to be declining in popularity.[10] It is being replaced by more informal scenarios, ranging from gruesome animal sacrifices to recitations of poems of Baudelaire to evocations of Satan in the manner of the ceremonial magicians. In the group mentioned, the room contained items which the leader was able to bring home from his work in a pathology laboratory. These included the traditional "Hand of Glory," a human head with the top of the skull neatly taken off, as well as an alleged ancient mummy. Expression in worship consisted of florid invocations to Satan, some in Latin, initiation of new members by their signing a pact and sealing it with blood, and a rite of exchange of psychic energy between a girl and the mummy. Many Satanic rites include liberal use of drugs.

Interpretations of the meaning of Satan vary from "traditionalist" views of him as the antagonist of the Christian God to modern perspectives which see Satan as a symbol of the "life-force," creative evolution, or the affirmation of innocent pleasure. Proponents of the first see Satan more or less as the Miltonic Lucifer, a proud but heroic rebel with whom they identify. He is, contrary to lies told about him by the churches, able to reward his followers with an eternity of pleasure, and with opportunity for revenge, around his dark throne.

A more sophisticated view is characteristic of the well-known Church of Satan founded in San Francisco by Anton LaVey in 1966 on Walpurgisnacht, the eve of Mayday when, in Germany, witches were believed to fly about and celebrate. On that macabre eve LaVey shaved his head and proclaimed himself priest of the new faith. With a background as animal trainer, criminologist, and ceremonial magician, he founded the Church of Satan, he says, because he felt the ordinary churches were twisting and distorting the nature of man, making it impossible for him to find true joy. He speaks of a doctrine of divine nonintervention. If there is a God, he is unable to intervene in human events. Spirituality, therefore, has no place on earth and its practice can only be self-deceptive, leading to the futility of a life based on a false premise. If humans are to worship anything, it ought to be their own natural desires, which are what is closest to them and control them. Satan is a symbol of the material world and this carnal human nature. LaVey believes it is necessary for one to indulge oneself, so long as one does nothing which hurts another who does not want to be hurt. To him Satan represents a counterbalancing force. God is remote and unconcerned natural law, but Satan embodies the life, joy, pleasure, and particularity intimate and important to humans.

The rituals of the group include a "black mass" with the body of a nude woman as the altar. They also include a rite of communal cursing in which members ventilate resentment and anger. In performances virtually approaching psychodrama Satanists act out means of coping with people and circumstances threatening to them.

In the 1980s the Church of Satan claimed to be continuing to grow, to have established overseas headquarters in London and Amsterdam. However, in the mid-1970s a portion of its membership split from it to form a new magical, though not explicitly Satanistic, organization called the Temple of Set.[11]

The need to identify oneself as a Satanist is a complex and devious thing. It indicates, certainly, a powerful inner rebellion. It usually goes with a strong power drive or, alternatively, a desire to be a "slave." It often expresses sociopathic traits, either mild or in some cases of highly disturbing intensity. Yet in other cases individuals appear to find self-acceptance and integration in the Satanist experience.[12]

Reading Selection: Satanism

Undoubtedly the most readable and systematic modern exposition of Satanism as a way of thought and life is Anton Szandor LaVey's *The Satanic Bible*. It also, no doubt, is the most moderate and sane, for while LaVey offers much bombastic invective against conventional religion and morality, obviously designed to titillate or shock, he is careful to avoid committing the Satanist to an exploitative or sadistic attitude toward man or beast. The Satanic religious mystique is what distinguishes it from the hedonism of a fundamentally normal salesman on a convention trip. There is no talk of orgy and sacrifice as rites, or of blood or vengeance.

Love is one of the most intense emotions felt by man; another is hate. Forcing yourself to feel indiscriminate love is very unnatural. If you try to love everyone you only lessen your feelings for those who deserve your love. Repressed hatred can lead to many physical and emotional ailments. By learning to release your hatred towards those who deserve it, you cleanse yourself of these malignant emotions and need not take your pent-up hatred out on your loved ones. . . .

Every pharisaical religionist claims to love his enemies, even though when wronged he consoles himself by thinking, "God will punish them." Instead of admitting to themselves that they are capable of hating their foes and treating them in the manner they deserve, they say: "There, but for the grace of God, go I," and "pray" for them. Why should we humiliate and lower ourselves by drawing such inaccurate comparisons?

Satanism has been thought of as being synonymous with cruelty and brutality. This is so only because people are afraid to face the truth—and the truth is that human beings are not all benign or all loving. Just because the Satanist admits he is capable of both love *and* hate, he is considered hateful. On the contrary, because he is able to give vent to his hatred through ritualized expression, he is far *more* capable of love—the deepest kind of love. By honestly recognizing and admitting to both the hate and the love he feels, there is no confusing one emotion with the other. Without being able to experience one of these emotions, you cannot *fully* experience the other.

ANTON SZANDOR LAVEY, *The Satanic Bible* (New York: Avon Books, 1969), pp. 64–65. © Anton Szandor LaVey, 1969.

NOTES

[1]The historical and ritual documents of the Golden Dawn have been published by the former secretary of Aleister Crowley, Israel Regardie, as *The Golden Dawn* (2nd ed.) (St. Paul, Minnesota: Llewellyn Publications, 1970).

[2]The best biography is J. Symonds, *The Great Beast* (New York: Roy Publishers, Inc., 1952). See also Symonds's *The Magic of Aleister Crowley* (London: Muller, 1958), and J. Symonds and K. Grant, eds., *The Confessions of Aleister Crowley* (New York: Hill and Wang, Inc., 1970). The latter is his autobiography, or "autohagiography," as he liked to call it.

[3]Starhawk, *The Spiral Dance: A Rebirth of the Ancient Religion of the Great Goddess* (San Francisco: Harper & Row, Publishers, 1979), pp. 77–78.

[4]See Gerald Gardner, *Witchcraft Today* (New York: Citadel Press, 1970).

[5]Henry Bailey Stevens, *The Recovery of Culture* (New York: Harper & Row, Publishers, 1953) is not as well known as the works of the other writers cited. But this book has had a deep influence on nature utopians like Frederick Adams. Stevens, an ardent vegetarian, argues that man was first a tender of trees, that there was a horticultural era before the "fall" into hunting and the subsequent sacrifice-linked agricultural period. This early horticultural paradise is symbolized in myth by such names as Hesperides, Avalon, etc.

[6]Frederick C. Adams, "The Kore," p. 1. © Feraferia, Inc. 1969.

[7]The Feraferian seasonal cycle is generally derived from the Celtic, although otherwise the group has been moving more and more in a Greek direction. The nine seasons represented by the nine pillars in the henge are: (1) *Ostara—East.* The birth of the divine male/female pair, Kouros and Kore; (2) *Beltane—Southeast.* The emergence of the Divine Maiden and the Kouros from childhood; pubescence and engagement. (3) *Midsummer—South.* The embrace of Kore and Kouros in the spirit of ripening love; marriage and coitus. (4) *Lugnasad—Southwest.* The congression in love of Kore and Kouros, revealing the Kore as a whole. (5) *Harvest Home—West.* Homecoming; Kore blossoms in the earth landscape; reaping the Harvest. (6) *Samhain—Northwest.* The Kore becomes sleepy and prepares to retire; the end of the harvest. (7) *Repose—The Center.* The Kore retreats beneath the earth, where all cosmic energy gathers, hidden from sight. The entire universe in a state of rest. (8) *Yule—North.* All life forces are gathered beneath the earth, converging inside the body of Kore. The life forces of the universe are thus impregnated in her body. (9) *Oimlec—Northeast.* The end of gestation; another divine Kore/Kouros pair is ready for birth. The seeds beneath the earth crack and begin to grope for the surface.

[8]This account of the sabbat of the Moon Birch Grove is based on the description in Cynthia Eller, *Feminist Spirituality and Social Transformation:* unpublished M.A. thesis, University of Southern California, 1984.

[9]For the outline of the three stages of a magical operation, we are indebted to the article "The Roots of Ritual Magic," in *Man, Myth, and Magic*, No. 11, pp. 297–300.

[10]See Arthur Lyons, *The Second Coming: Satanism in America* (New York: Dodd, Mead & Co., 1970).

[11]For a sociological study of a comparable group, see Jennie Graham Scott, *The Magicians* (New York: Irvington Publishers, 1983).

[12]See Edward J. Moody, "Magical Therapy: An Anthropological Investigation of Contemporary Satanism," in Irving I. Zaretsky and Mark P. Leone, eds., *Religious Movements in Contemporary America* (Princeton: Princeton University Press, 1974), pp. 355–82.

7

THE GANGES FLOWS WEST:
Indian Movements in America

The official Holy Land for most Americans is Palestine, a tiny, rocky, coastal strip of land at the eastern end of the Mediterranean. Here a few shepherd tribes exchanged contentiousness over wells and flocks for the rugged justice of a divine law. Burned by its righteousness, glowering prophets did not shrink from confronting kings. Later one of its children bloodied the wood of that symbol which has since haunted rampant and virile Europe.

But another holy land also worries the consciousness of the West. This land is also possessed by religion, but a land could scarcely be more different from Palestine. This land is not small and bare, but vast and lush with broad holy rivers, deep jungle noisy with parrots, and northern mountains gleaming white as the dawn of the day of creation. Here patriarchs and prophets tenaciously holding to God's law are replaced by sensuous and surrealistic gods and goddesses as brilliant and dreamlike and bizarre as tropical flowers.

Here palaces and temples raise towers so strange as to seem almost botanical. Matted-haired masters of the soul remain bent unmoving in red dawn and sunset. Shaven priests mutter in an old and sacred tongue before the holy flame. Here the rough equity of the law does not run, and here there have been human beings by birth so impure they could not emerge in the light of day, and others clad in peacock plumes and the shifting, colored gleam of jewels. This is India, whose very name and diversity suggests a wonder and imagination worthy of God.

One of the authors first visited a "native" Hindu temple on the island of Fiji where a large Indian population is found. It was by the side of a dusty road, and the oppressive, humid air and vegetation suggested southern India. First, upon entering the open-air precincts, was a great lingam, the vaguely phallic pillar which is the most common devotional symbol of Shiva. The emblem of this god, the Absolute from which all cosmic energies, creative and destructive alike, derive, was surrounded by open grillwork. Offering pans of colored rice placed in front of the lingam attracted innumerable birds, who flew in through the grill to peck at it. An image of Shiva's animal "vehicle," Nandi the bull, faced the shrine. Behind the bull stood Ganesha, the elephant-headed god, remover of worldly or spiritual obstacles, who is Shiva's son. The base of his open-air statue was piled with rotting fruit.

A little behind the lingam stood a temple building, a dark sanctuary with a black figure with ghostly oval white eyes. A single lamp flamed beside him. This was Krishna, the marvelous child, the divine lover, the hero, he whose every glance and word and breath has impenetrable mystery. On walls between the entrance and the image were crude paintings of the milkmaids who, consumed with inseparable passions of human and divine love, followed Krishna about on moonlight nights as he played his flute and danced and sported with them. On these dank, foul-smelling walls they ran decorously in full billowing skirts. About the grassy yard of the temples wandered children, domestic animals, and squadrons of birds.

The Hinduism of this temple complex is not the form in which it has been generally presented by its Western advocates. Yet this is the Hinduism of India's vast peasant culture which underlies the rest. Like all such cultures it has its deep wisdom and soaring mythical images, as well as its provinciality. Without taking this Hinduism into account, one cannot really understand the message of the "export versions" of Hinduism.

Most striking was the sense of continuity between the temple and the riotous, rotting organic life around it. This was no spotless American church, dead but for cut flowers, doors and windows shut tight against all incursions of nonhuman life. Although made by human hands, Hindu temples seem to grow out of the soil like prodigious plants. The human society and temples of India seem like growths stretching away from nature yet unsevered from its veins. They are products of some unfathomable biological interaction between our seething mental and physical drives and the primordial tropical energy of nature. It is to the *biological* flavor of Hinduism that one returns for understanding. Hinduism presses the potential of biology far beyond where others might set up dualisms of man and nature or mind and body.

Hindu society is not a contractual state, but a great organism. By means of the caste system, every individual finds a place through the biological process of birth and contributes to the whole like a cell of the body. The lingam suggests assimilation of the divine life-force to the sexual—a force creative and destructive, like God, and bearing the closest organic equivalents to eternity, the genetic molecules.

The numinous Hindu gods, dwelling in the dark cave-like interior of the temple (called the *garbha* or "womb"), are uncanny just because they are forms half-remembered, surfacings from the subtle deeps where mind grapples with such biological demigods as parents, sex, food, and shadowy recollections of the womb and the magically omnipotent infant. Yoga requires a skillful and persistent combined engineering of physiological and psychological forces. It says these two are ultimately one. It suggests the goal, *samadhi*, blissful unconditioned awareness, is the epitome or ultimate objective of the unceasing biological process. It is a total unveiling of that consciousness and perception which life seems to want, free of the limitations life ordinarily imposes. This attainment is, for Hinduism, the real transcendence. To Hinduism, the meaningful dualism is not of man and nature, or of mind and body, but of the infinite or unconditioned and the finite or conditioned. Mind, the unconscious, human society, and nature are all part of a biological continuum, all on one side of the dualism, because they are all alike conditioned; only the breakthrough which sees them all at once and so makes the many one moves to the other side. It is no blasphemy that birds and gods share the same offerings; it symbolizes they are alike in the circle of conception and consumption.

It is doubtless India's willingness explore and exploit the full magic of humankind's psychosomatic nature that has appealed to many Westerners. In the spiritual paths of India, there is, of course, place for self-denial, but no small psychological difference lies between the asceticism of respectful cooperation with the body and deliberate sexual sublimation, and the asceticism of warfare between the spirit and the flesh. Even more important, perhaps, the tales of fabulous lore and holy men of wondrous powers allow a new sanctification of the romantic faculties of marvel in days of minimalized belief—no wonder of India is greater than that of the splendid divine presence within. For some who have made the *Journey to the East* of Hermann Hesse's novel (often physically never leaving the West), it is the quest for the Distant which unlocks the Past, the sunrise East of ultimate origins—for the secret of lost identity, for the barely remembered splendor of the childhood world. The secret of this quest for the individual is to find the unity of mind, fantasy, and body; its myth is the shaman-like flight to a faraway and extraordinary land.

Consciously at least, the fundamental attraction of Hinduism for many Westerners has been the hope it holds up for the experience of radical nondualism. Nondualism or Advaita is a major strand of the message of Vedanta, the most important school of Hindu philosophy in recent centuries. Of course, most Hindus are not consciously so much Advaita Vedantists as "dualists" who worship one or another of the gods as personal and "other." Some quite sophisticated theistic philosophies have grown out of this tradition, whether of the "modified nondualistic" or radically dualistic type, to interpret that sense of difference from God which moves persons to worship God. The Krishna Consciousness movement has come out of one of those theistic traditions which sees Krishna as the single supreme God with whom we can exchange love. But despite this, one senses that there is a level on which Vedanta best explains much of Hindu culture, and that it is the quest for access to the nondualistic experience which activates most of the West's spiritual interest in India.

The realization of the unity of spirit and biology, of the splendid presence within, suggests leaving behind all the ambiguity of history, the nonintegrated personality, and the nonintegrated cosmos. India implies to Westerners that this experience is not dependent on time or place or creed, or need be despaired of, but can be attained anywhere, any time, with right help and right procedure, for it is the way things really are. There is only Brahman, the universal Absolute, who is the pure undifferentiated reality inside everything, to whom the world is just a drama or game. Probably many have come to Hindu groups, believing that if they could really comprehend and make real within such passages as this from one of the ancient Upanishads, they would know all that really needs to be known, and all would be well.

O Brahman Supreme!
Formless art thou, and yet
(Though the reason none knows)
Thou bringest forth many forms;
Thou bringest them forth, and then
Withdrawest them to thyself.
Fill us with thoughts of thee!

Thou art the fire,
Thou art the sun,
Thou art the air,
Thou art the moon,
Thou art the starry firmament,

Thou art Brahman Supreme:
Thou art the waters—thou
The creator of all!

Thou art woman, thou art man,
Thou art the youth, thou art the maiden,
Thou art the old man tottering with his staff;
Thou facest everywhere.

Thou art the dark butterfly,
Thou art the green parrot with red eyes,
Thou art the thunder cloud, the seasons, the seas
Without beginning art thou,
Beyond time, beyond space.
Thou art he from whom sprang
The three worlds.

One thou art, one only.
Born from many wombs,
Thou hast become many:
Unto thee all return.
Thou, Lord God, bestowest all blessings,
Thou the Light, thou the Adorable One.
Whoever finds thee
Finds infinite peace.[1]

The several sides of Hinduism have immigrated to the United States in different waves. The first and most influential, of course, has been philosophic. If one accepts the not unreasonable presupposition that there was some Hindu and Buddhist impact on Neoplatonism, then the whole alternative reality tradition in the West has never been without some savor of India. This Upanishadic strain of thought was rediscovered through direct access to the sources in modern translations such as those of Ram Mohan Roy in the early nineteenth century. Ralph Waldo Emerson was deeply affected by this kind of thought, as was Schopenhauer in Germany. The centrality of this teaching was affirmed by the first Hindu-inspired religious organizations established in the West, the Vedanta Societies.

Next to arrive were yoga groups, as though to supply means for attaining concretely the promises of Vedanta. Lastly, in the Krishna Consciousness group has come *bhakti,* devotional Hinduism. It is strongly opposed to the nondualistic interpretation of Hinduism, worshipping Krishna as a personal God other than man or the cosmos.

There are other aspects of Hinduism too. The careful, precise rituals of the Brahmans and the pious householder, so different in tone from the emotional waves of bhaktic fervor, have found less favor, although many Vedantists practice some of them. The caste system is little more than an embarrassment. On the other hand, karma yoga, the ideal of liberation through selfless action in the world made so famous and related specifically to the nonviolence of Mohandas Gandhi, has lastingly changed Western politics and manifested itself in such men as Martin Luther King. If this gift of Hinduism has produced no particular group, that is because its influence has been far too broad for such expression.

Let us not forget in our preoccupation with Hinduism, the dominant religious tradition of India, that there are other religions in India. Indeed, India is the land of religions *par excellence.* Buddhism had its birth there, although it later became virtually extinct in India. (There has been a modest revival of Indian Buddhism in recent decades.) Although the Indian subcontinent was divided between the Republic of India and the Islamic state of Pakistan following independence in 1947, there still remains a large Muslim population. And there are other religious communities. These include the Jains, who originated during the sixth century B.C., and, unlike the Buddhists, have had a continuous religious existence in India. The Sikhs, a community originating much later, on the borderline between Hinduism and Islam, incorporate some ideas and practices of each of these religions (for example, Islamic monotheism and Hindu reincarnationism). The Parsees, though not a large community, have exercised economic, educational, and charitable influences out of proportion to their numbers, and, religiously, have their base in the Zoroastrianism of seventh century Persia (hence "Parsee"), from which they fled the Muslim invaders of their homeland. The Christian communities of India include not only the converts of Western missionary efforts, but, significantly, Christian churches claiming to trace their origins back to the first century and the Apostle Thomas.

Two of the groups included in this chapter show the influence of these "other" Indian religions. Meher Baba, the *avatar* of the Baba Lovers, came from a Parsee family. The dominant religious influence on him, especially as regards his choice of religious language, was Sufism, the mystical dimension of Islam. Another, as we shall see, relates mostly to the Sikh tradition, though not so much to classical Sikhism as to Neo-Sikhism as it has found expression in particular groups, especially those of the Radhasoami tradition. Eckankar did not originate in India, but it is clear that its founder, Paul Twitchell, although eclectic and somewhat creative religiously, derived some of his more important religious ideas (for example, the divine "sound current") from Indian Sikhism.

But for limitations of space, we might well have included other American religious groups of Sikh origin, for example, the Divine Light Mission the 3HO ("The Happy, Healthy, Holy Organization"). Other Hinduistically inspired groups also might have been included and some attention given to certain individuals such as Baba Ramdass (Richard Alpert), formerly associated with Timothy Leary in the promotion of LSD, and, perhaps, Jiddu Krishnamurti, the erstwhile "Star of the East" of the Theosophical Society, who continued until his death in 1986 to communicate his personal spiritual ideas to receptive audiences.

What many of the groups emanating from or inspired by India have in common is a central charismatic figure, who seems, in a manner little encountered in the West, to personify a certain spiritual path—both means and goal. It is this immanential divine—not in pantheistic theory, but in persons—that makes India endlessly intriguing to God-seekers.

THE RAMAKRISHNA MISSION AND VEDANTA SOCIETIES

The first and most influential Hindu groups in the West, the centers affiliated with the Ramakrishna Order of India, draw from the spirituality of a modern saint, Ramakrishna (1836–86), who knew virtually nothing of Western learning, and who never travelled far. Yet had the movement drawn from any other person, it would have been less deep, for Ramakrishna as much as any man summed up within himself the breadth of Hinduism: Vedanta and devotion to the gods, priesthood, yoga, and tantric sexual sublimation. He expressed the peculiarly Hindu fashion of broad mindedness by trying the devotionalism of several other religions, including Islam and Christianity, and finding in them the same spiritual essence he knew in Hinduism.

Ramakrishna was born in a country village in Bengal of Brahmin parents. In the manner of Indian holy men, marvelous tales are told of his infancy and childhood. As a young man, he went with his brother to Calcutta where they were to serve as priests in the temple of a rich widow of low caste. The temple was to Kali, the great mother, consort of Shiva, who represents the phenomenal world which both masks and reveals God. Probably no Hindu deity is less calculated to win the understanding of the West than Kali, for she represents Time and the loving and devouring Mother at once; two of her four hands hold gifts and blessing, two hold terrible devices, a bloody sword and a severed head. But some say that to understand entirely this deity is to understand the full meaning of the harsh world and the joy that lies beyond its changes.

So it was that the gentle Ramakrishna loved her with deep passion, calling her "Mother." He would take no action without first referring it to her. When he married a child bride, as arranged by his family, he insisted on calling her "Mother," identifying her with Kali, and once placed her on an altar as a living idol and worshipped her the night through. But he was also initiated into Vedanta, and it is said that in the practice of nondualistic meditation he accomplished in a night what for others would take years. When he took up experimentally the practice of Krishna devotion, he (as is customary) spiritually identified himself with the milkmaids who followed the winsome Lord around, consumed with love, and we hear that Ramakrishna's dress and mincing step in this period were so authentically feminine that not even the market women could tell the difference. In the same "total immersion" mood, he practiced what he understood to be Muslim and Christian piety.

This was Ramakrishna: entirely consumed with spirituality, childlike, sometimes impetuously demanding of his followers, possessed of a subjective virtuosity, able to comprehend and participate in any path to God.

He summarized marvelously the rich, interior spirituality of India, and pioneered in showing its relevance to the paths of the other faiths. But such a man obviously calls for a St. Paul if his image and message are to endure. Such an apostle was found in the person of Swami Vivekananda (1863–1902). Through him Ramakrishna became the preeminent window into Hinduism for the West. Vivekananda had been a modern Indian educated in the Western scientific tradition. But, dissatisfied with naturalism and scepticism, he sought out the famous Ramakrishna, just before Ramakrishna's death. He was transformed and became Ramakrishna's leading disciple. After the master's passing, Vivekananda's powerful personality, great oratorical gifts, and organizational ability made the movement into something new: an international fraternity based on Hindu principles, dedicated to service as well as mysticism.

It was in 1893 that Vivekananda came into his own. He had heard about a World Parliament of Religions to be held in Chicago in connection with the Columbian Exposition, and was determined to attend. In those days, at the height of the colonial era, to presume to bring a message from Asia to the West was an unimaginably more audacious enterprise than today. The now well-walked trail had scarcely been disturbed since antiquity. Vivekananda, not even knowing the time of the Congress, arrived in America months too early. Robbed and cheated in his innocence, he ran out of money, went on to Boston, and was reduced to begging. But he met influential friends. When he finally addressed the Congress in his turban and dramatic orange and crimson habit, his striking personality and verbal fluency overwhelmed everyone; he won a raptuous following. He was popular, indeed a social lion, wherever he went.

Upon the heels of this success, the Vedanta Society of New York was founded by Vivekananda in 1896 to perpetuate his teaching and work. In its early years, Vedanta was influential in the highest ranks of society, attracting as it always has prominent, creative, and "interesting" people, such as Sarah Bernhardt, Nicolas Tesla, Paul Carus, and Ella Wheeler Wilcox. Some unlikely Westerners—including a former socialist and a former newspaperman—became swamis of the new movement. More recent ornaments of the Society have been the prominent novelists Aldous Huxley and Christopher Isherwood.

Leaving the American work in charge of Western and Indian leaders, Vivekananda went to Europe and finally triumphally returned to his homeland in 1897. He founded the admirable Ramakrishna Order to further the saint's work. In India, seeing the need there for social service work, the Society has labored among India's teeming poor. Believing the West's poverty was spiritual, Vivekananda established the Ramakrishna Mission as a vehicle for the Order's activities and sent swamis or trained teachers and spiritual masters of the Order to the "Vedanta Centers" which had appeared in the wake of his Western travels. All too soon, in 1902, Vivekandanda died.

The Ramakrishna Mission of the Ramakrishna Order in India is the real structure of the Vedanta Centers. Each American and European center is governed by a local board of trustees, but is given spiritual leadership by a swami of the Order invited to America; in this lies what relationship they have. There is no general American Vedanta Society. Some centers are not even called Vedanta Societies, such as the Ramakrishna-Vivekananda Center of New York. There are other groups in this country, not affiliated with the Ramakrishna Mission, which also call themselves Vedanta Societies.

In some ways, Ramakrishna Mission Societies remain expressions of the turn-of-the-century enthusiasm for the East upon which it so readily capitalized. Content with the belief that it enshrines the "perennial philosophy," the Mission and its societies have not sought to adjust very conspicuously to changing spiritual vogues and moods. Possibly for this very reason, though, they generally seem stable and well established.

The Vedanta temple will usually be set in beautiful, formally landscaped grounds. Within, a simple altar will have resting on it a picture of Ramakrishna. Probably there will also be a tasteful image of a Hindu deity such as the dancing Shiva, as well as Christian images, but they will not be blatant enough to offend those who might be attracted to Hindu philosophy but put off by "idolatry."

On entering the Temple before a lecture meeting, there will be a striking quality of meditative silence. The seats will be arranged rather as in a Protestant church, but the atmosphere is somehow neither the reverent hush of the Episcopal church, nor the intense mindfulness of the Zen hall. It is rather an inward, calm peace, still and full. Many persons, with heads bowed, will be apparently in deep meditation; often meditators can be seen in the temple throughout the week as well.

The swami enters in his orange robes. A choir may present a hymn. The swami will perhaps open with the ancient Upanishadic chant: "From the unreal lead us to the real, from darkness lead us to light, from death lead us to immortality." There may be scripture, prayer, silence, announcements, and an address. Sometimes, at the close, Indian music is played, suggesting some hint of the romance of India.

Typically, Vedanta temples offer weeknight classes in the Upanishads and the *Bhagavad Gita*. The swamis also spend much time giving private spiritual instruction to students. No particular technique is advocated. The Vedanta Societies are less concerned with hatha or physical yoga, taught in so many places, than with the impartation of the nondualist philosophy, and teaching a balanced spiritual life in which the four paths of devotion, work, discrimination, and meditation are practiced harmoniously.

The traditional Hindu ritualistic worship is also a part of the Ramakrishna tradition. It may be directed toward Ramakrishna himself, as a God-realized saint and (some believe) avatar of Vishnu, or toward his consort Sri Sarada Devi, or some other Hindu deity may be one's "Chosen Ideal." To do the worship properly, one must first receive *diksha,* or initiation by receiving a mantram. Ritual worship is offered daily in all the shrines and temples of the Vedanta Society of Southern California from 12 P.M. to 1 P.M. All monastics and many householders of the Society who find this form of discipline helpful participate. The worship combines elements of Vedic, bhaktic, and tantric ritual, as do most Hindu rituals nowadays. An *arati* or vesper service is offered daily also.

Almost all members of the Society have some kind of shrine in their home where they meditate daily. If they do not undertake a complete pattern of daily ritual worship, they at least offer incense and flowers to the deity.

On certain days a special worship or *puja* is held. There is then a long ritual worship, followed by *homa* (fire offering) and eating of *prasad* or food offered during the worship. At the Hollywood Temple this is done on Sri Ramakrishna's birthday, Sri Sarada Devi's birthday, Swami Vivekananda's birthday, Swami Brahmananda's birthday, Kali puja, Shiva ratri (Indian festivals of these deities), and Christmas day. Twice a month there is a Ram Nam, a song service to the god Rama.

In southern California the Vedanta Society maintains religious houses. There are convents and monasteries in conjunction with the temples in Hollywood and Santa Barbara, and a monastery on 300 acres of hilly grassland in Trabuco Canyon, Orange County. Here a handful of monks lead a life of work, study, and some three hours of worship and meditation daily.

In all these activities, the basic message is "three fundamental truths": That the real nature of men and women is divine; that the aim of human life on earth is to unfold and manifest this Godhead, eternally existent within, but hidden; that truth is universal. These three principles are the tests for all action and belief. The good is what aids in unfolding the divine within; man is one with every creature, for all are also the divine. That truth is universal means that all religion, all gods, are manifestations of the universal Being and the path to that Godhead. It is ignorance, not seeing clearly, which causes us to be lost from the One in the many and the separate, and which causes us to worship God under personalized and conceptualized forms. All this worship can also be accepted, for it is movement away from the toils of ego.

Reading Selection: The Vedanta Society

This selection is from a very interesting book offering statements by Westerners who have been attracted to Vedanta. The writer here is the well-known novelist Christopher Isherwood.

Vedanta is non-dualistic. Psychologically, this was of the greatest importance to me; because of my fear and hatred of God as the father-figure. I don't think I could ever have swallowed what *began* with dualism. Vedanta began by telling me that I was the Atman, and that the Atman was Brahman; the Godhead was my own real nature, and the real nature of all that I experienced as the external, surrounding universe. Having taught me this, it could go on to explain that this one immanent and transcendent Godhead may project all sorts of divine forms and incarnations which are, as the Gita says, its "million faces." To the eyes of this world, the One appears as many. Thus explained, dualism no longer seemed repulsive to me; for I could now think of the gods as mirrors in which man could dimly see what would otherwise be quite invisible to him, the splendour of his own immortal image. By looking deeply and single-mindedly into these mirrors, you could come gradually to know your own real nature; and, when that nature, that Atman, was fully known and entered into, the mirror-gods would no longer be necessary, since the beholder would be absolutely united with his reflection. This approach to dualism via non-dualism appealed so strongly to my temperament that I soon found myself taking part enthusiastically in the cult of Sri Ramakrishna, and even going into Christian churches I happened to be passing, to kneel for a while before the altar. Obviously, I had been longing to do this for years. I was a frustrated devotee.

CHRISTOPHER ISHERWOOD, in *What Vedanta Means to Me*, ed. JOHN YALE (London: Rider and Co., 1961), pp. 43–44 © The Vedanta Society of Southern California.

THE SELF-REALIZATION FELLOWSHIP

Over twenty years after Vivekananda's pioneering penetration of America as a spiritual envoy from India, another representative of that land, called Paramahansa Yogananda, repeated the journey. He too made his first impact in Boston, at a congress of liberal religionists (in his case, the International Congress of Religious Liberals in 1920, held under the auspices of the Unitarian Church), but soon was headquartered in Los Angeles, which was to become the nucleus for more than 150 Self-Realization Fellowship Centers on four continents. In contrast to Vivekananda's meteoric career, Yogananda (1893–1952) remained in America over thirty years, the first Hindu master to teach in the West for such an extended period of time. A vivid and winning personality combined with his willingness to use American publicity methods to promote what he believed was something America greatly needed, and the experienced value of his teachings for many people, made an indelible mark on the course of American spirituality.

He was a yogi rather than an intellectual Vedantist, and brought with him the fundamental teaching of traditional yoga philosophy, based on the ancient Yoga Sutras of Patanjali (approximately 100 B.C.), that we, underneath all apparent limitation and frustration, are an eternal divine soul. We have drives for love, joy, and power because we have a capacity for our true inheritance, infinite and divine love, joy, and power. But because of ignorance, limitation of sight, we misdirect it toward outer things in the material world. As a yogi, Yogananda brought with him not only this teaching, but techniques for doing something about it. Through yoga one can redirect one's life-energy (*prana*) from outward things towards the opening of the centers (*chakras*) which give the spiritual sight necessary for realization of one's true nature.

The man who more than anyone else has made this teaching available to the West was born Mukunda Lal Ghosh near Calcutta. He has given us a fascinating account of his life in the well-known *Autobiography of a Yogi,* a book widely distributed by the Self-Realization Fellowship. Yogananda was a Bengali; many of the Hindu missioners to the West have been of that quick, intelligent, poetic race. His father was a prosperous and devout railway official.

There are accounts that as a child Yogananda was endowed with remarkable psychic powers. There is an impression from his autobiography that as he grew up, he increasingly sensed an unusual spiritual drive which had to be realized. With a young man's warm enthusiasm, he was fascinated by the holy men of India. He visited one after another, observing their powers and ways of life. One could produce perfumes out of the air; another made tigers as gentle as house cats. In themselves, however, these abilities were not what the future teacher of the West, burning with a potential for divine cosmic consciousness yet to be unleashed, would settle for.

For all his spiritual seeking, Yogananda, as a youth and throughout his life, does not appear a stiflingly sober-sided pietist or an unapproachable paragon of godliness. In this is the real strength which he brought to his unique mission. He was less like the rocklike notoriously conservative and cross-grained conventional *sadhu,* and more like the strength of a bubbling, ever-fresh stream winning its course with liquid flexibility and persistence. He was clearly charming, popular with friends, endowed with intelligence and a light, almost romantic spirit, though his love was for the divine end of all loves. Rich, sensuous poetic language came naturally to him as he communicated his spiritual experiences and the vision of the cosmos they imparted to him. Compared to the impoverished world of many Westerners, his was one of fabulous wonder and beauty, the cosmos as it is opened to the eye of *samadhi*. It is also a world where seeming miracles, psychic feats, and phenomenal control of the physical body and even of life and death, are expected.

Yogananda's search for a master was fulfilled when he was initiated by Swami Yukteswar, a disciple of the family guru. Both in turn were said to be of the spiritual lineage of Swami Babaji, a master who had lived many centuries in the Himalayas and would remain in the body till the end of this age of the world. Swami Babaji is the highest patron of the Self-Realization Fellowship.

Upon coming to America in 1920, Paramahansa Yogananda ("Paramahansa" is the title of a Master Yogi, "Yogananda" is his name in religion) lectured, wrote devotional books, and founded the Self-Realization Fellowship as a vehicle for his teaching mission. In addition to the basic philosophy of the Yoga Sutras, he taught a specific technique, *kriya yoga*. It is a means for withdrawal of the life-energy from the outer concerns to the opening of the spiritual centers. The brain is an electric powerhouse for the body. Current goes from it down the spinal column. By right "magnetization" of this current, through techniques of *pranayama* or life-energy control, meditating on the cosmic syllable "Aum," and yogic exercise, one can open the centers and attain bliss. By the same token, one fantastically accelerates the speed of human evolution in his own case. Even conscious control of death is offered.

This half-metaphorical use of the vocabulary of modern, Western science to interpret to Western audiences the ancient wisdom of *kundalini yoga* is characteristic of the teaching skill of the yoga master in the West. A very basic point of his message is that yoga's philosophy and methods are scientific and entirely reinforced by the discoveries of Western science. Individual discovery and use of them can be empirical and experiential, like a laboratory experiment, and does not need to depend on scriptural or ecclesiastical authority, though in developing them sometimes trust is needed in the greater knowledge of one's guru.

Nonetheless, the Self-Realization Fellowship teaches that the yoga philosophy and methods, accessible as they are to empirical and scientific verification, underline all the great religions and scriptures. They are the essence, core, and substance of every religion. All the words and myths and symbols of the others can be seen as inevitably garbled expressions of man's intuitive sense of the truth of the goals of yoga and the stages by which it is attained. Patanjali's famous "Eight Steps" of Raja Yoga are: *yama* or negative rules for moral conduct, *niyama* or positive rules for living, *asanas* or postures, *pranayama* or control of the life-energy, *pratyahara* or "interiorization" of the mind and energy, *dharana* or concentration, *dhyana* or meditation, and *samadhi* or union and cosmic consciousness. Thus the Ten Commandments can be understood not as arbitrary laws but as articulations of *yama* or the preliminary moral stance necessary for further spiritual growth. Yoga teaching can help us to understand "hard sayings" of the Gospels, such as "If thine eye offend thee, pluck it out." This means not literal self-mutilation, but withdrawal of life-energy from the outer senses to the inner (*pratyahara*). Yogananda was convinced that Jesus and Paul and other spiritual masters of all times and places were yoga masters, with much the same message as his, though the message frequently needed to be accommodated to varying conditions of preparation, and was not always presented in its fullness. But it is the reality about man and his destiny which has given rise to all religions.

The Westerner with an attachment to Christianity or science, or both, could be assured that he or she could find nothing at odds with either in the message from the East. Even though it seems that today neither science nor Christianity have the prestige of some years ago, Yogananda's teaching is persuasive for many Americans. His Fellowship, his "Churches of All Religions," his classes and printed teachings have been greatly successful. His books sell well, and SRF lecturers easily fill large auditoriums in cities around the country.

The last remarkable event of Yogananda's life was the incorruptibility of his physical body for twenty days after his death, until the cover was placed on the casket for the last time. This was something of a sensation at the time, receiving nationwide attention in newspapers and magazines.

The Self-Realization Fellowship consists of laity and Renunciants. The latter have generally completed the introductory series of fifty-some lessons and begun the practice of kriya yoga, meditate at least two hours a day, and live a monastic life. The present head of the Fellowship is a nun whose religious name is Daya Mata, a Sanskrit name meaning "Mother of Compassion," chosen by the Paramahansa himself. The governing board, over which Daya Mata presides, consists of eight long-time members.

The Fellowship has branches all over the world, including India where, as the Yogoda Satsang, it is fairly extensive. In the United States nine of its forty-four centers are in California. A prominent landmark in west Los Angeles is the SRF "Lake Shrine," a beautifully landscaped park with such diverse attractions as lotus towers, a Dutch windmill, a houseboat, and some of the ashes of Mahatma Gandhi whom Yogananda had initiated into Kriya Yoga and whom he greatly admired. To the south, a seaside retreat is found at Encinitas.

Although the organization is controlled by persons whose experience goes back to the days of Yogananda himself, attenders and worshippers at SRF include old-timers, middle-aged seekers, and many young people. The Sunday morning worship or "lecture" is held in a chapel where many come to meditate through the week. The belief that what is taught and experienced here is the reality which underlies all religion is evidenced in the visible combination of cross and lotus, pictures of Yogananda and images of saints. The meeting begins with chants rather than hymns. The address, on a topic such as "How to Play Well Your Part in Life," "Filling the Mind with God," "Your Superconscious Power of Success," is presented by a personable Westerner wearing an ochre robe. His tone, and the whole atmosphere, is one of tranquility. During the week, most centers offer further lectures and yoga classes.

A typical SRF service was held in a small, crowded chapel. Persons of all ages were present, though the group tended toward middle age. The young people there seemed very serious. On the altar were six equal-sized pictures of Masters, including Jesus and Yogananda, but a large colored picture of Yogananada was set to the side and toward the front, with flowers before it as well as on the altar. Certain small SRF customs, striking to the visitor, established the atmosphere. Members greeted each other with the Indian *namaste* (bow with palms pressed together) rather than a Western handshake. Yogananda is often just referred to reverently as "Master." As they entered many stood before the pictures with folded hands a moment before sitting down.

Soft music played before the service. The minister, an American, began with an invocation of God as Father, Mother, and Friend, and of the saints and sages of all religions, and of "our guru." The closing blessing contained the same formula.

The service was drawn from many sources in a friendly and "low-key" style. Music consisted of Indian chants such as "Hymn to Brahma" accompanied by a harmonium. The last verse of the "Battle Hymn of the Republic" closes all services. Announcements, concerning conferences, classes, and the Sunday School, were rather lengthy. The address itself was a blending of scriptures (Genesis, the New Testament, the *Bhagavad Gita*, and the writings of Yogananda), chants, silent meditation, and words by the minister who used Vedantic and Christian language interchangeably. It should be emphasized that this syncretism is deliberate and wholly in accord with the premises of SRF. The "popular" level of some aspects of its public activity fits the spirit of Yogananda, who (like Jesus) was not concerned with intellectuals only, but with bringing his message in appropriate vesture to all sorts of people.

Yogananda has become an image—a remarkable, deep, sweet, poetic, ecstatic man enraptured of cosmic life—who has changed the map of American religious life. His image of the yogi has affected other movements. Others from India have built on it, but Yogananda started it in our day. Let him add a few words.

> When you find that your soul, your heart, every wisp of inspiration, every speck of the vast blue sky and its shining star-blossoms, the mountains, the earth, the whippoorwill, and the bluebells are all tied together with one cord of rhythm, one cord of joy, one cord of unity, one cord of Spirit, then you shall know that all are but waves in His cosmic sea.[2]

Reading Selection: The Self-Realization Fellowship

In this passage taken from his autobiography, Yogananda describes his first great experience of yogic cosmic consciousness. The mystical experience occurred when he was still a young man living and studying with his guru or master, Swami Yukteswar.

My body became immovably rooted; breath was drawn out of my lungs as if by some huge magnet. Soul and mind instantly lost their physical bondage, and streamed out like a fluid piercing light from my every pore. The flesh was as though dead, yet in my intense awareness I knew that never before had I been fully alive. My sense of identity was no longer narrowly confined to a body, but embraced the circumambient atoms. People on distant streets seemed to be moving gently over my own remote periphery. The roots of plants and trees appeared through a dim transparency of the soil; I discerned the inward flow of their sap.

The whole vicinity lay bare before me. My ordinary frontal vision was now changed to a vast spherical sight, simultaneously all-perceptive. Through the back of my head I saw men strolling far down Rai Ghat Road, and noticed also a white cow who was leisurely approaching. When she reached the space in front of the open ashram gate, I observed her with my two physical eyes. As she passed by, behind the brick wall, I saw her clearly still.

All objects within my panoramic gaze trembled and vibrated like quick motion pictures. My body, Master's, the pillared courtyard, the furniture and floor, the trees and sunshine, occasionally became violently agitated, until all melted into a luminescent sea; even as sugar crystals, thrown into a glass of water, dissolve after being shaken. The unifying light alternated with materializations of form, the metamorphoses revealing the law of cause and effect in creation.

An oceanic joy broke upon calm endless shores of my soul. The Spirit of God, I realized, is exhaustless Bliss; His body is countless tissues of light. A swelling glory within me began to envelop towns, continents, the earth, solar and stellar systems, tenuous nebulae, and floating universes. The entire cosmos, gently luminous, like a city seen afar at night, glimmered within the infinitude of my being. The sharply etched global outlines faded somewhat at the farthest edges; there I could see a mellow radiance, everundiminished. It was indescribably subtle; the planetary pictures were formed of a grosser light.

The divine dispersion of rays poured from an Eternal Source, blazing into galaxies, transfigured with ineffable auras. Again and again I saw the creative beams condense into constellations, then resolve into sheets of transparent flame. By rhythmic reversion, sextillion worlds passed into diaphanous luster; fire became firmament.

I cognized the center of the empyrean as a point of intuitive perception in my heart. Irradiating splendor issued from my nucleus to every part of the universal structure. Blissful *amrita*, the nectar of immortality, pulsed through me with a quicksilverlike fluidity. The creative voice of God I heard resounding as *Aum,** the vibration of the Cosmic Motor.

Suddenly the breath returned to my lungs. With a disappointment almost unbearable, I realized that my infinite immensity was lost. Once more I was limited to the humiliating cage of a body, not easily accommodative to the Spirit. Like a prodigal child, I had run away from my macrocosmic home and imprisoned myself in a narrow microcosm.

---

* "In the beginning was the Word, and the Word was with God, and the Word was God." John 1:1. [Note in original.]

My guru was standing motionless before me; I started to drop at his holy feet in gratitude for the experience in cosmic consciousness which I had long passionately sought. He held me upright, and spoke calmly, unpretentiously.

"You must not get overdrunk with ecstasy. Much work yet remains for you in the world. Come; let us sweep the balcony floor; then we shall walk by the Ganges."

PARAMAHANSA YOGANANDA, *Autobiography of a Yogi* (Los Angeles: Self-Realization Fellowship), pp. 149–51. Copyright © 1946, Paramahansa Yogananda.

THE MAHARISHI MAHESH YOGI'S TRANSCENDENTAL MEDITATION MOVEMENT

A bearded, white-robed guru left India for the United States in 1959 to start a movement known then as the Spiritual Regeneration Movement (SRM). He was Maharishi Mahesh Yogi. As his name indicates, he was a yogi, although rather different from Paramahansa Yogananda of the Self-Realization Fellowship who had preceded him by thirty-five years. As a young man he had studied physics at Allahabad University, but later turned to religion, studying under the renowned yoga master Swami Brahmananda Saraswati (also known as Guru Dev), leader of one of the monasteries founded by the great Shankara. It is said that the Swami urged his personable disciple to go to the West. In the United States he taught a simplified and popularized meditation technique he called "Transcendental Meditation."

Once in the United States, he began to seek publicity. His appearances were in the nature of spectacles. Many eager young persons filled auditoria in the 1960s to see the master, with his tiger-skin pallet, his long gray hair and beard, roses twirling in his hands, his twinkly eyes and bubbling giggle. He was obviously a figure with the other-worldly charisma of temple incense and Himalayan ashrams. He appeared on the various "talk shows" and the Sunday supplements contained the usual articles about him. He hired PR men and began to court personalities in the movies, TV, and sports. Mia Farrow, then married to Frank Sinatra, became a meditator, as did the Beatles, who soon became disenchanted, especially after visiting his training center at Rishiskesh in India. Other well-known meditators were Joe Namath, Buckminster Fuller, and Marshall McLuhan. TM became something of a vogue.

A major initiative of the Transcendental Meditation movement during the mid-seventies was the establishment of Maharishi International University in Fairfield, Iowa. The campus of the former Parsons College was acquired. It enrolls approximately 700 undergraduate and graduate students, offering bachelor's degrees in the usual fields. Its graduate division includes, besides an M.A. in business administration, a Ph.D. program in "Neuroscience of Human Consciousness." A unique feature of MIU is the twice-daily gathering of all students and faculty in the two "Golden Domes of Pure Knowledge" at the center of the campus for the collective practice of Transcendental Meditation. It is claimed that this twice-daily experience of transcendental consciousness "allows the mind and body of the student to experience a profound state of rest, creating a more fresh, vital, calm, stress-free, and orderly mental and physical state."

The basic teaching of TM is that it is possible fully to enjoy life by getting to the ground of joy through meditation. It is continually emphasized that transcendental meditation is a *natural* process. Unlike methods based on asceticism, yoga, and concentration, it never involves procedures which go against the normal functioning of the organism. Maybe after years of effort and association, one can condition oneself to experience a bliss-trance upon the stimuli of certain yogic actions, we are told, but this is essentially a reversal of what is natural.

TM employs the natural desire of the self to quest for expansion, joy, and ecstasy by seeking the subtlest level below biological, mechanical, chemical, molecular, atomic, and subatomic material reality—to the ground of being itself, which is of course the same as Brahman in Vedanta thought. The Maharishi's teaching is quite deliberately a popularized Vedanta. Thoughts in the mind are like bubbles rising up from great depths; we are ordinarily aware only of their surface manifestation. But by following thoughts back, or by exploring beneath phenomenal reality, we can move toward contact with original, unruffled consciousness. Too often we deal with problems just on their own level. We cannot solve the problem of darkness by rearranging darkness, but only by bringing light.

The natural tendency of the mind is to seek a field of greater happiness, and this is what it will do naturally once the distractions of thought, speech, and action have been stopped by withdrawal from them. This is meditation. It is not meditation *about* anything, or setting a mood, or giving oneself an emotional charge. It is stopping all subjective or external stimuli which keep the mind on the periphery, thereby releasing it to do what comes naturally to it, to go to its own center, the still point of greatest joy.

While reaching this point is not an end in itself apart from the enjoyment of life, it is said that it greatly enhances that joy. The movement presents much evidence from physiological experiments to the effect that the fifteen to twenty minutes of meditation twice daily by practitioners gives them deeper rest than deep sleep, reducing metabolism and oxygen consumption while the mind is fully awake. This is said to be a unique "fourth state" of consciousness. Physically and mentally refreshing, it energizes a person to use a vastly wider range of mental powers, and therefore become more creative, as well as happier.[3]

Since its founding in 1959 it has gone through several stages. During the halcyon sixties, the Maharishi and TM were highly colorful, highly publicized facets of the "youth culture." But the Beatles episode, pictures of the master riding in chauffered limousines, and an ill-advised speaking-concert tour with a famous rock group, produced an inevitable reaction as the bubble burst.

Then, in the 1970s, TM again burgeoned in popularity. It was now presented less as "pop" spirituality than as a scientific means to creativity and peace of mind, and its appeal was less to young people than to urban, upwardly mobile business and professional people. However, numbers fell off again toward the end of the decade. In the midst of this decline, the Maharishi surprised his followers with an announcement that meditators could be taught levitation. The publicity surrounding this apparently unverified claim, however, did little to enhance the movement's fortunes. But it continues to nourish adherents who report much benefit from its simple practice.

The movement has several wings, of which the most important are the Students International Meditation Society (SIMS), and the adult Spiritual Regeneration Movement. Of these, SIMS appears to be the most vigorous. Its program for initiating individuals into the practice of meditation is well honed. General lectures are presented in a series of two, the first dealing with general philosophy—the need, the psychology, the evidence. The second, presumably attended only by those seriously attracted by the first, gives more details on the process of meditation itself and initiation into it.

The Maharishi retains a rough, westernized approximation of the ancient guru's initiation of disciples. It is individual, requires a token sacrifice, and a personal impartation. Those who wish to be initiated must be off "non-prescribed drugs" for fifteen days. They must bring to the initiatory meeting twelve fresh flowers, some fresh fruit, a clean white handkerchief, and a contribution of money. It is said the money requirement can be waived in case of inability to pay, and is the only expected support for the work of the movement. The initiate should not have eaten for several hours before the initiation. The initiator gives the student his mantram and instructs him how to use it properly. The initiator also performs a ceremony of thanksgiving and purification, in which the articles the new meditator brought are used, as well as rice and water.

In any case, the initiate meets individually with a teacher, who instructs him in meditation and gives him his personal mantram, or sound, which he says "internally" to help him go into meditation. The mantram is to be kept secret, never to be said aloud, and is in harmony with the vibrations of the personality. Only initiators, who have been taught the principles of assigning mantras by the Maharishi in three-month training sessions, and initiated into this power, may impart them.

After receiving his mantra, the initiate practices meditation and meets daily with a small group to discuss his experiences for the next three days. He returns ten days later for checking, and once a month for as long as he wishes. The procedure from the first lecture to the final checking is called the "seven steps to bliss." There are books he can buy and read, and advanced classes he can take, and he may even become an initiator himself. But there is no great pressure in these directions; it depends on the bent of the individual meditator.

The meditation movement's adherents are attractive people with shining eyes and soft voices. They believe they know the most direct cure for the ills of the world, and the Maharishi has said that if only 10 percent of the world's population were to start meditating, the spiritual effect would be so great as to end war and strife.

Reading Selection: The Maharishi Mahesh Yogi's
Transcendental Meditation Movement

This passage from a Spiritual Regeneration Movement booklet describes in simple words the basic principle of why meditation works.

Children are unpredictable and difficult to control, yet any child's reaction, if you hold out a piece of candy to him, is easy to forecast. Water is not easy to confine, yet it, too, behaves predictably in certain circumstances: it will always run down hill; it will always find its own level, if permitted to.

By the same token, the mind, left to its own devices will always prefer to seek a field of greater happiness. Given the choice between an ugly and a beautiful sight, the eye will invariably be drawn to the beautiful. As between a harsh sound and a pleasing one, the ear will seek out the more charming.

It is not necessary to drag the attention toward attractive objects; to learn to prefer lovely and happy things requires no arduous instruction. The mind will automatically focus on them to the exclusion of other things, if given the opportunity.

The transcendental field, being true bliss, represents perfect happiness. It is the ultimate in "attractiveness." Were it made aware of this, the mind would seek out such a field with no need for any pointing and directing. It would automatically be drawn to it in increasing degree as the mind's consciousness and awareness of this contact developed and took hold.

The only thing that is needed, then, to take advantage of this natural inclination is a vehicle of some sort which will conduct the mind's attention surely and swiftly to the source it seeks, establish contact with it, and return the attention once again to the gross level from which it started.

To act as such a vehicle, Maharishi has chosen the medium of sound. The vibrations created by a sound or its mental image inexorably seek the source which gives rise to the thought, traversing the same path we have been describing, to reach eventually the thought's very genesis, which is none other than the absolute field. In the course of the journey the vibrations become progressively more refined and, by the same token, more powerful.

The attention, directed inward, is thus borne toward the field it is most naturally inclined to seek. It arrives eventually at the final threshold and transcends it, crossing the boundary line between the subtlest field of relative existence and the eternal, absolute ocean of pure Being.

M. B. JACKSON, *Transcendental Meditation as Taught by Maharishi Mahesh Yogi* (Los Angeles: Spiritual Regeneration Movement Foundation of America, 1967), pp. 14–15.

YOGA IN AMERICA

An athletic young woman in a leotard greets the television audience with "Namaste,"[4] begins to speak of proper breathing, and proceeds to demonstrate a variety of postures and physical exercises, urging the viewers to join in. She says that she is teaching yoga. The local bookstore, in its section on health and fitness, displays books on "Yoga and You," "Yoga for Executives," "Yoga for Couples," etc. Yoga is "in" among some persons who have little knowledge of or interest in its religious origins and associations. A smaller group, captivated by the mystique of yoga, searches avidly for yoga masters who can reveal its secrets and deep mysteries. Jean Varenne, in the preface to his book *Yoga and the Hindu Tradition,* reminds his readers that:

> . . . it is a "world view," a *Weltanschauung* that comprehends reality in its totality—material as well as spiritual—and provides the foundation for certain practices intended to enable those worthy of it to integrate themselves totally into that reality, if not transcend it. It is true that there is an element of the occult involved in this doctrine, because it requires a great deal of assimilating and because the help of a spiritual guide is indispensable if one is to succeed in doing so concretely. But there is nothing actually secret about it, the texts have all been published and the ashrams are open to anyone who presents himself. As for the gymnastic part of it, that is just one prescribed practice among many; the most picturesque, admittedly, but not the most important.[5]

Nevertheless, somewhere in the back of the mind of persons attracted by the spirituality of India lies a vision of deep Himalayan caves, or refuges in jungle forests, populated by scantily-clad recluses. Entranced and in strange postures, they are masters of yoga. Thought to know the secrets of combining the chemistry of diet and breath and the biophysics of posture with the subtler sciences of the psyche, they are able to attain both superb health and mental liberation.

Doubtless many stories of great yogis are fanciful, but some are not. Among the latter is Swami Sivananda (1887–1963), even though Mircea Eliade introduced him as a character in one of his fantastic tales.[6] Trained as a medical doctor, Swami Sivananda, after a successful career, renounced professional life to become a yogi. His worldly abilities were not lost, however, for Sivananda was innovative in establishing modern institutions centering around yoga—the Sivananda Ashrams, the Divine Life Society, the Sivananda Free Hospital, and the Vedanta Forest University. He wrote an extraordinary number of books. All of these activities centered in Rishikesh, traditionally a city of sages in the Himalayan foothills. Here those sick both in body and soul gathered around the sage, who lived in simple dignity and used his knowledge both of medicine and yoga to teach and heal.

A number of Indian yogis have brought versions of yoga to America, beginning, as we have seen, with Premahansa Yogananda's *kriya* yoga in 1920. The tradition of Sivananda was introduced by his disciple Swami

Vishnu Devananda (born 1927) in 1959. Americans were greeted with the improbable sight of a yogi flying his own plane (traditionally yogis were sometimes attributed the power of self-levitation!), establishing yoga centers everywhere. The Swami claims to have trained over two thousand yoga teachers. Three large yoga "camps" were established in Quebec, New York state, and the Bahamas. It is now possible to take a "yoga vacation" during which "the five basic principles of proper exercise, proper relaxation, proper breathing, proper diet, and proper thinking and meditation" are taught. Also interested in advancing yoga philosophy as a means to a better world, Vishnu Devananda initiated a movement called TWO (True World Order), on the basis of the yogic sense of harmony, mutual understanding, vegetarianism, health, and the sublimation of violence.

Swami Vishnu Devananda has emphasized the practice of *hatha* yoga, the physical yoga of breathing and postures, as his speciality, and has written a useful book on the subject.[7] Other masters have taught primarily other kinds of yoga, including *raja* yoga (sometimes referred to as "complete yoga"), the yoga of deep meditation which leads to liberation, or *kundalini* yoga, which employs techniques for raising the "serpent power" (kundalini) coiled at the base of the spine, which opens the psychic and spiritual centers along the spinal column.

The word *yoga* (derived from the same Indo-European root as the English word "yoke") means "union." However, it is a union which presupposes detachment from matter and emancipation from the phenomenal world. Its purpose is to unify the spirit, "to do away with the dispersion and automatism that characterize profane consciousness."[8] In theistically oriented, devotional yoga the ultimate union is that of the human soul with God.

Some confusion is created by the fact that the word *yoga* has sometimes been used so broadly as to include virtually any aspect of Hinduism regarded as a means of liberation. There is talk of *bhakti yoga,* the practice of devotion to a god conceived in personal terms; *karma yoga,* the path advocated in part of the *Bhagavad Gita* of doing one's duty (*dharma*) in the world; *mantra yoga,* or the recitation of verbal formulas (*mantras*); and so on. These do not, in themselves, involve the physical and meditational techniques commonly associated with the word at all. Perhaps it is clearer to use the term *marga* or path for these, and to restrict yoga to practices involving intense concentration, psychosomatic exercises, and a definite course of development under the guidance of a teacher or guru.

The classical tradition of yoga is based on the famous Yogas Sutras of Patanjali (around the first century B.C.).[9] Here the purpose of the discipline is to give the spirit independence of the conditioned existence of space and time and the body. This is done through gaining control of the whole system—body, emotions, and mind—by the highest levels of mind, so that the spirit can be allowed to shine forth as sovereign in its own house. That is, complete mastery of one's psychosomatic existence is achieved. It is for this reason, and not just for physical health, that one makes the physical and emotional systems into a finely tuned instrument—clean, supple, and amenable to the higher will. To attain the true end of yoga, these exercises are accompanied by meditations designed to stop the riotous activity of the stream of consciousness mind. Although theoretically hatha yoga comes before raja (meditative) yoga, most Western practitioners find that both go well together. Most modern Hindu teachers of yoga encourage a Vedanta philosophical interpretation of the experience. For them, the "spirit" isolated, put in control, and thereby liberated through the process is not merely the individual spirit, but Brahman, the universal mind and ground of being, the one real existent, realized within oneself.

While it is possible to find in the United States master yogis who offer guidance in the traditional forms of yoga, it is nevertheless the case, as was suggested above, that most Western yoga classes do not delve deeply into either the philosophy of yoga or Hindu religious practice. It seems to be understood that one may take yoga on whatever level and in whatever manner one chooses—as physical exercise only, or as an aid to meditation, or as a total way of life. The result may be a certain incongruity, as practitioners of yoga utilize *mudras* (traditional gestures of certain gods), and some breathing and other exercises that make sense only in the light of esoteric teaching about *kundalini* (the "serpent power"), *chakras* (psychic centers), and so on. Still, yoga is appreciated for its evident benefits as regards physical, and perhaps mental, health. For this reason, persons who have other religious commitments, or none at all, feel more or less comfortable in "doing" yoga.

Reading Selection: International Sivananda Yoga Society

These paragraphs are from an information sheet put out by the Sivananda Yoga Society. They summarize the yoga philosophy as understood by the Society and show how it interacts with the yogic concern for diet, health, and the body.

Yoga is a way of complete life. There are a number of different subdivisions in Yoga, but only *one* Yoga, with all paths leading to the same goal. Some teachers advise students to follow one path, and ignore the others. We feel that following a synthesis of all Yoga techniques is best suited for rapid progress. There are five requisites for this Yogic life: (1) proper exercise, (2) proper breathing, (3) proper diet, (4) relaxation, and (5) positive thinking and meditation. Regular day and evening classes are given here, and lectures in the philosophy are held Sundays at 7:30 P.M.

In this modern, mechanized world, our physical bodies are not given the necessary exercise to keep them in a state of health, and only in a healthy body can there be a healthy mind. In this healthy body one should have much flexibility, be a healthy mind. Unfortunately, most Americans have never even experienced the feeling of a relaxed, healthy body, let alone that in accord with a powerful, peaceful mind. In this healthy body, one should have much flexibility, as well as properly functioning glands and organs. Through Yoga exercises the whole body is restored to its natural health and vigor. For people who lead busy lives, you will find that time spent in practicing Yoga will more than make up for itself in peace of mind, relief from tension, and improved health.

To derive energy from the food we eat we must combine it with oxygen, so proper breathing is essential. Mind and thought are intimately connected with breath and relaxation. Proper breathing techniques aid one in achieving emotional control, physical health and inner calmness. Yoga breathing exercises (pranayama) are not dangerous, if learned from a competent teacher, but should never be attempted without proper guidance or from a book. Yoga techniques teach one to give the body and mind maximum relaxation and rejuvenation in a short period of time.

Food is an important limb in Yoga. The building blocks of our body and mind are the foods we eat. A vegetarian diet is advocated for physical, moral and spiritual reasons. Regular lectures are given explaining the advantages, enjoyments and practical hints to following such a diet.

Thought is the most powerful force on earth. Through meditation and focusing the mind, one is able to tap the hidden powers within and apply them to his daily life. To be truly content and have direction in life, we must have a goal and a philosophy. Vedanta philosophy shows man's relation to the universe and helps him answer the age old question "Who am I?" There is no dogmatism in Yoga Vedanta. Students may accept what they believe and experience to be true, and leave the rest. Some people who practice Yoga have little interest in the philosophy. However, they are undoubtedly interested in reaping peace of mind, relief from tension, and improved health.

SIVANANDA YOGA SOCIETY, "About the Sivananda Yoga Society and Yoga Philosophy," undated (about 1969).

THE INTERNATIONAL SOCIETY FOR KRISHNA CONSCIOUSNESS (ISKCON)

The "Hare Krishna" movement is among the most conspicuous of the new religious groups which have persisted in America since the 1960s. Its devotees, with their strict, conservative interpretation of the Krishna devotional tradition, with their orange or white robes, their ecstatic worship, and their close-knit communalism, have appeared to many a sharp intrusion into American spiritual life. In times past they have been notable for performing *kirtan,* religious singing and dancing, in the streets, and later for their controversial distribution of literature at airports and fairs. These practices have gradually diminished as they have chosen the more conventional means of lectures, building spiritual centers, and cementing friendships in various sectors of society to win understanding of their mission.

Visitors are always welcome to Krishna temples. But once there, the unprepared inquirer might wonder if he is in the right country, though with an open mind he will enjoy a fascinating, beautiful, and unforgettable afternoon. He will find himself in a room clouded with incense and full of a great number of the saffron-robed dancers. At one end will be a wide altar bedecked with images of Krishna the sweet divine lover as an infant, or playing his flute, or with Radha his freshfaced consort. Pictures bespangle the walls displaying Krishna and the milkmaids in idyllic pastimes, disporting themselves in perfumed, oriental gardens amidst peacocks, paradisal rivers, and blossoming trees under the full moon of an evening of love an aeon long. Other images and paintings suggest the somberer side of the things of God. The famous three faces from the Jagannath temple, part of the Krishna cultus, look like nightmarish primitive masks. Other illustrations show Krishna in earlier, more aggressive incarnations—he may be lion-headed, ripping the entrails out of demons in scenes splattered with blood and gore.

In time, after the song and dancing has risen to an ecstatic climax, the offerings begin. Devotees gracefully swing lamps and censers and offer food before the principal images. Following this, an address is given by a young, sincere devotee. A meal, full of strange spicy and sweet vegetarian dishes, is served on paper plates, perhaps eaten with the fingers, Indian-style.

At the back of the room is a large throne-like chair, probably gold and velvet. A photo of a bald, long-faced man with wreaths of flowers around his neck, and the vertical marks of a Vishnu devotee on his forehead, rests in the empty chair. This is His Divine Grace A.C. Bhaktivedanta Swami Prabhupada (1896–1977), the "Spiritual Master" of the Society.

All of the Indian religious movements have behind them a powerful charismatic leader. Like most of the others, Swami Bhaktivedanta (born Abhay Charan De) was a Bengali of a prominent and wealthy family, and received a Western education at the University of Calcutta. He studied under a leading Vishnuite swami as a youth, and was told by that master upon his death to spread Krishna consciousness to the English-speaking world. However, De spent thirty years in business before embarking upon this work in 1965 at the age of seventy. Stories are told of his arrival in America, virtually penniless, with nothing but zeal for his mission.

Bhaktivedanta did not come with precisely the same message or attitude as other swami envoys, and, in any case, his delay seems to have been no mistake, for his new gospel was clearly right for the sixties. The story is told by his followers that when he arrived in New York, and began working among the "hippies" and derelicts of the Bowery, he was taken to a reception with a group of other, established swamis, who told him that if he wished to be successful in America, he should wear Western clothes, eat meat, and stress the tolerant all-paths-lead-to-truth interpretation of Hinduism. But he went back to the Bowery. And he continued his work of training an order of Krishnaite devotees who follow four rules of conduct strictly: no eating of meat, fish, or eggs; no illicit sex; no intoxicants; and no gambling. They submit their lives in full obedience to the Spiritual Master, and are eager to proclaim that Krishna is the Supreme Lord, fully personal as well as impersonal, and that Vedantists and other impersonalists misrepresent Hinduism.

With this "hard line" Hinduism, Bhaktivedanta established centers as flourishing as those of the older groups. The movement is based on the Chaitanya Krishnaite sect, which makes central the life and teachings of Chaitanya Mahaprabhu (1486–1533). Chaitanya is believed by his followers to be an incarnation of Radha and Krishna. Appearing as a devotee he exemplified a "fundamentalist" Krishnaism which exalts Krishna as the personal and supreme Lord, and teaches that devotional ecstasy is the surest way to burn away ignorance and karma, and to attain to supernal bliss. Although the great majority of ordinary Hindus are doubtless bhaktic devotionalists of one of the great deities, Chaitanya Krishnaism differs from other Vishnuite groups which hold that Vishnu is the high god, and Krishna merely one incarnation of him. It differs from Vedantic Hinduism—hitherto most represented in the West—which holds all personal gods are but secondary manifestations or accommodations of the impersonal One.

The Krishna Consciousness Society maintains that the Vedas, *Bhagavad Gita,* and canonical lives of Krishna are literally and historically true. Krishna is the supreme personal Lord; he lives in a paradisal world. The souls of all individuals are eternal, and, though intended to love Krishna, are trapped in a series of material bodies owing to ignorance and sensory illusion. By love for Krishna the soul overcomes this identification with the temporary body and lives outside of karma. The devotee's acts are pure and no longer bring retribution. Devotionalism is higher to the Krishnaites than yogic or Vedantic meditation, or moralistic karma yoga, and definitely better than the much-criticized way of impersonalistic philosophy.

A bare doctrinal statement, however, does not reveal the transcendent beauty of Krishnaite devotion and belief. Its core is the accounts of Krishna's life on earth 5000 years ago. The secret meaning of its joyful dances and devotions is participation in the bliss of the milkmaids who loved him then. When Krishna was born in an infant's body in Vrindavan, he brought with him his eternal paradisical world, with all its jewel-like flowers, peacocks, and celestial devotees. For a short time, heaven dwelt before man's eyes in the midst of earth. As an infant, Krishna was as charming and exasperating as God, or the spiritual quest. As God sends earthquake and flood, so Krishna performed pranks like eating clay. But when his foster mother looked into his mouth to see if the clay was there, she saw instead the entire universe. On another occasion when she tried to tie him up, she found to her puzzlement that however much rope she uncoiled, there was never quite enough. In such charming ways, the *Srimad Bhagavatam* (life of Krishna) shows in the infant Krishna, and later in Krishna the mysterious lover whose flute-song in the moonlight draws the milkmaids from their homes to follow his revels, the incomprehensibility and seductive power of God.

The details of life are closely regulated. For example, each devotee was once encouraged to take two showers daily, and drink a cup of milk before retiring. There is to be no ordinary courtship or dating among devotees. However, marriages are fostered that will advance the cause of Krishna. As in every other area of life, living above personal karma and desire in the freedom of Krishna's love is the important thing. The Krishnaite group seems, above all, a family. Marriages are clearly secondary to the cohesion of the whole Krishnaite family. Most activities are done together: a member senses himself and his companions as a highly distinct body from the outside world. The creation of a family, with play, child-like joy, communality, and a highly structured life is evident.

As the Krishna movement has matured, inevitably its character has changed. Fewer new members are joining in the 1980s than in the 1960s, the sixties generation of members are reaching middle age, and children raised in the movement and its schools are approaching adulthood. Yet it remains a cause which fundamentally wants to bring as many human beings as possible to an appreciation of what its adherents have found to be the supreme joy.

Conversion to Krishna Consciousness is not simply religious, but has obvious cultural dimensions as well. To a significant degree devotees become Indian culturally as well as religiously. The process of initiation is clearly a rite of passage in which persons de-identify themselves not only with their bodies but with their past life history and culture, and acquire a new identification. The process progresses through several stages. It begins with a kind of novitiate, which includes not only the four basic rules of conduct mentioned above but a number of changes from one's ordinary previous life. A male devotee shaves his head except for a single lock (*sikha*) and dons the *dhoti*, a simple Indian-style garment. Women retain their hair but dress in *saris*. Devotees wear a string of small beads around their necks, signifying commitment to Krishna, and place clay markings (*tilaka*) on their forehead and nose, indicating that the body is a temple. These very obvious changes in appearance announce to all, including oneself, that he or she is no longer who they were in former life.

Further, one undertakes to de-identify oneself with the body, adopting an entirely new attitude toward it and treating it appropriately. Former possessions are given up. The process of leveling and stripping continues until the new devotee is no longer distinct from others in the group. Increasingly, a strictly regulated life is adopted, as well as a number of Indian ways of doing things (eating, sleeping, bathing, etc.). And, of course, neophytes participate fully in the *bhaktic* ritual life, including most importantly the performance of the "Hare Krishna" *mantra*, both individually and collectively.

The neophyte experiences what Victor Turner called liminality, the experience of being "betwixt and between" two distinct identifications (old and new).[10]

After six months the new devotee may undergo a definitive initiation. The *harynama* (holy name) ceremony, as its name indicates, involves principally the reception of a new (Sanskrit) name. The name signifies, further, a lifetime commitment to Krishna devotion. Six months later, a second, further initiation may be performed. In it the devotee receives a sacred thread (to be worn diagonally across the chest) and a secret *mantra*. In India those who are born as *brahmins* receive a sacred thread in youth at the time of initiation. In ISKCON devotees become what Prabhupada called "a brahmin by qualification" (rather than birth), and the reception of the sacred thread is its sign and symbol. In India it is from the brahmins that the priests are drawn. The new Krishna Consciousness brahmin is now considered a priest of Krishna and is permitted to perform the ISKCON rites and ceremonies. The initiation—the change of identification—is complete; one is no longer a liminal person.

It could be argued that no group breaks more thoroughly with more American values—religious, social, dietary, material—than Krishna Consciousness. But nothing is more disarming than the innocence, kindness, and inner joy of devotees. There is, of course, a "true believer" conviction, but it is not offensive unless one is unable to abide a few persons dancing and singing with sacred joy. The challenge is deeper than confrontation, and—in its love for a new image of a personal God—different from either social revolution or the impersonalist alternative reality tradition. Rather, here we see Krishna, the marvelous, eternal, omnipotent, and wise child, whose delights never end.

A. C. Bhaktivedanta Swami Prabhupada died in November 1977. The passing of the founder and central figure of a new religious movement is always a time of crisis. It was far from certain that the "Hare Krishnas" would survive the crisis. As we have observed, it is difficult to transmit charisma, especially from an individual to an institution. Seven years before his demise Prabhupada had wisely, as it turned out, established the Governing Body Commission (GBC), originally constituted by twelve senior devotees, each assigned a geographical area of spiritual and administrative responsibility. While Prabhupada reviewed the decisions of the GBC and occasionally vetoed some, the Commission gradually took shape as a semiautonomous, democratic body. After his death the GBC came into its own as a more or less effective instrument of corporate leadership. There were some strains, occasioned for the most part by the fact that Prabhupada had chosen some senior devotees as *gurus,* and these persons were presumed to have the traditional religious authority of *gurus.* Some were members of the GBC and others not. Again, there was some tension between individual, personal, "spiritual" authority and corporate, institutional authority. On the whole, institutional solidarity has been preserved, in the face of several abortive schisms by individual *gurus.*

In the beginning Krishna Consciousness was an urban movement; devotees chanted, sang, and danced on city streets. In recent years they have begun to move to rural areas. (For example, a temple is nearing completion on a farm some twenty miles from the city in which one of the authors resides.) The most impressive rural center of ISKCON is located near Moundville, West Virginia. There the devotees have constructed "Prabhupada's Palace of Gold," an elaborate and unique edifice dedicated to the spirit of the founder; a magnificent temple to Krishna is planned. New Vrindaban, named for the Vrindaban in India which was the scene of Krishna's marvelous play, has become a premier tourist attraction in the state of West Virginia, and has done much to improve the public image of the "Hare Krishnas." The images of Krishna offering *darshana*[11] witnesses to the religious convictions of the devotees, while at the same time, the development of New Vrindaban as a tourist attraction symbolizes a degree of accommodation to American society. Increasingly, visitors include Indian-American Hindus who appreciate this tribute to their traditional faith in their new homeland.

ISKCON has not only survived the demise of Prabhupada but, like some other new religious movements that have been around for several decades, is showing signs of maturing. Since 1977 it has not grown very much in North America. Its growth has been mainly in other parts of the world: Great Britain, Australia, Latin America, and India. Indians have witnessed the improbable phenomenon of American devotees attempting, with some success, to reintroduce Prabhupada's particular form of Krishna devotion in the land of its origin.

Reading Selection: International Society for Krishna Consciousness

This passage, from one of the shorter of Swami Bhaktivedanta's many books, treats the central phenomenon of Krishna Consciousness, the great mantra. The word *Hare* is a vocative form of the word for the energies of God. *Krishna* and *Rama* are both names of the supreme Lord. Rama belongs to an earlier divine descent from that of the marvelous Krishna. As Rama he was a heroic prince, and his deeds are described in the epic *Ramayana*. But in the mantra, all these showings of divinity are united in one attribution of praise.

The transcendental vibration established by the chanting of HARE KRSNA, HARE KRSNA, KRSNA KRSNA, HARE HARE/HARE RĀMA, HARE RĀMA, RĀMA RĀMA, HARE HARE is the sublime method for reviving our transcendental consciousness. As living spiritual souls, we are all originally Krsna conscious entities, but due to our association with matter from time immemorial, our consciousness is now adulterated by the material atmosphere. The material atmosphere, in which we are now living, is called *māyā,* or illusion. *Māyā* means that which is not. And what is this illusion? The illusion is that we are all trying to be lords of material nature, while actually we are under the grip of her stringent laws. When a servant artificially tries to imitate the all-powerful master, it is called illusion. We are trying to exploit the resources of material nature, but actually we are becoming more and more entangled in her complexities. Therefore, although we are engaged in a hard struggle to conquer nature, we are ever more dependent on her. This illusory struggle against material nature can be stopped at once by revival of our eternal Krsna consciousness.

Hare Krsna, Hare Krsna, Krsna Krsna, Hare Hare is the transcendental process for reviving this original pure consciousness. By chanting this transcendental vibration, we can cleanse away all misgivings within our hearts. The basic principle of all such misgivings is the false consciousness that I am the lord of all I survey.

Krsna consciousness is not an artificial imposition on the mind. This consciousness is the original natural energy of the living entity. When we hear the transcendental vibration, this consciousness is revived. This simplest method of meditation is recommended for this age. By practical experience also, one can perceive that by chanting this *mahāmantra,* or the Great Chanting for Deliverance, one can at once feel a transcendental ecstasy coming through from the spiritual stratum. In the material concept of life we are busy in the matter of sense gratification as if we were in the lower animal stage. A little elevated from this status of sense gratification, one is engaged in mental speculation for the purpose of getting out of the material clutches. A little elevated from this speculative status, when one is intelligent enough, one tries to find out the supreme cause of all causes— within and without. And when one is factually on the plane of spiritual understanding, surpassing the stages of sense, mind and intelligence, he is then on the transcendental plane. This chanting of the Hare Kṛṣṇa *mantra* is enacted from the spiritual platform, and thus this sound vibration surpasses all lower strata of consciousness—namely sensual, mental and intellectual. There is no need, therefore, to understand the language of the *mantra,* nor is there any need for mental speculation nor any intellectual adjustment for chanting this *māhamantra.* It is automatic, from the spiritual platform, and as such, anyone can take part in vibrating this transcendental sound without any previous qualification. In a more advanced stage, of course, one is not expected to commit offenses on grounds of spiritual understanding.

A. C. BHAKTIVEDANTA SWAMI, *Krsna Consciousness: The Topmost Yoga System* (Boston: Iskcon Press, 1970), pp. 32–33.

RAJNEESH INTERNATIONAL FOUNDATION

There is a tendency of long standing to assume that new groups considered religiously deviant are also necessarily morally deviant. Further, moral deviance has often been identified especially with sex. Even "puritanical" groups such as the Krishna devotees and the "Moonies" have sometimes been suspected in this regard (when they are not accused, conversely, of being "unnatural" in their denial or strict circumscription of sexual relations). Other groups may have beliefs or practices which seem to confirm the worst suspicions. Such was the case with the Mormons in the nineteenth century when their practice of polygamy gave rise to all sorts of rumors and horror tales.

Bhagwan Shree Rajneesh and his Neo-Sannyasins have been accused of sexual indulgence both in India and in the United States. Newspaper writers have called him "the sex guru."

India has a strong ascetical tradition. The *Sannyasin* represents the fourth and final stage of the ideal pattern of the life course of a Hindu. Its basic meaning is renunciation, by which is meant renunciation of attachment to all material and worldly things, including the human body and sexuality. Not so the sannyasins of Bhagwan. Theirs is not the way of denial. In his book *From Sex to Superconsciousness* Bhagwan has written:

> . . . sex is divine. The primal energy of sex has the reflection of God in it.
>   End this enmity with sex. If you crave a shower of love in your life, renounce this conflict with sex. Accept sex with joy. Acknowledge its sacredness. Receive it gratefully and embrace it more and more deeply.[12]

At the same time, Bhagwan insists that he does not advocate "free sex" or sexual indulgence, but recognizes that sex is a natural phenomenon which persons should experience "meditatively" so that it may become the first step on the road to superconsciousness.

Most of the religious teachers who have come to the West from India have emphasized the spirituality of India against the materialism of the West. Their message has been that while the West has made great progress in science and technology and has produced the highest standard of living (in material terms) the world has known, it has not been able to create a true spirituality. That must come from the East, we are told, the fountainhead of spiritual life. Rajneesh has a different message, one which he proclaimed in India, and that has given rise to surprise and controversy. He has described himself as "a materialist-spiritualist," who teaches a sensuous religion. "I want Gautama the Buddha and Zorba the Greek," he says, "to come closer and closer; my disciple has to be Zorba-the-Buddha. Man is body-soul together. Both have to be satisfied."[13]

Rajneesh was born in a small village in Madhya Province, India, in 1931. His family was Jain.[14] One cannot, however, simply identify Rajneesh as a Jain in his religious orientation, for he has been quite eclectic. While there are Jain elements in his teaching, one can also find Hindu, Buddhist, and Tantric elements from India as well as the outside influences of Zen, Gurdjieff, and psychologists of what is often referred to as the Human Potential Movement.

He studied philosophy and was a university professor for eleven years. He resigned his professorship in 1966, having decided to devote the rest of his life to the task of human enlightenment and liberation through meditation. Meditation is usually assumed to be quietistic, an act of concentration and withdrawal. Again, not so with Bhagwan. He developed a number of methods and techniques of meditation, including, most importantly, "Dynamic Meditation."

Dynamic Meditation is a technique designed for cerebral people with repressions. It is intended to overcome their social and psychological conditioning and to rid them of suppressed impulses and emotions. It may involve shouting, screaming, wild dancing, taking off one's clothing, and other equally unconventional and intense actions. The technique borrows perhaps as much from some modern psychological theories as from religious sources. Only after such preliminaries, according to Bhagwan, can the silent meditative state be experienced. It has been described as a state of inward receptivity to all that is in the moment and as essentially a state of "no-mind" in which the truth is known directly. One witnesses one's own body, emotions, and thoughts as if they did not belong to him or her, as an impartial witness. All the energies of the body, including the sexual energy, are transmuted, as if alchemically. By alternately engaging in strong, cathartic activity and in silent witnessing the transformation of energy occurs.

In 1981 Rajneesh left his ashram in Poona to come to the United States, where he has remained. Shortly thereafter the Rajneesh Foundation purchased 64,000 acres of land near Antelope, Oregon, and incorporated part of it as the new city of Rajneeshpuram, the site of a "Rajneeshee" commune. Religious and political conflict shortly ensued between the Rajneeshees and the local inhabitants. The latter resisted what they saw as a strange, foreign invasion. The Rajneeshees insisted on their religious and civil rights. The struggle has continued at the polls and in the courts.

Rajneesh has been extraordinarily prolific. He has lectured extensively and written well over one hundred books. He sees his life pattern as divided into three phases, as represented by the *gunas*, the three qualities or properties that according to Indian thought are to be found in all things: *tamas* (the quality of inactivity, inertia), *rajas* (activity, passion), and *sattva* (serenity, calmness, wisdom). His *rajas* period coincided with his time of extraordinary productivity. His *sattva* period began decisively with his announcement on April 10, 1981, that he would henceforth be silent (reminiscent of Meher Baba). He claimed that his disciples would now be able to enter into spiritual communion with him on a deeper level because of his silence. He maintained silence for several years.

Prior to 1971 Rajneesh used the title "Acharya," a traditional title for a teacher. Since that time he has called himself "Bhagwan," which can be translated variously as "the Blessed One" and "God." As teacher he had communicated through the head; now he would communicate, as he said, heart to heart with those in love with him. Those who came to him as disciples (Sannyasins) were initiated during *darshans* and were henceforth identified by four things:

1. orange-colored clothing (symbol of the rising sun);
2. a *mala* (a necklace of 108 beads with a locket containing a picture of Bhagwan, and symbolizing devotion to him);
3. a new name (beginning with "Swami" ["Lord"] for males and "Ma" ["Mother"] for females); and
4. a daily meditation given each Sannyasin individually.

Rajneeshees are taught to destroy their old identity and to create a new one. Rajneesh speaks of it mainly in terms of the destruction of the Ego, which must be destroyed if one is to experience Enlightenment, the ultimate goal of the Sannyasin. He claims to have experienced Enlightenment himself on March 21, 1953, when he was 21 years old. It was the time when, according to an astrologer who did his horoscope when he was an infant, he could expect to die. He interpreted his Enlightenment experience as a fulfillment of the prophecy, in the sense that he died to his old life and entered into deathlessness.

Bhagwan Shree Rajneesh came to prominence in the United States, though controversially, at a time when most other Indian "gurus" had either died or were fading from the scene. Although Rajneeshees are to be found in some numbers in Great Britain, Western Europe, and India as well as in a number of centers in the United States, it appeared that Rajneeshpuram in Oregon was the place where he hoped to realize his vision of a new physical-spiritual community. His choice of a sparsely settled area of the American West in which to establish it on an impressive scale recalled the strategy of the Mormons in the early nineteenth century. Also, unlike most religious groups of Indian origin, Bhagwan was able to attract middle-aged persons as well as the young to his following.

In words reminiscent of the Three-fold Refuge of the Buddhists, the Sannyasins recite:

I go to the feet of the Awakened One.
I go to the feet of the Commune of the Awakened One.
I go to the feet of the Ultimate Truth of the Awakened One.[15]

As this is being written, however, all is not well in "paradise." The Bhagwan's former secretary, Ma Anand Sheela, and several other leaders have defected, and have been denounced by the Bhagwan for theft and attempted murder. In November, 1985, he was incarcerated and charged with multiple violations of the immigration laws. These charges resulted in his deportation to India. It is unlikely that he will return. The future of Rajneeshism in the United States is uncertain.

Reading Selection: Rajneesh International Foundation

In the following selection Bhagwan Shree Rajneesh explains the technique and meaning of his primary method of meditation: Dynamic Meditation.

Dynamic Meditation is a contradiction. "Dynamic" means effort—much effort, absolute effort. And "Meditation" means silence, no effort, no activity. You can call it dialectical meditation. . . .

My system of Dynamic Meditation begins with breathing, and I suggest ten minutes of chaotic breathing in the first stage of the technique. By chaotic breathing I mean deep, fast, vigorous breathing, without any rhythm. Just taking the breath in and out . . . as deeply, as intensely as possible. . . .

This chaotic breathing is to create a chaos within your repressed system. . . .

This chaotic breathing is to destroy all your past patterns. . . . Unless a chaos is created you cannot release your repressed emotions. And those emotions have now moved into the body.

You are not body *and* mind, you are body-mind; you are both together. So whatever is done with your body reaches the mind, and whatever is done with the mind reaches the body. Body and mind are two parts of the same entity.

Deep, fast breathing gives you more oxygen. The more oxygen in the body, the more alive you become, the more animal-like, vibrating, vital.

With more energy in your blood, more energy in your cells, your body cells will become more alive. This oxygenation helps to create body electricity— or you can call it "bioenergy." When there is electricity in the body you can move deep within, beyond yourself. . . .

The second step . . . is a catharsis. I tell you to be *consciously* insane. Whatever comes to your mind—*whatever*—allow it to express itself; cooperate with it. No resistance: just a flow of emotions. If you want to scream, then scream. A deep scream, a total scream, in which your whole being becomes involved is very therapeutic, deeply therapeutic. Many things, many diseases, will be released just by the scream. If the scream is total, your whole being will be in it. . . .

With this second step, when things are thrown out, you become vacant. And this is what is meant by emptiness: to be empty of all repressions. In this emptiness something can be done. Transformation can happen; meditation can happen.

Then, in the third step, I use the sound *hoo.* Many sounds have been used in the past. Each sound has something specific to do. . . .

Sufis have used *hoo,* and if you say *hoo* loudly, it goes deep to the sex center. So this sound is used just as a hammering within. When you have become empty and vacant, this sound can move within you. . . .

This *hoo* goes deep down and hits the sex center, and the sex center can be hit in two ways. The first way is naturally. Whenever you are attracted to a member of the opposite sex, the sex center is hit from without. And that hit is also a subtle vibration. . . .

Hoo hits the same center of energy but from within. And when the sex center hits from within, the energy starts to flow within. This inner flow of energy changes you completely. You are transformed; you give birth to yourself.

You are transformed only when your energy moves in a totally opposite direction. Right now it is flowing out, but then it begins to flow within. Now it is flowing down, but then it flows upward. This upward flow of energy is what is known as *kundalini.* You will feel it actually flowing in your spine . . . and the higher it moves, the higher you will move with it. When this energy reaches the *brahmarandhra* (the last center in you, the seventh center located at the top of the head) you are the highest man possible—what Gurdjieff calls "man number seven." . . .

The fourth step is the jump. In the fourth step I tell you to stop. When I say "Stop!" stop completely. Don't do anything at all because anything you do can become a diversion and you will miss the point. Anything—just a cough or a sneeze—and you may miss the whole thing because the mind has become diverted. Then the upward flow will stop immediately because your attention has moved. . . .

When the energy moves upward you become more and more silent. Silence is the by-product of energy moving upward and tension is the by-product of energy moving downward. Now your whole body will become so silent—as if it has disappeared. You will not be able to feel it. You have become bodiless. And when you are silent, the whole existence is silent, because existence is nothing but a mirror. It reflects you. In thousands and thousands of mirrors it reflects you. . . .

In your silence I will tell you to just be a witness, a constant alertness—not doing anything but just remaining a witness, just remaining with yourself; not doing *anything*—no movement, no desire, no becoming—but just remaining then and there, silently witnessing what is happening.

These first three steps will make you ready to remain with the moment. They will make you aware. That is meditation. In that meditation something happens that is beyond words. And once it happens you will never be the same again. . . .

After ten minutes of silence, the Dynamic Meditation concludes with ten minutes of celebration—singing, dancing, and expressing whatever bliss or ecstasy is there.

> RAJNEESH FOUNDATION PRESS INFORMATION FILES (Poona, 1975–1981), quoted in Vasant Joshi, *The Awakened One* (San Francisco: Harper and Row, 1982), pp. 194–97.

THE SATYA SAI BABA MOVEMENT

The Satya Sai Baba is a new American religious movement whose founder and teacher has never been to the United States. But in these days of jets and intercontinental telephone, that matters little. Devotees from around the world can fly to India in a few hours, or exchange verbal communication instantaneously.

Not that such physical contact would be entirely necessary in this case, for the center of attention, a smiling and winning holy man in the south of India, is believed to be an *avatar,* a divine incarnation, of Krishna, and of Shiva and his *shakti* or consort. He is a wonder-worker to whom distance and natural law mean little. He embodies the same spontaneous, unassuming, effortless marvel and power as the child Krishna. There are other signs of his presence also—total aversion to meat and the slaughter of animals; childlike whimsy, humor, and charm; and almost pranksterish gaiety mingled with deep insight and appeals to righteousness.

All of this seems to be brought together in a living man in India. A prominent lawyer says that Sai Baba cured him of Parkinson's disease with a wave of his hand. Sai Baba continually produces small objects, like rings, pictures of himself, statues of the gods, or prayer beads from out of the air to hand to visitors and devotees as talismans. He materializes out of his body an aromatic gray ash, called *vibhuti.* His followers treasure it as a token of the holy man, and as beneficial for healing and benediction. By now the saint must have distributed tons of the substance. Most remarkable of all, once a year on a festival of Shiva, Sai Baba produces from his mouth one or two small, oblong, stone *linga*—the symbol of Shiva.

Needless to say, such performances have drawn controversy and charges of charlatanism. But believers have not been deterred.

Sai Baba was born on November 23, 1926 in a small village, Puttaparthi, in south India, and he has the flamboyance, religious fervor, and lithe grace of that region. As might be expected, stories are told of marvels at his birth. Musical instruments played of their own accord; a harmless cobra appeared under his bed. Even as a child, he could foretell the future and produce flowers and candy just by waving his hands. He also went through strange moods and seizures. He would be quiet, he would writhe like a terrifying deity; he would sing or proclaim that he saw gods passing across the sky. He was god-intoxicated, and no one knew what to make of him.

Then, on May 23, 1940, at the age of thirteen, the fey period—so like the shamanistic initiatory psychopathology—ended as the boy announced, "I am Sai Baba." That was the name in religion of a notable saint who had died in 1918. The new Sai Baba took the title and began to show signs of being a reincarnation of the old holy man. He materialized pictures and displayed knowledge and mannerisms of the former Sai Baba. Yet Sai Baba had lived in a part of India culturally and geographically remote from the tiny southern village where the young boy was brought up; it is not likely that anyone would have even heard of him in the new Sai Baba's obscure village.

In any case, from 1940 Sai Baba left school and all traces of ordinary life. He began his legendary miracles and his life amid his disciples and devotees as teacher and healer. The most famous of all the events occurred in 1963, the same year he declared himself an incarnation of Shiva and his *shakti* or consort as well as of Krishna. He suffered a stroke and four heart attacks, refused medical help, and then miraculously cured himself before an audience of 5,000 in his prayer hall.

In India, Sai Baba's work is no small-scale affair. His village has become a great pilgrimage center. Some 50,000 pour into it annually for festivals. His movement has built schools, dispensaries, and centers all over India. The workers in Sai Baba's Indian organization rebuild homes and feed victims after floods and hurricanes. They were quietly at work after the Bhopal disaster and have regular programs for feeding the poor. Sai Baba asks his followers to set aside a little grain each day for the hungry, rather than give money, for, as he says, money is a source of trouble for spiritual groups. Sai Baba has attracted attention in the highest educational and intellectual circles, and counts leading public figures among his followers.

Even so, this is only prelude, according to Satya Sai Baba. His believers say that he is an avatar or "descent" of God, rather than just a holy man who by his asceticism and piety has become "God-realized," for the following reasons: there was no obvious period of preparation in his life, and an infinite power seems to flow effortlessly through him. Satya Sai Baba seems altogether of a different order from the "ordinary" enlightened man of holy India to his followers. But Sai Baba himself says that he is only the second of a series of three avatars. The first was the former Sai Baba, the second is himself; he will live to be ninety-eight. Then, eight years after his death, he will be reborn as the third avatar, Prema Sai Baba, who will complete the work and will fully manifest God in himself to the world.

So far he has not won the attention outside India that he has in his own country. Sai Baba and his mystique is a very Hindu kind of phenomenon, well understood and accepted by his compatriots, but more baffling perhaps than anything else to those in less fervent lands. Although he has gone to west Africa (where his triumphal tour was mainly among the Hindu population), he has not come to the West, despite many promises and postponed dates. For this reason, he has not emulated Vivekananada or Yogananda or Bhaktivedanta's successes.

But an informal and devoted movement centered around acceptance of Sai Baba's claims, and interest in his phenomena, is growing. At first, enthusiastic pilgrims returning to America, such as Elsie and Walter Cowan of California, Hilda Charlton of New York, and Indra Devi of Tecate, Mexico, informally shared their experiences with Baba by teaching the lessons and songs they had learned. Later, as interest grew, meetings became more structured, and guidelines approved by Sai Baba were introduced.

At the time of his revelation at thirteen, Sai Baba said "Worship me every Thursday," and that is the main day for activities at the several Sai Baba centers in the West. Usually there will be yoga classes, discussion, and *bhajan* or the chanting of devotional hymns to altars which include pictures of the saint. Books and magazines are available.

It is in hearing the conversation of Sai Baba enthusiasts, however, that the real spirit of the movement becomes evident. Many have been to India, and others are eager to go. Those who have been there tell story after story of the avatar's powers. They wear rings and show pictures materialized by him and tell of remarkable healings, or prophecies, or ways in which inexplicable rescues from accidents seemed to involve the presence of relics, or even visions, of the saint. It is as though they were caught up in a different world, a world of grace and miracle different from ordinary America. And even more is expected of the future. The liberal press in India has, however, attempted to debunk the Sai Baba phenomenon.

The religious teachings of Sai Baba are perhaps less remarkable than his miracles. In India he talks of reestablishing the authority of the Vedas and sounds, in Hindu terms, rather conservative. But he does not seem to feel that Vedantic orthodoxy need be expected of non-Hindus attracted to him. He emphasizes the values of vegetarianism and purity of diet and action characteristic of the Vishnuite tradition. He talks of the central function of the avatar, the restitution of *dharma* or divine law, but in fairly general terms. At his best he rises to the simplicity of the true mystic as he speaks of the love of God rather than of the world, which can never satisfy man's deepest yearnings.

Sai Baba is a vivid personality. He wears brilliant red robes, his dark smiling face looks oddly like a composite of every human race, his long black hair (which, it is said, no scissors can cut) wreathes around his head. In seeing films of him walking through rows of his devotees, healing, distributing *vibhuti*, teaching, one is struck by the thought that the scene suddenly makes the New Testament seem contemporary. He is the holy, charismatic, miraculous personality, walking the dusty roads of a peasant society full of sick and poverty-stricken yet eagerly believing people. We see this in the midst of the twentieth century, recorded on film.

In 1984 seventy-six Satya Sai Baba Centers and Study Circles were listed in the directory issued by the Satya Sai Baba Council of America. The largest centers are located in New York, Los Angeles, and Chicago. California has the largest number of centers, but New England, the Southeast, and the Southwest are well represented. In 1983 it was decided that every recognized center would participate in service projects, thus establishing in the United States the service-oriented tradition of the Indian followers.

Every five years Sai Baba holds a World Conference. The fourth was held in November 1985. At that time Sai Baba's sixtieth birthday was celebrated. He has said that henceforth he will not be as readily accessible to the general public as he has been in the past.

Reading Selection: The Satya Sai Baba Movement

The passage below is by an American writer who devoted considerable time to investigating Sai Baba and his movement. He left Baba impressed with the strange and inexplicable physical and spiritual works he had seen wrought, but uncommitted as to interpretation of it. Here he describes his first meeting with Baba. The phenomenon described is typical of that recorded by countless persons who have been in his presence.

The writer heard of Baba during his first stay in India and through a friend, an Indian novelist, had arranged to meet him.

Baba, in his early forties, was slightly over five feet tall. He wore a bright orange silk dress that hung loosely down to his chunky bare feet; but the first thing one noticed was his Afro-electric hair standing straight out from all parts of his head like a black, kinky halo five or six inches wide. His coloring was the soft beige of a Brahmin. He spoke gently and with great sweetness to each of the seven people in the room, but did not reveal anything about anyone's past or future. He confined his remarks to platitudes about God, love, and devotion. Then, just before Baba ended the audience, he materialized a ruby ring, which he gave to the novelist, and a handful of ashes, which he gave to a woman in the group. Baba was talking to someone else on the other side of the room when suddenly he had stopped in the middle of a sentence and turned to the woman.

"I will cure your appendicitis," he said, as he materialized ashes. "Take this in water three days."

She had suffered an attack of appendicitis the night before and was in great pain. No one had mentioned her attack.

She followed his instructions and three days later, when the pain had completely disappeared, she had two reputable doctors in another town examine her thoroughly. Neither of them could find any trace of appendicitis.

THE LOVERS OF MEHER BABA

Those who recall the enthusiasms of the 1930s and those familiar with the religious counter-culture of the 1960s will remember posters, newspaper pictures, pins, and rings bearing the photograph of a smiling, avuncular man in Indian dress. No untidy holy man, his black hair is neatly combed back in the Western manner, and he is cleanshaven save for a great bushy moustache which makes his broad, brilliant smile as warm as the sun. This is Meher Baba, a son of India and in some ways the most enigmatic of all the figures we have discussed. For he has made the greatest claim of all, saying, "I am God personified," and has seemingly done the least to demonstrate the claim as the world would judge proof. Yet with only quixotic efforts toward organization, and frequently changing plans, he has convinced thousands that his enigmatic charm and unpredictibility is indeed the fascination and inscrutibility of God focused into the world.

This man was born Merwan S. Irani in 1894 in Poona, India. His background reflects a religious universalism. Of Persian lineage, his parents were Parsees or Zoroastrians. But his milieu was, of course, Hindu, and he was much influenced by Sufi mystics. He was educated at a Christian high school.

Clearly his chief concept was the cult of holy men so central to Sufism and one strand of Hinduism. According to this tradition, there are always a certain number of true holy men or "Perfect Masters" alive in the world. Beside what they have, the vagaries of religious belief and practice are unimportant. The essential thing is to find them—or be found by them—love and serve them, and emulate them. In them is all grace and love.

Meher Baba's contact with such persons began when he was nineteen. He encountered an aged Muslim woman, Hazrat Babajan, who was famous as a saint. She kissed his forehead, and thereby began a process which made him God-realized and conscious of himself as an avatar or personification of God. He went through an ordeal virtually like a shamanistic initiation. For three days he lay as though dead, and for a long time he wandered in an ecstasy of infinite bliss but dissociated from his surroundings. Gradually he readjusted, but he was never again able to live a "normal" life. He contacted the Hindu master Sai Baba (the same whom Satya Sai Baba claims to reincarnate), and worked for three years under an advanced disciple of his, Upasni Maharaj. All of these were what Meher Baba called "Perfect Masters." He said that there are at all times five Perfect Masters in the world who sustain it in occult ways. He was recognized by all of them as an avatar (a Hindu term meaning divine "descent" or incarnation), greater than a God-realized master, because the avatar is a showing or self-revelation of God Himself from the other side. Past avatars have been such figures as Krishna, Jesus, the Buddha, and other religious founders, and occur about every 700 years.

In 1921 Meher Baba established his first ashram and gathered about him disciples, called *mandali*. Their life was never easy nor secure. Baba's work included the establishment of many orphanages, hospitals, schools, and shelters for the poor. But under Baba's direction, the works seemed erratic. One is reminded of Gurdjieff at the Institute at Fontainebleau. He would order a flourishing and worthwhile philanthropy terminated for no evident reason. He would lead his disciples on trips and turn them around before they reached the announced destination. In all of this, Baba seemed to be either unstable or as mysterious as God.

Baba believed that he must identify with both the highest and lowest of society. In India and his journeys to the West, he was lionized by government officials and movie stars. But he also devoted what some might have considered an inordinate amount of time to searching out the many deranged, God-possessed holy men of India he called *masts*. These strange people, bizarre in utterance, often catatonic, living in filth in dumps, public toilets, and railway stations, he embraced and cleaned and sometimes brought lovingly to his ashram. And in his travels, Meher Baba would visit the sites of past avatars and Perfect Masters, including Jesus and St. Francis, to perform mysterious actions alone there. His Eastern and Western followers believe that he still knows and affects everything that is going on in the world.

Meher Baba is most noted for his silence. From 1925 until his physical death on January 31, 1969, he spoke nothing. Although he wrote books and gave lectures with the help of an alphabet board, the silence of the personification of God in the midst of a world so given to continual communication through so many media no doubt bore a deep message. Later he gave up use of the alphabet board and communicated only through hand gestures. Baba said that he would break his silence by speaking the One Word which would spiritualize the world, manifest his true nature, and open a new age of love. Although on several occasions he indicated he would break his silence, and set dates, the time was always postponed. His death caused some to feel he had not lived up to his promise to speak the One Word. Others understood "the breaking of the silence" as an inner awakening of the heart. His devotees point to several veiled predictions he made earlier that he would suffer disease and humiliation before he spoke the "Word of Words" and was glorified. While the previous impression was that the prophecies indicated events that would happen before he "dropped the body," his followers now tell that on the day of his death he wrote, "Today is my crucifixion." They say that only now is the meaning of his humiliation—the taunts of the scoffers—really clear. They remain loyal to him in the expectation that in due time he will vindicate himself. In all of this Baba's lovers, convinced by his radiance and the strange psychic effect he had on them, believe there is enigmatically divine meaning behind his seeming capriciousness and defeat.

Meher Baba's writings and lectures place him definitely within the Sufi tradition, though he is most in the line of those Indian poets like Kabir and Nanak who have dwelt with great creativity on the borderline of Hinduism and Islam, combining Islamic monotheism with a Vedantic sense of divine nondualism and immanence, and Sufi-bhakti fervent devotionalism with its ideal of the fool for the love of God. Baha'i, Subud, and the Meher Baba movement are the three religions in the West most affected by that attractive Muslim mystical current called Sufism.

Meher Baba's formal teachings, most fully expounded in his book *God Speaks,* use mainly Sufi language and quotations from Sufi masters, together with some Vedanta terminology. The basic concept is that God "loses" himself in creation, and then "finds" himself by exterior evolution through stone, metal, vegetation, worms, birds, animals, and man to develop complete consciousness. Then for man there are seven interior states of "involution" or spiritual realization wherein what man understands as full consciousness is lost to be replaced by divine awareness. Those on the seventh plane of this ascent are God-realized. Some of them function as Perfect Masters. The avatar may, however, for reasons of divine policy, appears a Master on any of the higher planes. Meher Baba appears on the seventh, but Jesus, who because of his cultural environment had to retain some concern for miracles and dualistic attitudes, was embodied on the fourth plane. The appealing devotional writing of Meher Baba is pure Sufi celebration of intoxication with the wine of God's love, and of the comparison of the love of God with the love of fair women, and displays the charm of the babbling fools of this love.

To a remarkable extent, the lovers of Meher Baba carry to the streets of our cities this Sufi love. So it was in a meeting of Meher Baba followers held in the back room of a Meher Baba bookstore. From the outside the store appeared drab, and it was located in a "skid row" block. But within, the rooms were enlivened by many giant posters of the Master's beaming face, and by the harlequin dress of his devotees who were mostly young and of the new generation of seekers. About twenty-five were present, seated on couches and cushions in a big circle.

The unofficial leader, a bright-faced young man with a brown beard, opened the meeting by remarking that the center needed certain objects, including a vacuum cleaner and refrigerator. He then said that recently he had been with his wife to a natural childbirth class. It was in a Catholic hospital. During a break he wandered into the bookstore and picked up a paperback copy of *The Little Flowers of St. Francis.* He had apparently been unfamiliar with this classic before, but remembering that Baba had said St. Francis was the only Perfect Master the West had produced, he read this delightful and moving collection of incidents in the life of the saint of Assisi. Finding it real "heart stuff," full of the divine fool's love of God and man, he wanted to share it. He read aloud several incidents from the book, such as the conversion of Brother Bernard and the taming of the wolf of Gubbio. The group discussed the stories. Several had read Nikos Kazantzakis's novel about St. Francis. One boy, who could not have been more than twelve or thirteen, remarked that Francis's saying to Brother Leo that perfect joy is found in suffering for God reminded him of the same theme in the life of the Tibetan mystic Milarepa. Parallels in Baba's teachings were also continually brought out.

Next another member of the group read an installment of a continuing Sufi love story—one of those stories of wine and romance which can be taken on two levels. A little earlier, an obviously very drunk denizen of the neighborhood had wandered in, slouched down on the floor, and sat dozing. As the Sufi story was being read, he roused himself, looked at the reader, and broke in, saying, "Shcuse me, I wanna ask you a question. Are you happy?"

The reader with some aplomb smiled at him and said, "Yes. I'm happy because Baba is happy."

The visitor replied, "Who's Baba?"

"Baba is like our father."

"I'm sorry," he said.

"That's all right. Thank you, friend." The word of thanks seemed to amaze the guest as he sank again back into a stupor.

The group, like most religious groups centered around affective experience, is informal with emphasis on the creation of a fellowship of coequal love. Baba insisted he did not want to found an organization or "religion," and that there be no central structure. The Avatar Meher Baba Trust, set up by Baba years ago, is run by the disciples and is responsible for Meherabad, where his tomb is located, and the various charitable projects there (free clinic, pilgrims' quarters, etc.). There is a Baba center at North Myrtle Beach, South Carolina, where Baba himself spent time on three of his five visits to the United States. A San Francisco organization, Sufism Reoriented, makes Meher Baba as avatar a very important part of its vision, but is concerned with the main Sufi tradition too. In general, though, the followers of Baba form only scattered groups, usually meeting in Meher Baba bookstores (run by enthusiasts without much financial profit) or private homes. No permission to organize or join is needed save a love for Baba, and a delight in hearing and talking about him.

It was expected that the movement would decline sharply after 1969, in part because of Baba's death and in part because of the diminishing of the counterculture and mysticism which fed into it during the 1960s. In fact, it has held up better than anticipated. Figures are difficult to come by, mainly because membership criteria are lacking by which one can say precisely who is or is not a Baba Lover. Most persons in the United States and Europe who consider themselves Baba Lovers have come to know of him since 1969. Very few of his followers in the West actually met Meher Baba. In Myrtle Beach, for example, where about 300 Baba Lovers have moved to be near the Meher Spiritual Center, there are only six who met Baba. In 1984 the Center is said to have had 2,200 retreat guests; of these, more than 500 were new to Baba. (It is claimed that in India 10,000 pilgrims came to Meherabad on January 31, 1985—the anniversary of his passing— for a four-day celebration.)

During the past ten years there has been a growing interest among Baba Lovers in annual gatherings held in various locations in the United States and Europe. These are often called "Sahavas" gatherings (Baba used the term "Sahavas" when he would call together his lovers for an intimate time in his company). The oldest of these gatherings is in Southern California where two to three hundred persons come together each year.

Many Baba Lovers consider Meher Baba to be very much alive, guiding his lovers personally and directly, even though they have not met him physically. They believe, rather, that they have met him inwardly. Many Baba Lovers will say that this outpouring of love from Baba and to Baba is part of his manifestation, whatever else the "breaking of the silence" may mean.

Reading Selection: The Meher Baba Movement

In the following intriguing passage, the Master Meher Baba himself purports to describe his own consciousness for those who are not yet able to intuit it directly. The sense of mission, the Bhakti-Sufi sense of divine playfulness are there. To allow one like this to work in oneself is, for Baba's lovers, joy and the promise of more joy.

Believe that I am the Ancient One. Do not doubt that for a moment. There is no possibility of my being anyone else. I am not this body that you see. It is only a coat I put on when I visit you. I am Infinite Consciousness. I sit with you, play and laugh with you; but simultaneously I am working on all planes of existence.

Before me are saints and perfect saints and masters of the earlier stages of the spiritual path. They are all different forms of me. I am the Root of every one and every thing. An infinite number of branches spread out from me. I work through, and suffer in and for, each one of you.

My bliss and my infinite sense of humour sustain me in my suffering. The amusing incidents that arise at the expense of none lighten my burden.

Think of me; remain cheerful in all your trials and I am with you helping you.

MEHER BABA, *The Everything and the Nothing* (Sydney, Australia: Meher House Publications, 1963), p. 56.

ECKANKAR

Eckankar, "the ancient science of soul travel," is difficult to place in the classification of religious groups employed in this book. A case could be made for including it among the "ancient wisdom" groups, as its founder, Paul Twitchell, claimed to be the 971st Living ECK Master of the Order of Vairagi in a line said to begin before recorded history. But Eckankar also has a special connection with India (and Tibet) in that Twitchell claimed to have been initiated into soul travel and the ancient mysteries by former Masters Sudar Singh in India and Rebazar Tarzs in the Himalayas of Tibet. More than that, it is reasonably clear that he, like the founder of the Divine Light Mission, was heavily influenced by one of the neo-Sikh groups; in his case it was probably the Ruhani Satsang, founded by Kirpal Singh, which derived from the Radhasoami Satsang Beas. According to David Christopher Lane, author of *The Making of a Spiritual Movement,*[16] Paul Twitchell was initiated by Kirpal Singh during a tour of the United States in 1955. More substantially, certain concepts that appear prominently in Eckankar are remarkably similar to those of the Radhasoami tradition of India,[17] in particular, the ideas of the Perfect Master (*satguru*), of the divine as manifesting itself as sound current, and of the path of return to God.

Eckankar has a spiritual cosmology which distinguishes between higher and lower worlds or planes. It distinguishes specifically twelve planes, beginning with the lowest (the physical) and climaxing with the plane of Sugmad, the Eckists' name for God (while allowing that there are yet higher planes not yet realized). The four lowest planes constitute the totality of the physical and psychic worlds (the usual habitat of humans, because of karma and reincarnation). Above them are the spiritual worlds in ascending order. The world of Sugmad is the source of all life; all life flows down from Sugmad. This cosmic current, which flows downward and returns in wavelike fashion, is referred to as Eck; it is comparable to the *Shabd* of the Ruhani Satsang. The human soul is identified with Eck, the essence of God, the divine spark that dwells in every human. Eck can be known and experienced, for it manifests itself as sound and light, which can be heard and seen by those who attune themselves through spiritual exercises.

In broad terms, Eckankar is a variation on the familiar theme of return to God through ascension. Because the soul (*atma sarup*) is separable from the body, it is able to travel progressively to the higher worlds in the course of which it becomes Self-Realized, God-Realized, and, ultimately, a "co-worker with God" (the meaning of the term Eckankar). Individuality is preserved throughout eternity.

"Soul travel" can be experienced on all levels, beginning with the astral plane (immediately above the physical plane). Travel on the astral plane ("astral projection"), however, is little more than a curiosity and a play; it is the exploration of the higher, spiritual worlds that is religiously significant. Eckankar teaches its students (called "chelas") a large number and variety of spiritual exercises, including the use of dreams, imagination, and direct projection, by means of which they may begin to explore the worlds of Eck. For the higher explorations one needs a spiritual guide who can initiate him or her into the higher planes. Such is the essential function of the Eck Masters, especially of the Living Eck Master (comparable to the *satguru* of the Radhasoami tradition). He can be contacted, as it were, and become accessible not only physically but by means of various spiritual exercises. Many chelas say they meet the Eck Master in their dreams. The Living Eck Master ultimately delivers the chela from the chains of reincarnation by linking him or her with the divine, cosmic Eck current. The path is long and difficult, however. It begins with overcoming the obstacles to spiritual progress (the five passions: lust, anger, greed, attachment, and vanity). One is then ready to experience the wisdom, charity, and freedom which come from the practice of Eck and to begin the journey through the spiritual planes to the world of Sugmad. Thus one is led to realms where complete spiritual freedom is finally attained.

The key word in the appeal of Eckankar is freedom. It offers the experience of freedom of the soul from the body and freedom from the fear of death, for the Eckist knows that death is only an illusion. It offers freedom from confusion about one's place in the cosmos because the soul traveller can view the whole picture from above and see how each piece fits into the cosmic puzzle. Finally, Eckankar offers freedom from the cycle of birth and death. Through Eckankar, the soul, the divine spark of God, can soar freely through the worlds and witness at firsthand the beauty of all Sugmad's creations. Most importantly, the divine spark can experience the greatest freedom of all—the freedom to return to the heavenly kingdom of God.

The 971st Living Eck Master, Paul Twitchell, the founder of Eckankar, was in some respects a mysterious figure. There is a biography,[18] but questions have been raised about its reliability. Curiously, it does not give the year of his birth, which may have been as early as about 1910. (He died in 1971.) Similarly, the place of his birth is uncertain. Was it China Point, Mississippi, as the biography has it, or was it, perhaps, Paducah, Kentucky? The question is not intrinsically important, but it is indicative of some elements of mystery that surround Twitchell—mystery which continued with his accounts of visits to India and Tibet, and initiations and soul travels with past Masters.[19]

Questions also exist about his involvements with other religious groups (besides Neo-Sikhism) in the United States before the founding of Eckankar.[20] Our intention is not to denigrate him, but to suggest that in the case of Paul Twitchell, as in some others encountered earlier in this book, an air of uncertainty and mystery is characteristic. As we have seen, it often adds to the appeal and power of the persons possessing it.

Paul Twitchell was succeeded by the 972nd Living Eck Master, Darwin Gross, when after the former's "translation" (death) in 1971 "the Rod of Power" was passed to him. Eckists claim, however, that after his translation "Shri Paul" is more accessible than ever to the chelas, having been released from such limitations as those associated with physical life. Eckankar grew substantially under the leadership of Darwin Gross. He is a musician and encouraged Eckists to become interested in music and other arts, relating it all to spiritual growth. He was also chiefly responsible for the establishment of an impressive international headquarters in Menlo Park, California. After ten years the Rod of Power was passed to Harold Klemp on October 22, 1981. (October 22nd seems to have been Paul Twitchell's birth date—whatever the year—as well as the date of the official founding of Eckankar in 1965. It also marks the close of the old and the beginning of the new spiritual year in the Eckists' religious calendar.)

Eckankar has an initiatory structure, the details of which are not made public. However, initiates of the fifth grade or higher are called "Mahdis." Some are chosen to make Eck teaching available to the public and to oversee the satsang classes for chelas. They also perform sacredotal functions, including Eck weddings, initiations, and funerals. "Arahatas" are eligible to teach the satsang classes, in which there is study and discussion of the Satsang Discourses, written by Twitchell. The Satsang Group, composed of chelas, is Eckankar's principal social expression of its religious experience. At the same time, each chela is said to be under the personal tutelage and guidance of the Living Eck Master.

Although Eckankar was founded in 1965 and has experienced significant growth during two decades, it is one of the less widely known new religious movements. Eckankar has maintained a rather low profile, although it has done some advertising (for example, advertisements of some of Twitchell's books in *Time* magazine and occasionally on television). Eckists are not readily identifiable by dress or other means and do not propagate their faith aggressively. They assume, rather, that when individuals are ready for what Eckankar has to offer, the seekers will somehow present themselves and the connection will be made. They respect the religious freedom of others. The experience of the writers is that Eckists tend to be thoughtful, gentle, concerned persons who are "ordinary" in most respects; they hardly fit the stereotype of a "cult member."

Reading Selection: Eckankar

In the following selection Paul Twitchell writes of the basic principles of soul travel. Elsewhere he describes a number of specific techniques for effecting the separation of the soul from the body.

The key to soul travel, separation of spirit from body, is made up of three essential, basic principles.

The trio of these principles are: thought, light, and sound. Each of these has a part in the leaving and returning to the physical body by one's own volition. Unless those interested in the art of soul-travel-at-will know and use these three basic elements as an integrated media, their success will be limited to the three visible worlds only.

Thought, that principle we call action, is done by the faculty of imagination. By placing the idea somewhere in some action, thought will be followed by the inner body within the first three worlds. The essential idea here is to make contact with a spiritual traveler who can give assistance in acquiring experience in the state of being outside the body.

The second part of the three principles is concerned with the cosmic light, which is a study within itself. The true nature of this phenomenon is that it brings wisdom, love, and bliss to those who are fortunate enough to receive it in its purer form. Often this light will present itself like a rosy glow, a mantle wrapped around the person whom it has chosen as a channel. . . .

Sound is the third and most important part of the three principles in the study of soul travel. It is the central theme in every religion, and the creating and sustaining power of the entire universe, including the physical worlds. When St. John wrote in the beginning of his Gospel that the word was God, and all things were made by Him, and without Him nothing was made, he was speaking of the sound, which is found in every religious scripture of the world.

This sound stands for all that the Supreme Being is, and what He does in all worlds. In other words, it is the whole of the Divine Being in action, and includes all of His qualities. It is through light and sound that the universal spirit can manifest itself to the human consciousness.

Once the spiritual consciousness is awakened in one, especially in one who has learned soul travel, he may hear the sound, and when he feels it, he feels the power of God. This sound is the Divine Being expressing Himself in something that is both audible and visible.

Once anyone has developed the ability for soul travel, the spiritual hearing can pick up the sound and purification of the mind and soul. These are then cleared to be attuned to the higher vibrations.

Anyone wishing to do soul travel can practice it by sitting in silence and being completely relaxed. Once this has been experienced in a few sessions of practice, the practitioner will find the sound will begin to be heard by the inner sense, and the light will begin to appear to his spiritual eyes. It takes practice, although other techniques by which one can gain this spiritual phenomenon are always available. One can gain this spiritual phenomenon by these methods much more quickly than having to wait for it.

The three principles must be integrated: thought, light, and sound. Once out of the body, the great self encounters massive areas of light, but it can move anywhere within these regions by thought—the actions of the other worlds—and pass to wherever desired on beams of sound, for that desire will be according to self's thought command.

These principles become an integrated part within soul and can be used for beneficial aspects for man himself or for a universal need among his fellowmen.

PAUL TWITCHELL, *Eckankar: The Key to Secret Worlds* (Menlo Park, CA: Illuminated Way Press, 1969), pp. 101–103. Reprinted by permission.

NOTES

[1] Swami Prabhavananda and Frederick Manchester, trans., *The Upanishads: Breath of the Eternal* (New York: The New American Library, Mentor Books, 1961), pp. 123–25. Copyright 1957 by the Vedanta Society of Southern California.

[2] Paramahansa Yogananda, *Metaphysical Meditations* (Los Angeles: Self-Realization Fellowship, 1964), p. 36.

[3] See Charles T. Tart, "A Psychologist's Experience with Transcendental Meditation," *Journal of Transpersonal Psychology*, 2, (1971), 135–40; Robert Keith Wallace, "Physiological Effects of Transcendental Meditation,: *Science*, 167 (March 27, 1970), 1751–54; Robert Keith Wallace and Herbert Benson, "The Physiology of Meditation," *Scientific American*, February 1972, pp. 85–90; Anthony Campbell, M.D., *Seven States of Consciousness: A Vision of Possibilities Suggested by the Teaching of Maharishi Mahesh Yogi* (New York: Harper Torchbooks, 1973).

[4] The traditional Indian greeting accompanying palms of the hands pressed together.

[5] Jean Varenne, *Yoga and the Hindu Tradition*, trans. Derek Coltman (Chicago: University of Chicago Press, 1976), p. ix.

[6] Mircea Eliade, "Nights at Serampore," in *Two Tales of the Occult*, trans. William Ames Coates (New York: Herder & Herrder, 1970), pp. 3–60. Eliade practiced yoga at Rishikesh under the direction of Sivananda for six months during his youth.

[7]*The Complete Illustrated Book of Yoga* (Bombay: Ananda Press, 1967).

[8]Mircea Eliade, *Yoga: Immortality and Freedom*, 2nd ed. (Princeton: Princeton University Press, 1969), p. 45.

[9]See, for example, Mircea Eliade, *Patanjali and Yoga*, trans. Charles Lam Markmann (New York: Schocken Books, 1975).

[10]Victor Turner, *The Ritual Process* (Chicago: Aldine, 1969), p. 95.

[11]*Darshana* is the Hindu practice of seeing and being seen by a divine image.

[12]*From Sex to Superconsciousness* (Poona: Rajneesh Foundation, 1973), pp. 32f.

[13]Quoted in Vasant Joshi, *The Awakened One* (San Francisco: Harper and Row Publishers, Inc., 1982), p. 1.

[14]The Jains are a religious community that goes back to the sixth century B.C. The traditional founder, Mahavira, was a contemporary of Gautama Buddha. Traditionally, the Jain religious way of life has emphasized asceticism.

[15]Lay Buddhists used a similar formula, taking "refuge" in the Buddha (the Enlightened or Awakened One), the *sangha* (the religious community), and the *dharma* (the doctrine, truth).

[16](Del Mar, CA.: Del Mar Press, 1983), p. 22.

[17]On the Radhasoami tradition, see Philip Ashby, *Modern Trends in Hinduism* (New York: Columbia University Press, 1974), Ch. 4.

[18]Brad Steiger, *In My Soul I Am Free* (Menlo Park, CA.: Illuminated Way Press).

[19]See, for example, his book *The Tiger's Fang* (Menlo Park, CA.: Illuminated Way Press, 1967), an account of his soul travels in the worlds of Sugmad with Rebazar Tarzs.

[20]Including the Self-Revelation Church of Absolute Monism, related to the Self-Realization Fellowship of Paramahansa Yogananda; and Ron Hubbard's Scientology.

8

THE EAST IN THE GOLDEN WEST:
Other Oriental Movements

This chapter offers a discussion of a collection of groups based on non-Indian sources. Three are Buddhist, two are primarily mystical Muslim in inspiration, one is an unusual oriental version of Christianity. Their geographical origin is even more diverse: Japan, Iran, Indonesia, Korea, and Tibet.

But these oriental movements have certain points in common. While they all have charismatic leadership, no one has been able to equal the Indians (especially the Bengalis) in fascinating Americans by sheer force of personality and in sweeping all before them amid waves of publicity. These movements have been sometimes less centered on one personality. They have flourished mainly by reason of the appeal of the actual technique or philosophy of the movement, and have been propagandized more by convinced Westerners in the West than by their Eastern advocates.

It would first be well to examine Buddhism and Islam with a view to understanding what it is in them which has made movements based on their experience appealing to some Americans.

Buddhism can be considered an "export version" of Hinduism in the same sense that Christianity is of Judaism. It encapsulates in the saving experience of a single member of that tradition its universal essence. But both new export religions do not bring with them whole societal and cultic traditions, such as the caste system and Brahman sacrifices in Hinduism. For the Buddha, the essential experience was that of *anatman*, or "no self."

This term puts in convenient negative form the basic Upanishadic discovery of the unity of the self with the universal, Brahman. The Buddha discovered during the night of his enlightenment, as he sat under the fig tree vowing not to move from there until he had obtained the object of his quest, that our sense of being an independent separate self is the product, not of experience of reality, but of anxieties created by blind needs and desires. We are actually just collections of elements. In the Buddha's dying words, "All aggregates are transitory." But there is hope, hope keener than the seeming despair of this analysis and sharper than desire. By mindfulness of ego illusion one can live in freedom and unconditionedness, swimming in the tides of the universal. One can be an expression of the universal, as adamantine and joyful and fearless as the Whole.

All Buddhist techniques are ultimately means of "turning on" this kind of consciousness. Anything that can stop for a moment the "monkey mind" and give one even a flash of what is left when the anxiety-desire syndrome is halted is precious. Therefore valuable is the numinous wonder of a cool, dark, incense-laden Buddhist temple, with its other-worldly glittering gold lotuses and inward-gazing image; the deep frenzy of Tibetan visualizing of strange Buddhas and gods; the silence of the Zen meditator cut off from external sensual stimuli; the powerful steady chanting of "Nam Myoho Renge Kyo" by adherents of Nichiren Shoshu.

Most modern Westerners who have been interested in following Buddhist practices have taken up with Mahayana, the Buddhism of China, Tibet, and Japan. This great tradition puts most emphasis not on the historical Buddha but on the universal presence of the "Buddha-nature" in every blade of grass and every grain of sand and every sentient being. The Buddha-nature is really an ontologizing of the Buddha's enlightenment experience. It is the true nature of reality, which he let irradiate his being at that moment. Because the Buddha-nature is present everywhere, it can be realized as one's true nature at any moment, whenever we loosen our grasp on ego-illusions. To aid in this realization, the universe is seen as continuous with the ground of the mind. The universe is visualized as full of Buddhas and Bodhisattvas (beings in enlightenment-consciousness who operate in this world at the same time), who are, as it were, projections of the ideal or enlightened self. Creation of such figures who have psychological rather than historical or "out there" reality, of course, is an important part of the "esoteric" Buddhism of Tibet and some other places. Chanting, rituals, and yogic psychosomatic exercises are among the techniques used to make the "meditation" Buddhas appear.

This tradition employs the archetypes and images of the mind—the same which appear in myth and dream—as doorways into the state of consciousness in which burdensome selfhood disappears. Another popular tradition, Zen, takes an opposite tack. It teaches that all such conceptualizations only perpetuate the structures of self, and that one must be able to break through all forms and images. One can do this through "sitting quietly doing nothing," or by the psychological tension created by the *sesshin,* or intensive Zen training session. The *sesshin* participant barely eats or sleeps for several days. He practices meditation, and has often painful interviews with the *roshi,* or master, through the long days. Finally, the tension builds up until, like water breaking over a dam, he suddenly is struck by the surprise of *satori,* the awareness of seeing things on the Buddha-nature level.

These are all ways of capturing the secure joy of being in tune with ultimate Oneness. The other major religion which lies behind the groups under consideration in this chapter, Islam, is also profoundly concerned with Oneness, but in a very different way. In Islam psychological and cosmic Oneness mean setting to rights the relationship of two entities, the omnipotent personal God and the individual, through submission of the latter to God, a submission deepened by the exchange of love.

The fundamental tenet of Islam, proclaimed every day by the muezzin from the minaret of every mosque, is that there is no god but God ("Allah" is "The God" in Arabic) and Muhammad is his Prophet, or Envoy. Islam (which means "submission," submission to the absolute will of God) is a supreme example of the emissary style of religious communication. Muhammad is emphatically human. He was selected by God as his final prophet solely by God's will and not on the basis of any great psychic or mystical recommendations, even though orthodox Muslims also talk of him as a paragon of virtue.

Nonetheless, the powerful emphasis on the singleness and omnipotence of God gave rise to currents in Islam capable of making contact with the alternative reality tradition in the West, especially as Islam encountered Hellenism, Zoroastrianism, and India on its fringes. On one hand, the tremendousness of the Muslim God encouraged great concern about the legitimacy of lines of communication between this mighty being and ordinary men. Muslim arguments about true *imams,* prophets, and masters provided some fuel for the speculative flames of Theosophy, and also provided prophesies and models for teachers of new gospels like Baha-'u'llah of Baha'i. On the other hand, the greatness and personality of the Islamic God favored a type of mysticism called Sufism marked by yearning, freedom, ecstasy, and awareness of immediacy expressed exquisitely in its classical literature through the language of love and intoxication.

These two traditions often interacted in the Shi'ite Islam of Iran and neighboring areas. That land was one homeland of Shi'ite eschatologists and Sufi mystics. Shi'ah taught that an infallible human teacher is needed to interpret Islam, and that he should be found in the descendants of Ali, Muhammad's cousin. Ali was brought up by the Prophet, married his daughter Fatimah, and was his constant companion. But after the death of Muhammad there was no peace between the heirs of this lineage, the *imams,* and the politico-religious leaders of two successive dynasties called caliphs who usually held the actual power in the expanding Muslim Empire. Indeed, the first eleven *imams* all died violently; the death of the third, Husain, in 680 in the month of Mukarram is mourned annually by Shi'ite Muslims with rites of wailing so fervently emotional as to be reminiscent of the ancient wailing for Tammuz or Osiris, and to have seasonal-soteriological overtones.

Against the background of this dark and tragic scenario of the fate which befell the family of the envoy of God, Shi'ah believes that the twelfth *imam*, who was not murdered but who disappeared, is still living. For sixty-nine years he was in hiding, but communicated to the faithful through four ambassadors; he then went into a great hiding, and sent no ambassadors. But he is the Coming One, the *Imam* for all time, and will reappear when the world is full of evil. One can readily understand that this kind of teaching could blend easily into belief in secret Masters, and charge the air with electric apocalyptic expectation. The flavor of Shi'ah's belief in infallible teachers, true though hidden succession, and new revelation is carried over directly in Baha'i, and has deeply tinctured other mysteries of central Asian background, including Theosophy, for the lands where knowledge of the hidden *Imam* was rife were probably among those through which the young Helena Blavatsky wandered.

The Sufis also believed that a hidden hierarchy of saints ruled the world of Islam. This authority was for them based more on spiritual attainment and occult transmission than physical descent from the Prophet. Sufis in the Shi'ite areas claimed that a special secret knowledge of the inner meaning of Islam was passed from Muhammad through Ali and the *Imams*. This tradition was more mystical than the outer husks of the Koranic law.

The further east from its Arabian homeland Islam moved, by and large, the more mystical in temper it became. The lush, tropical islands of Indonesia, with their graceful, smiling people, are in sharp contrast to Saudi Arabia. Although they are predominantly Muslim, it is an Islam modified by an animistic, Hindu, and Buddhist past. Sufism found fertile ground in the islands' pantheistic milieu. Like Sufis, especially dervishes, everywhere, many Indonesian orders have produced religious ecstasy by shouting loud rhythmic praises of Allah, jumping, and dancing strange circular dances. In Java, some members of Sufi orders even stabbed themselves with iron daggers at the height of the ecstasy. Against this background, one can well understand the emergence of the techniques of Subud.

In general the transmittal of these Eastern teachings to the West has been conditioned by two factors: (1) They have made their distinctive experience independent and absolute. They say, in other words, that the truth of their expression of Buddhism or Islam is more important than Buddhism or Islam itself, and of unconditioned universal validity. This makes them rather heterodox in their homelands, but gives them great universality and makes them able to become part of the alternative reality tradition in the West. (2) An unusual teacher or special set of historical circumstances has made transmittal to the West possible.

Tibet and Subud come West in part because something in the troubled Western psyche needs them in the same way it needs the alternative reality tradition. The new gospel of Baha'i does not come to the West to communicate Shi'ite Islam, which on its conscious level is no part of it, but because we also need a new messiah and a vision of world unity, and find this movement so detached from its cultural sources as to convince us of its claim to universality.

WESTERN ZEN

Zen today is not quite as big a symbol of the spiritual counterculture as it was in the 1950s, before LSD and maharishis and astrology had come forward to share the new milieu with it. Indeed, something in the cold water austerity and hard antisymbolism of Zen was incompatible with the luxuriant surrealist fancy of the sixties. But in an earlier day, when "beatniks" talked philosophy over cheap wine in dreary flats unadorned by psychedelic posters, Zen seemed the chief religious token of a total reversal of Western values. It was the day of Kerouac's *Dharma Bums,* whose heroes wandered the littered American hinterland seeing the crown of ten-wondered Avalokiteshvara in the stars and the laughing cosmic Buddha-nature in the heart of the drabbest railway tramp. There were some who were more than just romantics in the Kerouac style. Some went to Japan to practice; some started serious Zen meditation halls in the United States, often under the supervision of masters brought from Japan; some underwent the gruelling spiritual marathon of the *sesshin.*

I once attended a typical Thursday-evening *zazen,* or seated meditation, at an American center of the Rinzai denomination of Zen.* The *roshi* or master was from a Japanese monastery, but most of the members of this center were Caucasian. Some were students at nearby universities, usually in Asian studies, who lived a communal life in the center and were intending to become Zen monks or priests. Most were persons in the city who came to "sit" fairly often, and to receive guidance from the *roshi.*

As I crossed the flagstoned courtyard of the center, I was met by a courteous European-accented lady who, rightly taking me for a newcomer, instructed me to enter the hall, bow to the image of the Buddha on the altar, and take a seat on one of the two rows of mats on either side of the hall. This I did, sitting cross-legged with spine erect, and eyes pointed toward the floor three feet in front of me. With some thirty other people, I sat in this manner for half an hour. A proctor, one of the students, walked around the hall with a stick on his shoulder. When he saw someone whose mindfulness seemed to be lagging, or whose posture was poor (often the case with me), he would sound the stick sharply on the floor before him, or if it was a stable and experienced member who requested it, would administer a smart but harmless blow on the shoulder.

At the end of a half hour, everyone silently arose, moved to the courtyard, and snaked around it at a half-running pace hands folded for a minute or two, then returned. There was another half hour of meditation, exercise, and then another.

I was then asked if I would like to have an interview with the *roshi.* I said that I would, and was led to a small anteroom. A low table, with a gong on it, was the only piece of furniture; three or four persons were seated on the floor in *zazen* posture beside the table. Beyond this room was the *roshi* in a private audience hall. When he had finished with an interviewee, he rang

*It seems appropriate to present this personal experience of Robert Ellwood in the first person.

a bell. The next in line responded by sounding the gong in the audience hall. He would then enter, kowtow (bow touching the forehead to the floor) to the *roshi* as he entered his room, and kowtow once again just before him.

The small, round Zen master, seated high on a vast cushion, wearing a sashed and starchy-winged gown of old Japan, toying with a Japanese fan, greeted me gravely. He took a note of introduction from me.

"So," he said, eyeing me shrewdly, "You're a professor of religion. Do you believe in God?"

Stumbling around, having no real idea how one expressed such things to a Zen master, I tried to say something about my belief in God as the ground of my being and the universe's.

I was cut short. I felt a surprising sting as the master slapped me on the thigh with his folded fan, and said "Not good! NOW how do you believe in God?"

This time I stumbled even more. "Perhaps in the immediacy of the experience . . ."

"Not good!" he retorted, slapping me again with the fan. "This is your Zen koan. Meditate on it. NOW how do you believe in God?"

The Zen koan is a puzzle-like conundrum (famous ones are "Where was your face before you were born?" "What is the sound of one hand clapping?") designed to bring the mind up against a stoppage of its rational machination, and move it into the empty and marvelous void of enlightenment. I thought I knew what this one, "NOW how do you believe in God?" meant: How do you rub against God in the immediate NOW? Not in reflection upon study or experience of God two years, or two seconds, ago; not in anticipation of God's future disclosures, but NOW, in the flashing moment before the dimensionless NOW has escaped into memory and reflection and its content become thereby twisted into words and concepts, where is God?

I ruminated upon this for a time after a return to the *zazen* position, in the main hall, and tried to push my mind beyond the verbal boxes into which we put all experiences as soon as we are aware we are having them, or only a split-second later. Then I began, if only dimly, to have some feeling of the potential of Zen enlightenment.

I sensed a timeless euphoria. I was lightly floating, as though I might be a half-inch above the mat. All times except the NOW fell away, like something seen through the wrong end of a telescope. I might have been in that Zen meditation hall two hours, which was actually the case, or two weeks, or two years, or two centuries; it didn't matter and wouldn't have felt much different whichever it was. This was my life, the center of my being. I remembered, as a small child, going out in the back yard, lying under the peony bushes. I imagined that I was floating in the midst of black, empty space, with only stars and planets as companions, and that my house, my family, and my life were only a story I was telling myself.

But soon enough this meditation was over, tea was served, and the *roshi* came out to give an address, translated by a Japanese-American member of the group. (The interpreter is a simple gardener by day, but some in the temple say he is a bodhisattva.) Finally, the evening ended with the chanting, in Japanese, of the Heart Sutra. ("Form is emptiness, and emptiness is form . . . The wisdom that has gone beyond, and beyond the beyond; O what an awakening, all hail!")

On a later occasion, when I told about this experience in speaking to a church group, a medical doctor said to me afterwards that this experience wasn't necessarily "spiritual." The euphoria and timelessness were probably results of the cutting off the circulation in my legs by the unaccustomed posture; Doubtless this is true, but a Zen master would probably have said, "So what?" If man is a unity of mind and body, set over against the One, what difference does it make how much one part of the unity helps the other to realize the One? The spiritual quest is not a battle of spirit against flesh in the East, but a struggle of each to find the other and thereby the Whole. If an experience of the Ecstasy of the One is induced in part by physiological means, does this make it any less "valid"?

The point of Zen is to induce an experience which stops the activity of the "monkey mind," with its continual bouncing from one thing to another. Anything which throws sand in the mind's gears, which brings the mind up against a blank wall, is to the point. It can be counting breaths (from one to ten), merely maintaining mindfulness of breathing, following thoughts until they dissipate like soap bubbles, reflecting on the koans.

This experience is central to Zen, but, of course, its popularity in America depends on more than that. Zen is also a delight in the strange stories told about the old Zen masters, juicy with whimsy and fierce joy. There is, among many Western Zen enthusiasts, a desire to adopt a culture as well as a faith in their passion for the tea ceremony, the painting and architecture and gardens of Zen. In all of these forms the essence which represents the One in it is reached through taking away all that is superfluous and "unnatural." A bird on a bamboo is represented by a half-dozen strokes of the brush. The whole of Buddhism is capsulized in a *haiku* poem:

> An old pond;
> A frog jumps in:
> The sound of water.

And in the art of swordsmanship as taught by masters steeled in Zen, the adept is supposed to be able to cause his opponent to flee without striking a blow, simply by the poise of his pose and visage.

The Buddhist Society of America, called after the Second World War the First Zen Institute of America, was founded in New York in 1930 by Shigetsu Sasaki (1882–1945), called Sokei-an. The struggling center made some impression and published a delightful periodical, *Cat's Yawn*,[1] until the *roshi* was imprisoned during the war. He was released in 1943, but died before peace was reestablished with his homeland. His widow, an American, Ruth Fuller Sasaki (1893–1967), continued the work. After the New York Center had been well launched in postwar American culture, she moved permanently to Japan. Her labor toward establishing Western Zen on a firm basis of commitment, scholarship, and discipline was indispensable.

The postwar Zen boom, however, was too explosive to be attributed to one line of transmission. The greatest influence was probably not any Western Zen center, but the writing of D. T. Suzuki (1870–1966). The almost countless books on Buddhism and Zen he authored in English, and also those of his American wife, Beatrice Lane Suzuki, and of those Westerners who learned Zen from him—Edward Conze, Hubert Benoit, Christmas Humphreys, Alan Watts—have in very large part been Zen as it has appealed to the West. The intense intellectual interest in Zen in the fifties can be traced directly to Suzuki's lectures in Columbia University early in the decade. The strengths (universality, psychological awareness, freedom) of Zen in the West, and also its weaknesses (limited concern for the actual practice of monastic Zen in the East, impatience with discipline) stem from his and his disciples' predilections.

One counterbalance has now come forward in Philip Kapleau's book, *The Three Pillars of Zen*.[2] For him, Zen is less a romantic or existential or crypto-psychoanalytic experience than a hard monastic discipline, even when experienced by laymen. He stresses, unlike Suzuki and Watts, the techniques of sitting and the ordeal of the *sesshin*, and insists that the true fruits of Zen cannot be attained without them.

Out of all this, there are now ten or twelve serious Zen centers in the United States, with legitimately trained masters, including Kapleau's in Rochester and the Zen Center of Los Angeles. The largest is undoubtedly the San Francisco Zen Center, with hundreds of students, many resident, in its four locations in the Bay Area. It operates the already-legendary Zen Mountain Center at Tassajara Hot Springs, in the rugged country east of Big Sur. Almost as hard to reach as *satori*, the Center was once a fashionable hot springs resort. The hills are steep, the forests deep and murmuring, the moon large and bright as in ancient myth.

Zen students come to Tassajara to spend several months combining work and meditation and recreation under the direction of the *roshi*. They eat simple but delicious organic vegetarian food, and sit in front of blank brick walls. The *roshi* asks meditators to count breaths for forty minutes without losing count (not easy!) before doing more. In the meantime, nature and time move at different rates than in the city. The "Tassajara Calendar, Herbal & Bestiary" records such events as:

February—Canyon Wrens sing
        lots of thrushes
        some lavender Shooting Stars

March 19—planted—Chard, green and red.
        Suzuki Roshi:"When it is hot we are hot Buddhas.
            When it is cold we are cold Buddhas."

Mid-June—a desert dryness
        Scattered on the hills Yucca plants send up phallic green stalks
        from the middle of spiked fortresses, then burst into tall
        candles of pure white flowers blazing in the Sun, glowing
        under the Full Moon.

Reading Selection: Western Zen

Of many writings by Westerners who have experienced "the taste of Zen," perhaps this account of an experience of *kensho*, the breakthrough to enlightenment, best catches its potentialities. *Dokusan* is the interview between the *roshi* or master and the student. *Mu*, "nothingness" or the wondrous void, was the koan or riddle-like word to focus meditation given this lady, an American schoolteacher. The experiences took place during a *sesshin*, or period of intensive Zen practice.

The morning of the fifth day I stayed home to take care of the children. I should mention that neither my husband nor I attended sesshin full time. We took turns going to the 4 A.M. sitting and went home for almost all meals. I stayed overnight once, my husband not at all.

A little embarrassed at dokusan that afternoon, I confessed that I had not done zazen at home because of too many interruptions. I was told that two people had already reached kensho and that if I exerted myself to the utmost, I could also get kensho. So that night my husband allowed me to stay overnight.

With Mu I went to bed, with Mu I arose the sixth day. "Don't get nervous," Tai-san cautioned, "just concentrate." I listened to these words of wisdom, but was too tired to meditate. My energies were drained. After breakfast I lay down to rest, doing Mu in a horizontal position, when suddenly a glow appeared in front of my eyes as though sunshine were hitting them directly. I clearly heard sounds I had not heard since I was a little girl sick in bed: my mother's footsteps and the rustling of her boxes. Having had so many strange experiences already at this sesshin, I paid no further heed but continued my concentration on Mu throughout the entire morning's sitting. As I was awaiting dokusan a familiar aroma tantalized my nostrils; it was the tempting smell of my mother's cooking. My eyes glanced at a red cushion on a brown table, the same colors of my grandmother's living-room furniture. A door slammed, a dog barked, a white cloud sailed through a blue sky—I was reliving my childhood in makyo, hallucinations.

At noon, with the roshi's permission, my husband told me that he had achieved kensho. "Now or never!" I told myself. "A pumpkin wife cannot be married to an enlightened husband!" I vividly recalled the story of the youth with the knife and incense. "Death or deliverance!" became my watchword.

I inhaled deeply and with each exhalation concentrated with all my might on Mu. I felt as though I were all air and would levitate any second. I "crawled" into the belly of a hideous, hairy spider. "Mu! Mu! Mu!" I groaned, and I became a big, black Mu. An angel, it seemed, touched me ever so softly on the shoulder, and I fell backwards. Suddenly I realized that my husband and Tai-san were standing behind me, but I could not move; my feet were absolutely numb. They practically carried me outside, and I sobbed helplessly. "I was already dead," I said to myself. "Why did they have to bring me back to life?" At dokusan the roshi told me that this was but a foretaste of kensho, it was not yet realization.

Then I took a little walk and suddenly the whole experience of the last few days seemed utterly ridiculous to me. "That stupid roshi," I remember thinking, "he and his Oriental hocus-pocus. He just doesn't know what he's talking about." At dinner, half an hour later, as I was fumbling with my chopsticks, I felt like getting up and handing him a fork. "Here, old boy, let's get used to Western ways." I giggled at my own joke. Throughout the evening chanting I could hardly keep a straight face. After the roshi's final words I wanted to pick up my bag and walk out, never to return, so unreal did it all seem.

In his first lecture the roshi had told us that Mu was like a red-hot ball stuck in the throat which one can neither swallow nor spit out. He was right, so right. As I look back, every word, every move was part of the deliberate plan of this venerable teacher. His name, "White Cloud" [Hakuun], indeed fits him. He is the greatest, whitest cloud I have ever experienced, a real antidote to the dark atomic mushroom.

Now I was in bed, doing zazen again. All night long I alternately breathed Mu and fell into trances. I thought of the monk who had reached kensho in just such a state of fatigue. Eventually I must have dozed off in complete exhaustion. Suddenly the same light angel touched me on the shoulder. Only this time I awoke with a bright "Ha!" and realized I was enlightened. The angel was my kind, tired husband tapping me on the shoulder to waken me to go to sesshin.

A strange power propelled me. I looked at the clock—twenty minutes to four, just in time to make the morning sitting. I arose and calmly dressed. My mind raced as I solved problem after problem. I arrived at the sesshin before four o'clock and accepted an offer of coffee with such a positive "Yes" that I could not believe my own ears. When Tai-san came around with his "sword" I told him not to bother hitting me. At dokusan I rushed into the little cottage my teacher was occupying and hugged and kissed him and shook Tai-san's hand, and let loose with such a torrent of comical verbosity that all three of us laughed with delight. The roshi tested and passed me, and I was officially ushered through the gateless gate.

A lifetime has been compressed into one week. A thousand new sensations are bombarding my senses, a thousand new paths are opening before me. I live my life minute by minute, but only now does a warm love pervade my whole being, because I know that I am not just my little self but a great big miraculous Self. My constant thought is to have everybody share this deep satisfaction.

I can think of no better way to end this account than with the vows I chanted at sesshin every morning:

All beings, however limitless, I vow to save. Fantasy and delusion, however endless, I vow to cut off. Dharma teachings, however immeasurable, I vow to master. Buddha's Way, however lofty, I vow to attain.

PHILIP KAPLEAU, *The Three Pillars of Zen* (New York and Tokyo: John Weatherhill, Inc., 1965), pp. 243–45.

TIBETAN BUDDHISM IN AMERICA

"OM MANI PADME HUM"—the low, guttural sounds of the chanting of Tibetan lamas is heard in Berkeley, Boulder, Barnet, Vermont, and other places in the United States.[3] It would seem to be the fulfillment of the strange prophecy attributed to Padmasambhava, who brought Buddhism to Tibet in the eighth century: "When the iron bird flies, and horses run on wheels, the Tibetan people will be scattered like ants across the world, and the Dharma will come to the land of the Red Man."

In 1959 a hundred thousand Tibetans, including the Dalai Lama and many lesser lamas, fled Tibet before the Chinese occupiers. They sought exile in India, Nepal, Bhutan, Sikkim, and, to some extent, the West. Their desperate plight led Houston Smith to make a film in India to preserve a record of their chanting and ceremonies. He entitled the film poignantly "Requiem for a Faith." It seems, however, that the demise of the Tibetan form of Buddhism, regarded by Westerners as either extraordinarily sophisticated philosophy and psychology or a mixture of superstition and magic, was announced prematurely. Although the Chinese have attempted systematically to secularize Tibet—destroying monasteries, laicizing monks, persecuting believers, and educating the young in communist ideology— the complete eradication of Tibet's deeply rooted and pervasive tradition of "Lamaism" (as Tibetan Buddhism is sometimes called) is doubtful. Just as the destruction of Jerusalem spread Judaism over the world, so the destruction of the Tibetan homeland has created a Tibetan diaspora, not only of ordinary refugees but also of lamas able to teach the spiritual methods long treasured in the monasteries of the "Land of Snows." The tradition survives among the refugees in the border lands south of Tibet, and, surprisingly, in the West, especially the United States.[4]

Briefly, Tibetan Buddhism, like other forms of Buddhism, seeks the ultimate release of all sentient beings from *samsara*, the endless cycle of birth, death, and rebirth, through enlightenment. It may come through bodhisattvas, who, though themselves liberated, forego Nirvana in order to help others along the way. These bodhisattvas include not only saints of the past but have contemporary expression in lamas, who are incarnations of the power of enlightenment. They combine wisdom and compassion. Through disciplined meditation and other acts the mind is ultimately enabled to realize that the gods and demons that trouble it are but projections of the mind itself and *karma*. Thus is realized the "emptiness" of the world and the self that is Nirvana.

The introduction of Tibetan Buddhism in the United States was largely due to the initiatives of young lamas, most notably Chogyam Trungpa (who died April 4, 1987 at age 44) and Tarthang Tulku. Both were thoroughly schooled in the religious and cultural traditions of Tibet, and possessed great energy and impressive organizational skills.

The dramatic story of Chogyam Trungpa's narrow escape from Tibet, leading a band of 300 refugees, is told in his book, *Born in Tibet*.[5] Although then only twenty, he had been abbot of a group of monasteries and was recognized as the reincarnation of the tenth Trungpa Tulku (incarnate lama). After learning English in India, he went to Oxford University on a scholarship in 1963 where he plunged into the study of Western philosophy and art. He also prepared a new *sadhana* (meditation text) intended to exorcise the materialism he believed to pervade modern spiritual disciplines, and in 1967 established the Samye-Ling Meditation Center in Scotland as the initial base for his teaching in the West. However, he left Scotland after deciding he could function more effectively as a layman, renouncing his exalted status as guru. His new lifestyle was upsetting to some of those who had looked to him as Rinpoche ("guru").

Trungpa arrived in the United States in 1970, going first to a farm near Barnet, Vermont, purchased by some Americans who had meditated at Samye-Ling. It became the Tail of the Tiger community. After a lecture tour to the West Coast he was invited to teach at the University of Colorado and settled in Boulder, where another center (Karma Dzong) was established. In rural northern Colorado the Rocky Mountain Dharma Center soon came into existence. In the summer of 1974 the Naropa Institute held its first session. It drew 2000 persons to Colorado. The Institute continued to develop as a place of meeting of the Western intellectual mind and Buddhist meditation and experience, and attracted psychologists, philosophers, physicians, and poets as well as religionists and Buddhologists, both as faculty and students. Naropa became, in effect, a Buddhist university, offering degrees (A.B. and M.A.) in psychology and the performing arts, as well as in Buddhist studies.

Chogyam Trungpa's disdain for the role of guru did not mean that he eschewed the function of teacher, or that he was not intent on bringing the religion and art of Tibet to the United States. He recognized, however, that Americans are not Tibetans, and should not try to imitate them. Therefore, he discouraged fascination with the externals of Tibetan Buddhism, seeing them as a trap in which some might be caught. Moreover, he realized that Tibetan Buddhism in America would be practiced in the midst of society, not in monasteries. He was convinced that Americans would have to begin at the beginning, which meant learning and understanding the basic Buddhism of the early centuries and progressing spiritually through the development of Buddhism in its Mahayana forms towards the realization of its highest development in Tibetan ritualism and esotericism. One should begin with the exoteric and move slowly and gradually toward esoteric Buddhism.

In 1977 Chogyam introduced Shambhala Training. In Tibetan (and Indian) tradition Shambhala is a mythical kingdom, the spiritual center of the world, where an enlightened society of goodness and peace dwells. It was the model for Shangri-la in James Hilton's novel, *Lost Horizon.*[6] Whether or not it exists as an actual place, it can be reached only by those who are spiritually advanced.

As a meditative technique Shambhala Training has some resemblance to Zen. Like Zen, it is a discipline of sitting meditation and, besides talks and group discussion, involves interviews similar to those offered by Zen *roshis*. Reminiscent of the *samurai* relations of Zen, it is presented as "the warrior's way" rather than that of the monk or yogin. Shambhala Training is said to begin with the discovery through meditation of one's intrinsic quality of goodness; proceed with the expression of "warriorship" in terms of dignity, confidence, courage, and fearlessness; and issue in a way of life appropriate to the modern world. Chogyam Trungpa saw the training as a means of combining ancient traditions and techniques with the special needs and capabilities of Westerners. Needless to say, he was criticized by more traditional lamas and teachers who claimed that although he knew Tibetan religion and culture well, both his teaching and lifestyle promulgated a Dharma so adapted to Western, particularly American, culture as to preserve little of the Tibetan heritage. We see in this case, as we have seen in that of various Hindu gurus (notably Maharishi and Prabhupada) disagreement as to how much and in what ways adaptations should be made to American conditions.

In 1976 Chogyam Trungpa empowered Thomas F. Rich, an American long-time disciple, as his regent and as holder of both the Kagyu and Nyingma lineages. He was given the name Osel Tendzin and became Chogyam's appointed successor. In the ceremony that marked this signal event, Chogyam Trungpa observed:

> This is a long-awaited situation in the introduction of buddhadharma into the Western hemisphere, which has become a very large and energetic task. . . . There is a possibility that members of the sangha, Western people, can take over from the Tibetans. We are not trying to transplant culture, particularly. Our main concern is to transplant buddhadharma, with or without culture. Buddhism is such a clear, precise and sane, nontheistic tradition that it can fit in anywhere, even the middle of the Gobi desert or the Black Hole of Calcutta. And in the midst of America it is flourishing.[7]

Tarthang Tulku's exit from Tibet was not as dramatic and daring as that of Chogyam Trungpa, but he lived as a refugee in India. In Tibet, he had been recognized as a reincarnate lama (*tulku*) as a child, and from the age of seven had been trained in meditation and scholastic studies. From 1962 to 1968 he taught at the Sanskrit University in Benares as a representative of the Nyingma school. Partly through the assistance of an American studying in India he was able to emigrate to the United States in 1968. After a winter in New York City he made his way to the Bay area of California, and soon proved as enterprising as Chogyam Trungpa. Eight months after his arrival in the United States he established the Tibetan Nyingma Meditation Center in Berkeley as the first Vajrayana group in this country.

Briefly, Vajrayana is the tantric path to enlightenment. It is considered the way of direct "assault" on enlightenment, and, as such, is difficult and dangerous, requiring extraordinary commitment and discipline. A skillful and sure guru is indispensable. Vajrayana emphasizes the use of "skillful means" (*upaya*) more than any other form of Buddhism. The tantric way engages the mind and body in the full range of their capabilities. Chanting, visualization, complex rituals of many kinds, intense meditation, profound philosophical and psychological study, and much more besides, are part of the vast "arsenal" of the practitioners of Vajrayana. Tarthang Tulku realized, as did Chogyam Trungpa, that Americans could not begin at other than the preliminary stages of practice. He instructed them to begin simply, with a hundred thousand prostrations, which were followed by other hundreds of thousands of repetitions (of mantras, bodhisattva vows, meditations on mandalas, etc.), all with their appropriate visualizations. These were regarded as only preliminary to the real beginning of the *sadhana* (spiritual path).

Since the late seventies Tarthang Tulku has taught his students primarily through emphasis on work, as set forth especially in his book *Skilful Means* (1978), rather than through formal *sadhanas*. It has seemed appropriate to do so with American students, given their cultural work ethic. He evolved a new philosophy of work whereby it may become a meaningful expression of knowledge and energy—a means of realization—rather than a burden or merely a means to an end.

A practical expression of the emphasis on work was the establishment of the Dharma Press and Dharma Publishing in 1970, with the purpose of communicating essential Buddhist teachings to the West and, very ambitiously, preserving the vast Tibetan canon. Students were trained in the many skills required for major editing and publishing ventures, including, most impressively, the Nyingma edition of the Kanjur and Tanjur, an excellently printed 120-volume set of the canon.

Another impressive work of Nyingma students has been the manufacture and installation of massive (the largest ten tons in weight) prayer wheels. The prayer wheels contain millions of mantras which when turned, as it is believed, emanate a force for universal harmony and order integrating the chaotic energies of both humans and the cosmos. Nearly two thousand prayer wheels turn continuously at the Nyingma Institute (Padma Ling) and the Odiyan temple ("Copper Mountain Mandala") located in rural Sonoma County, California.

Comparable to the Naropa Institute founded by Chogyam Trungpa is Tarthang Tulku's Nyingma Institute, opened in 1973 with a human development training program intended to bring the insights and experiences contained in the religious, philosophical, and psychological tradition of Nyingma Buddhism to academicians, mental health professionals, and others. Its purpose, which it has pursued assiduously, is to integrate Western science and knowledge, wisdom, and experiences found in the Nyingma tradition, as well as to train some students in Tibetan language, history, culture, and religion.

Although they came from different Tibetan Buddhist Orders (Karma Kagyu and Nyingma, respectively), both Chogyam Trungpa and Tarthang Tulku devoted themselves to the preservation of Tibetan Buddhism, still threatened in its homeland. Both extraordinarily energetic in propagating the Dharma in the West, they exhibited considerable creativity and inventiveness in pursuing this enterprise.

Jacob Needleman writes of Tibet as the intriguing "land of lost content":

> Gradually, Tibet is coming into view. Instead of a romantic land haunted by a primitive or perverse mystical spirituality, we see the outlines of something breath-taking: an entire nation defined and ruled by the search for inwardness.[8]

It remains to be seen whether Americans will succeed in appropriating this most newly arrived form of Buddhism. In Tibet, initiation by transmission of the spiritual power to perform at particular *sadhana* is very important. Power is passed first of all from master to disciple. But even after initiation a long training, up to twenty years, remains before the full fruits of the path can be attained. It is not just a matter of apprehending fleeting illuminative "insights," but of psychological training and practice that is necessary for visualization of deities and perfection of psychic powers that give one the control over the mind finally to reach the "Diamond State," and know experientially that all is Mind. Needless to say, we cannot presume to present in a few pages a spiritual tradition so rich and yet so alien to Westerners.

We now have in the West nearly all major forms of Buddhism. It is interesting to note that the Buddhism popular in the West in any given period usually says more about the state of the West in any given period than of Buddhism. In the early years of the century, the supposedly atheistic rationalism of Theravada philosophy was most celebrated, and was much contrasted with the alleged superstition of Mahayana, not to mention Tibet, considered "debased" forms.

In the 1950s, as something of a reaction against science, psychoanalysis, and Western materialism set in, the Zen of D. T. Suzuki and the "beatniks" was in greatest favor. Then, the psychedelic explosion of the 1960s, with its exploration of the strange populations of the unconscious, and its feel for the uncanniness of psychic and mystic states of awareness, made suddenly clear what works like *The Tibetan Book of the Dead* were about. The growing interest is esoteric Buddhism seems to parallel that in Neo-Paganism and ceremonial magic: both create a transformed state of consciousness by creating a sacred visual and auditory environment through visualization and ritual.

Reading Selection: Tibetan Buddhism in America

Tibetan Buddhism has traditionally emphasized spiritual lineages and the relationship between guru and disciple. This emphasis has continued in the American setting. Although there are religious texts of many kinds, including Tantras, the Dharma and the meditative techniques for its realization are still communicated fundamentally "from mouth to ear," that is, personally and orally. In the following excerpt Tarthang Tulku speaks of the relationship between "teacher and student".

The teacher-student relationship can be the most stimulating experience of our lives, catalyzing and enriching a growth process in more ways than we thought possible. It can also encourage an open attitude, making it possible for us to receive all that the teacher has to offer. Difficult tasks may be asked of us, but sometimes destructive habit patterns can only be broken by great perseverance on our part. The teacher is there to show us our potential and capabilities. When we finally connect the teacher's advice with our experience, and come to realize the value of his teachings, we will be able to see ourselves more clearly and thus be able to work with our problems more effectively. In looking in retrospect at our changes, we will be able to perceive the teacher's ability to transform negative factors into what is wholesome and valuable. So we should remain confident in the teacher, and filled with trust; then real learning—which often occurs in unexpected and disappointing ways—can take place.

In the relationship between student and teacher, there are external, internal, and secret teachings that can be transmitted—all sewn together by the thread of the relationship. Without contacting this lineage of teachings in an intimate, personal way, it is very difficult to experience what "realization" means. But once we do, we understand the kindness of the teacher— and a very fine relationship develops that is based on honesty, caring, and confidence. At this time compassion flows forth from our openness, and we begin to understand the responsibility we have to ourselves and others.

The teacher, the teachings, and we ourselves are the foundations necessary for spiritual development. These three must be intimately linked for genuine progress to take place, and if any one of the three is missing, our growth is hampered. Together they are like good friends who trust and rely on each other. In order for the teachings to be transmitted we must remain open and accepting—like a white robe which is dyed the color of the teachings. Or, like film within a camera, we become transformed into the image of the teacher when exposed to the light of the teaching.

When the transference from teacher to student is full and open, we actually experience the teacher, the teachings, and ourselves as one. When we have this realization, it is as if we previously lived in a tiny dark room, with only a lantern for light; then suddenly were introduced to a vast, unlimited sunlit place. The joy and clarity of this experience make all the hardships of the teacher-student relationship worthwhile. The importance of this relationship cannot be emphasized enough. Unless the links to experiential knowledge are transmitted and carried on in this generation vast stores of wisdom will be lost.

Tarthang Tulku, *Gesture of Balance* (Emeryville, CA: Dharma Publishing, 1977), pp. 160–62.

NICHIREN SHOSHU ACADEMY

The house was a neat, white bungalow in a modest residential neighborhood. It might have been the home of an honest working-class family, or of a young organization man on the way up. But it wasn't; it was the district headquarters of a dynamic Japanese Buddhist denomination which has grown phenomenally in its homeland and has now invaded the West. The living room contained, that evening, about seventy-five people, mostly young and mostly Caucasian. They were not dancing or drinking cokes together; they were chanting the profound words of an ancient Eastern formula in the strange language of another time and place: *Nam Myoho Renge Kyo.* It is an affirmation that all needful wisdom is subsumed in the

Buddhist Lotus Sutra, and that merely reciting the formula of ascription of praise to this book will put one in harmony with the lines of force radiating from all the resplendent Buddhas mentioned in it, and from the central Being of the universe itself, and can unite the phenomenal world and absolute reality.

It was a weekly district meeting of Nichiren Shoshu. The chanting had already begun. The crowd was seated on the floor facing a dark black wooden box of an altar containing a white sheet of paper with Sino-Japanese characters on it radiating out from the center; this is the Gohonzon, visual focus of the cultus. It contains the names of important figures in the Lotus Sutra. The assembly recited, in Japanese, verses from the Lotus Sutra and the chant called the Daimoku: *Nam Myoho Renge Kyo*. The recitation was to the accompaniment of the dry rustle of 108 bead rosaries and drums; the resultant sound was an uncanny low jungle-like roar, suggesting unspeakable power.

The chanting ended in a grand rhythmic crash of voices. Next came the seemingly incongruous melodies of American hymns and folksongs, with English words praising the virtues of chanting and propagating the new faith, such as "I've been doing *shakubuku*," to the tune of "I've Been Working on the Railroad." *Shakubuku*, literally "break and subdue," is the Nichiren Shoshu term for aggressive evangelism.

The giving of testimonials followed. This was perhaps the most significent and impressive part of the meeting. The vivacious members of the group were not merely willing to tell what chanting the Daimoku had done for them, but were irrepressible in their enthusiasm. They not only raised their hands to be called upon by the middle-aged leader, but threw their arms into the air, dozens at a time, and even jumped up and down with eagerness.

When they spoke, they told often long-winded but clearly heartfelt tales of deep personal change and acquisition of power. There were people who, before starting to chant, had been virtual zombies due to drugs, alcoholism, habitual failure, and sense of meaninglessness. They had no friends, no purpose, no abilities they could believe in. They, when introduced to the simple practice of chanting *Nam Myoho Renge Kyo*, saw remarkable changes occur with the first fall of its mantic syllables from their lips—friends gathered around, grades in school improved markedly, strength arose to give up drugs or drink, marriages were saved, great improvements resulted in employment and material prosperity. The contrasting blacks and brilliant sunlight tones of conversion stories in general were evident; clearly here was a faith which dealt in that psychology.

Others reported more modest, but no less striking, results. One young man had wanted a new guitar, but there appeared no means by which he could get one. However, he had "chanted for it," and a few days later, through a strange series of coincidences, money came into his hands in the necessary amount. It was even said that if a parking place in a crowded business section of town was needed, chanting would make the place appear!

The leader, a personable American, gave a short lecture. It concerned Buddhist doctrine as interpreted by Nichiren Shoshu, and was saved from tediousness by a quite articulate manner and wholly Western style, despite holding firm to Nichiren Shoshu orthodoxy. He spoke of the ten basic states of life: hellish suffering, the incessant hunger of wandering ghosts, animality, angry titans, human tranquillity, heavenly rapture (the six traditional Buddhist planes where karmic reincarnation is possible), learning, following the path, the aspiration for enlightenment of the bodhisattva, the bliss of Buddhahood (four traditional stages of the spiritual ascent). These are all conditions of the present, he said; they are not afterlife conditions, but here and now. A person may move through all ten several times in one day. They can all be brought into "one thought" through the chanting of the Daimoku. This radical drive toward unification of all realities mundane and spiritual into one unity in the immediate present is characteristic of Nichiren Shoshu.

Finally it was announced, after cheers like college yells, that "The meeting is over, the *shakubuku* begins!" Scores of eager faces poured out to transform the world through the Daimoku.

Nichiren Shoshu can indeed be persuasive. One student, sent to do a report on the organization, joined some of its exuberant youthful members in invading university dormitories doing *shakubuku*, and ended up being converted himself! The movement is surrounded by happy smiles, creativity, and almost frenetic energy. In the American headquarters building in Santa Monica, California, or any district headquarters, when chanting is not going on, there is likely to be music practice—a fife and drum corps, popular music, chamber music.

The real impact of Nichiren Shoshu comes into being at the great annual conventions. They draw thousands of participants who fill the largest municipal halls. The convention days are packed with parades, stirring lectures, and memorable music performances. Behind them one rightly envisions brisk executive-type men talking on telephones and meeting planes, countless committee meetings, and the expenditure of considerable funds.

This vigorous extroverted activism scarcely fits the conventional Western (and Eastern) image of Buddhism. Instead of rows of monks in silent inward meditation, and a gentle aetherial tolerance of attitude, here are prepossessive people chanting vigorously and acting vigorously, hardly pausing for any "mindfulness" but that of the active moment, and trying to persuade others that their religion is the only truth. Further, they are convinced that beginning in Japan their faith will win the world, and provide the basis of a "Third Civilization" in which Buddhism and society will be one.

But if this is not a conventional Buddhism, its real founder, Nichiren (1222–82) was not a conventional Buddhist saint. He seems rather a transplanted Old Testament prophet, or a Muhammad. He taught an exclusivist religion of the Lotus Sutra, led a great popular movement, feared not to denounce the faithless in the highest places, and predicted national disaster if the nation failed to repent. Though there have been other Buddhists like him in Japan, and there is something in the Japanese temperament which makes him understandable, Nichiren is really unique, like his movement.

Nichiren was trained in the great Mt. Hiei monastery of the Tendai tradition, an ancient Buddhism deeply dyed with esoteric teaching. But amid the social upheavals of the Middle Ages, when feudal warlords rebelled against the old imperial court in Kyoto and the whole country was convulsed with a search for new social and spiritual values, he found himself asking new questions. More can often be told about a religious movement by the questions it is asking than the answers it gives. The old quasi-esoteric Buddhism of the Heian (Kyoto) period was asking the question, "How can all Buddhist philosophy and all human experience be brought into a grand synthesis?" But Nichiren, and other Buddhist figures of the subsequent Kamakura period, like the Protestant reformers of Europe, were asking more personal and mundane religious questions: "How can I be sure that I am saved?" "How can the events of human history be reconciled with Providence?" In this last particular, Nichiren was much disturbed as a young man by the fact that the imperial loyalists were defeated by the warlord insurgents despite the incantations of innumerable Buddhist priests and abbots on behalf of the imperial forces.

Like all who ask the religious question in terms of "How can I be sure that I am saved?" Nichiren ended with a simple key, a sure, entirely sufficient minimum requirement for salvation beyond which all else is just confusing superfluity. For him, that sure key was the Lotus Sutra, considered the embodiment of all necessary Buddhist truth. This great document, whose images remind one of the New Testament Book of Revelation, envisions millions of Buddha worlds and tells that the historical Buddha is but a manifestation of the eternal Buddha-nature, and that since these mysteries are beyond comprehension, simple devotion is as certain a key to liberation as meditation or philosophy. It is not necessary that one study the Lotus Sutra; to chant the Daimoku is to attune oneself mystically with all that it contains, which is all that is needed. It is advantageous, though, to chant before the Gohonzon since it holds the names, and so the power, of the principal Buddhas and bodhisattvas in the book.

Nichiren taught devotion to the Lotus Sutra with monolithic firmness. If the nation did not reject all other forms of Buddhism in favor of the Lotus, it would suffer calamity. If the nation were converted to his Buddhism, it would become the center of a new world civilization. For moderns, Nichiren is the one authority; Nichiren Shoshu teaches that he is the Buddha for the present age. The Lotus Sutra is the one book—only faith is necessary. In this one central focus, everything is unified; all seeming polarities meet. The three Buddha expressions—as essence of the universe, as heavenly lord, and as earthly teacher of saving wisdom—are brought together. Nichiren Shoshu also employs such expressions as *shikishin funi*, "body and mind not two," *esho funi*, "individual and environment not two," *obutsu myogo*, "the state and Buddhism one society," and so forth. This radical simplicity and unity, focusing all down to a single intense point, is the secret of Nichiren: one scripture, one man, one country, one object of worship, one practice, all potentialities realized in one moment which is the present. Nichiren Shoshu was one of two major Buddhist denominations established by immediate disciples of Nichiren. Its head temple, containing allegedly Nichiren's tooth and the original Gohonzon drawn by him as principal relics, is on the slopes of Mt. Fuji.

The radical nature of this tradition was revived in our day by T. Makiguchi, who founded an organization for laymen in 1930 called Soka Gakkai, "Value-creation study society." He and his followers soon joined Nichiren Shoshu. Soka Gakkai was based on an "Essay on Value" Makiguchi had written, in which he had substituted "benefit" for "truth" in the traditional triad of "goodness, truth, and beauty." Not all truth is beneficial to man, but benefit, including material benefit, by definition is. It is, of course, chanting the Daimoku which delivers benefit.

This unsubtle secular pragmatism sets the tone for the appeal of the faith, although it should be recognized that it is consistent with its deepest assumptions. If it says, "Other religions promise good things after you die, but only Nichiren Shoshu can deliver them now," or, "Try chanting just for something you want to see if it works," that is not because Nichiren Shoshu is solely materialistic. It is rather because of its premise that there must be unity between all aspects of being rather than mutual exclusiveness. If chanting brings material benefits, the real message is that this affirms the inseparability of matter and nonmatter; chanting should lead deeper into the mysteries of the Buddha-nature that unites them.

Because of his refusal to participate in Shinto, Makiguchi fell out of favor with the militaristic government, and he ended his days in prison in 1944. Soka Gakkai was a tiny, obscure sect with the coming of religious freedom in 1945. But its leadership fell into the hands of J. Toda (1900–58), one of the most remarkable religious administrators of modern times. Under his masterful, hard-driving guidance the faith became undoubtedly the fastest-growing religion in the world in the 1950s, increasing from a few thousand to some ten million adherents in Japan by the end of the decade. More than any other faith, it filled the spiritual void left in Japan by the discrediting of traditional forms of Shinto and Buddhism, and by the materialism of the phenomenal economic recovery. To lonely people transplanted to the great industrial cities, it offered participation, activity, and a sense of direction.

Soka Gakkai warred fearlessly and often successfully with the great Marxist-oriented trade unions for the loyalty of the working class. The techniques of *shakubuku* were highly developed. Regarded as an act of mercy, *shakubuku* was often effected with a ruthlessness—business boycotts, midnight phone calls, argumentative interruption of the meetings of other religious groups—which brought Soka Gakkai much criticism, but also many converts. Anyone with real familiarity with modern Japan, however, will realize how much fulfillment has been brought by the new faith to millions of plain people whose lives and past values were shattered by war and social transformation. The progress of Soka Gakkai in Japan was climaxed by the creation of its own political party, the Komeito, now the third strongest in the Diet. While the meteoric growth of the faith seems to have let up somewhat in the period since the fifties, it is still one of the most important social forces in Japan.

Until 1960, Soka Gakkai (still, in Japan, technically a layman's organization within Nichiren Shoshu) showed little interest in spreading to the West. But so close have been ties between the United States and Japan in the postwar era that it would be hard to keep a movement so powerful in one nation from touching the other. A few Americans stationed in Japan on military service had been converted, mostly by Japanese wives and girlfriends. Many Japanese "war brides" came to America as missionaries of the faith; some Japanese-Americans were converted through home contacts. Thus Soka Gakkai acquired an American foothold.

Daisaku Ikeda, Toda's successor, was eager to spread the faith overseas. In 1960 he sent Masayasu Sadanaga (who later changed his name to George M. Williams) to the United States. Sadanaga there found about five hundred members, nearly all of them Japanese brides of American servicemen. He set about to organize and to create enthusiasm, and succeeded impressively. While Nichiren Shoshu is one of the lesser known of the new religious movements in the United States, its numbers and the extent of its geographical distribution exceed that of the better-known groups. At the time of its first convention in 1963 in Chicago, there were only ten chapters. Nichiren Shoshu met again in Chicago fifteen years later (1978); it claimed to have 150 chapters and about 300,000 members. (The figure is based on the number of "households" which have accepted a Gohonzon, and so is indefinite and doubtless in excess of the number of actual practitioners. However that may be, Nichiren Shoshu is able to turn out crowds numbering in the many thousands for its major public events, such as its cultural festivals.)

Activities center in the American headquarters in Santa Monica, California, under the leadership of the Director General, George Williams. The name Soka Gakkai is not used in this country. Nichiren Shoshu of America (NSA) is probably the most thoroughly organized of all the new religious movements. The basic unit is the District, which meets several times a week; within it are groups and units of five to ten members under the supervision of experienced individuals for communication purposes. Above the District are regional Chapters and General Chapters. In addition, there are men's and women's divisions, a student bureau, a bureau for control of pilgrimages to Japan, the important Min-on which handles the characteristic music groups, and an active publications department, including the newspaper *World Tribune*. Organizational activism is a key part of the spirit of Nichiren Shoshu. But the faith also has two temples in America, one in Honolulu and one in Etiwanda, California. In these, ceremonies such as formal weddings and consecrations of Gohonzons requiring ministrations of Nichiren Shoshu priests are held.

In addition to group meetings, members carry out daily worship called *gongyo*. This consists of reciting certain chapters of the Lotus Sutra, in Japanese, five times in the morning and three times in the evening, followed by chanting the Daimoku until one feels satisfied. This worship is done in front of the Gohonzon, the mandala made by Nichiren enshrined in a box-like wooden altar. The Gohonzon is owned by Nichiren Shoshu, but upon entering the faith one receives, after payment of a small donation, a lifetime loan of one, which is installed by officers of the District in a brief home ceremony. This is the real initiation into Nichiren Shoshu. Of course, chanting is also done silently throughout the day—wherever one is.

The late sixties were days of fantastic growth for Nichiren Shoshu. As the organization entered the seventies and then the eighties, it appeared to be slowing in numerical expansion. However, better than most new religious groups Nichiren Shoshu has been able to retain members and to mobilize them effectively. This is in part because Nichiren Shoshu is not only well organized but the charisma of its leaders has been diffused effectively throughout the organization. It has been able to develop a tight organizational structure without suffering the impersonalism of bureaucracy. In 1975 representatives from fifty-one countries gathered to create Soka Gakkai International, an umbrella organization for all Nichiren Shoshu national groups. Daisaku Ikeda became the first president of SGI. His extended visit to the United States in 1984 was a major event in the recent history of NSA and generated the characteristic enthusiasm of its members in the many cities he visited.

In recent years there has been an emphasis on the education and nurture of members. As in Japan, overaggressive *shakubuku* had in some cases produced a negative image. Now, in the addresses of leaders and the evangelism of ordinary members, there is less emphasis on promise of immediate phenomenal benefits from chanting, and more on serious points of Buddhist philosophy as interpreted by Nichiren.

Nichiren Shoshu communicates itself in its own way through the impressive testimonials of those who have given it a chance, and in the pure enthusiasm and joy of its crowds, full of fellowship, music, and the euphoria of group chanting. They are as clean-cut as midwestern 4-H kids. Nichiren Shoshu encourages no extreme politics, dress, or lifestyle. Its young people seem able to enjoy bus excursions wearing identical sweaters, county fair style parades, and campfire songs. But if Nichiren Shoshu culture may seem to some to border on the over-organized and the banal, it has given many a home. More than that, it has given many a sparkle. Life, they say, is like a rocket rising and flashing within the infinite lotus depths of the Buddha-nature. Let it glitter as it rises.

Reading Selection: Nichiren Shoshu of America

The following conversion story, typical of those continually published in Nichiren Shoshu periodicals and recited at meetings, shows the kind of radical change in the style and meaning of life the movement strives for and frequently achieves. The picture of a happy, outgoing, active life, full of friends and success and inner power, suggests the image of the ideal Nichiren Shoshu member the organization wants to project. The searching, counterculture background of the convert points toward the source of much of its recruitment and indicates its close relation to that scene even though Nichiren Shoshu's own style is as radically different as the psychology of deep conversion requires.

Picture a frantic nineteen-year-old girl, constantly running from her environment, moving eight times in one year from her nice middle class home to a swanky college in Arizona and finally ending up in Haight-Ashbury. This was Rochelle Byrd's life three years ago.

Her fantasy world was one of drugs, books, peace movements, and finally, depression. Inside, she cried to change, but couldn't. She could not control her life. People would come into her life and then leave just as easily. Of herself, Rochelle says, "They could not tolerate my nature. I was on the verge of losing another circle of friends, when fortune really came my way." Here, of course, she was referring to the Gohonzon and Nam-myoho-renge-kyo.

When she met the members, she saw smiling, confident faces of people who really seemed to care. Because of this, she chanted the "weird sounding words," thinking too that she would go on some kind of a faraway trip. She went on a trip all right—lots of them—Los Angeles, Japan—all over. But most of all, she went on a real "happiness" trip, a place she had never been to before.

Now, after two years of practice, she's found the things that she'd always been searching for—a happy family, good job and most of all, a rhythmical daily life.

She still runs a lot—to study meetings, discussion meetings, chorus and dance practices, visiting members, and most of all to the Gohonzon. In Rochelle's words, "It's a beautiful trip and a beautiful life!"

> "Waking to Reality—'It's Beautiful,'" *World Tribune,* Friday, May 1, 1970, p. 6.

THE BAHA'I FAITH

North of Chicago along the shore of Lake Michigan in the suburb of Wilmette is a splendid building which looks almost as though it might have been transplanted from a Persian paradise. Its grounds are gorgeously landscaped, and above its nine sides looms a dome spun of such lacy, light filigree as to seem to be floating above the lakeshore. This is the American temple of the Baha'i Faith, a worldwide religion of Iranian origin which holds that its teacher, Baha'u'llah, is the prophet of God for our age, and that its institutions set the pattern for a new universal world order of liberty and peace.

While some may have been drawn to the Baha'i Faith because of its imposing temple, many more in large and small communities have been reached through the peculiar tradition known as the Baha'i fireside. Leading members of Baha'i hold weekly discussions in their homes to introduce inquirers to the world of this new religion which claims to give an answer to the tortured spiritual quest of modern man in this day of transition.

A Friday evening fireside was held in the home of the secretary of the local Baha'i group. Unlike most Baha'is, she was reared in a Baha'i Faith family. About a dozen members were present, with a predominance of females. The group was interracial. Most were middle-class, well educated persons, including a biochemist and several in the health-care professions. The membership of the local group is approximately thirty, with additional Baha'is in the area. The question for the evening was "What is liberty?" It was introduced by a member who read relevant passages from the writings of Baha'u'llah and other Baha'i authorities. All joined in the ensuing discussion on the nature of liberty, contributing from their own observations and experiences. They agreed that true liberty comes only with a disciplined life lived in obedience to the law of God, which for them meant the teachings of Baha'u'llah. During the refreshments which followed there was easy, friendly conversation about both the coming activities of the local assembly (including meetings to be held on a local university campus) and the wider world concerns of Baha'is.

The quiet, verbal manner with emphasis on social rather than mystical experience suggests that Baha'i is geared to the emissary style, even if more Muslim than Judaeo-Christian in background. In the West, it has lost most of the Sufi immediacy it had at the beginning.

It is appropriate and significant that this new prophet for a new age should have appeared in Iran, for that land may be considered the homeland of eschatology, or religious beliefs concerning the future and the end of history. It is thus a homeland of the emissary style; and eschatology is the emissary's greatest tool—work and sacrifice now, eschew ecstasy now, for greater glory in the Lord's Day. There, some 2500 years ago, the mighty prophet Zoroaster taught that man must choose between sides in a great cosmic war between the principles of good and evil, and that at the end of the war—the end of history—a new prophet would appear, and the victorious good God, Ahura Mazda, would end the sentence of the wicked in hell and create a new paradisical heaven and earth. Many scholars believe that the subsequent eschatologies of Judaism, Christianity, Islam, and Hindu and Buddhist teachings about the future avatar of Vishnu and the coming Buddha Maitreya were deeply influenced by Zoroaster's primordial vision of man living not in cosmic, eternal-return time, but on the battlefield of a history in which he is judged and which will end in a glorious divine victory.

When Zoroastrianism gave way to Islam in Iran, the Shi'ite wing of the latter faith which took root there was, as might be expected, more strongly eschatological than the legalistic Sunni school of most other Muslims. Shi'ites looked forward eagerly to the coming of the Mahdi, the twelfth *Imam* or successor of Muhammad who, it was believed, had hidden himself but would appear at the right time as a Messiah surrounded by glorious hosts to raise the dead and deliver final revelations and effect the ultimate victory of righteousness. Yet the Shi'ites also had a cultus of the quasi-redemptive sufferings of Husain, the Christ-like grandson of Muhammad martyred in 680. Moreover, Iran is a homeland of the Sufis, the God-intoxicated Muslim mystics whose ecstatic devotionalism tempers the harshness of Islamic fervor.

All of these historical strands met with the incipient modern world to produce the new Baha'i faith. Its first manifestation was in the figure known as the Bab, or "Gate," born Mirza Ali Muhammad (1819–50). As a young man he became involved with a Sufi sect expecting an imminent divine revelation, and in this atmosphere first declared himself the Bab, then that he was the Mahdi himself in 1844. A great number of his Sufi sect accepted his claims, and with their help a fervent Babi religious movement swept through the land. The Bab taught that resurrection and judgment, heaven and hell, are here now in the new divine manifestation, depending on whether individuals accept or reject it. If one accepts, he lives in a universal love and holy ecstasy no power can destroy. This original ecstatic immediacy was quickly tempered by the incursion of history in the form of suffering. Perhaps out of this came its new futurism. Like most enthusiastic religious revivals, Babism was considered blasphemous and disturbing by the unenthusiastic. It suffered persecution from the backward Persian government of the day. Finally in 1850, the Bab himself was martyred. But among his followers was another God-possessed young man, Baha'u'llah (1817–92).

The death of the Bab did not mark the end of the Babi religious movement. When in 1852 a deranged member made an attempt on the life of the Shah, fierce persecution broke out anew. A number of Babis were thrown into dungeons, including Baha'u'llah. But, as is so often the case, persecution only strengthened faith. Baha'u'llah became convinced that he was called to regenerate the movement. After four months of imprisonment, Baha'u'llah was exiled and went to Baghdad. Later the Ottoman government moved him to Adrianople, then to Constantinople, and finally to the grim prison city of Acre. Just before leaving Baghdad in 1863, he declared that he was the One whose coming had been announced by the Bab, the Chosen of God. He ended his life in house arrest at Acre, though in the later years restrictions were much relaxed and he lived in some comfort and dignity, visited by high and low. According to Baha'is the Bab and Baha'u'llah are Co-Founders of the Faith, though Baha'u'llah represents a culmination of the revelation.

Baha'u'llah was succeeded as leader by his son, called Abdu'l-Baha, (1844–1921), who wrote extensively and lectured in Europe and America, doing much to extend the new teaching. He did not, however, rank himself with the Bab or Baha'u'llah, but saw himself merely a conservor of their faith.

Upon Abdu'l-Baha's death, he was succeeded by his grandson, called Shoghi Effendi, as Guardian of the Faith. Both could add nothing, but were "infallible" interpreters of its meaning. Upon Shoghi Effendi's passing in 1957, this authority passed to the cabinet-like body called the Hands of the Cause of God, and in 1963 to the Universal House of Justice, now constituted as the supreme governing body and prototype of a world government. It is elected world-wide and sits in Haifa, Israel. There, on Mount Carmel, one finds the Shrine of the Bab. Nearby, in Bahji, north of Abba, is the Shrine of Baha'u'llah. Both are important places of pilgrimage for American Baha'is.

One God and one world: this is the essence of the Baha'i vision. With this goes the concept of progressive revelation. The founders of all major faiths, Krishna, Buddha, Zoroaster, Moses, Jesus, Muhammad, and now Baha'u'llah, are all manifestations and messengers of God. But they have each spoken the message needed by a particular time and place, and so should not be followed exclusively after their day has passed. The great message of the present founder, Baha'u'llah, is the oneness of mankind. Like all great religious teachers, he was concerned with love and devotion toward God, and with the deep matters of suffering and death and ultimate destiny. But he was especially concerned with making the unity of humankind and its practical structures—a world tribunal; equality of all races, nationalities, and sexes; universal peace; universal education; a world calendar; a universal auxiliary language—part of religious faith and vision. The attainment of practical unity was made the object of that most powerful of human drives, the religious. *This* is the day when the unity of humankind can be attained because of universalizing culture and communication. It is desperately needed. It is God's desire and so is the burden of his true prophet for our time. Perhaps a couple millennia or so in the future, the next prophet will come with a new message beyond our present comprehension.

The Baha'i concept of the history of religion is essentially one of continuing revelation through great men. One is reminded of Carlyle's view of history as the strokes of heroes. Baha'i seems to presume that all of a religion, except the life and words of the founder, is deterioration. It has likened the history of a religion to the seasons of a year. It begins with spring—new, fresh, and vital—but declines through summer and fall until the religion reaches its wintertime—formal, fixed, and frozen. Perhaps this accounts for the very great zeal to preserve uncorrupted the sayings of Baha'u'llah.

The Baha'i Faith sees itself as a new vision of the meaning of history, and a light of hope in mankind's present dark and stormy and often desperate passage from one age to another—the efficacious plan for the next and far better era is already here. Just as Christianity retained some incidentals and externals of Judaism, so Baha'i has retained some externals of its womb-faith, Islam. There are daily prayers and a month-long fast reminiscent of the Muslim Ramadan. It could be argued that Baha'i's basic concepts—radical monotheism, prophet and scripture-centeredness, suspicion of priesthood and soteriology and rite—all suggest a perhaps unconscious carry-over of Islamic assumptions about the very nature of true religion. Indeed, for a long time the Baha'i Faith was considered a Muslim sect. But some Baha'is are willing to allow the providential nature of this—and rightly point out that these Islamic biases also correspond with the biases of many present-day European and American religious liberals, those who have left "Puritan" theology, but not an ingrained "Protestant ethic" and a negative reaction to anything suggestive of medieval Catholicism.

Concerning life after death, Baha'is like to talk about this present life as comparable to the life in the womb, and death as a rebirth, a prelude to infinite further growth. Heaven and hell are not places but states of consciousness.

Baha'i life for the believer centers around the local Baha'i community. It does not have the usual Sunday worship, although temples like the one in Wilmette have a Sunday lecture. But in addition to the firesides there is a monthly feast. It is "monthly" according to the Baha'i calendar of nineteen months of nineteen days each (plus four or five intercalary days). The nineteen-day feast, for Baha'is only, consists of three parts: devotional, business, and social. The devotional part will be simple prayers and readings from the Baha'i writings. The governing body of a Baha'i community is the Spiritual Assembly, consisting of nine persons selected by secret ballot without nominations. Throughout the year there are nine festivals, mostly based on Baha'i history, when Baha'is stay away from work or school if possible, and the spring nineteen-day fast when they take no food or drink from dawn to dusk.

Moral and religious discipline is not taken lightly in Baha'i circles. The local Spiritual Assembly is consulted about the marriage of members, and regardless of the age of bride and groom, they must also obtain the consent of all four parents if living. Drinking and narcotics are not allowed. Many people who might otherwise be attracted by the idealism of Baha'i are put off by its prohibition of participation in clearly political demonstrations and partisan politics. The local Spiritual Assembly may reprimand erring members, though the member may appeal to national and world assemblies. The life style often suggests "deferred reward" and "inner asceticism," work rather than ecstasy now to produce a good society later. In his suffering and verbal-legal teachings, Baha'u'llah seems a model of these values, even though some of his devotional writing tends toward Sufi mysticism.

The enthusiasm of committed Baha'is who have been seized by its vision of a new revelation and new world order is splendid. Some become "Baha'i pioneers," who move, at their own expense, to new places where the Faith is not yet planted to sow its seeds. It has now spread to some 280 countries and major territories. Presently it seems to be growing most rapidly in the underdeveloped world. Its mission appeals to those for whom work and sacrifice as spiritual values correspond to current historical experience. For them, Baha'i is a vehicle of modernization.

But the Baha'i Faith is also making headway in the West. The total American membership is about 75,000. A new Seven Year Plan, instituted in 1979, for heightening public awareness of the Baha'i Faith, increasing the number of assemblies, and intensifying work among minorities met with some success. Many of the new adherents are young people retaining idealism but disillusioned with the "instant" realization offered by sheer mysticism and revolutionary ideology alike. The Baha'i Faith retains a personal God, a legal and emissary as well as exemplary concept of the prophet, and a social as well as mystical experience orientation in spiritual life.

Members of the Baha'i Faith have been especially active in calling attention to the desperate plight of their co-religionists in Iran who are continuing to suffer severe persecution under the new Shi'ite fundamentalist regime.

Reading Selection: The Baha'i Faith

The following passage from a classic introduction to the Baha'i Faith by an early Western convert sums up well some of the Faith's most important characteristics—

love for God and the wide world, continual happy references to the words of Baha'u'llah and Abdu'l-Baha, insistence that while on the one hand it is important to recognize and nourish the good in all religions, on the other it is now a day when new envoys from God have come who must be heard.

When asked on one occasion: "What is a Baha'i?" Abdu'l-Baha replied: "To be a Baha'i simply means to love all the world; to love humanity and try to serve it; to work for universal peace and universal brotherhood." On another occasion He defined a Baha'i as "one endowed with all the perfections of man in activity." In one of His London talks He said that a man may be a Baha'i even if He has never heard the name of Baha'u'llah. He added: "The man who lives the life according to the teachings of Baha'u'llah is already a Baha'i. On the other hand, a man may call himself a Baha'i for fifty years, and if he does not live the life he is not a Baha'i. An ugly man may call himself handsome, but he deceives no one, and a black man may call himself white, yet he deceives no one, not even himself."

One who does not know God's Messengers, however, is like a plant growing in the shade. Although it knows not the sun, it is, nevertheless, absolutely dependent on it. The great Prophets are spiritual suns, and Baha'u'llah is the sun of this "day" in which we live. The suns of former days have warmed and vivified the world, and had those suns not shone, the earth would now be cold and dead, but it is the sunshine of today that alone can ripen the fruits which the suns of former days have kissed into life.

J. E. ESSLEMONT, *Baha'u'llah and the New Era* (Wilmette, Illinois: Baha'i Publishing Trust, revised edition, 1970), pp. 83–84. Original edition published 1923.

SUBUD

The spiritual association called Subud does not advertise and has not been in the news much in recent years, but nearly everyone with any knowledge of the religious counterculture has heard of it. It has a certain reputation as the most "far out," or the most "deep in," of them all.

In most of the seventy-some American cities with Subud centers, the only notice of the organization is a modest listing in the telephone directory. By calling this number, inquirers will be able to find the time and place of Subud's only corporate act of worship, the *latihan*.

This soft Indonesian word points to the land of origin of this movement, but scarcely anything of its dynamics. The address the inquirer receives over the telephone may be a church, rented hall, private house, or, perhaps, Subud-owned facility. Upon entering, he or she will see a group of persons in leisure clothes. From their dress it might not appear that some of them are professors, physicians, psychologists, and executives, all drawn to the *latihan*.

The visitor will be met by someone called a "helper" who will tell what the *latihan* is. It may seem to the visitor quite different from anything he or she has previously known as a spiritual exercise. Members enter a large, lighted room (in earlier days it was usually darkened). There they stand with eyes closed, and begin to allow themselves to be completely open to the motions of the Spirit. This leads in most cases to external manifestations as each person gets into his or her "exercise": shouting, crooning, jumping and leaping about, weeping, glossolalia, etc. It is said that each person's *latihan* is unique and its manifestations differ accordingly. Generally, there are some resemblances to the manifestations associated with participation in the Christian charismatic movement of recent years.

Men and women have *latihan* in separate rooms, mainly because the *latihans* of the two sexes are said to be different, not because of inequality. Only those who have been "opened" are permitted in the room, although visitors and applicants for membership may be permitted to sit outside the door. They can hear the sound of the *latihan* but see nothing. The visitor will probably find fifteen or twenty minutes of listening unforgettable. There is a strange luring attraction to the sound of total spiritual expression. It is the sound of earliest childhood, the child leaping and crying about the nursery, free to shout and weep, and the primitive festival, the return to chaos and renewal. One hears animal sounds, sounds of frenzy and joy, and deep, utterly strange and moving wordless hymn-like chants. Sometimes the action is individual; sometimes all move in one direction around the room, moving and singing in concert as though participating in some great cosmic dance. Despite the spontaneity of individual activity, participants in the *latihan* rarely collide with each other. As though led by a sixth sense, they move around and past their companions.

There is a feeling of being pulled almost magnetically toward the *latihan,* if susceptible to it, as toward a vortex. It is the discovery of total freedom. Members say that participation in *latihan* twice a week—the norm—leads to the opening up of the person one really is, the person as known to God. It leads also to purification, to the falling away of undesirable habits, and to the acquisition of buoyancy and power. Some report that they have received physical and emotional healings in the *latihan.* Others claim that they have received clear and unmistakable guidance in personal decisions, guidance that may have seemed contrary to prudence at the time, but which turned out in the end to be right.

The originator of this movement is an Indonesian named Muhammad Subuh, now generally called "Bapak," a conventional Javanese term meaning "father." He was born in 1901, and it is said that his childhood was marked by strange psychic occurrences. This, and a prophecy of early death, led him to seek out spiritual teachers as a young man. In Indonesia these are not difficult to find. Bapak contacted many sages of the dervish and Sufi traditions, but none satisfied him. Allegedly, some claimed his was a destiny beyond their ken, and reversed custom by paying the applicant honor. So Bapak took up family life and a minor government job.

Then, on his twenty-fourth birthday in 1925, as he was walking alone on a dark, moonless night, Bapak had a new and clearly initiatory experience. A sphere of light brighter than the sun appeared above him and seemed to enter his body through the top of his head. He felt himself filled with coursing, vibrating light. It is said the preternatural light was visible miles away. For three years after, he felt an experience like that of the *latihan* trembling through him frequently, so that he was always full of energy and joy.

Inexplicably, when he was twenty-seven years of age in 1928, the spontaneous *latihan* stopped. Bapak passed through a period of confusion, a "dark night of the soul," in his interior life, even though his outward life as a government official and husband and father continued normally, and he was beginning to acquire a reputation as a counselor.

This stage ended on his thirty-second birthday, when Bapak's mission was revealed to him. He was to pass the experience he had received to others. This unfolding restored Bapak's own spiritual life, and gave him an all-consuming vocation. Leaving his former work, Bapak henceforth devoted himself entirely to the movement he subsequently called Subud. Unlike other methods, the Subud experience, he claims, can be communicated wholly and entirely by "contact," and others can immediately receive—if the receiver's intellectual mind does not interfere—the same energy Bapak received when the illumination greater than the sun descended.

From 1933—the real birthday of Subud—until after the Second World War, Subud spread very quietly on the island of Java, and had won the attention of a few Europeans. Beginning in 1956, however, it moved rapidly around the world. Since then Bapak has spent much of his time travelling and visiting one center after another. He last visited the United States in 1981 during the course of a world tour. His travelling is now restricted considerably by his advanced age and some health problems, but he continues to lead Subud from Jakarta.

In countries like Britain, where Gurdjieff's teachings had been strong, Subud cut a particularly wide swath through the adherents of the south Russian philosopher. The situation is vividly described in the autobiographical book by Anthony Bright-Paul, *Stairway to Subud*. Gurdjieff had paved the way by mysterious allusions to a coming Indonesian teacher, and some of his followers had felt that no real headway could be made until the "higher emotional center" was opened. When Bapak arrived in Britain with Subud, the Gurdjieff center at Coombe Springs was swept by enthusiasm for the *latihan*. One is reminded of Krishnamurti's equally radical rejection of the intricate intellectualism of Theosophy and the dilemma this created for his devotees. Shortly after, in 1959, Subud was well launched with an International Congress held in England. A few days after the Congress, the well-known Hungarian actress Eva Bartok gave Subud a burst of favorable publicity by being "opened" by Bapak and in the process healed of childbirth complications.

The word Subud is derived from the Sanskrit *susila*, which Bapak interprets as living in accordance with the will of God; *budhi*, which refers to the divine power in each human being; and *dharma*, by which he means complete surrender to the will of God. For Bapak, *dharma* is a process, not a teaching. The process is the *latihan*, which enables the *budhi* to become effective in human beings and leads to lives characterized by *susila*. While the three basic terms (*susila, budhi,* and *dharma*) that enter into the name Subud (su-bu-d) are Buddhist (or Hindu), they are not interpreted Buddhistically.

Bapak and his adherents say that Subud is not a religion. It is, rather, a kind of religious exercise or training that can be participated in effectively by persons of various religions, including Christians and Jews as well as adherents of other religions. One can therefore continue conventional religious affiliation while practicing the *latihan.*

At the same time, the predominant religious influence on Subud is Islamic. Subud is not only theistic, but monotheistic. In its own way Subud emphasizes the basic meaning of the word *islam,* which is submission or surrender to the will of Allah (literally, "the God"). Bapak considers himself a Muslim, as do many of his Indonesian followers, and he observes the traditional Muslim religious duties, for example, the annual fast during the month of Ramadan. Most of his followers in the West are not Muslims, although they too may observe an annual fast, whether in the Muslim manner or in other ways. Some add a Muslim element to their name. It would be a mistake, however, to consider Subud a Muslim sect, in part because Subud maintains that its characteristic religious experience is possible for adherents of all religions, not just Islam. Members of Subud are fond of saying: "All we have is the *latihan.*"

The verbal expression of Subud, found primarily in the writings of Bapak, affirms that there is a higher, purifying, and joyous consciousness to which one can be opened, and which gives its own definition of reality. Bapak and most Subud followers definitely believe in God, though without excessive talk about the nature of God. What is required is complete surrender to the divine will and gifts. The surrender in the *latihan* room is what makes the experience work. Bapak says, "We do not have a teaching, there is nothing to learn to do, because all that is required of us is complete surrender. A person who claims to know the way to God is really one who is anticipating God's gifts without having received them." But if one surrenders, God will give immediate guidance, and that person will find the right way toward God.

"Opening," the initiation by which this happens, is no elaborate ritual, although the present preparatory requirements in the United States—that one has registered as a candidate, met with the local "helpers" approximately twice a month for three months, and is at least seventeen years of age—are normative. Usually something like this is done at an "opening": the applicant meets with a "helper," who reads some words from Bapak to him, then goes into the *latihan* room with him and says, "Close your eyes and begin."

The *latihan* room will typically be bare except for a rug on the floor. The *latihan* itself will be initiated by a "helper" saying "Begin," and ended when he or she says, "Finish." "Helpers" may also go to the homes of sick members to assist them in experiencing the *latihan* there.

Locally, Subud has two kinds of meetings: the *latihan* and business meetings. Each center has a committee (distinct from the "helpers," spiritual guides appointed by Bapak). Social get-togethers are also held from time to time. Usually Subud people are convivial and enjoy these occasions. Everything is discussed except possibly the "meaning" of Subud, for some members have a certain anti-intellectual bias and greatly resist such talk. Others speak freely of the *latihan* to outsiders who show genuine interest, responding warmly to inquirers.

The organization of Subud is not complex. The key to it is the "helper." "Helpers" exist on the regional, national, and international levels as well as the local. The social service and humanitarian activities of Subud are coordinated and directed by the Susila Dharma International Association.

Subud shares with the seeming converse Gurdjieff tradition with which it is oddly linked in the West—and with the alternative reality tradition—a belief that if one finds the right key or technique, one can "short" oneself into a very different and higher kind of consciousness that makes life suddenly meaningful. Its technique is perhaps the most open and direct, reminding one of such psychotherapeutic methods as primal therapy. Unlike others, it does not provide much of a given symbol system, visual or verbal, to associate with the new consciousness. Perhaps one could say that the *latihan* is its own symbol, or that it provides a clearing in which the person can erect his or her own symbols evoked out of newly released parts of the consciousness.

Reading Selection: Subud

This passage by a Westerner who experienced Subud after being very active in the Gurdjieff movement, when Bapak (Pak Subuh) first brought it to England, enables one to experience the *latihan* in company with the leader himself and several Indonesians of Muslim background as well as Western novices.

The whole of that Whit weekend, except for its culmination on the Monday evening, has now been blotted from my memory. I can remember only that sometime on Monday afternoon, about fifteen men gathered upstairs in Mr. Bennett's study, prior to being "opened." He gave us a very brief introductory talk. We were to take off our shoes and ties and watches. We were simply to stand and to be open in our feelings. If we experienced the spontaneous arising of movements within our bodies we were not to resist but simply to follow. We were not to make any effort to control our mental associations, but were to let them wander freely, constraining nothing.

We then filed downstairs to the dining room, the floor of which had been covered by a number of new carpets, and the curtains had been drawn. We were placed in a rough sort of circle in the room. Pak Subuh was already in the room, together with a number of other Indonesians. I recall a very fine exquisite odour, such as I had never smelt before.

Pak Subuh said a few words in Indonesian that were translated haltingly by one of the Indonesian helpers. He said something about coming to the true worship of God, and that in the way of Subud we should not use our thoughts for meditation but simply receive. Then, "Close your eyes and we begin."

Almost at once a number of people began a very strange singing. They sang quite independently, but it did blend in a curious way. The singers also seemed to be moving about in the room. Someone else began to pray in a loud voice in a language that I presumed to be Arabic. The words "Akbar Allah" were repeated a great number of times. But if I simply say prayed in a loud voice, such as one has heard from a priest or muezzin, this would give entirely the wrong impression. This prayer seemed to be heaved from the very depths of his being, as if he was in an agony of remorse, sorrow and supplication. It had a strong effect upon my feelings and I began to feel very small and utterly unworthy. At the same time I began to be afraid and I tensed up. I heard a friend on my left crash to the ground. At the other end of the room someone began to weep, as if he would burst in two. Yet another began to laugh as if at the most huge joke in the world. And still others were obviously moving about quite rapidly, to judge from the panting and the feet padding on the floor.

The longer the exercise lasted the more afraid I became, till I was holding on to myself, determined to resist anything that might come. Suddenly, one word was called out—"Finish!"—and the pandemonium stopped. I opened my eyes and saw that six or seven of my friends were still standing as I was, while the rest had obviously been moving about. A half-hour had passed.

I went next door to put on my shoes and jacket. A friend tried to catch my eye with a questioning look, but I avoided him. I quickly gathered my things together and went down to the station to catch the train to London. Four of us shared the same compartment who had been to the exercise, but not one of us spoke a word.

> ANTHONY BRIGHT-PAUL, *Stairway to Subud* (New York: Dharma Book Company, Inc., 1965), pp. 165–66.

UNIFICATION CHURCH

In the original edition of this book there was an entry on "The United Family," a name by which the Unification Church was known at that time. This new religious movement was not well known in this country, although it had been introduced by a Korean Unification missionary, Miss Young Oon Kim, on the West Coast in 1959. Its founder, Sun Myung Moon, came to live in the United States in 1971, the time of writing of the first edition. Since then the Unification Church has become perhaps the best known new religious movement in this country, rivalled in this regard only by the "Hare Krishnas" and, perhaps, the Scientologists. It has also become one of the most controversial.

Its inclusion in this book is somewhat questionable, because it is not clearly an alternative religious movement. It claims to be a Christian, though not a traditionally Christian, group. Nevertheless, because of its importance and notoriety, we have chosen to include it in the new edition.

In the Unification Church one could say that American Christianity is meeting itself coming back from the mission field, for it is based on an interpretation of the Christian Bible by an Asian convert. It is not unusual for new and different interpretations of Christianity to appear in the Third World. What is unusual is for them to make their way to the West. In this regard, Unificationism may be a harbinger of things to come, though perhaps more likely from Latin America and Africa than Asia.

Sun Myung Moon was born in what is now North Korea in 1920. While he was a child his family joined a conservative Presbyterian church established by American missionaries. At the age of sixteen he had a dramatic and decisive religious experience. He says that on Easter Day, 1936, Jesus appeared to him and told him to "complete my mission," referring to the mission Jesus began nearly two thousand years ago. He was to be responsible for establishing the Kingdom of God on earth. He is said later to have communicated with other great religious personalities, including Abraham, Moses, and the Buddha, as well as with God. For nine years after his initial meeting with Jesus Moon felt himself engaged in a bitter struggle against Satanic forces that tortured him spiritually and physically. Finally, by persevering, he discovered the secret crime Adam and Eve committed in the Garden of Eden, the crime that destroyed the proper divine-human (and interhuman) relationship. Sun Myung Moon believed himself called to restore this God-intended relationship. Unfortunately, it was 1945 and the place he chose to begin his mission was Pyongyang, which became the capital of Communist North Korea in the same year. No sooner had he gathered a small following than he was arrested by the Communist authorities. He is said to have suffered terrible tortures in a labor camp where he spent two and half years. These sufferings have more than ordinary significance for Unificationists, for they are interpreted as a payment of "indemnity" for the sins of the first parents and their descendants. He was released from the camp by United Nations forces during the Korean War and made his way to South Korea. There he began to speak of a "divine principle" which should rule all of life. In 1958 he established a Divine Principle religion, which was known as Tong Il. In the United States it came to be known by various names, including the Holy Spirit Association for the Unification of World Christianity (HSA-UWC), the United (or Unified) Family, the Unification Church, and by the general public most commonly as the "Moonies."

This movement in Korea had all the marks of a Far Eastern new religion like the Japanese. Indeed, it spread to Japan during the late 1950s where it achieved some success. In Korea it has many thousands of members and, showing strong traces of the traditional shamanism of the Korean countryside as well as of missionary Christianity, emphasizes clairvoyance, clairaudience, healing, and spiritualistic phenomena. Believers feel spiritual fire and electricity, and communicate mediumistically with spirits, Jesus, and God. One of his early Korean associates described Rev. Moon's religious experiences of encounters and travels with Jesus to one of the authors in clearly shamanistic terms. However, this early and pervasive shamanism is not emphasized by American "Moonies."

It was not until Rev. Moon moved to the United States that the movement began to make progress in this country. Showing great energy and ingenuity, he went on lecture tours (although he had to speak through an interpreter), held large rallies for which "Moonies" assembled crowds through prodigious publicity efforts, sponsored lavish dinners and receptions for public officials and dignitaries, and organized international conferences to which distinguished scholars and scientists were invited. The media began to report his activities and those of his followers. Widely reported was the rally held on the Capitol steps in Washington in support of President Richard Nixon during the Watergate crisis, as well as his private meeting with the president. In the public eye also were the "Moonies," young, earnest, conservatively dressed men and women who sold flowers, candy, and Unification literature on street corners across the country as members of "mobile fundraising teams."

The basic theological document of the Unification Church is the book called *Divine Principle.* It is not, properly speaking, the bible of the Unification Church, as is sometimes said, but an interpretation of the Christian Bible (Old and New Testaments), communicating the "divine principle" the Unificationists believe the Bible contains. The book relates that the universe is founded on certain laws establishing the right relations of things, of which the most fundamental are Polarity and the Four Position Foundation. All things come in pairs in "give and take" relationship (recalling the Ying-Yang of Chinese Taoism): God as both male and female, God and humans, male and female, subject and object, inner and outer, positive and negative, etc. Within the reciprocal polarities is the proper fourfold hierarchy: God as head; male and female, coequal, in the middle; and the child, on the bottom, as new life.

According to *Divine Principle,* God intended that the first human beings, Adam and Eve, should relate as brother and sister until they matured. Thereafter they were to unite in marriage in obedience to the divine will and produce godly offspring, populating the world with persons who would love and serve God in proper relationship with him and one another. Unfortunately, something went wrong. According to *Divine Principle,* God had entrusted the archangel Lucifer with the responsibility of looking after Adam and Eve. However, Lucifer became jealous of God's love for the first humans and seduced Eve. She had "spiritual intercourse" with him. Eve, in turn, tempted Adam, who had physical intercourse with her, prematurely, thus perverting love, as Unificationists believe. In other words, sex was the "apple" eaten by the progenitors of the human race. Their transgression was transmitted to all their descendants. Of their union were born Cain and Abel, the former especially identified with Satan (Lucifer). Thus was the proper fourfold foundation disrupted, Satan taking the place of God in relation to the first couple and all their descendants.[9]

Unification theology is strongly restorationist. It holds that only through a Messiah, who is the New Adam, will the proper, God-intended relationship be restored and the world achieve perfection. Only the Messiah *and his wife*, standing in the place of the first Adam and Eve, can effect the longed-for restoration. *Divine Principle* teaches that throughout human history God has been seeking to restore the proper four position foundation, through Abraham, Moses, and others, including Jesus. None of these succeeded, although Jesus came closest. He is described as the Second Adam and the Messiah. It was God's intention that he marry a Second Eve and that they produce godly offspring. Unfortunately, before he could do so he was condemned by his enemies and abandoned by his disciples with the result that he was unable to fulfill the divine plan, which would have restored the human family, and ultimately the whole of human society, under God. In the end he could only submit to crucifixion, which was a payment of "indemnity" to God for human sinfulness. By doing so he effected partial salvation ("spiritual salvation") for humans, but not complete salvation, which would have been physical and material as well as spiritual. It is for this reason that Jesus instructed the young Sun Myung Moon: "Complete my mission."

Before the Messiah can succeed it is necessary for humans to establish a "foundation" on which to receive him. This can be done only by the payment of "indemnity," which consists essentially of sacrificial good deeds that constitute payment for the sins of the past. Not only Rev. Moon but all "Moonies" are expected to pay indemnity, which accounts for their apparently unflagging efforts at fundraising, witnessing to possible converts, and other activities in furtherance of the cause. "Moonies" are consequently perhaps the most sacrificial and hardworking of the members of all the new religious movements.

Unificationists are also expected to be celibate before marriage and to remain single for several years after they have joined the movement. At the proper time they are matched with a mate by Rev. Moon in preparation for periodic mass wedding ceremonies known as Blessings. This is clearly the most important ritual in a group that has comparatively little ritual.

In recent years provision has been made for members of another kind. They belong to what is called "home church," and are persons who are sympathetic to Unification thought, but who do not devote their full time to the movement. They live and work in the general society.

Although *Divine Principle* does not say so unequivocally, it is clear that it means to affirm that Rev. Moon is in the position, as Unificationists put it, of the Third Adam, the Lord of the Coming Advent, the new Messiah. It is not certain that he will succeed in effecting the hoped for restoration, thus inaugurating the New Age, but he has accepted this vocation, paying indemnity through his suffering and beginning to create a new human family through his marriage to Hak Ja Han (the new Eve) and his offspring, both physical (the children of this marriage) and spiritual (the "Moonies," to whom he is father). It is in this light that one should understand the mass marriages, amounting to thousands of couples at a time, performed by Rev. and Mrs. Moon, the "True Parents." Further, it is Sun Myung Moon's vocation to battle against Satan, who is still alive and active in the world, especially through communism at the present time. It is this struggle that gives Unificationism its pervasive apocalypticism and right-wing politics.

During the early years of the Unification movement in the United States the "Moonies" were usually equivocal when asked directly whether Rev. Moon is the new Messiah, probably for the reason that they anticipated hostile reactions from Christians to the claim that Jesus did not effect total salvation for the human race and could have a successor as Messiah. Recently, they have become less equivocal, although the messiahship of Rev. Moon is not official church teaching. However, most Unificationists believe it.

Also in recent years the Unificationists have tried to reach a wider audience of academicians and others, not so much, it seems, in the hope of making converts as in gaining a degree of acceptance as a valid American religious community. This they have attempted to do through conferences and seminars on various topics usually having some relationship to Unification thought, and organizations related to the Unification Church.[10] They have also tried to relate to more conventional religious groups, undaunted, it appears, by the rejection of their application for membership in the ecumenical National Council of Churches.

All the while, the Unification Church has had very bad "press" and has replaced the Children of God as the group most criticized and opposed by the anticult movement. More than any other group, with the possible exception of the "Hare Krishnas," it has been accused of "brainwashing" and disrupting families. Rev. Moon has been depicted as the personification of the stereotype of the "cult" leader who lives lavishly on the labors of his obedient followers. The Unification Church has vigorously denied and defended itself against these charges.

The conviction of Rev. Moon on charges of income tax evasion and his imprisonment in 1984 would seem to have dealt the Unification Church a serious blow in its quest for credibility. However, before one concludes that the effects are all negative, it is well to observe that a number of American religious groups, including some major Protestant denominations, have come partially to his defense, questioning both his conviction and the interference of the state in the internal financial affairs of a religious group. Also, while the most vocal religious opposition to the "Moonies" has come from churches belonging to the "religious right," the active involvement of the Unification Church in support of current conservative causes (patriotism, anticommunism, pro-family, antiabortion, noninterference in "Christian" schools, etc.) has softened somewhat their opposition to the "Moonies." It remains to be seen whether the Unification Church will find an enduring place in the American religious economy.

Reading Selection: Unification Church

Toward the end of Divine Principle it is revealed that the "Lord of the Second Advent" will come from an Eastern nation, specifically Korea, and, in fact, is already in the world. The period of the Second Advent is said to have begun shortly after the First World War. Rev. Sun Myung Moon was born in 1920.

First, the nation to which the Messiah comes must be the object of

God's heart. In this view, Korea is the land God has prepared. God, since the fall of the first human ancestors until today, has lived in deep despair and unfulfillment. Too often we refer to God as a being of utmost glory who is so far above us, but this is because we do not know God's heart. Due to the fall of man, who is His only child, God has been grieving with the heart of a parent who has lost his child, and to save that rebellious child, He has wandered through the sinful world of hell in search of him. Therefore, the individual, or family, or nation which fights against Satan on earth in God's place can hardly avoid the path of tears and suffering. How could a filial and faithful son, who shares the agony of his parent's heart, lead an easy life?

Since the Messiah is the one who comes bearing the grieving heart of God, to relieve God's sorrow here on earth, he cannot come among a people who are satisfied by their material abundance. Since the nation which is to receive the Messiah must become the object of God's heart—since its people must become sons and daughters of the same heart as God's—that nation cannot avoid the way of suffering.

The First and Second Israel both had to tread the way of suffering and hardship; likewise, the Third Israel must tread the same way. The history of the utmost misery, especially the extreme example of suffering in modern times, has been the model course which the Third Israel had to take. Thus, even while undergoing the life of suffering and misery, this nation, Korea, has been faithfully inheriting the good tradition of filial piety and loyalty, and even at the height of its national power, never provoked or first invaded a neighboring nation. God's strategy has been that of winning victory from the position of being attacked, quite different from the intent of invasion or aggression. Despite innumerable foreign invasions, the fact that the Korean people have maintained their homogeneous lineage and subjectivity of culture is simply amazing. Even amidst its persistently sorrowful history it has cherished its education as a nation.

Second, Korea is meaningful as the nation bearing fruit of many religions. Korea has a strong inclination toward religious life. The Korean people revere God. Many of the world's great religions, such as Confucianism and Buddhism, have flourished in this land and borne fruit. In recent centuries Christianity arrived and achieved the highest pinnacle of Christianity. Religion has deeply blended with daily life in exquisite harmony. A nation matching this description is indeed hard to find in the world.

The Lord does not come to save Christians alone. Of course Christianity is the central nation in God's providence, but God Himself has created and guided all the major religions for the restoration of their particular region, time period, or circumstance. Therefore, the Messiah, who is to accomplish the ultimate purpose of God's providence must simultaneously fulfill the purpose of all other religions as well.

In this view, the nation which bears the fruits of all the major religions becomes the land suitable to receive the Lord.

Third, the nation in which our Lord comes must be the front line of both God and Satan. As we can understand from God's words to Adam and

Eve not to eat of the fruit or they would die, the point where they fell became a dividing line of heaven and earth and life and death, and thus good and evil also split apart from this point.

Thus, our Lord comes to the same basic type of point, where again life and death and good and evil confront one another. He then goes on to fulfill the providential history and solve the current problems.

God's providence to restore the world to His own side, after Satan took the initiative, can also be seen as the dispensation of dividing Cain and Abel. The separation of the worlds of Cain and Abel before the coming of the Messiah is manifested in the Communist and democratic worlds. Thus, this can be called a horizontal development of the vertical providence which God has wrought throughout history.

Therefore, where our Lord comes is where the two powers of democracy and Communism confront one another; it is the focal point of both God's love and Satan's hate. That very line of confrontation is the 38th parallel in the Korean peninsula. Therefore, this line is not only the front line of democracy and Communism but also the front line of God and Satan as well.

Since the nation and race in which the Lord comes in the East are an offering for the restoration providence, the Korean nation, which is the offering, must be divided. Thus, the Korean War which broke out along the 38th parallel was not merely the civil conflict of a nation due to territorial separation. It was the confrontation between the democratic and Communist blocs and furthermore, between God and Satan. The fact that many nations (16) not immediately concerned with the conflict nonetheless participated and helped the providence of restoration has divine significance.

Fourth, the nation in which the Lord comes must establish a national foundation for the providence of restoration. In order for Korea to become the nation to receive the Messiah, just as did the First and Second Israel, it must establish the national foundation to separate from Satan. The Israelites had to establish a condition of separating from Satan by suffering in slavery for 400 years in Egypt, which represented the Satanic world. The Second Israel established a condition to separate from Satan by enduring persecution for four centuries in the Roman Empire, which also represented the Satanic world.

Thus at the time of the Second Advent, the Third Israel, Korea, must also endure suffering at the hands of a particular nation on the satanic side in order to separate from Satan. In this case, it was Japan, and for 40 years it brought unimaginable torment upon Korea. In 1905, Japan forcibly deprived Korea of its diplomatic rights and this brought on a period of loss of national sovereignty which lasted until 1945, the year of its defeat in World War II. During this period, the Korean people were completely deprived of their freedom by Japan, and countless numbers were imprisoned, slaughtered, and underwent all sorts of extreme persecution. Especially in 1910, after Japan annexed Korea, the persecution of Christianity, which was the major foundation for Korea's independence movement, was unparalleled in its cruelty. When Christianity was enjoying its freedom under God's providence all around the globe, the suffering of the Korean nation, of which Christians were the core, became the condition of national indemnity to qualify it as the Third Israel.

Fifth, this nation must have prophetical testimonies among the people. When God sends his beloved Son, how can He do it quietly? Certainly, He would reveal it to all prepared souls on earth, hand them the good news and have them prepare themselves. Just as the Jewish people knew through the prophets that the Messiah would come as a king and save them, for 500 years Korea also had a strong messianic faith through the Chung-Gam-Nok, a book of prophecy. It was written in the time of the providence when God's salvation through the Messiah was not immediately available. It is characteristic of Korea to have been nurtured by this unique messianic thought.

Also, many spiritually gifted clergy and laymen have received specific revelations regarding the Second Advent of the Lord in Korea. Furthermore, many deeply religious people have had the common revelation that Korea will be the center of world salvation.

"Divine Principle–Six Hour Lecture," The Holy Spirit Association for the Unification of World Christianity, 1977, pp. 47–49. Reprinted by permission.

NOTES

[1]The thirteen numbers of this magazine published in 1940 and 1941 by the Buddhist Society of America have been reprinted with a foreword in a bound volume called *Cat's Yawn* (New York: First Zen Institute of America, 1947).

[2]Philip Kapleau, *The Three Pillars of Zen* (New York and Tokyo: John Weatherhill, Inc., 1965).

[3]Jacob Needleman, in *The New Religions* (New York: Doubleday & Co., Inc., 1970), Chapter 7, gives a fascinating account of one Tibetan center in the West, the Tibetan Nyingmapa Meditation Center in Berkeley, California, founded by Tarthang Tulku in 1969. Probably the best introduction to the actual practice of Tibetan methods in a Western setting is John Blofeld, *The Way of Power* (London: George Allen & Unwin, 1970). The books of Lama Govinda, Alexandra David-Neel, David Snellgrove, Herbert Guenther, and W. Y. Evans-Wenz have also been very influential and sympathetic, but not always uncritical, presentations of the Tibetan heritage.

[4]When asked by a reporter in 1974 why he had come to the United States, Rangjung Rigpe Dorje, head of one of the Tibetan orders, replied: "If there was a lake, the swans would go there." His charming, though somewhat enigmatic, reply was appropriated by Rick Fields as the title of his narrative history of Buddhism in America, *How the Swans Came to the Lake* (Boulder, CO: Shambhala Publications, 1981).

[5]Boulder, CO: Shambhala Publications, 1977.

[6]James Hilton, *Lost Horizon* (New York: William Morrow & Co., Inc., 1933).

[7]*Garuda*, edited by Chogyam Trungpa. (Boulder, CO: Shambhala Publications, 1977), Vol. 5, p. 98.

[8]*The New Religions,* p. 170.

[9]The idea that the transgression of Adam and Eve was sexual in nature has appeared from time to time in Christian thought. It is not unique to *Divine Principle* and the Unificationists.

[10]For example, the New Ecumenical Research Association, the International Cultural Foundation, and the International Conference on the Unity of the Sciences.

9

NEW RELIGIOUS MOVEMENTS:
Sociological and Psychological Approaches

Although new religious movements of various kinds have been a significant and continuing feature of American religious life, they have not received the attention they deserve until recently. In the past, historians and social scientists have been interested in dominant movements and processes in American society to the neglect of those considered marginal. The general public and, nearly as much, the scholarly community have thought of American religion in the terms suggested by the title of Will Herberg's book *Protestant, Catholic, Jew,*[1] and were not attentive to religious groups that did not fit this tripartite scheme. Rarely did general books on the history of American religion give attention to marginal groups. A breakthrough of sorts occurred with the publication of Sidney E. Ahlstrom's two-volume *A Religious History of the American People.*[2] Toward the end of the second volume the author gave some attention to "Harmonial Religion" (e.g., New Thought) in the nineteenth century and "Piety for the Age of Aquarius" (Theosophy, occultism, and non-Western religion) in the twentieth. Even so, it was a sort of add-on, almost an afterthought. Written a decade later, Catherine L. Albanese's book *America: Religions and Religion*[3] recognized the "manyness" of religion in America and devoted major sections to a much wider range of nineteenth and twentieth century new religions, occult and metaphysical movements, and Eastern religions, as well as native American and Afro-American religions—all without losing sight of elements of "oneness" of religion in America. Similar perspectives emerge in some of the writings of the historian of American religion Martin E. Marty.[4] Scholars in the history, phenomenology, and comparative study of religion, whom one would think uniquely equipped to investigate marginal religions, have been slow to take up this area of study, still preferring to direct their attention mainly to extra-American religious phenomena.

There now exists, however, a considerable and growing body of reputable, scholarly study of new religious movements, including studies of particular groups as well as general and topical studies.[5] Both theoretical and, increasingly, empirical studies are being produced. Most of them come from sociologists and psychologists.

The sociology of religion, as sociology generally, recognizes the existence of social structures and social processes that are not reducible to individual psychology or explainable as the effects of ideas. It studies these structures and processes both in themselves and in relation to individual motivation, ideas, and values. It may do so in terms of functional theory, based mainly on the insights of Emile Durkheim[6] and the cultural anthropologists, who see religion as interdependent with other aspects and the whole of society, and functioning to maintain the social system. Alternatively, it may take a developmental point of view, based on the works of Ernst Troeltsch, Max Weber, and Joachim Wach.[7] In the latter case it attempts to explore the relation between religious phenomena and the variety of social factors so as to follow the development of religious institutions.

The psychology of religion is usually, by contrast, an individualistic orientation and assumes that there are relations between mental states and overt actions. Although they share this assumption, specific psychologies of religion diverge from one another, depending on their relations with "schools" (psychoanalytical, gestalt, behaviorists, etc.).

We were introduced to sociological and psychological approaches in the discussion of the meanings of "cult" in the first chapter. Sociologists of religion, in particular, have long been interested in types of religious association, including "sect" and "cult." Their interest, especially in the latter, has grown since the 1960s, as they have become aware of the presence of numerous new, alternative religious groups in the American religious economy.

In this chapter we shall focus on several questions which arise from the study of new religious movements, and to which sociologists and psychologists have made important contributions. We shall have in mind mainly the 1960s' type of groups of the intensive kind to which we referred in the first chapter in connection with Erving Goffman's concept of "total institutions." They require a high degree of commitment and conformity. It is around them that swirl the controversies about "cults," "brainwashing," and "deprogramming." We recognize that there are many non-normative religious groups—in fact, most of those included in this book—that are not of this type. By contrast, they are less demanding and enveloping, less subject to controversy and opposition, and more diffuse in influence.[8]

RELIGIOUS CONVERSION

Conversion is best understood as a process of identity change, potentially a total change of identity. It is a kind of rebirth. Conversion also changes the way one looks at the world. It is more than and different from alternation, for it involves a radical break with the past. Religious alternation occurs when, say, a Methodist becomes an Episcopalian (perhaps because one's spouse is an Episcopalian or the local Episcopal Church is more conveniently located); religious conversion occurs when, say, a Methodist becomes a "Moonie." Conversion is "a radical reorganization of identity, meaning, and life."[9]

The true convert who becomes a "Moonie", for example, is observed by family and friends to have changed, sometimes almost beyond recognition. He or she is full of new-found faith and fervor, a son or daughter of the True Parents (Rev. and Mrs. Moon), a brother or sister of other "Moonies," a participant in the ongoing work of God to restore humanity to its proper order and harmony, willing to "pay indemnity" and to accept the ostracism that comes from membership in a group widely considered deviant.

The question most frequently asked about new religious movements, especially those considered "cults," is why and how persons are converted to them. Conversion to "cults" elicits a great deal more interest than conversion to conventional religious groups. Society does not expect that persons will be attracted to religious groups it considers deviant; consequently, it requires explanation. Further, such conversions appear often to be surprisingly rapid. Bromley and Shupe in their study of a group of Unificationists found that about fifteen percent made the decision to join the church within three days of their first contact with it.[10] Another fifteen percent joined within one week. By the end of a month sixty percent had made the decision. A number of theories of the conversion process have been generated by, mainly, sociologists and psychologists to account for such conversions.

Deprivation Theory

Half a century ago Louis Richard Binder puzzled over the phenomenon of apparently intelligent and knowledgeable persons joining "cults." He ventured the opinion that their intelligence was offset by a psychological deficiency or emotional complex.[11] Binder was expressing a version of what has come to be known as the *deprivation* theory of religious conversion. In general, the deprivation theory holds that potential converts are predisposed by psychological, economic, and social deficiencies and problems to seek membership in religious "cults." The nature of the deprivation varies somewhat from one researcher to another, but the emphasis in any case is on the individual psychology, situation, and motivation of the potential convert. Conversion may be attributed to sexual inadequacies, for example. In his study of the Church of Satan Edward J. Moody claimed that through participation in its sexual rites some members were able to overcome not only their sense of personal powerlessness but, specifically, their sexual inadequacy.[12] Conversely, a study of conversion to the Unification Church concluded that its asceticism reduced neurotic stress for some young adult members.[13] Other researchers find other problems lying at the base of conversion, as, for example, Glock and Stark, who included various kinds of physical, ethical, and social status deficiencies.[14]

The deprivation theory can be criticized. Deprivations of many kinds are widespread in society; conversions to "cults" are not. Why then do only some of those who have the predisposing conditions actually convert? Also, is it in fact the case, as is often assumed, that "cults" contain more emotionally unstable and mentally ill persons than do conventional religious groups? The evidence does not indicate that it is. For example, Bromley and Shupe, interviewing converts to the Unification Church, concluded that there was not much evidence of serious deprivation. Further, deprivation theories neglect the social and cultural dimensions of conversion in favor of the individually psychological. They focus on individuals with private problems—personal pathologies—who seek resolution through religious affiliation. Moreover, such theories depict conversion as essentially a passive process, as something which happens *to* the individual, not something he or she does. The element of voluntariness in conversion is minimized or denied. Finally, deprivation theories often evidence psychological reductionism, in that a religious phenomenon is reduced to or explained in terms of psychological pathology.

Interactionist Theory

Anson D. Shupe, Jr., has given the name *interactionist* to a second theory or model of conversion, which does not necessarily deny the deprivational or motivational theory, but questions its adequacy alone to account for conversion to fringe religious groups.[15] Social factors, as well as possible deprivations, are taken into account. These social factors are both internal (relations among members) and external (relations with the general society).

A well-known example of the interactionist model is that presented by John Lofland and Rodney Stark.[16] It was developed in connection with a study of the Unification Church, but the authors held, cautiously, that it possesses generalizable features. In brief, Lofland and Stark distinguished two kinds of conditions or factors in conversion: Predisposing conditions and situational contingencies. The former comprise the attributes of persons prior to their contact with the new religious group. The latter are the conditions which lead to the successful recruitment of such predisposed persons. Successful conversion requires both the predispositions and the proper situational conditions. Briefly, there are three predisposing conditions. The first is acutely felt tension, which Lofland and Stark defined in terms of discrepancy felt between an imaginary, ideal state of affairs and the actual state in which persons find themselves. The second is a religious problem-solving perspective (rather than, say, a political or psychiatric perspective which might lead one to a political movement or an HPM ("human potential movement") group. The third is a self-definition as a religious seeker, that is, a person searching for a system of religious meaning and value that can explain and resolve discontent. The situational contingencies are four: first, encountering the new religious group at a turning point in one's life; second, forming an affective bond with one or more members; third, the absence (or neutralization) of extra-group attachments; and, finally, exposure to intensive interaction with core members of the group. It is the last which transforms one from a verbal convert into a fully committed member.

In a sense, this model is not in fact interactional, but essentially passive, for the potential convert is viewed as a more or less neutral medium through which social forces operate. Lofland has recognized this characteristic of the theory and has begun to ask what active part individuals play in their own conversion.[17] A further criticism of the theory is that it does not explain why persons who have little or no interest in religion, thus lacking an important predisposition, convert to fringe religious groups. As with the deprivation theory, much is made of tensions, but tensions, even acutely felt ones, are widespread if not universal. Unlike the deprivation theory, however, the interactionist theory, by invoking situational contingencies, does provide an answer to the question why only some of those who experience acute tension are converted.

Role Theory

A third model of conversion is known as the *role* theory. Conversion is seen as beginning essentially with the acceptance of a social role advocated by a religious group. Interest focuses on the continuing process by which an individual assumes roles and statuses and is to all appearances a member and believer. In this perspective conversion is a gradual affair, being marked by the adoption of successive roles within a religious group. The perspective is organizational and sociological. While there may be predispositions, not much significance is attributed to them in determining who joins a religious group. In fact, the emphasis is more on *how* one joins than why. For the most part, roles in religious groups are clear and usually not difficult to learn and assume. They can be assumed without much understanding of the meanings implicit in them, and with a minimum of belief. Understanding and belief may increase over time. It has been said that "one bows the knee to become religious." The role theory would agree.

Robert W. Balch was a participant-observer in a millennial UFO group led by "the Two," who called themselves Bo and Peep.[18] The group gained public attention in the mid-1970s when several hundred persons gave up all their worldly attachments, including their material possessions, jobs, families, and friends after hearing Bo and Peep in public meetings in which they predicted that UFOs would arrive shortly to carry off members to the "Next Evolutionary Kingdom." Balch, who joined the group for a time and observed it closely in the course of its peregrinations, found that individuals soon acted like believers although belief usually came gradually (and was perhaps never complete). Acting like a believer meant conforming to a set of expectations specified by the Two. The first step in conversion was learning to act like a convert. If firm conviction developed, it did so behind a façade of total commitment. Balch observed that appearances can be deceiving, for some members continued to play the role long after they had begun seriously to doubt. The defections, of which there were many, often came as a complete surprise to others.

Bromley and Shupe studied a Unification Church fundraising/proselytization team and found the role theory more appropriate than the deprivational.[19] They found an affiliative process at work, consisting of five conceptual components: (1) predisposing factors, (2) attraction, (3) incipient involvement, (4) active involvement, and (5) commitment. They observed also that behavior changed greatly as persons increased their involvement, but that these changes could not be correlated with psychological conversion as usually understood. Instead, behavior changes preceded belief changes, and psychological commitment issued from active role performance. Moreover, they found, as had Balch, that frequent defections indicate that the commitment of individuals may not be as great as appears from their behavior.

One of the values of the role theory is that it recognizes the conscious, active participation of persons in their own conversion. In this respect it differs markedly from the brainwashing theory, to which we shall turn next, with its image of persons as passive, helpless victims.

Brainwashing Theory

The *brainwashing* theory denies that conversion is in fact conversion. It sees the individual as having been transformed involuntarily into a "cult" member and subsequently held captive, as it were, by psychological means.

The proximate origin of this theory of psychological conditioning is the Korean War, during which some captured American servicemen were subjected to "brainwashing."[20] Following the war there was considerable interest in the phenomenon. Especially influential was the psychologist Robert Jay Lifton's book *Thought Reform and the Psychology of Totalism*.[21] A more recent popular presentation of brainwashing, going far beyond Lifton in dramatizing the phenomenon, is the book *Snapping: America's Epidemic of Sudden Personality Change,* written by Flo Conway and Jim Siegelman.[22] As the subtitle indicates, conversion is viewed as a disease. "Snapping" is the term the authors use for the sudden loss of free will and freedom of thought through external control. They contend that the entire personality "snaps," resulting in, as they put it, a new person inside the old—a personality completely different and thus unrecognizable. Conversion to "cults" is said to provide the best example of the phenomenon. Under the cumulative pressures of a physical, emotional, and psychological "blitz," self-identity and control and personal beliefs surrender. According to Conway and Siegelman, this process is facilitated by isolation, poor diet, exhaustion, "love bombing," intimidation, and the like. At length, persons are no longer able to think and decide for themselves. They reach a state of explosive overstimulation and emotional collapse. Paradoxically, say the authors, they consider what has happened to them positively, as a rebirth. They learn to accept and value their captivity. So goes the "snapping" version of conversion.

The brainwashing model was developed with certain intensive groups mainly in mind—the Children of God,[23] the Unification Church, the "Hare Krishnas," and Scientology—but it was quickly extended to other new religious groups and even to "old" new religious groups such as the Mormons.

Brainwashing as a general, comprehensive theory of religious conversion has few scholarly proponents. Much of the evidence brought forth in support of it is anecdotal, including the atrocity tales of ex-"cult" members who are perhaps predisposed to interpret their experiences in such a way as to relieve themselves of responsibility for their own actions. Statistical analyses of the "thought reform" efforts of the Chinese Communists during the Korean War indicate that they were relatively unsuccessful. Also, instances of coercive conversion result in high rates of defection. All in all, the brainwashing theory is most notable for its usefulness for parents, defectors, and the public opposed to "cults," not for its adequacy as an interpretation of conversion to religious groups. It relieved both parents and their offspring of any responsibility or stigma in the matter. In a sense, it is a modern version of the medieval doctrine of satanic possession.

By our criticism of the brainwashing theory, we do not mean to suggest that none of the groups we have studied, especially those of the intensive type, do not use questionable methods of persuasion. Some groups do not identify themselves readily, for fear that their name will "turn off" potential converts before they have the opportunity to present themselves. Potential converts are sometimes taken to relatively isolated places for intensive interaction with the group, where they experience overt, perhaps excessive, affection. Strategies of psychological conditioning, frequently employed in advertising and sales and in the political (and religious) realms in American society, are utilized. In general, groups present themselves in the most favorable light and hope for positive response. That should not surprise us, for these groups are intensely serious and enthusiastic about "evangelizing," and are quite convinced that they are doing a good thing. Americans, with their tradition of religious voluntarism and history of religious revivals, should be well prepared to understand this phenomenon as it appears among alternative, new religious groups. There is little new about it. A good deal of suspicion and exaggeration is required to call it "brainwashing."

Transformation Theory

Almost diametrically opposed to the brainwashing theory is a psychological theory proposed by J. Gordon Melton and Robert L. Moore in *The Cult Experience: Responding to the New Religious Pluralism*.[24] To "snapping" they oppose "transformation."

Melton and Moore observe that the majority of persons who enter alternative religious groups do so in their early twenties. They call attention to the existence of more or less predictable crises at certain points in the life cycle,[25] including the transition from adolescence to young adulthood. These crises, although difficult and disturbing, are normal developmental phenomena and not expressions of psychopathology. The authors utilize insights from the work of the late psychosocial anthropologist Victor Turner.[26] It was he who renewed the analysis of rites of passage, originally investigated by the Belgian psychologist Arnold van Gennep.[27] Briefly, van Gennep held that rites of passage (birth, marriage, and funeral rites; initiations; pilgrimages; etc.) exhibit a tripartite structure: separation, margin, and aggregation. By this is meant (1) separation from a previously existing role and/or status, (2) transition, and (3) incorporation into a new role and/or status. Turner explored in particular the second phase (margin, transition), which he interpreted as the phase of being betwixt and between. He gave this phase the name *liminal* (from *limen*, "threshold").[28] According to Melton and Moore, conversion to "cults" frequently coincides with or comes shortly after the onset of a period of transition or liminality in the life cycle. The sudden personality change much touted by Conway and Siegelman is actually a movement over the threshold into liminality.

The behavior of converts which Conway and Siegelman described dramatically may be expected among persons experiencing liminality. For example, the disoriented look which new converts are said to have may well be due to the trauma of transition rather than brainwashing. Similarly, the apparently uncritical acceptance of the authority of and obedience to "cult" leaders has its parallel in the attitude of tribal initiands to their initiating elders in so-called "primitive" societies. Further, the experience of "communitas"[29] which often obtains among members of new religious groups that function as surrogate families is common among initiands in the liminal phase of their initiation. In this phase they have separated themselves from the old social structure and relations. That converts to "cults" tend to separate themselves from their families, breaking off old relationships, should not surprise us. In these and other respects there are striking parallels between the new convert and liminal persons in other contexts. Melton and Moore are also able to account for subsequent defections, seeing them as evidence of the completion of transition.

Among the various theories of conversion the transformation theory seems to provide the best general framework within which to understand conversion to alternative religious groups. It enables one to understand how it is that at a certain point in their lives young persons who may or may not previously have shown religious interests begin to do so. It also accounts for the typically rather short-lived involvement of members of new religious groups. Moreover, it provides a general theory and pattern within which deprivation, interaction, and role-playing may be seen to operate, and is a counter to the "brainwashing" theory.

It seems to us, however, that none of the theories is sufficiently attentive to what converts say about their own conversion. While their interpretations of their experience should not simply be taken at face value, sociologists and psychologists may be too reluctant to consider these interpretations with sufficient seriousness, being predisposed to believe that things are never what they seem or are said to be. Too much skepticism at this point may be as great a hindrance to understanding as too little.

It seems to us also that sociologists and psychologists ignore something which for many converts is of great importance, namely, that one converts to a particular religious way. Much of what is written about conversion to new religions seems to assume that they are simply interchangeable—that it does not matter much what the religion is—and that an individual would as likely be converted to one as to another if the opportunity presented itself. The new religious movements are not homogeneous; they represent *different* ways of being religious, as Frederick J. Streng has reminded us.[30] Some persons seem to be attracted to some ways rather, or rather more, than others. These individual differences, which may have to do with temperament, imagination, previous experience, and much besides, should be recognized.

CHARACTERISTICS OF MEMBERS

Who joins new religious movements? What are the characteristics of those who do? Is there a profile of the typical "cult" member? It is commonly assumed that potential members must be different from most persons in significant ways, simply for the reason that most persons do not join unconventional religious groups. There are stereotypes, which have been created largely by the anticult movement and, to a considerable extent, by the media. A common stereotype is that the typical member is an idealistic, yet gullible, young person who is experiencing some personal problems and has gotten into the clutches of a "cult" leader or his agents. Another stereotype, especially in the case where the person is older, is that he or she is an "odd" person who is maladjusted and probably a "loser." Unable to get along in ordinary society, he or she retreats to a safe haven. Undoubtedly one finds persons who conform to these stereotypes in fringe religious groups, but one also finds them in conventional groups. More significantly, one finds many persons who do not conform to these stereotypes in all kinds of religious groups, including those considered deviant. There is considerable variety in the characteristics of members of new religious groups. This observation holds true whether one is examining a particular group or a number of groups.

However, on the basis of sociological data obtained through the study of particular groups, especially those of the intensive type, some broad generalizations may be made, provided one recognizes that there are many exceptions. We are describing tendencies, not drawing a profile.

1. Most members of new religious movements, especially those of the intensive type, are young persons. Eileen Barker's study of the Unification Church in Great Britain found that half of the members were between twenty-one and twenty-six years of age.[31] The proportion for American Unificationists is similar. Much the same holds true for such groups as the "Hare Krishnas,"[32] the "premies" of the Divine Light Mission, the Baba Lovers, and some other groups. Members usually join while in their early twenties and defect well before they are thirty. All these groups have some members in their thirties and above, but the great cluster consists of younger persons. In contrast, some religious groups, usually of the less intensive

variety, attract older persons. For the most part, these are the older "new" religious movements: the Theosophists, Anthroposophists, Rosicrucians, Builders of the Adytum, and some others. They attract middle-aged and older persons.

There are reasons why various groups appeal predominantly to certain age groups. Among them are differences in religious style and in the kind and degree of involvement required. The Anthroposophical Society, for example, still has about it something of an Old World atmosphere which does not appeal to the young, although they may find some of the ideas of Rudolf Steiner interesting. The Theosophical Society's emphasis on books and lectures similarly does not attract youthful adherents as much as older ones. Nichiren Shoshu, however, with its enthusiastic rallies, musical groups, and infectious chanting does attract the young, as do some other religious groups of foreign origin (various forms of Buddhism, Hinduism, Sikhism, etc.) with their exoticism. Age responses are also related to the demands groups make. One is much more likely to join a high demand group, say, the Krishna Consciousness Society or the Unification Church or Nichiren Shoshu, if he or she does not have the responsibilities of older adults. Also, the young are perhaps better able to bear the ostracism which commonly attaches to membership in these groups. However, youthful membership is a mixed blessing, for it also results in high rates of defection, with the consequence that groups have to recruit constantly in order to maintain their numbers.

2. Most members of new religious groups are somewhat isolated, unattached individuals. They are likely to be unmarried at the time of joining, and to remain so. They are also likely to be away from home when they are first contacted, perhaps travelling, in college, in a new town, or on a new job; that is, they probably do not live in a family setting or have close family ties. New religious movements are not examples of "familiar religion."[33] Sometimes families are established within the group, the striking example being the Unification Church with its periodic mass marriages and its encouragement to produce "godly offspring." The recent "Home Church" initiative among the Unificationists has furthered this family trend. The Home Church members tend to be older than full-time "Moonies," married, and often were introduced to the movement by their offspring. This is, however, exceptional among new religious movements and is directly related to the particular ideology of the Unification Church. The dominant tendency, as we have said, is for members of marginal religious groups to be single, unattached individuals. The religious group is likely more or less to function as a surrogate family.

3. Most members come from the middle or upper-middle classes. Questionnaires and interviews of young members about their parents' occupations and incomes substantiate this generalization. For example, Rochford's questionnaires (1980) from "Hare Krishnas" indicated that 58 percent of the devotees came from families with annual incomes in excess of $20,000 (38 percent over $30,000), which was a considerable income for the time.[34] As regards occupations of fathers, 66 percent were professionals, executives, managers, or owners of small businesses.[35] Although the

members may themselves be underemployed and not concerned to maintain their family's class status, they are likely to have had a relatively privileged background. Economic and social deprivations are found more commonly among members of religious sects[36] than "cults," except ethnically based ones.

4. Most members are relatively well educated. A high proportion have been to college. Of Rochford's "Hare Krishnas," for example, 61 percent had attended college.[37] The proportion is similar among other intensive groups. While some are college "drop-outs," others possess one or more degrees. The idea that they are typically persons lacking in intelligence and education is without foundation.

5. The experience of disaffection is often found among members of intensive new religious groups. It is well known that one of the main sources of converts to new religious movements in the 1960s and 1970s was the counterculture. (The decline of the counterculture in recent years has dried up an important source of adherents.) Many members have experienced alienation, which may include alienation from their families, society, and, perhaps, conventional religious institutions. Some are escaping from bad family situations, hoping to find, as mentioned above, a surrogate family in the group. This is not to say, however, that such alienation is a necessary condition for membership. Anthony and Robbins found in their study of the Baba Lovers that members did not necessarily come from broken homes, but, on the contrary, sometimes came instead from close, loving families.[38] They suggested that religious groups that serve as surrogate families may provide their members the possibility of a *recovery* of family-like relationships they have lost in the highly competitive worlds of school and work since leaving home. We observed in Chapter 1 that a personal problem which has often led young persons to some new religious groups is the need for a tight social structure. It appears that in fact converts come from both close-knit families and their opposite.

Interviews with members of new religious movements often indicate alienation from conventional religion. They frequently include statements to the effect that they found their family religion (if there was one) seriously wanting, while those with no family religion remark negatively about conventional religious institutions (formal, cold, hypocritical, etc.). This recurring theme seems to be more than simply a justification for current religious affiliation and seems to express a significant disaffection from conventional, "mainstream" religion. At the same time, there are many converts who have not had any relations with conventional religion and for whom involvement in a new religious movement is their first personal religious encounter. The growth of these movements is not to be explained simply as the result of the failure of the churches and synagogues, as some conventional religious elements claim.

6. Religious seekership seems to be a characteristic of many members of new religious groups. By seekership is meant the search for a satisfactory system of meaning and value. In the case of the young this religious "bent" often surprises their parents who are not religious seekers themselves and puzzle over the apparently strange preoccupation of their son or daughter.

It has been observed that it is not unusual for such a seeker to belong successively to several new religious groups and to consider his or her spiritual peregrinations a pilgrimage.

Although we do not present it as a generalization, it is clear from studies of the backgrounds of converts that some new religious groups, again particularly those of the intensive type, attract persons who have experienced the drug culture and found it wanting. While drugs may have altered consciousness, they did not support other countercultural values (love, noninjury, etc.).[39] Krishna Consciousness and the Baba Lovers, as well as some other new religious groups, alter consciousness without the negative effects of drug "trips," and, additionally, provide a structure and discipline missing in the chaos of the drug culture. These groups have been an effective way out of drugs for many persons.

THE LEADER

As we observed in Chapter 1, one of the characteristics of the group is that it has authoritative and, often, charismatic leadership. New religious movements center around strong leaders, usually a single leader, who is often the founder. The centrality, authority, and power of the leader are such as to promote in the public mind a stereotype of the "cult" leader as one who *completely* dominates the members of the group so that they obey him or her totally and without hesitation. The leader is often thought to be cunning and nefarious as well as powerful, and to live grandly on the forced labors of the followers. As with all stereotypes, this one should not be accepted uncritically.

Types of Prophets

The German sociologist Max Weber distinguished two types of "prophets," one the emissary type and the other exemplary.[40] By the emissary prophet he meant the type familiar to readers of the Hebrew scriptures, that is, a prophet who believes he has received a message and is commissioned to communicate it to others. By exemplary Weber meant one whose own religious experience serves as an example for others. Such was Gautama the Buddha whose enlightenment experience under the Bodhi tree awakened other human beings to their own possibility of having this experience. Most of the leaders of new religious movements are prophets of the exemplary type. So it was in the case of, say, Prabhupada with his ecstatic experience, Frederick Adams with his experience of the feminine modes of sacrality, and Georges Gurdjieff with his experiments in human self-transformation. Not all the "prophets" presented in this book are of the exemplary type. Sun Myung Moon, founder of the Unification Church, claims, as we have seen, to have a religious message which is communicated through the book called *Divine Principle*, but even he evidences something of the exemplary type through the shamanistic aspects of his religious experience.[41] UFO "contactees"[42] are also of the emissary type. These are exceptions, however, to the generalization that most leaders are of the exemplary type.

Charisma

Sociologists often speak of "charisma" as a characteristic of some persons. Charisma is difficult to define, but it refers to a personal quality or qualities that make one striking, attractive, fascinating, mysterious, powerful, effective. Some persons have it and others do not. Max Weber described the charismatic type of leader as one who is ". . . set apart from ordinary men and treated as endowed with supernatural, superhuman, or at least specifically exceptional powers or qualities. These are such as are not accessible to the ordinary person, but are regarded as of divine origin or exemplary, and on the basis of them the individual concerned is treated as a leader."[43] It has to do with such things as appearance,[44] voice, "presence," intimations of prescience, confidence and assuredness, aura of mystery, effective power, and, perhaps, sexuality. It is not so much something one claims for oneself as something recognized by others. However, it has to be demonstrated, "proved," as it were. Yet, the charismatic leader does not derive his or her authority from the election of followers, for the reverse holds true. It is their duty to recognize the charismatically qualified leader and to obey.

Charisma does not lend itself to transfer from one person to another, which complicates the problem of succession to charismatic leaders in new religious movements by persons lacking in charisma. A common solution to this problem, as we mentioned in Chapter 1, is the "routinization" (institutionalization) of charisma by way of attempting to invest the charisma in an office rather than a person. Consequently, the incumbent of the charismatic office may come to possess some of the power that charismatic persons would possess, although apart from the office he or she lacks charisma. The maximum effect occurs when a personally charismatic person occupies a charismatic office. (A contemporary example, from the realm of conventional religion, is Pope John Paul II, who combines the charismatic office of the papacy with attractive personal qualities that appeal far beyond the limits of Roman Catholicism.) Many of the leaders of new religious groups we have encountered in this book possess personal rather than official charisma. If their movements endure, however, dependence on official, institutional charisma is likely to increase.

The Magus

In Chapter 2 we wrote of the magus, whom we characterized briefly as the shaman-in-civilization. Some leaders of new religious movements, especially originators of the first generation, are magus-like. Clear examples are Helene Blavatsky and Georges Gurdjieff. Others, such as Ron Hubbard and Paul Twitchell aspired to become magi by creating appropriate autobiographies. The magus is not simply one who possesses charisma. In addition to the aura of mystery and power, the magus has certain characteristic experiences. We find that the magi typically claim to have had unusual, indeed strange, childhoods in which extraordinary powers were manifested and special destinies forecast. We also find mysterious encounters and transforming initiatory experiences as well as claims of travels to distant, exotic places. Confrontations with danger, including brushes with death (and even death, with subsequent revival), feature as motifs. All this and more recalls the atmosphere and experiences of the shaman of archaic and traditional cultures, although it takes place on the civilizational level.

We should bear in mind also that originators of new religious movements have authority and power not simply because of charisma or magus-like qualities, but because they have discovered something thought by their followers to be of great value. It may be a secret, a kind of experience, a religious technique (for example, a chant), a teaching, or something else which enables one to establish a relationship with a transcendent source of meaning and value. In defining "cult" in Chapter 1 we emphasized its orientation toward inducing powerful subjective experiences.

INTERNAL DYNAMICS

What is life on the "inside," that is, within a new religious movement? Some books, motion pictures, and television programs have attempted to depict the life of the member and, in doing so, have contributed to its stereotyping. We have referred already to the image of the leader as all powerful, requiring and eliciting the unquestioning obedience of the members. As regards the followers, it is frequently assumed that they live together and devote virtually their full time to the service of the leader. If they work on the "outside," it is in order to earn money which will necessarily be turned over to the leader. If they possessed money or property when they joined, they will have turned it over to the group and now live on the sufferance of their master for their daily necessities. They are deprived of adequate food and medical care. Further, the members will have cut off all unnecessary contact with the outside world, including most probably members of their natural families. Other members of the group are considered brothers and sisters, and the leader, father or master. The world of the follower is reduced to a microcosm.

It is not difficult to show that most new religious groups do not conform to this stereotype. Only in the most intense groups is there anything approaching it, and it is not completely realized in any of them. None of the leaders we have presented are Jim Joneses (see Appendix), who possessed, as it seemed, the power of life and death over his followers.[45]

If one compares the expectations made of members of some alternative religious groups with those in most conventional religious groups, it is clear that the expectations of the former are often greater, and, also, that there is typically a greater willingness to fulfill them. It may be that the rather low level of expectation found in the latter accounts for the surprise at what members of some new religious groups are willing to do. It is not easy to be part of an alternative religious group, especially of the intensive type. Not only does one have to endure a degree of ostracism, depending on how "deviant" the particular group is thought to be, but other members, and not only the leaders, expect a high level of commitment and participation. It is therefore not surprising that in intensive groups persons exert themselves as never before and live at the limits of their physical and emotional energy. The rewards, in terms of group approval and personal satisfaction, are seemingly sufficient to sustain them, at least for a time.

Adherents of intensive groups are drawn into a life different from what they have previously known. Accordingly, they separate themselves from the familiar and enter into the new—the other—attributing to it a higher value. With the zeal of converts they give themselves, with perhaps occasional doubts, to a new and energizing commitment. Having committed themselves, and defending that commitment, they enter as fully as possible into the microcosmic world of the group, which they expand to macrocosmic dimensions. The problem then becomes how to avoid encapsulation in this special "world," which would void all relationship with the ordinary world to which one needs to relate in order to communicate effectively. This is a perennial problem for many new religious movements.

Some of the groups included in this book do not, in fact, make heavy demands on their adherents. Transcendental Meditation, as we have seen, boasts that it takes only a few minutes a day to benefit measurably from the practice of its method of meditation. Members of the Rosicrucian AMORC read their weekly lessons, answer the written questions, perform their little rituals, and otherwise go about their lives much as their neighbors. Subud, for example, has somewhat higher expectations. The meetings for the common experience of *latihan* may be intense, but are soon over. As regards private *latihan* by individuals, they are advised to limit its practice, as too much is considered dangerous. In other words, although the characteristic religious experience of members of Subud is intense, often ecstatic, in other respects participation in Subud is relatively undemanding and left to the discretion of the individual. The members of Gurdjieff groups engage in "the work," George King's members of the Aetherius Society are alerted when Mars Sector VI or another extraplanetary ship comes into invisible orbit around Terra (Earth) and join their efforts (powers) to those of the extraterrestrial visitors, and participants in Feraferia come together for ritual performances at crucial times in the turning of the calendar (solstices, equinoxes, etc.); but none of these requires full-time, total, exhausting commitment and involvement. And so we find that new religious movements differ considerably from one another both in what they expect of members and what they obtain. It is, as the terminology already suggests, the intensive groups that expect and obtain the most—for example, the "Moonies"[46] and the "Hare Krishnas." It is these that have been most strenuously opposed and given rise to the stereotype.

It is often assumed that "cults" are communes, that is, that members live together. Some new religious groups form new communities, including communal living. Obviously, groups that have at their center a monastic order, as does ISKCON, are predominantly communal. Even in the case of ISKCON, however, not all members live together in the temple. There are also nonmonastic communes, such as Stephen Gaskins's The Farm in Summerton, Tennessee. The original group trekked across the United States from California (the opposite of the usual East to West movement of new religious groups) to settle on the Tennessee property. Other groups have special centers to which members come from time to time where they may experience communitarian "togetherness" for an interval. Such is the Meher (Baba) Spiritual Center in North Myrtle Beach, South Carolina, and, to a lesser extent, various yoga camps and Tibetan Buddhist study centers. Most new religious groups, however, do not feature communal living. They are likely to have at most some sort of meeting place, frequently in members' homes, a bookstore, or perhaps a hired hall. Thus it is with the Baha'is with their "firesides," many of the ritual magic groups (The Satanist Brotherhood of the Ram met in a nightclub), and lecture-oriented groups (e. g., the Theosophical Society).

Mobilization

New religious movements also differ considerably in what they exact from their members in labor, money, and other goods. Some groups engage in labor-intensive activities for self-support. So-called deviant religious groups, like conventional ones, have to find and develop sources of income to sustain themselves. It is not surprising that when the group has at its disposal a considerable corps of willing workers, it engages in labor-intensive activities. Usually these involve manufacture and sales, such as the making of incense for sale by Krishna devotees and the sale of flowers by "Moonies." The former also sell the books of Prabhupada, which are produced by their own printing house (the Bhaktivedanta Book Trust) staffed by devotees. In addition to selling flowers and other items, the Unificationists have in recent years gone into the fishing business, competing effectively with local fishermen.

Other groups, although they may sell books for the propagation of their religious ideas and derive some income from them, rely importantly on dues and payments for services by members to sustain the group. In some cases (e. g., AMORC and the Church of Satan) dues are not high. Transcendental Meditation expects payment of an initiation fee, which has increased over the years, presumably in pace with inflation, but its exactions do not begin to compare with the most expensive of all the new religious groups, L. Ronald Hubbard's Church of Scientology, in which various "auditings," courses, "run-downs," and "degrees" (not academic) cost many thousands of dollars. By comparison the costs of most other new religious groups are modest.

It is often said that "cults," especially their leaders, amass fortunes. Perhaps some of them do; most do not. The accusation is a ready one among their opponents. Most groups struggle along, trying to keep going, and sometimes failing. Others do better and are able to sustain themselves. Such is obviously the case with the various "old" new religious groups: Theosophy, Anthroposophy, Gurdjieff Groups, and the like. The relatively small number of groups that do well financially make the news.

Progression

What are the opportunities for members within the groups to which they belong? They expect, of course, to make what might be called spiritual progress, however that is defined within the group. Members of the Self-Realization Fellowship hope to progress in *kriya* yoga so as to be able to redirect the *prana* ("life energy") to open the *chakras* ("centers"), which leads to the realization of one's essential nature. Students of Gurdjieff hope through "the work" to be able to effect at least partially the difficult human awakening and self-transformation he offered as an unlikely possibility. Rev. Moon's followers hope that by paying "indemnity" they will contribute to the restoration of the originally intended divine-human relationship. And so it goes for other groups, each with its goals for its adherents. These are, as it were, spiritual goals. Membership in new religious movements also offers other possibilities. Earlier, in discussing the role theory of conversion we called attention to the roles and statuses offered by new religious movements. These, too, are available for those who continue in the movement. Indeed, there are those who find greater opportunities of this kind within the religious group than on the outside. While they may be ostracized on the outside (because of their participation in a "deviant" religious group), they may be esteemed on the inside (partly because of their willingness to bear ostracism).

Some religious groups are highly structured in terms of a member's progression. The AMORC Rosicrucianism provides a good example, for it has adopted, as have some other religious groups, the basically Freemason pattern of successive "degrees." Among the newer groups Scientology has outdone all others in this regard. New "levels" are added and announced regularly. The old Dianetics goal of becoming a "clear" has been surpassed by "Operating Thetan" (OT). In general, groups that emphasize initiatory experiences tend to have a progressive structure, for there is usually a progressive series of initiations, not just one. Less structured groups, however, also recognize some distinctions among members. These may be informal, as in the case of acknowledging that there are individuals who surpass others in ardent devotion to the cause, or are "old timers" (a status that comes quickly in new religious movements with much coming and going), or have survived attempted "de-programmings." Then, too, there are offices to which one may aspire: Temple presidents among the Krishna devotees, captains of mobile fundraising teams among the "Moonies," Transcendental Meditation initiators, and Subud "helpers." It has been observed that such opportunities within "cults" sometimes bring out the unsuspected potentialities for initiative and leadership in persons who prior to joining the group were shy, retiring, and lacking in self-confidence.

Dropping Out

Dropping out is always a possibility, despite the insistence of deprogrammers that one can only be liberated by intervention. The fact is that members do drop out. They do so for many reasons, even as they join for many reasons. It is a mistake to think that they drop out simply because they no longer "believe." In the popular mind too much is made of "belief" both as the reason for joining and the reason for dropping out. In both cases the perspective is too intellectualistic, as if persons are to be defined as minds. We suggested earlier that in the case of groups that require virtually full-time involvement the pressures of career prospects, children, and the like may lead to a decision to make a break after a certain age. So may changes in relationships with other members of the group. One suspects also that discouragement and fatigue lead to defection from groups which promise manifest changes in the outer world as well as within oneself, and urge one to ever more strenuous efforts to bring them about. Also, if Melton and Moore are correct with their transformation theory, there comes the time when the "project," so to say, is completed; membership in the group has served its function of transition.

It is difficult to drop out of groups that are closeknit and intensive, in part because one cannot readily do it gradually, by stages. Also, the defector can expect a high degree of ostracism from remaining members, for whom the defector is a renegade or worse. The role theory has relevance here. One may continue to play the role long after commitment has gone. Defection then comes as a surprise to other members. Dropping out is much easier with less intensive groups. A Rosicrucian can simply stop paying the dues and receiving the literature. The mail order nature of the transaction between AMORC and the Rosicrucian member makes for easy cessation. In the case of the Baba Lovers, for example, there is such indefiniteness of membership that defection is difficult to define and detect. In still other cases participation is of the nature of dabbling, and so can be terminated easily as interests change. Such may be the case for some individuals who get "into" witchcraft, ritual magic, soul travel, and the like. Also, there are those who go from one religious interest to another—someone has called them "metaphysical bums"—and consequently from one group to another, usually with some tentativeness. They "drop in" and subsequently "drop out." But, again, the situation is different with groups of the intensive kind, in which defection is both difficult and traumatic. However, it is obviously possible, for it is done by a significant proportion of the membership of these groups each year.

RELATIONS WITH THE LARGER COMMUNITY

The appearance of new religious movements both within and without the Christian religious orbit is a characteristic feature of American religious history. However, it still remains difficult for a new religious movement to gain acceptance in the wider community. To the extent that there has been a religious "settlement" in the United States it has been, as we said at the beginning of this chapter, in terms of a tripartite division: Protestantism, Catholicism, and Judaism. This settlement allowed for varieties of each, especially of Protestantism, but there existed a sense, if not a definition, of limits. Groups claiming a Christian connection but exhibiting peculiar beliefs or practices were doubtful. (Hence the difficulties faced by the Mormons for most of their history.) Groups claiming no Christian (or Judaic) connection or associating themselves with other religions were often ostracized, if not simply ignored. For the current crop of new religious groups little has changed in this regard. Some of them, especially those readily referred to as "destructive cults," receive the kinds of criticisms and attacks that in earlier times were directed against the Mormons (and even the Catholics).

How do the various new religious movements relate to the larger society? Clearly, some of them return the antagonism they receive. The Children of God (which we have not included in this book because they consider themselves Christians) are a case in point. COG identifies American society with the biblical Egypt (place of bondage, worthy to be despoiled) and with Babylon (place of exile and whoredom), and calls for separation. There is a certain logic in the strategy of the Children of God in abandoning these shores, as they have now largely done, for overseas missions. The Unificationists, on the contrary, are hopeful about America, although they are critical of the present state of its society. They see America as having ultimately a strategic role in restoring the "divine principle." Other groups fall between these extremes.

Most new religious groups, as we have said, are in fact more concerned with the problems of individuals than of society. Their relations with society are therefore likely to be concerned with the practical matters of their own existence within it. They are aware that their existence and future are precarious, depending not only on their own efforts, but also on the attitudes and actions of society toward them. The kinds of groups with which we have dealt in this book cannot be as disdainful of society's reactions to them as are some religious sects. Sects often criticize the social as well as the religious institutions and take pride in negative social responses.

The Anticult Movement

Americans became aware of the existence of "cults" during the 1960s. Initially, there was some curiosity and uneasiness about them, but not much opposition. The 1970s saw the beginning of organized opposition.[47] The source of the opposition was parents of young persons who had joined certain groups, mainly the Children of God, the "Moonies," the "Hare Krishnas," and Scientology. Organized resistance began specifically in 1972 in San Diego when the parents of a young adult woman founded an organization known originally as The Parents' Committee to Free Our Sons and Daughters from the Children of God Organization (later shortened to Free the Children of God [acronym FREECOG]). The parents, Mr. and Mrs. William Rambur, had tried unsuccessfully to rescue their young adult daughter. They publicized their efforts and the menace of "cults." Soon there were other, similar organizations in various parts of the country, usually spearheaded by parents of members. Among them, briefly, were Citizens Engaged in Reuniting Families, Inc. (Scarsdale, New York), Love Our Children, Inc. (Omaha, Nebraska), and Citizens Organized for Public Awareness of Cults, Inc. (Greensboro, North Carolina). Attempts to create national organizations met with only modest success.[48]

Parents were joined by other elements of society, including some religious groups. The "mainline" churches, for the most part, did not get caught up in the anticult movement. Conservative, sectarian, and fundamentalist Christians were its main religious supporters. The Spiritual

Counterfeits Project in Berkeley, California, a place viewed by many as the hotbed of "cults," published "exposés" of a number of groups. There was also some Jewish participation in the ACM (anticult movement), mainly by rabbis, of whom Maurice Davis, founder of Citizens Engaged in Reuniting Families, was the most notable. The Jewish community believed that Jewish youth are the special target of religious "cults," although that does not seem to be true.

What were the activities of the ACM? To begin, it publicized the threat of "cults" to the young and to society generally. Perhaps its greatest effectiveness was in this activity. Also, the various organizations provided a place for parents to turn and receive support when their youth were involved in "cults." The movement also tried to work out strategies for utilizing the police and the courts in its efforts, and for getting legislation at various levels, including, at the extreme, laws to criminalize conversion. These efforts were usually unsuccessful, except possibly at the local level. They were frequently opposed by such groups as the American Civil Liberties Union and the National Council of Churches through its Division on Civil and Religious Liberty. One of the most effective strategies of the ACM was the use of the atrocity tale, a genre much cultivated in wartime. (The anticultists believed they were engaged in a war.) We refer to the accounts, often dramatic, written or told by ex-members who typically claimed they were duped and that terrible things happened to them before their defection or deprogramming.[49]

As mentioned earlier, the anticult movement was able to utilize the writings of various professionals in psychology, mental health, and psychiatry who claimed that participation in "cults" is pathological and has deleterious effects on individuals. We referred to Robert Jay Lifton's work on "thought reform." Other claimed allies were the Harvard psychiatrist John G. Clark, Jr., and the psychologist Margaret Singer.[50] Through the combination of negative publicity, sensational charges, and the testimony of some "experts" the anticult movement succeeded in creating a highly unfavorable social climate for all groups that could by any definition be considered "cults."

Why did the anticult movement and, more broadly, highly negative evaluations of new religious movements arise? Consider what is likely to be the reaction of parents who receive a letter from a daughter who graduated *magna cum laude* from a top college and has received a fellowship for graduate study at a distinguished university, who writes to say that she has met a wonderful group of people who love one another and are going to change the world, and that she is travelling across the country in a van to help them in "fundraising" (as "Moonies" call their sale of flowers and other items). She says she isn't going to graduate school because she has found something much more important and intends to give her life to it. She adds that she is very happy.[51] Or, again, a son writes just as he is about to take the MCAT[52] tests to say that he is living in a Krishna temple, has changed his name to Vasudeva Dasa, and chants "Hare Krishna, Hare Krishna, Hare Rama, Hare Rama" all day long.

Bromley and Shupe maintain that there are two main reasons for parental opposition to membership in such groups. The first is that they are seen as endangering parental expectations, principally that their sons and daughters will prepare for suitable careers. Such expectations are high within the middle and upper-middle classes from which many converts come. Second, "cults" are seen as a threat to the family's authority structure.[53] Parents see "cult" leaders substituted for biological parents. In the case of the Unification Church it is said that Rev. and Mrs. Moon are the "true parents." As we have said before, new members of "cults," whether "Moonies" or others of the intensive kind, have often broken off relations with their biological parents. Mate selection by leaders, again as in the case of Rev. Moon, is onerous to parents.

Parents are puzzled as well as shocked by what has happened. How can this strange behavior be accounted for? Who would have thought that, say, Greg or Sharon would do such a thing? Something must be wrong; something must have happened to them. As we suggested earlier, the most common and convenient answer is "brainwashing." The term itself conjures up images and thoughts well fitted to scandalize, and it rallies public opinion against "cults." As we also suggested earlier, it removes responsibility. Neither Sharon nor her parents are responsible for what has happened to her, for what she has become. She has no will of her own; she is a victim. Thus no stigma attaches to her or her parents. One can readily see what a useful weapon the charge of "brainwashing" is in the arsenal of the anti-cultists.

Deprogramming

Deprogramming is controversial, for it may violate the civil and religious rights of the individual, violate the law (especially if kidnapping is part of it), and employ psychological manipulation. It is not advocated by all who oppose "cults." However, those who support or engage in it see it as the necessary antidote for the "poison" of "cults."

Most deprogramming, especially of the coercive type, is performed by "professionals," who offer their services for a fee. The best known deprogrammer is Ted Patrick, who claims to have deprogrammed 1600 persons, almost all successfully.[54]

The first requirement for deprogramming is to gain access to the individual. Usually he or she is unwilling to submit voluntarily. Resort may be made to ruses, *habeas corpus*, or other means to gain custody. Anticultists have also tried to use conservatorship laws in states that have them. Such laws are intended to give temporary custody in cases of emergency when an individual (often an elderly, senile relative) is about to do injury to self. They are not intended to give custody of offspring to parents who are offended by their children's religious affiliation, but, in fact, have been so used. The extreme action of kidnapping is sometimes resorted to, although its patent illegality has limited its use.

Once the individual is in custody, by whatever means, the deprogramming begins. Briefly, he or she is taken to some isolated, secure place where a psychological and religious assault is carried out with the intention of "snapping" the victim back (the reverse of the original "snapping"). By the use of more or less non-stop questioning, ridicule, shame and humiliation, exposés of the "cult" and its leaders, and other means, the individual is brought to the breaking point. The whole affair is typically noisy, intimidating, insulting, and abusive. It is in essence a reprogramming, as the individual's prior values and commitments are reinstalled and the family's authority structure reinstated.

Critics of coercive deprogramming point not only to the violations of the personal and legal rights of young adults, but to the fact that most members of "cults" from which it is claimed they must be rescued actually defect on their own after a time, about 75 percent within two years.

The groups that have been the main targets of the deprogrammers have reacted, sometimes appealing to the authorities and the courts. They have made deprogramming a hazardous profession. In some cases parents have been sued successfully by their offspring.

After Jonestown

The world was shocked by the mass suicide and murder of over 900 members of the Peoples Temple in Jonestown, Guyana, in November, 1978.[55] This bizarre and tragic event was seized upon by some anticultists, who said in effect: "This is what happens! We are not surprised. Your sons and daughters are in mortal danger if they belong to a cult!" It began to be rumored that the "Moonies" routinely teach their members how to commit suicide rather than submit to deprogramming, and that they hold mass suicide rehearsals (like Jim Jones's "white nights"). There was nothing to these and similar rumors associating other groups with suicide plans, but they circulated nonetheless. Also, some congressional hearings were held as part of the post-mortem investigation of Jonestown. Various persons and organizations managed to get called as "witnesses" and to broaden the scope of the hearings to encompass other religious groups. The shock and horror of the Jonestown suicides created an atmosphere in which the public was receptive to every accusation and warning about "deviant" religious groups. Jonestown did more for the anticult movement than it had been able to do for itself.

New religious movements cannot but be aware of the widespread suspicion and even fear they evoke in American society. Understandably, they are uneasy and usually uncertain about how to respond to this negative social environment. They would like to think they can rely confidently on the constitutional guarantees of religious and personal freedom, but they perceive disparities between theory and practice. They hesitate to acquiesce when their rights and those of their members are violated. If they defend themselves vigorously—for example, by resorting to the courts to sue those who violate these rights—they risk escalation of the confrontation. Also, American religious history seems to show that the new religious movements that survive are those that effect at least a partial accommodation with American society.

How New Religions Succeed

How do new religious groups survive, and possibly "succeed," in American society? Rodney Stark has given an instructive model.[56] He argues that new religious movements are likely to succeed to the extent they meet certain conditions. He emphasizes, first, the need for *cultural continuity* with the conventional religions of the society. This means that converts must not be asked to discard their entire religious tradition, but, rather, add something new to it. There must be elements of continuity. Second, Stark points to the need to achieve a *medium* level of *tension* with the environment in which the new religious movements exist, which is to say that they must be somewhat deviant (for otherwise there is little reason to exist), but not too deviant (so as to be rejected out of hand). Third, they must achieve *effective mobilization.* This requires both strong leadership and a high level of personal, individual commitment by members. Fourth, says Stark, groups, in order to succeed, must manage to achieve and maintain a *normal age and sex* ratio. Groups that attract and retain predominantly persons of one sex or age group have little chance for long-term success. (Most current "cults" of the intensive type, as we have seen, attract mostly the young.) Fifth, it is necessary that there be a *favorable ecology.* Such exists, according to Stark, when there is a relatively unregulated religious economy and the conventional religions are experiencing the debilitating effects of secularization or social disintegration. Sixth, Stark emphasizes the need to maintain *dense internal network relations* while avoiding becoming isolated. That is, individuals need to be strongly attached to one another and the group without becoming unduly exclusive in relation to the outside world. Seventh, secularization must be resisted. Finally, the socialization of the young is crucial, for by it pressures toward secularization are limited, as is defection.

Stark's requirements for "success" are very demanding. He maintains that *all* the requirements must be met, at least minimally, if a movement is to succeed. Similarly, his definition of success is stringent. He defines it in terms of "the degree to which a religious movement is able to dominate one or more societies." By "dominate" he means "to influence behavior, culture, and public policy in a society."[57]

Given Stark's definition and conditions for success, it is very doubtful that any of the groups presented in this book will "succeed," which is not to say that they will necessarily pass out of existence or will fail to find a niche in the American religious ecology. For Stark, only one American new religious movement has succeeded in the past. It is the Church of Jesus Christ of Latter Day Saints: the Mormons. One suspects that Stark derived his model of success from his study of the Mormons, for there is remarkable congruence between important aspects and characteristics of Mormonism and the elements of Stark's model.

We cannot confidently predict the religious future, especially in a society as changing as the American, but we expect that many of the religious groups presented in this book—how many and which ones, we hesitate to predict—will survive into the twenty-first century. Some of them will become the "old" new religious groups, as the Theosophical Society is today. A few may do even better, although it is unlikely that any will become, as it were, the new Mormons. Whatever the fate of the groups we have presented, we are confident that *new* "religious and spiritual groups" will continue to appear in America, offering its citizens religious options its founders could hardly have imagined.

NOTES

[1](Garden City, NY: Doubleday, & Co., Inc. 1955). Herberg averred that "to be a Protestant, a Catholic or a Jew are today the alternative ways of being an American," p. 274.

[2](New Haven, CN: Yale University Press, 1972).

[3](Belmont, CA: Wadsworth Publishing Co., 1981).

[4]For example, *A Nation of Behavers* (Chicago: University of Chicago Press, 1976). See also "The Occult Establishment," Social Research, 37(2):212–30.

[5]These studies include David G. Bromley and Anson D. Shupe, *Strange Gods* (1981); Robert S. Ellwood, Jr., *Alternative Altars: Unconventional and Eastern Spirituality in America* (1979); Steven M. Tipton, *Getting Saved from the Sixties* (1982); Robert Wuthnow, *The Consciousness Reformation* (1976) and *Experimentation in American Religion* (1978); *In Gods We Trust* (ed. by Thomas Robbins and Dick Anthony, 1981); *The New Religious Consciousness* (ed. by Charles Y. Glock and Robert N. Bellah, 1976); *Religion in Sociological Perspective* (ed. by Charles Y. Glock, 1973); *Religious Movements in Contemporary America* (ed. by Irving I. Zaretsky and Mark P. Leone, 1974); *The Social Impact of New Religious Movements* (ed. by Bryan Wilson, 1981); and *Understanding the New Religions* (ed. by Jacob Needleman and George Baker, 1978).

[6]*The Elementary Forms of the Religious Life* (New York: The Free Press, 1976).

[7]See especially E. Troeltsch, *Social Teachings of the Christian Churches* (New York: Macmillan, Inc. 1931); M. Weber, *The Protestant Ethic and the Spirit of Capitalism* (New York: Charles Scribner's Sons, 1930); and J. Wach, *Sociology of Religion* (Chicago: University of Chicago Press, 1941).

[8]On the distinction between intensive and diffuse "excursus" religious groups, see Ellwood, *Alternative Altars: Unconventional and Eastern Spirituality in America* (Chicago: University of Chicago Press, 1979), pp. 33ff.

[9]Richard Travisano, "Alternation and Conversion as Qualitatively Different Transformations," in Gregory Stone and Harvey Faberman (eds.), *Social Psychology through Symbolic Interaction* (Waltham, MA: Ginn-Blaisdell, 1968), p. 600.

[10]David G. Bromley and Anson D. Shupe, " 'Just a Few Years Seem like a Lifetime': A Role Theory Approach to Participation in Religious Movements," *Research in Social Movements, Conflicts and Change*, Vol. II, edited by Louis Kriesberg (Greenwich, CT: Jai Press, 1979), p. 173.

[11]*Modern Religious Cults and Society* (New York: AMS Press, 1933).

[12]"Magical Therapy: An Anthropological Investigation of Contemporary Satanism," in *Religious Movements in Contemporary America*, edited by Irving Zaretsky and Mark Leone (Princeton: Princeton University Press, 1974).

[13]Marc Galanter, Richard Rabkin, Judith Rabkin, and Alexander Deutsch, "The Moonies: A Psychological Study of Conversion and Membership in a Contemporary Religious Sect," *American Journal of Psychiatry*, Vol. 136 (Feb.), pp. 165–70.

[14]Charles Y. Glock and Rodney Stark, *Religion and Society in Tension* (Chicago: Rand McNally & Co., 1965).

[15]*Six Perspectives on New Religions* (New York: Edwin Mellen Press, 1981).

[16]"Becoming a World Saver: A Theory of Conversion to a Deviant Perspective," *American Behavioral Scientist*, Vol. 30 (July/August), pp. 887–908.

[17]"Becoming a World Saver Revisited," *American Behavioral Scientist*, Vol. 20 (July/August), pp. 805–18.

[18]See Robert W. Balch, "Bo and Peep: A Case Study of the Origins of Messianic Leadership," in Roy Wallis (ed.), *Millennialism and Charisma* (Belfast: Queen's University, 1982); Robert W. Balch and David Taylor, "Salvation in a UFO Cult," *Psychology Today*, Vol. 10, 1976, pp. 58–66; and Balch and Taylor, "Seekers and Saucers: The Role of the Cultic Milieu in Joining a UFO Cult," *American Behavioral Scientist*, Vol. 41 (1980) pp. 137–43.

[19]"Just a Few Years Seem Like a Lifetime."

[20]The term used by the Chinese is more accurately translated "thought reform."

[21](New York: W. W. Norton & Co., Inc., 1961).

[22](Philadelphia: J. B. Lippincott Co., 1978).

[23]We have not included the Children of God, more recently known as The Love Family, in this book, for it developed out of the Jesus Movement of the 1960s, becoming the radical wing of that movement. Also, in recent years, COG, as it is familiarly known, has largely

deserted its American base in favor of missionary work in Europe, the Middle East, Africa, and Asia.

24(New York: The Pilgrim Press, 1982).

25See, for example, Daniel J. Levinson, *The Seasons of a Man's Life* (New York: Alfred A. Knopf, Inc., 1978).

26A good introduction to Turner's thought is his book *The Ritual Process: Structure and Anti-Structure* (Ithaca, NY: Cornell University Press, 1977). Robert S. Ellwood has utilized some of Turner's insights for the study of alternative religions in *Alternative Altars: Unconventional and Eastern Spirituality in America* (Chicago: University of Chicago Press, 1979).

27*Rites of Passage*, translated by Monika Vizedom and Gabrielle L. Caffee (Chicago: University of Chicago Press, 1960).

28See, for example, Turner's essay "Betwixt and Between: The Liminal Phase in Rites of Passage," in his book *The Forest of Symbols* (Ithaca, NY: Cornell University Press, 1967), pp. 93–111.

29Turner's term for the sense of unstructured, spontaneous human togetherness.

30*Understanding Religious Life*, 2d ed (Belmont, CA: Dickenson Publishing Co., Inc. 1976), pp. 66ff.

31"Who'd Be a Moonie?," in *The Social Impact of New Religious Movements*, edited by Bryan Wilson (New York: Rose of Sharon Press, 1981), pp. 59–96. See also Barker, *The Making of a Moonie: Brainwashing Or Choice* (New York: Rose of Sharon Press, 1984).

32Rochford found that 96 percent of the Krishna devotees were under thirty when they joined ISKCON. See E. Burke Rochford, Jr., *Hare Krishna in America* (New Brunswick, NJ: Rutgers University Press, 1985), p. 78.

33By familiar religion is meant religion intertwined with the ethnic and community structures communicated through one's family (*familia*). See Robert S. Ellwood, *Alternative Altars: Unconventional and Eastern Spirituality in America* (Chicago: University of Chicago Press, 1979), p. 21.

34Rochford, *Op. Cit.*, p. 51.

35*Ibid.*, p. 50.

36See H. Richard Niebuhr, *The Social Sources of Denominationalism* (New York: Henry Holt, 1929).

37*Op. Cit.*, p. 49.

38Dick Anthony and Thomas Robbins, "The Meher Baba Movement: Its Effect on Post-Adolescent Social Alienation," in *Religious Movements in Contemporary America*, edited by I. Zaretsky and P. Leone (Princeton: Princeton University Press, 1974).

39See Steven M. Tipton, *Getting Saved from the Sixties* (Berkeley, CA: University of California Press, 1982).

40*The Sociology of Religion*, translated by Ephraim Fischoff (Boston: Beacon Press, 1963), pp. 46ff.

41Unificationism is eclectic and syncretistic, combining elements of Taoism, a Presbyterian form of Christian Fundamentalism, and Korean shamanism.

42As described earlier, these are persons who claim not only to have seen unidentified flying objects but to have been contacted by extraterrestrials who gave them a message for earth-lings, and who seek to gain a hearing and following.

43*The Theory of Economic and Social Organization* (Glencoe, IL: The Free Press, 1964), pp. 358f.

44It should not be assumed that appearance necessarily refers to impressive stature. There come to mind "short" persons recognized as charismatic, such as "Father Divine" (George Baker) of the Peace Mission of the 1930s and, more recently, Elijah Muhammad, leader of the so-called "Black Muslims." Both were strikingly short. The paradox of shortness of stature, yet powerful presence, was evidently impressive in its own way.

45Even this statement should be qualified, according to Judith Mary Weightman, author of the book *Making Sense of the Jonestown Suicides* (New York and Toronto: Edwin Mellen Press, 1983), who argues that most of the Jonestown inhabitants committed "revolutionary suicide" willingly, for they were living in a different "reality" from that in which most Americans live, and within that reality the mass suicide made sense.

46Bromley and Shupe have studied the "Moonies" specifically in terms of resource mobilization. See their book *"Moonies" in America: Cult, Church, Crusade* (Beverley Hills, CA: Sage Publications, Inc., 1979).

47On the origin and development of the anticult movement see especially Anson D. Shupe, Jr.

and David G. Bromley, *The New Vigilantes: Deprogrammers, Anti-Cultists, And The New Religions* (Beverley Hills, CA: Sage Publications, Inc., 1980) and Shupe and Bromley, *Strange Gods: The Great American Cult Scare* (Boston: Beacon Press, 1981).

[48]Two such organizations were founded: The Citizens' Freedom Foundation (CFF) and the National *ad hoc* Committee Engaged in Freeing Minds (CEFM). Neither fulfilled the hopes of its originators.

[49]Representative accounts include Christopher Edwards, *Crazy for God* (Englewood Cliffs, NJ: Prentice-Hall, Inc., 1979); Barbara and Betty Underwood, *Hostage to Heaven* (New York: Clarkson N. Potter, 1979); and Allen T. Wood and J. Vitsek, *Moonstruck* (New York: William Morrow & Co., Inc., 1979).

[50]See John G. Clark, Jr., "Cults," in *Journal of the American Medical Association*, Vol. 42 (July 20, 1979), pp. 279–81; and Margaret T. Singer, "Coming Out of the Cults," *Psychology Today*, Vol. 12 (January 1979), pp. 72–82. More recent articles in *Psychology Today* have been more positive. See, for example, Saul V. Levine, "Radical Departures," *Psychology Today*, Vol. 18 (August, 1984), pp. 20–27.

[51]This and the following account are actual "cases," known to one of the authors.

[52]Medical Colleges Admission Test.

[53]*The New Vigilantes: Deprogrammers, Anti-Cultists, and the New Religions* (Beverley Hills, CA: Sage Publications, Inc., 1980).

[54]For Patrick's interpretation and justification of his activities, see Ted Patrick and Tom Dulack, *Let Our Children Go!* (New York: Ballantine Books, Inc., 1976).

[55]We have included Jim Jones and the Peoples Temple in the Appendix.

[56]"How New Religions Succeed: A Theoretical Model," in *The Future of New Religious Movements*, edited by David G. Bromley and Phillip E. Hammond (Macon, GA: Mercer University Press, 1987).

[57]*Op. Cit.*, p. 12.

APPENDIX
The "Black Muslims" and the Peoples Temple

In defining the scope of this book the authors have deliberately excluded Jewish and Christian groups. We have omitted them because they are not alternative religious groups in the sense in which the groups included in this book are alternative; they are part of or relate to the dominant, conventional religious tradition of American society. We have also excluded largely ethnic (and racial) religious groups because they are not open to all persons in the society. We have chosen rather to include only groups that have some appeal (and membership) across ethnic and racial lines. To have done otherwise would, for example, have required us to give attention to the large number of black religious groups. They are an important part of the American religious scene but have been studied by others more qualified than we.[1]

Nevertheless, we are including in an *appendix* two religious groups that fall outside the scope of this book: the "Black Muslims" (as they used to be called) and the Peoples Temple. Until recently the "Black Muslims" were an exclusively black group; the Peoples Temple was predominantly black in membership (about 80 percent). Also, the Peoples Temple existed within a mainline Protestant denomination known as "Christian Church (Disciples of Christ)." We are giving exceptional attention to the "Black Muslims" because they were the principal means by which an alternative religion, Islam, became present initially in the consciousness of Americans. Islam has long existed in the United States in small immigrant communities

(Lebanese, Syrian, etc.), but these communities have been quiescent and of low profile. The Islam of the "Black Muslims" has been striking in its contrast; theirs is a confident, aggressive Islam. Further, the group is no longer exclusively black. Following the death of the founder, Elijah Muhammad, the group under new leadership opened itself even to the "white devil," as persons of the Caucasian race were formerly called. While strong racial and ethnic identifications remain, the main group has progressively transformed itself into "The American Muslim Mission."

The principal reason for adding the Peoples Temple is that the tragic events of Jonestown in 1978 traumatized the American public and deeply influenced the way it thinks about "cults." Although the Peoples Temple was not a "cult" in the sense in which we have used the term in this book, it was almost universally called a "cult" in the media and was widely considered an example of all that is worst in a "cult." As we indicated in the last chapter, many new religious groups came to be viewed in the light of the Peoples Temple and its horrendous end. Although it no longer exists, the Peoples Temple continues to haunt the consciousness of Americans who recall the events of 1978. Despite the flood of books and articles which followed its dramatic demise it has yet to be fully comprehended.[2]

THE "BLACK MUSLIMS" (AMERICAN MUSLIM MISSION)

In the early 1960s one of the authors lived in Chicago across the street from "Muhammad's Temple of Islam No. 2." It was the national headquarters of the "Black Muslims" (also known as the Lost-Found Nation of Islam), a black religious group that originated in the ghetto of Detroit in 1930. Outside the black community it was little known. However, it was soon to become very well known through the biting indictment of racism and "the white man's religion" (Christianity) by its leader, the Honorable Elijah Muhammad (as he was called by his followers), and Malcolm X, an articulate spokesman for the Muslims. Soon the public at large became aware of this expression of militant Islam found, of all places, in the black community.

The "Black Muslims" trace their beginnings to the activity of a mysterious peddler who appeared in the Detroit ghetto in 1930. He called himself variously Wali Fard, Wallace Fard, and W. D. Fard, and claimed to be an Arab from the Holy City of Mecca come to America to reveal to American blacks that they are members of the "lost-found" tribe of Shabazz and that their original religion is Islam, not the "slave religion" of the white man. He gained a following and created an organization. Among those attracted was Elijah Poole, son of an itinerant Baptist preacher, who had migrated earlier from Georgia. Upon becoming a Muslim he took the name Elijah Muhammad, giving up his slave name, Poole. After Fard's mysterious disappearance in 1934 Elijah Muhammad secured the leadership and moved his headquarters to Chicago. There the movement grew and prospered, all the while at the center of controversy, mainly because of its indictments of white society and religion, and its racial separatism. It demanded a separate black state within the United States. It was seen, rightly, as a radical protest movement, representing an extreme among the various Black groups engaged in the rights struggle. Many blacks who did not actually become Muslims nevertheless understood and sympathized with Muhammad's analysis of the situation of American blacks. Those attracted to the movement included not only convicts (prisons were an important recruiting ground) but sports and entertainment personalities, including Cassius Clay (who took the Muslim name Muhammad Ali).

The appearance of Islam among American blacks came as a surprise, for they were thought of religiously as Christians from an African "pagan" background. Virtually nothing was known of the fact that some of the blacks brought as unwilling immigrants to this country were Muslims, mainly from the Islamic kingdoms of West Africa. Their Islam did not survive. In a sense the emergence of the "Black Muslims" represents its revival. There had been earlier attempts, notably the effort of Noble Drew Ali, a North Carolinian who in 1913 established the Moorish Science Temple in Newark, New Jersey, but they were not successful.

Elijah Muhammad's Islam was significantly different from orthodox Islam, but that did not seem to bother him. He was intent on introducing a version of Islam that would be relevant to the situation of blacks as he understood it. At the same time, there were important Islamic elements: Muslim prayers, reading of the Qur'an, dietary restrictions, and identification as "Muslims." The late Islamicist Marshall Hodgson once referred to them in conversation with one of the authors as "would-be Muslims."

Briefly, Islam is a religion that affirms that the One God (Allah) who created all things, including humans, is a compassionate and merciful God who gives guidance to erring and straying human beings so they will know how to live in this world and prepare for the next, learning all the while how to relate to one another and their Creator. Allah has given his guidance through a series of messengers, of whom Muhammad in the seventh century C.E. was the last ("the seal of the prophets"). The guidance is contained in the holy book—the Qur'an—which Allah revealed to Muhammad. The Islamic law, or *Shari'ah,* is an elaboration of the guidance, based mainly on the Qur'an and the Traditions (*hadith*) which present Muhammad as a model of *Islam* (in its basic meaning of submission or surrender to the will of Allah). Islam is eschatological in orientation, for it holds that on the Last Day Allah will judge the living and the dead, and consign each person to the Garden (*jannah*) or the Fire (*jahanam*).

Elijah Muhammad's version of Islam differed from the above at crucial points. He claimed that Allah is the Supreme Black Man, sharing his divinity with all black men, obviously violating the strict Islamic monotheism. Moreover, W. D. Fard was said to be Allah incarnate. Incarnationism is a particular form of the error of polytheism and idolatry, according to Islamic teaching. Further, Elijah Muhammad claimed to be the messenger and prophet of Fard. Islam teaches that there are no prophets after Muhammad. As for judgment, Elijah held that it is rendered in this world, not in the world to come. There is no heaven or hell. Temporal divine judgment will soon be rendered on the white man in particular.

Blacks should separate themselves from whites racially, socially, and economically as well as religiously. Such separation is counter to the traditional Islamic nonsegregation of the races. Muslim's pride themselves, rightly, in having succeeded better than most religious communities in avoiding discrimination based on color. Elijah Muhammad created a myth of the origin of the white race. According to his myth, all humans derive originally from the black race, the white man coming into existence as the result of a genetic experiment by a black scientist which went wrong, resulting unfortunately in "blue-eyed devils" without true humanity.

Positively, Elijah Muhammad's Islam included the performance of the traditional five daily prayers said facing Mecca, the use of the Islamic greeting ("As-salam alaikum"), and other ritual duties as well as Islamic dietary proscriptions (chiefly against eating pork) and the ban on the use of alcohol. They were supplemented by additional requirements (e.g., prohibition of many foods common among blacks, especially from the South, as well as tobacco) and a stringent code of morality (dress, sex, etc.).

Elijah Muhammad succeeded in establishing the "Black Muslims" as the major Islamic presence in the United States, the question of orthodoxy aside. His choice of Islam was not arbitrary. Not only does Islam have a distinguished past on the African continent—in black Africa as well as in North Africa—but in recent decades it has grown more rapidly in black Africa than Christianity. It has also related to African culture far more successfully. It can be considered an African alternative to white Christianity. Elijah was also aware of the traditional antagonism between Christians and Muslims, which is not limited to Africa. Further, he was aware of the Islamic emphasis on a disciplined, responsible personal and corporate life, which could serve well in helping blacks recover pride and uplift themselves.

The Honorable Elijah Muhammad, Chief Minister of the Nation of Islam, died in 1975 and was succeeded by his fifth son, Wallace Deen Muhammad, who proceeded to transform the movement in the direction of Islamic orthodoxy by a process of decultification of the "Black Muslims." He began by denying that his father had been a prophet, affirming that there has been no prophet since the seventh century founder of Islam. In 1976 he changed the name of the movement to "The World Community of Al-Islam in the West," signaling his intention to make the "Black Muslims" part of the worldwide Islamic community (*Ummah*). (Later he would change the name to the American Muslim Mission, making his intention clearer still.) He boldly opened the group to the membership of whites and little was heard of the myth of the origin of the "blue-eyed devil." The separatist theme was no longer sounded. The Chief Imam (as he now began to be called), having also changed his name from Wallace to the Arabic Warith, called for Muslim participation in the economic, political, and religious life of the American nation. Muslims began to study the Arabic language more seriously in their schools, the ritual duties of Muslims were more strictly observed, and these American Muslims began to travel and study in the Islamic world, which travel often included the obligatory pilgrimage (*hajj*) to Mecca. (Elijah Muhammad had himself visited Mecca in 1959. The fact that he was then permitted to enter the forbidden [to non-Muslims] city indicated some degree of acceptance of his Islam even then.)

The group has existed in Durham, North Carolina, for more than a quarter of a century. In the 1960s, its meeting place was identified as "Muhammad's Temple of Islam No. 34" (meaning that it was the 34th temple established). After Elijah's death the identification began to change, each change marking a stage in the decultification and transformation of the movement. It became successively "Muhammad's Mosque" (replacing the non-Islamic term "temple" with "mosque" [for the Arabic *masjid*]), "Muhammad Masjid" (using Arabic instead of English), and, finally, simply "Durham Masjid" (no longer identifying it with Elijah Muhammad).

Warith Muhammad's transformation of the movement rapidly and assuredly in the direction of Islamic orthodoxy did not come without opposition from within. It resulted in a splinter, rival movement under the leadership of Minister Louis Farrakhan. Farrakhan's group represents continuity with the Islam and ideology of Elijah Muhammad. It is this latter group to which the media now frequently refer as the "Black Muslims." The decultification of the American Muslim Mission is now virtually complete, most of its members considering themselves *Muslims* who happen to be black.

Reading Selection: The "Black Muslims" (American Muslim Mission)

The following selection is taken from a letter which Malcolm X, Elijah Muhammad's most prominent and articulate lieutenant until his withdrawal from the Black Muslims in March, 1964, wrote from Mecca to friends in America at the conclusion of his pilgrimage. In fulfilling the traditional duty of Muslims to make the pilgrimage to Mecca he experienced the wider world of Islam at first hand, which, among other things, affected his racial attitudes and expectations. In a sense, Malcolm X anticipated the modification of the movement that followed the death of Elijah Muhammad.

Never have I witnessed such sincere hospitality and the overwhelming spirit of true brotherhood as is practiced by people of all colors and races here in this Ancient Holy Land, the home of Abraham, Muhammad, and all the other prophets of the Holy Scriptures. For the past week, I have been utterly speechless and spellbound by the graciousness I see displayed all around me by people *of all colors.*

I have been blessed to visit the Holy City of Mecca. I have made my seven circuits around the Ka'ba, led by a young *Mutawaf* named Muhammad. I drank water from the well of Zem Zem. I ran seven times back and forth between the hills of Mt. Al-Safa and Al-Marwah. I have prayed in the ancient city of Mina, and I have prayed on Mt. Arafat.

There were tens of thousands of pilgrims, from all over the world. They were of all colors, from blue-eyed blondes to black-skinned Africans. But we were all participating in the same ritual, displaying a spirit of unity and brotherhood that my experiences in America had led me to believe never could exist between the white and the non-white.

America needs to understand Islam, because this is the one religion that erases from its society the race problem. Throughout my travels in the Muslim world, I have met, talked to, and even eaten with people who in America would have been considered "white"—but the "white" attitude was removed from their minds by the religion of Islam. I have never before seen *sincere* and *true* brotherhood practiced by all colors together, irrespective of their color.

You may be shocked by these words coming from me. But on this pilgrimage, what I have seen, and experienced, has forced me to *re-arrange* much of my thought-patterns previously held, and to *toss aside* some of my previous conclusions.

From the *Autobiography of Malcolm X,* by Malcolm X, with the assistance of Alex Haley, (New York: Grove Press, 1966), pp. 339–40. Copyright © 1964 by Alex Haley and Malcolm X. Copyright © 1965 by Alex Haley and Betty Shabazz. Reprinted by permission of Random House, Inc.

THE PEOPLES TEMPLE

In the afternoon of November 18, 1978, 912 persons, members of the Peoples Temple, died at Jonestown in Guyana. Most of them committed "revolutionary suicide"; others were killed. At first the outside world discounted the news of a mass suicide, thinking it a rumor or an exaggeration. After several days, with the news confirmed and the body count rising, the true dimensions of the tragic event began to emerge, sending a shudder through the collective psyche.

The Peoples Temple was the creation of James ("Jim") Warren Jones, born in 1931 in the small town of Lynn, Indiana, where the principal industry was, ironically, casket-making. Attracted to religion at an early age, he drifted into the Christian ministry with no formal training. The early fifties saw him in the inner city of Indianapolis where he sought ministerial opportunities, first among the Methodists and then independently. It was here that he became aware of racism and poverty, especially among inner-city blacks. In 1956 he established the Peoples Temple, and four years later affiliated it with a mainline Protestant denomination headquartered in Indianapolis, known as "Christian Church (Disciples of Christ)."[3] Inasmuch as the denomination was rather loosely organized and prized the autonomy of local congregations, the Peoples Temple was able to develop its own distinctive style within it.

A man of great energy and considerable charisma—and a self-styled miracle worker—Jim Jones was able to attract a following, predominantly of black persons. He gradually transformed this following into a new community, interracial in character, which was highly demanding of the time, devotion, and loyalty of its members, giving them in exchange a sense of belonging, relative security, and relevant activity. At a time when other ministers were talking about the problems of people in the inner city, Jim

Jones was doing something about them, and so attracted support from persons who overlooked his showman, self-aggrandizing style. He soon became chairman of the Indianapolis Human Relations Commission.

In 1965 Jim Jones shared his apocalyptic vision of thermonuclear war with his congregation and advised all to take refuge in northern California. About a hundred members of the Peoples Temple trekked across the continent with him to Redwood Valley, near Ukiah, California. There the Peoples Temple was re-established. More at home in a large urban environment, however, the congregation soon expanded as the "Peoples Temple Christian Church" in the Fillmore district of San Francisco. It became the chief base of the Temple.

Jim Jones continued to attract ghetto blacks, mostly elderly but some young—a remarkable feat for a white preacher. He also attracted some whites, including not only blue collar, lower-middle-class persons, but young professionals (social workers, teachers, and attorneys) who shared his vision of an interracial community dedicated to love and justice.

Life within the Temple became increasingly regimented, Jones demanding strict conformity and loyalty. After a visit to Father Divine he began to have his followers call him "Father," more commonly, "Dad." As Father he alternated between expressions of affection for his followers and stern judgments and punishments, which at length brought some defections.

Jones's influence grew in San Francisco, notably among politicians, because of his ability to rally his people in campaigns. A newly elected and grateful mayor appointed him chairman of the Housing Authority. At the same time, there began to be rumors of ugly goings-on in the Peoples Temple, spread initially by defectors and finally by investigative reporters. The climax came with the impending publication of an exposé by the magazine *New West*. Despite his best efforts Jones was unable to stop publication. The time had come for another trek, this time to Guyana on the northern coast of South America, where the Temple had already made plans for an agricultural commune. The date was August 1977. "Jonestown" was established in the jungle of Guyana through arrangements with the leftist government.

Jim Jones's attitude toward religion was complex. He began as an evangelical, conservative preacher in search of a congregation. Gradually he became involved with the problems of black people and the inner city, believing that social, economic, and political issues and activities are primary in changing the conditions of their lives. At the same time, he utilized the attractions of religion, especially spirited religious services and miraculous healings, to build his constituency. At some point—one cannot say just when—he began to consider himself a Marxist (socialist and communist), which he was of sorts. However, he continued to use religious language (mixing it frequently with obscenities). Unlike Marx he did not see religion as necessarily an "opiate" but as something that could be used; indeed, religion could be used to destroy religion, he said. At the same time he used it positively, which he did in part by declaring himself an embodiment of the divine. He claimed variously to be God, Christ, and a prophet, as well as the reincarnation of great historical figures, including Lenin.

Jim Jones had about him something of the magus. His frequent illnesses, real and feigned, remind one of the initiatory illnesses of the shaman. Moreover, he claimed to have died and revived more than once. He claimed also to have raised the dead. He created an air of mystery and secret power by such simple devices as dark glasses and the complex claim to be an embodiment of "Principle" (which he left vaguely undefined). As with some other magi, there was also a trickster side to Jim Jones, which is seen in his unpredictableness, erratic behavior, cunning, exaggeration, and grossness, including sexual license.

Although Jonestown was deep in the jungle, reachable only by air or a long boat journey from the capital, Georgetown, and much farther still from the United States, it was not completely isolated. A defector couple brought suit to recover their young son held by Jones, who claimed to be the biological father. Jim Jones became a virtual prisoner in Jonestown in order to avoid legal actions. To complicate matters further a California congressman, Leo Ryan, insisted on visiting Jonestown, leading a group of "concerned relatives" (of Peoples Temple members in Guyana) and reporters in order to investigate rumors and accusations about the Temple. Jones was not able to prevent the visit. During the visit fourteen members expressed their desire to leave Jonestown and were offered transportation by the congressman. As Ryan was leaving, an unsuccessful attempt was made on his life by a member of the Peoples Temple. Shortly after the departing group arrived at the nearby airstrip, members of the "Red Brigade" (the Temple's paramilitary unit) appeared and opened fire on the party, killing Congressman Ryan, three newsmen, and a defector, and wounding others.

Meanwhile Jim Jones and his followers had gathered around the central pavilion of Jonestown. He told them that they had no choice but to commit revolutionary suicide, for the congressman and others had been killed, and Jonestown would soon be attacked in retaliation. He warned that the children would be taken and the adults captured or killed. To those who proposed that the group make an "airlift" to Russia he replied that it was too late. Overcoming all opposition, he was able to convince most of the group to "end it all," beginning with the children into whose throats a cyanide-laced "potion" was forced. Next came the turn of the adults. Most of them apparently drank the potion willingly, as they had done many times before during the "white night" suicide rehearsals when the potion was innocuous. Those who resisted were forced to drink or injected or shot. Several managed to escape to tell the story. Jones himself was among the last to die. He died from a gunshot wound, inflicted at close range. It is not clear whether it was self-inflicted. Thus ended Jonestown.

There are many questions to be asked, but two of the major ones are: (1) why did Jones choose to end the Peoples Temple in this way, and (2) why did most of his followers (children aside) willingly commit suicide. As for the first question, several things may be observed. First, Jones was seriously ill, physically as well as mentally, and may have been within weeks or even days of death. He was also frequently at the point of exhaustion. It may be that the mass suicide was Jones's suicide writ large. Further, it may be seen as his final demonstration and exercise of power, the absolute power of life and death, and thus in a sense a personal vindication in the face of evident defeat. More importantly, the mass suicide represents the end of a trail; in religious terms, a pilgrimage. It was a pilgrimage that began in Indianapolis, continued to the Redwood Valley and San Francisco, and ended in the jungle of Guyana (with discussions toward the end of emigrating to Cuba or the Soviet Union). By the afternoon of November 18, 1978, there was nowhere to go—in this world. What was the quest, the goal, of this long pilgrimage? It was to realize a new community, an interracial community of mutual love and justice. It had not been possible in Indianapolis, a center of Ku Klux Klan activity and Midwestern racism. (The move to northern California was not motivated solely by the fear of thermonuclear war.) But in California, noted for its openness and liberalism regarding lifestyles, there were the prying reporters and the defectors who threatened the realization of the new community. And in Guyana? There came the congressman and the news photographers and the "concerned relatives," leaving with a fresh group of defectors. It seemed to Jones and his committed followers that the world would not permit such a community to exist—anywhere. As one of his followers said at the end, with a sigh of sadness and resignation: "We might as well end it now." (It is ironical that through his exploitation, including sexual exploitation, of members of the Peoples Temple, his tendency to make most black members second-class citizens when it came to positions of authority [young white women held much of the power under him], and his acts of cruelty toward individuals, he had already vitiated the possibility of realizing the community he envisioned.) Jones saw an apparently futile act as paradoxically a final affirmation with somehow positive consequences. At the least, his name would go down in history, as indeed it has.

The question that incredulous Americans asked when they learned the full extent of the Jonestown tragedy was why hundreds of persons were willing to commit suicide. Historical parallels were immediately sought— the Jews at Masada, Japanese soldiers jumping *en masse* into the sea—but none of them fit or made the event comprehensible. Judith Mary Weightman wrote in her book *Making Sense of the Jonestown Suicide:*

> The mass suicide of the members of the Peoples Temple was a phenomenon so far out of the reality of our society that there was an instant paralysis before any attempt to make sense of it could be undertaken. Once that attempt was started, however, it was only natural that any—and all—explanations should be framed in terms of our reality, a reality in which such an act is impossible. In a very real sense, there is no room for the Peoples Temple's reality within our reality.[4]

It is not surprising that most of the explanations given were in terms of pathology and deviance, invoking brainwashing and mental illness, for these are explanations that make sense within *our* reality.

The Peoples Temple had its own reality, created along the way and completed in the isolation of the Guyana jungle. While it was the creation fundamentally of Jim Jones, the maintenance of the social reality required the participation and commitment of its members. Indeed, their world became real as they lived in it as real. Their microcosm became the container and bearer of all meaning and value. They responded to its imminent destruction with their own.

Reading Selection: The Peoples Temple

The following are excerpts from an audio tape recording believed to have been made in Jonestown during the afternoon of November 18, 1978, when Jim Jones addressed his followers for the last time, urging them to "revolutionary suicide":

How very much I have tried my best to give you a good life. In spite of all that I've tried a handful of our people with their lies have made our life impossible. There's no way to detach ourselves from what's happened today. Not only are we in a compound situation; not only are there those who have left and committed the betrayal of the century; some have stolen children from others and they are in pursuit right now to kill them because they stole their children. And we are sitting here on a powder keg. . . . What's going to happen here in a matter of a few minutes is that one of those people on that plane is going to shoot that pilot. I know that; I didn't plan it but I know it's going to happen. He's going to shoot the pilot and down comes that plane in the jungle, and we had better not have any of our children left when it's over 'cause they'll parachute in on us. . . . So my opinion is that we'd be kind to children and be kind to seniors and take the potion like they used to take in ancient Greece, and step over quietly because we are not committing suicide; it's a revolutionary act. We can't go back; they won't leave us alone. They're now going back to tell more lies, which means more congressmen, and there's no way—no way—we can survive. . . . I made my manifestation and the world was not ready for me. Paul said I am a man born out of due season. I've been born out of due season, just like we all are, and the best testimony we can make is to leave this god-dammed world. . . . It's all over, all over. What a legacy, what a legacy. They invaded our privacy. They came into our home. They followed 6000 miles away. The Red Brigade showed them justice. The congressman's dead. Please get us some medication.[5] It's simple, it's simple. There's no convulsions with it. It's simple. Please get going before it's too late. The GDF [Guyanese Defence Force] will be here. I tell you get moving, get moving, get moving. Don't be afraid to die. . . . I tell you I don't care how many screams you hear. I don't care how many anguished cries. Death is a million times preferable to ten more days of this life. If you knew what was ahead of you, you'd be glad to be stepping over tonight. Death, death, death is common to people. . . . We said—1000 people said—we don't like the way the world is. Take our life from us. We laid it down. We got tired. We didn't commit suicide; we committed an act of revolutionary suicide protesting the conditions of an inhumane world.

NOTES

[1]See, for example, the publications of C. Eric Lincoln, including *The Black Experience in Religion* (Garden City, NY: Anchor Press, 1974), and *The Black Muslims in America,* rev. ed. (Boston: Beacon Press, 1973).

[2]The latest, and in some ways best, effort is Judith Mary Weightman's book *Making Sense of the Jonestown Suicides* (New York and Toronto: The Edwin Mellen Press, 1983).

[3]The "Disciples of Christ," originating on the American frontier in the early nineteenth century, has about a million and a half members nationwide.

[4]Weightman, *op. cit.,* p. 205.

[5]The poison "potion."

BIBLIOGRAPHY

This bibliography is intended to provide starting points for the study of new religious movements in America. For further resources, including the extensive sociological and other literature available in journals and periodicals, the reader is referred to the several excellent book-length bibliographies in print, particularly those of Choquette on the new religions generally, the works of J. Gordon Melton, and the series of bibliographies on various movements available from Garland Publishing, Inc., all listed below. For the publications of movements themselves, the reader is referred to the groups themselves, whose addresses are listed after the bibliography.

Chapter 1: The Several Meanings of "Cult," and Chapter 9: New Religious Movements: Sociological and Psychological Approaches, Together with General Reference Works.

A. General Discussions

BARKER, EILEEN, ed., *Of Gods and Men: New Religious Movements in the West.* Macon, GA: Mercer University Press, 1983.

BROMLEY, DAVID G., and ANSON D. SHUPE, JR., *Strange Gods: The Great American Cult Scare.* Boston: Beacon Press, 1981.

GLOCK, CHARLES Y., and ROBERT N. BELLAH, eds., *The New Religious Consciousness.* Berkeley: University of California Press, 1976.

HALPERIN, DAVID A., ed., *Psychodynamic Perspectives on Religion, Sect, and Cult.* Boston: John Wright, 1983.

MELTON, J. GORDON, and ROBERT L. MOORE, *The Cult Experience.* New York: Pilgrim Press, 1982.

MOSATCHE, HARRIET S., *Searching: Practices and Beliefs of the Religious Cults and Human Potential Groups.* New York: Stravon Educational Press, 1983.

NEEDLEMAN, JACOB, *The New Religions.* New York: Doubleday & Co., Inc., 1970.

———, and GEORGE BAKER, eds., *Understanding the New Religions.* New York: Seabury, 1978.

PAVLOS, ANDREW J., *The Cult Experience.* Westport, CT: Greenwood Press, 1982.

RICHARDSON, HERBERT W., ed., *New Religions and Mental Health. Understanding the Issues.* New York: Edwin Mellon, 1980.

RICHARDSON, JAMES T., ed., *Conversion Careers: In and Out of the New Religions.* Beverly Hills, CA: Sage Publications, Inc., 1978.

SHUPE, ANSON D., JR., *Six Perspectives on New Religions: A Case Study Approach.* New York: Edwin Mellon, 1981.

STARK, WERNER, *The Sociology of Religion,* 4 vols. London: Routledge and Kegan Paul, 1966.

TIPTON, STEVEN M., *Getting Saved from the Sixties.* Berkeley: University of California Press, 1982.

TIRYAKIAN, EDWARD A., ed., *On the Margin of the Visible: Sociology, the Esoteric, and the Occult.* New York: John Wiley & Sons, Inc., 1974.

UNGERLEIDER, J. THOMAS, *The New Religions: Insights into the Cult Phenomenon.* New York: Merck, Sharp, and Dohme, 1979.

WACH, JOACHIM, *Sociology of Religion.* Chicago: University of Chicago Press, 1944.

WALLIS, ROY, ed., *Sectarianism: Analyses of Religious and Non-Religious Sects.* New York: John Wiley & Sons, Inc., 1975.

WILSON, BRYAN, ed., *The Social Impact of New Religious Movements.* Barrytown, NY: Unification Theological Seminary, 1981.

WUTHNOW, ROBERT, *The Consciousness Reformation.* Berkeley: University of California Press, 1976.

———, *Experimentation in American Religion.* Berkeley: University of California Press, 1978.

YINGER, J. MILTON, *Religion, Society, and the Individual.* New York: Macmillan, 1957.

———, *The Scientific Study of Religion.* New York: Macmillan, Inc., 1970.

ZARETSKY, IRVING I., and MARK P. LEONE, eds., *Religious Movements in Contemporary America.* Princeton, NJ: Princeton University Press, 1974.

B. Encyclopedias, Directories, and Bibliographies

CHOQUETTE, DIANE, *New Religious Movements in the United States and Canada: A Critical Assessment and Annotated Bibliography.* Westport, CT: Greenwood, 1985.

FOX, SELENA, *Circle Guide to Pagan Resources.* Mt Horeb, WI: Circle, periodically revised.

MELTON, J. GORDON, *The Encyclopedia of American Religions,* 2 vols. Wilmington, NC: McGrath, 1978.

———, *Biographical Dictionary of American Cult and Sect Leaders.* New York: Garland Publishing, 1986.

———, *Encyclopedic Handbook of Cults in America.* New York: Garland Publishing, 1986.

———, and JAMES V. GEISENDORF, *A Directory of Religious Bodies in the United States.* New York: Garland, 1977.

ROBBINS, THOMAS, *Civil Liberties, "Brainwashing" and "Cults": A Select Annotated Bibliography.* Berkeley: Graduate Theological Union, 1981.

SALIBA, JOHN A., *Psychiatry and the Cults: An Annotated Bibliography.* New York: Garland, 1987.

SHUPE, ANSON D., JR., *The Anti-Cult Movement in America: A Bibliographic History.* New York: Garland, 1984.

SINGH, PARMATMA, *The New Consciousness Sourcebook: Spiritual Community Guide.* Berkeley: Spiritual Community Publications, periodic revisions.

Chapter 2: The History of an Alternative Reality in the West.

A. The Hellenistic Period

BUTLER, E. M., *The Myth of the Magus.* New York: The Macmillan Company, Publishers, 1948.

CONYBEARE, F. C., trans., *The Life of Apollonious of Tyana.* New York: The Macmillan Company, Publishers, 1912.

DILL, SAMUEL, *Roman Society from Nero to Marcus Aurelius.* London: The Macmillan Company, Publishers, 1904.

DODDS, E. R., *The Greeks and the Irrational.* Berkeley: University of California Press, 1951.

GRANT, FREDERICK C., *Hellenistic Religions*. New York: Liberal Arts Press, 1953.
GRANT, ROBERT M., *Gnosticism and Early Christianity*. New York: Harper & Row, Publishers, 1966.
JONAS, HANS, *The Gnostic Religion*. Boston: Beacon Press, Inc., 1963.
MEAD, G. R. S., *Echoes from the Gnosis*. London: Theosophical Publishing Society, 1908. Vols. VIII–IX, *The Chaldean Oracles*.
PAGELS, ELAINE, *The Gnostic Gospels*. New York: Random House, Inc., 1979.
PHILIP, JAMES A., *Pythagoras and Early Pythagoreanism*. Toronto: University of Toronto Press, 1966.
SCOTT, WALTER, *Hermetica*. Oxford, England: Clarendon Press, 1924–36.
TARN, WILLIAM W., *Hellenistic Civilization*. New York: World Publishing Co., 1961.
VAN MOORSEL, GERARD, *The Mysteries of Hermes Trismegistus*. Utrecht: Kemink & Zoon, 1955.

B. The Middle Ages

BUTLER, E. M., *Ritual Magic*. Cambridge: Cambridge University Press, 1949.
DEGIVRY, GRILLOT, *A Pictorial Anthology of Witchcraft, Magic, and Alchemy*. New York: University Books, 1958.
ELIADE, MIRCEA, *The Forge and the Crucible*. New York: Harper & Row, Publishers, Inc., 1962.
HUGHES, PENNETHORNE, *Witchcraft*. London: Longmans, Green and Co., 1952.
MURRAY, MARGARET, *God of the Witches*. New York: Doubleday & Company, Inc., Anchor Books, 1960. (First published 1933.)
RUNCIMAN, STEVEN, *The Medieval Manichee*. Cambridge: Cambridge University Press, 1960.
SCHOLEM, GERSHOM G., *Major Trends in Jewish Mysticism*. New York: Schocken Books, Inc., 1967.
———, *On the Kabbalah and its Symbolism*. New York: Schocken Books, Inc., 1969.
SUMMERS, MONTAGUE, *The Geography of Witchcraft*. New York: University Books, 1958.
WILLIAMS, CHARLES, *Witchcraft*. New York: Meridian Books, 1959.

C. The Renaissance

ALLEN, DON CAMERON, *Doubt's Boundless Sea: Skepticism and Faith in the Renaissance*. Baltimore: Johns Hopkins Press, 1964.
HARGROVE, JOHN, *The Life and Soul of Paracelsus*. London: Gallancz, 1951.
JACOBI, JOLANDE, *Paracelsus: Selected Writings*. New York: Pantheon Books, Inc., 1951.
YATES, FRANCES, *Giordino Bruno and the Hermetic Tradition*. Chicago: University of Chicago Press, 1964.
———, *The Occult Philosophy in the Elizabethan Age*. London: Routledge & Kegan Paul, 1979.

D. The Rosicrucians

CRAVEN, JAMES BROWN, *Doctor Robert Fludd*. Kirkwall, Scotland: William Peace & Son, 1902.
DEBUS, ALLEN G., *The English Paracelsians*. New York: Franklin Watts, Inc., 1966.
JONES, MERVYN, "The Rosicrucians," in *Secret Societies*, ed. Norman Mackenzie. New York: P. F. Collier, Inc., 1971.
MAGRE, MAURICE, *Magicians, Seers, and Mystics*. New York: E. P. Dutton & Co., Inc., 1932.
SHELLEY, PERCY BYSSHE (1792–1822), *St. Ivryne or The Rosicrucian: a Romance* (1811).
STOUDT, JOHN JOSEPH, *Sunrise to Eternity: A Study in Jacob Boehme's Life and Thought*. Philadelphia: University of Pennsylvania Press, 1957.
WAITE, A. E., *The Brotherhood of the Rosy Cross*. New York: University Books, 1961.
———, ed., *The Works of Thomas Vaughan*. New York: University Books, 1968.
YATES, FRANCES, *The Rosicrucian Enlightenment*. London: Routledge & Kegan Paul, 1972.

E. The Eighteenth Century

COOPER-OAKLEY, ISABEL, *The Count of Saint-Germain*. Blauvelt, New York: Rudolf Steiner Publications, 1970. (Originally published 1912.)
DUMAS, F. R., *Cagliostro*. New York: Grossman Publishers, Inc., 1968.
JONES, MERVYN, "Freemasonry," in *Secret Societies*, ed. Norman Mackenzie. New York: P. F. Collier Books, Inc., 1971.
KATZ, JACOB, *Jews and Freemasons in Europe 1725–1939*. Cambridge: Harvard University Press, 1970.
PILK, FRED, et al., *Pocket History of Freemasonry*. New York: International Publications Service, 1969.

SWEDENBORG, EMANUEL, *The World of Spirits and Man's State After Death*. New York: Sweden-borg Foundation, 1940.

TOKSVIG, SIGNE, *Emanuel Swedenborg, Scientist and Mystic*. New Haven: Yale University Press, 1948.

TROWBRIDGE, W. R. H., *Cagliostro*. London: Allen & Unwin, 1910.

WAITE, A. E., *New Encyclopedia of Freemasonry* (2 vols). New York: University Books, 1970.

———, *The Unknown Philosopher: The Life of Louis Claude de St. Martin*. Blauvelt, New York: Rudolf Steiner Publications, 1970.

BURANELLI, VINCENT, *The Wizard from Vienna*. New York: Cowand, McCann, and Geoghegan, 1975. On Mesmer.

F. Spiritualism

ANDREWS, ERNEST DEMING, *The People Called Shakers*. New York: Oxford University Press, 1953.

BROWN, SLATER, *The Heyday of Spiritualism*. New York: Hawthorne Books, Inc., 1970.

CROSS, WHITNEY R., *The Burned Over District: The Social and Intellectual History of Enthusiastic Religion in Western New York*. New York: Harper & Row, Publishers, 1965.

FORNELL, EARL W., *Unhappy Medium: Spiritualism and the Life of Margaret Fox*. Austin: University of Texas Press, 1964.

KERR, HOWARD, *Mediums, and Spirit-Rappers, and Rearing Radicals: Spiritualism in American Literature 1850–1900*. Urbana: Univ. of Illinois Press, 1972.

NELSON, GEOFFREY K., *Spiritualism and Society*. New York: Schocken Books, Inc., 1969.

NORDHOFF, CHARLES, *The Communistic Societies of the United States*. New York: Dover Publications, Inc., 1966.

PRICE, ROBERT, *Johnny Appleseed, Man and Myth*. Gloucester, Massachusetts: Peter Smith, Publisher, Inc., 1967.

G. Theosophy

CAMPBELL, BRUCE F., *Ancient Wisdom Revived: A History of the Theosophical Movement*. Berkeley: Univ. of California Press, 1980.

GREENWALT, EMMETT A., *The Point Loma Community in California, 1897–1942: A Theosophical Experiment*. Berkeley: University of California Press, 1955.

NEFF, MARY K., *Personal Memories of H. P. Blavatsky*. Wheaton, Illinois: Theosophical Publishing House, 1937, 1967.

NETHERCOT, ARTHUR HOBART, *The First Five Lives of Annie Besant*. London: R. Hart-Dabis, 1960.

———, *The Last Four Lives of Annie Besant*. Chicago: University of Chicago Press, 1963.

OLCOTT, HENRY STEELE, *Old Diary Leaves: The True Story of the Theosophical Society*, Series I–IV. Adyar, Madras, India: Theosophical Publishing House, 1895–1910.

H. New Thought

BRADEN, CHARLES S., *Spirits in Rebellion: The Rise and Development of New Thought*. Dallas: Southern Methodist University Press, 1963.

JUDAH, J. STILLSON, *The History and Philosophy of the Metaphysical Movements in America*. Philadelphia: Westminster Press, 1967.

SCHNEIDER, LOUIS, and SANFORD DORNBUSCH, *Popular Religion: Inspirational Books in America*. Chicago, Illinois: University of Chicago Press, 1958.

I. Eastern Imports

JACKSON, CARL T., *The Oriental Religions and American Thought: Nineteenth-Century Explorations*. Westport, CT: Greenwood Press, 1981.

LANDAU, RON, *God Is My Adventure*. London: Unwin Books, 1935, 1964.

NEEDLEMAN, JACOB, *The New Religions*. New York: Doubleday & Company, Inc., 1970.

THOMAS, WENDELL, *Hinduism Invades America*. New York: Beacon Press, Inc., 1930.

J. The Sixties

Definitive books on the spiritual story of this decade have yet to appear. For perspectives see Chapter II, Notes 27 to 33, and bibliography on specific groups.

K. *General Books on the American History of New Religious Movements*

BRADEN, CHARLES S., *These Also Believe: A Study of Modern American Cults and Minority Religious Movements.* New York: Macmillan, Inc., 1949.

BRIDGES, HAL., *American Mysticism: From William James to Zen.* New York: Harper & Row, Publishers, Inc., 1970. Reprint: Lakemont, Ga.: CSA Press, 1977.

DARE, PHILIP N., *American Communes to 1860: An Annotated Bibliography.* New York: Garland, 1986.

ELLWOOD, ROBERT S., JR., *Alternative Altars: Unconventional and Eastern Spirituality in America.* Chicago: University of Chicago Press, 1979.

FIELDS, RICK, *How the Swans Came to the Lake: A Narrative History of Buddhism in America.* Boulder, CO: Shambhala, 1981.

JACKSON, CARL THOMAS, *The Oriental Religions and American Thought: Nineteenth Century Explorations.* Westport, CN: Greenwood Press, 1981.

JUDAH, J. STILLSON, *The History and Philosophy of the Metaphysical Movements in America.* Philadelphia: Westminster Press, 1967.

KERR, HOWARD, and CHARLES L. CROW, eds., *The Occult in America: New Historical Perspectives.* Urbana: Univ. of Illinois Press, 1983.

LAYMAN, EMMA MCCLOY, *Buddhism in America.* Chicago: Nelson-Hall, 1976.

PREBISH, CHARLES, *American Buddhism.* North Scituate, Mass.: Duxbury Press, 1979.

RASCHKE, CARL A., *The Interruption of Eternity: Modern Gnosticism and the Origins of the New Religious Consciousness.* Chicago: Nelson-Hall, 1980.

VEYSEY, LAURENCE R., *The Communal Experience: Anarchist and Mystical Communities in Twentieth-Century America.* Chicago: University of Chicago Press, 1978.

WEBB, JAMES, *The Occult Establishment.* La Salle, IL: Open Court, 1976.

———, *The Occult Underground.* La Salle, IL: Open Court, 1974.

Chapter 4: New Vessels for the Ancient Wisdom

A. *Theosophy. See also Section a, biblio. for Ch. 2, above.*

BARKER, A. T., ed., *The Mahatma Letters to A. P. Sinnett.* London: Rider and Company, 1933.

BLAVATSKY, HELENA PETROVNA, *Collected Writings.* Boris de Zirkoff, compiler (10 volumes), varying dates and publishers.

BRADEN, CHARLES S., *These Also Believe: A Study of Modern American Cults and Minority Religious Movements.* New York: The Macmillan Company, Publishers, 1949.

CAMPBELL, BRUCE, *Ancient Wisdom Revived.* Berkeley: Univ. of California Press, 1980.

JUDAH, J. STILLSON, *History and Philosophy of the Metaphysical Movements in America.* Philadelphia: Westminster Press, 1967.

LILJEGREN, STEN BODVAR, *Bulwer-Lytton's Novels and Isis Unveiled.* Cambridge: Harvard University Press, 1957.

RANSOM, JOSEPHINE, *A Short History of the Theosophical Society.* Adyar, Madras, India: Theosophical Publishing House, 1930.

B. *Full Moon Meditation Groups*

BAILEY, ALICE A., *Works.* New York: Lucis Publishing Company, varying dates.

———, *The Unfinished Autobiography of Alice A. Bailey.* New York: Lucis Publishing Company, 1951.

JUDAH, J. STILLSON, *History and Philosophy of the Metaphysical Movements in America.* Philadelphia: Westminster Press, 1967.

C. *Anthroposophy*

BARFIELD, OWEN, *Romanticism Comes of Age.* London: Anthroposophical Publishing Co., 1944.

HARWOOD, A., *The Faithful Thinker.* London: Hodder and Stoughton, 1961.

LANDAU, RON, *God Is My Adventure.* London: Unwin Books, 1935, 1964.

D. *Modern Gnosticism*

ANSON, PETER, *Bishops at Large.* London: Faber and Faber, 1964.

E. The "I Am" Movement

BRADEN, CHARLES S., *These Also Believe: A Study of Modern American Cults and Minority Religious Movements*. New York: The Macmillan Company, Publishers, 1949.

F. The Liberal Catholic Church

ANSON, PETER, *Bishops at Large*. London: Faber and Faber, 1964.
BRADEN, CHARLES S., *These Also Believe: A Study of Modern American Cults and Minority Religious Movements*. New York: The Macmillan Company, Publishers, 1949.

Chapter 5: The Descent of the Mighty Ones

A. Spiritualism

BRADEN, CHARLES S., *These Also Believe: A Study of Modern American Cults and Minority Religious Movements*. New York: The Macmillan Company, 1949.
BROWN, SLATER, *The Heyday of Spiritualism*. New York: Hawthorne Books, Inc., 1970.
CARMER, CARL LANSON, *Listen for a Lonesome Drum*. New York: Farrar and Rinehart, 1956.
ELLWOOD, ROBERT S., JR., *Alternative Altars: Unconventional and Eastern Spirituality in America*. Chicago: University of Chicago Press, 1979.
FORNELL, EARL W., *Unhappy Medium: Spiritualism and the Life of Margaret Fox*. Austin: University of Texas Press, 1964.
GOODSPEED, EDGAR T., *Modern Apocrypha*. Boston: Beacon Press, Inc., 1956.
JUDAH, J. STILLSON, *History and Philosophy of the Metaphysical Movements in America*. Philadelphia: Westminster Press, 1967.
KERR, HOWARD, and CHARLES L. CROW, eds., *The Occult in America: New Historical Perspectives*. Urbana, Illinois: University of Illinois Press, 1983.
MOORE, R. LAURENCE, *In Search of White Crows: Spiritualism, Parapsychology, and American Culture*. New York: Oxford Univ. Press, 1977.
NELSON, GEOFFREY K., *Spiritualism and Society*. New York: Schocken Books, Inc., 1969.
WEBB, JAMES, *The Occult Underground*. La Salle, IL: Open Court, 1974.

B. UFO Movements

BALCH, ROBERT W., "Looking Behind the Scenes in a Religious Cult: Implications for the Study of Conversion," *Sociological Analysis*, XXXI (1980), 137–43.
CATOE, LYNN E., *UFO's and Related Subjects: An Annotated Bibliography*. Detroit: Gale Research, 1978.
CURRAN, DOUGLAS, *In Advance of the Landing*. New York: Abbeville, 1985.
FESTINGER, LEON, HENRY W. RIECKEN, and STANLEY SCHACTER, *When Prophecy Fails*. Minneapolis: University of Minnesota Press, 1956.
JUNG, CARL G., *Flying Saucers: A Modern Myth of Things Seen in the Sky*. New York: Signet Books, 1969.
STORY, RONALD D., ed., *The Encyclopedia of UFOs*. Garden City, New York: Doubleday, 1980.
WALLIS, ROY, "The Aetherius Society," in Roy Wallis, ed., *Sectarianism: Analyses of Religious and Non-Religious Sects*. New York: John Wiley and Sons, Inc., 1975.

Chapter 6: The Crystal Within

A. Gurdjieff

ANDERSON, MARGARET, *The Unknowable Gurdjieff*. New York: Samuel Weiser, 1973.
DE HARTMANN, THOMAS, *Our Life with Mr. Gurdjieff*. Baltimore: Penguin Books, 1972.
DRISCOLL, J. WALTER, and THE GURDJIEFF FOUNDATION OF CALIFORNIA, *Gurdjieff: An Annotated Bibliography*. New York: Garland, 1985.
GURDJIEFF, G., *All and Everything*. New York: Harcourt, Brace & World, Inc., 1950.
LEFORT, RAFAEL, *The Teachers of Gurdjieff*. New York: Samuel Weiser, 1973.
NOTT, C. S., *Teachings of Gurdjieff, The Journal of a Pupil*. New York: Samuel Weiser, 1962.
OUSPENSKY, P. D., *In Search of the Miraculous*. New York: Harcourt, Brace & World, Inc., 1949.
———, *The Fourth Way*. New York: Random House, 1971.

PAUWELS, L., *Gurdjieff*. New York: Samuel Weiser, 1972.
PETERS, FRITZ, *Boyhood with Gurdjieff*. Santa Barbara: Capra Press, 1980.
WALKER, KENNETH, *A Study of Gurdjieff's Teaching*. New York: Samuel Weiser, 1974.
WEBB, JAMES, *The Harmonious Circle: The Lives and Work of G. I. Gurdjieff, P. D. Ouspensky, and Their Followers*. New York: G. P. Putnam's Sons, 1980.

B. *Scientology*

MALKO, GEORGE, *Scientology: The Now Religion*. New York: Delacorte Press, 1970.
O'BRIEN, HELEN, *Dianetics in Limbo*. Philadelphia: Whitmore Publishing Company, 1966.
WALLIS, ROY, *The Road to Total Freedom: A Sociological Analysis of Scientololgy*. New York: Columbia University Press, 1977.

C. *Astrology*

HOWE, ELLIC, *Urania's Children: The Strange World of the Astrologers*. London: Kimber, 1967.
MCINTOSH, CHRISTOPHER, *The Astrologers and Their Creed*. London: Hutchinson, 1969.

Chapter 7: The Edenic Bower: Neo-Paganism

A. *Neo-Paganism and Witchcraft*

ADLER, MARGOT, *Drawing Down the Moon: Witches, Druids, Goddess-Worshippers & Other Pagans in America Today*. New York: Viking Press, 1979. Rev. ed. Boston: Beacon, 1986.
FARRAR, JANET and STEWART, *The Witches' Way: Principles, Rituals and Beliefs of Modern Witchcraft*. London: Robert Hale, 1984.
GARDNER, GERALD, *Witchcraft Today*. New York: Citadel Press, 1970.
MELTON, J. GORDON, *Magic, Witchcraft and Paganism in America*. New York: Garland, 1982.
STARHAWK, *Dreaming the Dark*. Boston: Beacon, 1982.
———, *The Spiral Dance: A Rebirth of the Ancient Religion of the Great Goddess*. San Francisco: Harper and Row, Publishers, Inc., 1979.

B. *Ceremonial Magic*

BARDON, FRANZ, *Initiation into Hermetics*. Kettig uber Koblenz: Osiris-Verlag, 1962.
———, *The Practice of Evocational Magic*. Graz-Puntigam, Austria: Rudolf Pravica, 1967.
BURLAND, C. A., *The Magical Arts*. New York: Horizon Press, Inc., 1966.
BUTLER, W. E., *Apprenticed to Magic*. London: Aquarian Press, 1962.
CAVENDISH, RICHARD, *The Black Arts*. London: Routledge and Kegan, Paul, 1967.
CROW, W. B., *Witchcraft, Magic, and Occultism*. Los Angeles: Wilshire Book Company, 1968.
CROWLEY, ALEISTER, *Magic in Theory and Practice*. New York: Castle Books, n.d.
KING, FRANCIS, *Ritual Magic in England*. London: Neville Spearman, 1970.
LEVI, ELIPHAS (A. L. Constant), *Transcendental Magic*. New York: Samuel Weiser, 1970.
———, *History of Magic*. New York: Samuel Weiser, 1970.
MATHERS, S. L., *The Sacred Magic of Abra Melin*. New York: Wehman Brothers, 1948.
REGARDIE, ISRAEL, *The Golden Dawn* (2nd ed.). St. Paul: Llewellyn Publications, 1970.
———, ed., P. R. STEPHENSEN, *The Legend of Aleister Crowley*. St. Paul: Llewellyn Publications, 1970.
———, *My Rosicrucian Adventure*. Chicago: Aries Press, 1936.
SCOTT, JENNIE GRAHAM, *The Magicians*. New York: Irvington, 1983.
SYMONDS, J., *The Great Beast*. New York: Roy Publishers, Inc., 1952.
———, *The Magic of Aleister Crowley*. London: Muller, 1958.
SYMONDS, J., and K. GRANT, eds., *The Confessions of Aleister Crowley*. New York: Hill and Wang, Inc., 1970.
WAITE, A. E., *The Book of Ceremonial Magic*. New York: University Books, 1961.

C. *Satanism*

LAVEY, ANTON, *The Satanic Bible*. New York: Avon Books, 1969.
LYONS, ARTHUR, *The Second Coming: Satanism in America*. New York: Dodd, Mead & Company, 1970.
RHODES, H. T., *The Satanic Mass: A Sociological and Criminological Study*. New York: Citadel Press, 1955. (Reprint, Wehman.)

Chapter 8: The Ganges Flows West

A. The Vedanta Society

BRIDGES, HAL, *American Mysticism: From William James to Zen*. New York: Harper & Row, Publishers, 1970.

DAMRELL, JOSEPH, *Seeking Spiritual Meaning: The World of Vedanta*. Sociological Observations, no. 2. Beverly Hills: Sage Publications, Inc., 1977.

FRENCH, HAROLD W., *The Swan's Wide Waters: Ramakrishna and Western Culture*. Port Washington, NY: Kennikat Press, 1974.

ISHERWOOD, CHRISTOPHER, ed., *Vedanta for Modern Man*. New York: P. F. Collier, Inc., 1962.

———, ed., *Vedanta for the Western World*. Hollywood: Marcel Rodd, 1946.

———, *My Guru and his Disciple*. New York: Farrar, Strauss, and Giroux, 1980.

———, *Ramakrishna and His Disciples*. New York: Simon & Schuster, Inc., 1965.

THOMAS, WENDELL, *Hinduism Invades America*. New York: Beacon Press, Inc., 1930.

VEYSEY, LAURENCE R., *The Communal Experience: Anarchist and Mystical Communities in Twentieth-Century America*. Chicago: University of Chicago Press, 1978.

YALE, JOHN, ed., *What Vedanta Means to Me*. London: Rider, 1961.

B. Self-Realization Fellowship

THOMAS, WENDELL, *Hinduism Invades America*. New York: Beacon Press, Inc., 1930.

C. The Maharishi Mahesh Yogi's Transcendental Meditation Movement

BAINBRIDGE, WILLIAM SIMS, and DANIEL H. JACKSON, "The Rise and Decline of Transcendental Meditation," in Bryan Wilson, ed., *The Social Impact of New Religious Movements*. New York: The Rose of Sharon Press, Inc., 1981.

CAMPBELL, ANTHONY, M. D., *Seven States of Consciousness: A Vision of Possibilities Suggested by the Teaching of Maharishi Mahesh Yogi*. New York: Harper Torchbooks, 1973.

D. Yoga

ELIADE, MIRCEA, *Yoga: Immortality and Freedom*. Translated from the French by Willard R. Trask. 2d ed.; Princeton: Princeton University Press, 1970.

———, *Patanjali and Yoga*. Translated from the French by Charles Lam Markmann. New York: Schocken Books, 1975.

JARRELL, HOWARD R., *International Yoga Bibliography, 1950 to 1980*. Metuchen, N. J.: Scarecrow Press, 1981.

VARENNE, JEAN. *Yoga and the Hindu Tradition*. Translated from the French by Derek Cottman. Chicago: University of Chicago Press, 1976.

E. Krishna Consciousness

DANER, FRANCINE J., *The American Children of Krsna: A Study of the Hare Krishna Movement*. New York: Holt, Rinehart and Winston, 1976.

———, "Conversion to Krishna Consciousness: The Transformation from Hippie to Religious Ascetic," in Roy Wallis, ed., *Sectarianism: Analyses of Religious and Non-Religious Sects*. New York: John Wiley & Sons, Inc., 1975.

GELBERG, STEVEN J., ed., *Hare Krishna, Hare Krishna: Five Distinguished Scholars on the Krishna Movement in the West*. New York: Grove Press, 1983.

JOHNSON, GREGORY, "The Hare Krishna in San Francisco," in Charles Y. Glock and Robert N. Bellah, eds., *The New Religious Consciousness*. Berkeley: University of California Press, 1976.

JUDAH, J. STILLSON, *Hare Krishna and the Counterculture*. New York: John Wiley and Sons, Inc., 1974.

ROCHFORD, EDMUND BURKE, JR., *Hare Krishna in America*. New Brunswick, NJ: Rutgers University Press, 1985.

SHINN, LARRY D., *The Dark Lord*. Philadelphia: Westminster, 1986.

SINGER, MILTON B., ed., *Krishna: Myth, Rites, and Attitudes*. Honolulu: East-West Center Press, 1966.

F. Meher Baba

NEEDLEMAN, JACOB, *The New Religions*. New York: Doubleday & Co., Inc., 1970.

PURDOM, CHARLES B., *The God-Man: The Life, Journeys, and Work of Meher Baba.* London: Allen and Unwin, 1964.

G. *Eckankar*

LANE, DAVID CHRISTOPHER, *The Making of a Spiritual Movement: The Untold Story of Paul Twitchell and Eckankar.* Del Mar, CA: Del Mar Press, 1983.

Chapter 9: The East in the Golden West

A. *Western Zen*

BENOIT, HUBERT, *The Supreme Doctrine.* New York: Viking Press, Inc., 1968.
BRIDGES, HAL, *American Mysticism: From William James to Zen.* New York: Harper & Row, Publishers, Inc., 1967.
ELLWOOD, ROBERT S., JR., *Alternative Altars: Unconventional and Eastern Spirituality in America.* Chicago: University of Chicago Press, 1979.
FIELDS, RICK, *How the Swans Came to the Lake: A Narrative History of Buddhism in America.* Boulder, CO: Shambhala, 1981.
GRAHAM, DON ALFRED, *Zen Catholicism.* New York: Harcourt Brace Jovanovich, 1963.
GUSTAITIS, ROSA, *Turning On.* New York: Macmillan, Inc., Publishers, 1969.
KAPLEAU, PHILIP, *The Three Pillars of Zen.* Boston: Beacon Press, Inc., 1967.
LAYMAN, EMMA MCCLOY, *Buddhism in America.* Chicago: Nelson-Hall, 1976.
NEEDLEMAN, JACOB, *The New Religions.* New York: Doubleday & Company, Inc., 1970.
SUZUKI, D. T., *Zen Buddhism.* New York: Doubleday & Company, Inc., Anchor Books, 1956.
TIPTON, STEVEN M., *Getting Saved from the Sixties.* Berkeley: University of California Press, 1982.
WATTS, ALAN, *The Way of Zen.* New York: Pantheon Books, Inc., 1957.
————, *The Spirit of Zen.* New York: Grove, 1958.
ZEN CENTER OF SAN FRANCISCO, *Wind Bell,* VIII, Nos. 1–2 (Fall 1969). (Issue devoted to history of Zen Centers in America.)

B. *Tibetan Buddhism*

ANDERSON, WALT, *Open Secrets: A Western Guide to Tibetan Buddhism.* New York: Viking Press, 1979.
CLARK, TOM, *The Great Naropa Poetry Wars.* Santa Barbara, CA: Cadmus Editions, 1980.
COX, HARVEY, *Turning East: The Promise and Peril of the New Orientalism.* New York: Simon and Schuster, Inc., 1977.
FIELD, RICK, *How the Swans Came to the Lake.* Boulder, CO: Shambhala, 1981.
PREBISH, CHARLES, *American Buddhism.* North Scituate, MA: Duxbury Press, 1979.

C. *Nichiren Shoshu*

ANESAKI, MASAHARU, *Nichiren: The Buddhist Prophet.* Cambridge: Harvard University Press, 1916.
BRANNEN, NOAH S., *Soka Gakkai: Japan's Militant Buddhists.* Richmond, VA: John Knox Press, 1968.
DATOR, JAMES ALLEN. *Soka Gakkai, Builders of the Third Civilization: American and Japanese Members.* Seattle: University of Washington Press, 1969.
EARHART, H. BYRON, *The New Religions of Japan: An Annotated List of Books Published in English, 1971 through 1975.* 2d ed. Michigan Papers in Japanese Studies, No. 9. Ann Arbor: Center for Japanese Studies, University of Michigan, 1983.
ELLWOOD, ROBERT S., JR., *The Eagle and the Rising Sun: Americans and the New Religions of Japan.* Philadelphia: Westminster Press, 1974.
FIELDS, RICK, *How the Swan Came to the Lake: A Narrative History of Buddhism in America.* Boulder, CO: Shambhala, 1981.
HASHIMOTO, HIDEO, and WILLIAM MCPHERSON, "Rise and Decline of Sokagakkai in Japan and the United States," *Review of Religious Research,* XVII, 2 (Winter 1976), 83–92.
MCFARLAND, H. NEILL, *The Rush Hour of the Gods.* New York: Macmillan, Inc., 1967.
PREBISH, CHARLES, *American Buddhism.* North Scituate, MA: Duxbury Press, 1979.
THOMSEN, HARRY, *The New Religions of Japan.* Rutland, VT: C. E. Tuttle Co., 1963.

WHITE, JAMES W., *The Sokagakkai and Mass Society.* Stanford, CA: Stanford University Press, 1970.

D. The Baha'i Faith

BJORLING, JOEL, *The Baha'i Faith: A Historical Bibliography.* New York: Garland, 1985.
ESSLEMONT, J. E., *Baha'u'llah and the New Era.* Wilmette, IL: Baha'i Publishing Trust, 1970.
FERRABY, JOHN, *All Things Made New.* London: G. Allen & Unwin, 1957.
GAVER, JESSYCA, *Baha'i Faith.* New York: Award Books, 1968.
HATCHER, WILLIAM, and JAMES D. MARTIN, *The Baha'i Faith: The Emerging Global Religion.* New York: Harper & Row Publishers, Inc., 1984.
MOMEN, MOOJAN, ed., *The Babi and Baha'i Religions 1844–1944: Some Contemporary Accounts.* Oxford: George Ronald, 1981.
RICHARDS, J. R., *The Religion of the Baha'is.* Macmillan, 1932.

E. Subud

BENNETT, JOHN G., *Concerning Subud.* New York: University Books, 1959.
COHEN, DANIEL, *The New Believers.* New York: M. Evans, 1975.
NEEDLEMAN, JACOB, *The New Religions.* New York: Doubleday & Company, Inc., 1970.
ROFE, HUSEIN, *The Path of Subud.* London: Rider, 1959.
SUBUH, MUHAMMAD, *The Meaning of Subud.* New York: Dharma Book Company, 1961.

F. The Unification Church

BARKER, EILEEN, "Who'd Be a Moonie?," in Bryan Wilson, ed., *The Social Impact of New Religious Movements.* Conference series, No. 9. Barrytown, NY: The Unification Theological Seminary, 1981.
———, *The Making of a Moonie: Choice or Brainwashing.* New York: B. Blackwell. 1984.
BROMLEY, DAVID G., and ANSON D. SHUPE, JR., *"Moonies" in America: Cult, Church, and Crusade.* Beverly Hills, CA: Sage Publications, Inc., 1979.
———, "The Moonies and the Anti-Cultists: Movement and Counter Movement in Conflict," *Sociological Analysis,* 40 (1979), 325–34.
———, "Repression and the Decline of Social Movements: The Case of the New Religions," in Jo Freeman, ed., *Social Movements of the Sixties and Seventies.* New York: Longman, 1983.
BRYANT, M. DARROL, and HERBERT W. RICHARDSON, eds., *A Time for Consideration: A Scholarly Appraisal of the Unification Church.* New York: Edwin Mellen Press, 1978.
LOFLAND, JOHN, *Doomsday Cult: A Study of Conversion, Proselytization, and Maintenance of Faith.* Enlarged edition. New York: Irvington Publishers, 1977.
MICKLER, MICHAEL L. *The Unification Church in America: A Bibliography.* New York: Garland, 1986.
SONTAG, FREDERICK, *Sun Myung Moon and the Unification Church.* Nashville: Abingdon Press, 1977.

Appendix

A. "The Black Muslims" (American Muslim Mission)

ABILLA, WALTER D., *The Black Muslims in America: An Introduction to the Theory of Commitment.* Kampala: East African Literature Bureau, 1977.
BALDWIN, JAMES, *The Fire Next Time.* New York: Dial Press, 1963.
FAUSET, ARTHUR H., "Moorish Science Temple of America," in J. Milton Yinger, ed., *Religion, Society, and the Individual.* New York: Macmillan, 1957.
HALL, RAYMOND L., *Black Separatism in the United States.* Published for Dartmouth College by the University Press of New England, 1978.
LINCOLN, C. ERIC, *My Face is Black.* Boston: Beacon Press, 1964.
———, *The Black Muslims in America.* Boston: Beacon Press, 1973.
LITTLE, MALCOLM, *Malcolm X Speaks.* New York: Grove Press, 1965.
LOMAX, LOUIS E., *When the Word is Given: A Report on Elijah Muhammad, Malcolm X, and the Black Muslim World.* Cleveland: World Publishing Company, 1963.
MALCOLM X, with the assistance of Alex Haley, *The Autobiography of Malcolm X.* New York: Grove Press, 1964.

MUHAMMAD, ELIJAH, *Message to the Blackman in America*. Chicago: Muhammad Mosque of Islam No. 2, 1965.

————, *The Supreme Wisdom: Solution to the So-called Negroes' Problem*. 2d ed.; Chicago: The University of Islam, 1957.

PINKNEY, ALPHONSO, *Red, Black, and Green: Black Nationalism in the United States*. New York: Cambridge University Press, 1976.

B. Jim Jones and the Peoples Temple

FEINSOD, ETHAN, *Awake in a Nightmare*. New York: W. W. Norton & Co., Inc., 1981.

HALL, JOHN R., "Apocalypse at Jonestown," in Thomas Robbins and Dick Anthony, eds., *In Gods We Trust: New Patterns of Religious Pluralism in America*. New Brunswick, NJ: Transaction Books, 1981.

HALPERIN, DAVID A., *Psychodynamic Perspectives on Religion, Sect, and Cult*. London: John Wright, 1983.

KERNS, PHILIP, *People's Temple, People's Tomb*. Plainfield, NJ: Logos, 1979.

KILDUFF, MARSHALL, and RON JAVERS, *The Suicide Cult: The Inside Story of the People's Temple Sect and the Massacre in Guyana*. New York: Bantam Books, 1978.

KLINEMAN, GEORGE, SHERMAN BUTLER, and DAVID CONN, *The Cult that Died: The Tragedy of Jim Jones and the Peoples Temple*. New York: G. P. Putnam's Sons, 1980.

KRAUSE, CHARLES A., *Guyana Massacre: The Eyewitness Account*. New York: Berkely, 1978.

LANE, MARK, *The Strongest Poison*. New York: Hawthorn Books, Inc., 1980.

LEVI, KEN, ed., *Violence and Religious Commitment: Implications of Jim Jones's People's Temple Movement*. New York: Dale Books, 1978.

LEWIS, GORDON K., *Gather with the Saints at the River: The Jonestown Guyana Holocaust*. Rio Pedras, Puerto Rico: Institute of Caribbean Studies, University of Puerto Rico, 1978.

MAGUIRE, JOHN, and MARY LEE DUNN, *Hold Hands and Die*. New York: Dale Books, 1978.

MILLS, JEANNIE, *Six Years with God: Life Inside Rev. Jim Jones' Peoples Temple*. New York: A & W, 1979.

NAIPAUL, SHIVA, *Journey to Nowhere: A New World Tragedy*. New York: Simon and Schuster, Inc., 1981.

NUGENT, JOHN PEER, *White Night*. New York: Rawson and Wade, 1979.

REITERMAN, TIM, with JOHN JACOBS, *Raven: The Untold Story of the Rev. Jim Jones and His People*. New York: E. P. Dutton, 1982.

RESTON, JAMES, JR., *Our Father Who Art in Hell: The Life and Death of Jim Jones*. New York: Times Books, 1981.

ROSE, STEVEN. *Jesus and Jim Jones: Behind Jonestown*. Boston: Pilgrim Press, 1979.

SMITH, JONATHAN Z., *Imagining Religion: From Babylon to Jonestown*. Chicago: University of Chicago Press, 1982.

WEIGHTMAN, JUDITH MARY, *Making Sense of the Jonestown Suicides: A Sociological History of the People's Temple*. New York: Mellen Press, 1984.

WOODEN, KENNETH, *The Children of Jonestown*. New York: McGraw Hill Book Company, 1981.

YEE, MIN S., and THOMAS N. LAYTON, *In My Father's House: The Story of the Layton Family and the Rev. Jim Jones*. New York: Holt, Rinehart, and Winston, 1981.

ADDRESSES OF GROUPS

The following current (1987) addresses of groups discussed in this book are provided to assist those who may wish to undertake further investigation of particular groups.

Chapter 3: New Vessels for the Ancient Wisdom

Theosophy

The Theosophical Society in America, Box 270, Wheaton, Illinois 60187.

The Krotona School of Theosophy, 46 Krotona Hill, Ojai, California 93023.

The Theosophical Society, Post Office Bin C, Pasadena, California 91109.

The United Lodge of Theosophists, 245 West 33rd Street, Los Angeles, California 90007.

Full Moon Meditation Groups

Lucis Publishing Company and the Arcane School, 866 United Nations Plaza, Suite 566–7, New York, New York 10017.

Meditation Groups for the New Age, P. O. Box 566, Ojai, California 93023.

Other Groups

Anthroposophical Society in America, Rudolf Steiner Information Center, 211 Madison Avenue, New York, New York 10016.

The Rosicrucian Fellowship, Oceanside, California 92054.

Rosicrucian Order (AMORC), Rosicrucian Park, San Jose, California 95114.

Sophia Gnostic Center, 4516 Hollywood Blvd., Los Angeles, California 90027.

"I Am" Movement, Saint Germain Foundation, 1120 Stonehedge Dr., Schaumburg, Illinois 60194.

Liberal Catholic Church, St. Alban Press, P. O. Box 598, Ojai, California 93023.

Church Universal and Triumphant, Bx A, Livingston, Montana 59047.

Chapter 4: The Descent of the Mighty Ones

National Spiritualist Association of Churches, General Offices, P. O. Box 128, Cassadaga, Florida 32706.

(World) Understanding, Inc., P. O. Box 614, Alamogordo, New Mexico 88311-0614.

Amalgamated Flying Saucer Clubs of America, P. O. Box 39, Yucca Valley, California 92284.

The Aetherius Society, 6202 Afton Place, Hollywood, California 90028.

Chapter 5: The Crystal Within: Initiatory Groups

The Gurdjieff Foundation, 123 East 63rd Street, New York, New York 10021.

Church of Scientology, Los Angeles Continental Organization, 4810 Sunset Boulevard, Los Angeles, California 90027.

Builders of the Adytum, 5105 North Figueroa Street, Los Angeles, California 90042.

Chapter 6: The Edenic Bower: Neo-Paganism

Moon Birch Grove, 4111 Lincoln Blvd 211, Marina del Rey, California 90292.

Covenant of the Goddess, Bx 1226, Berkeley, California 94704 (National Pagan organization).

Circle, Bx 219, Mt. Horeb, Wisconsin 53572 (Pagan information).

Dreamweavers, Bx 846, Montrose, California 91020. For information on other activities of the Native American spirituality movement, see the periodical *Shaman's Drum*, Bx 2636, Berkeley, California 94702.

Ordo Templi Astartes, Bx 40094, Pasadena, California 91104.

Church of Satan, Bx 210082, San Francisco, California 94121.

Feraferia, Bx 41363, Eagle Rock Station, Los Angeles, California 90041.

Chapter 7: The Ganges Flows West: Indian Movements in America

Vedanta Society of Northern California, 2323 Vallejo Street, San Francisco, California 94123.

Vedanta Society of Southern California, 1946 Vedanta Place, Hollywood, California 90068.

Ramakrishna-Vivekananda Center, 17 East 94th Street, New York, New York 10028.

Self-Realization Fellowship, 3880 San Rafael Avenue, Los Angeles, California 90065.

Transcendental Meditation Program, 17310 Sunset Boulevard, Pacific Palisades, California 90272.

Transcendental Meditation Program, 220 East 23rd Street, New York, New York 10010.

Sivananda Yoga Society, 243 West 24th Street, New York, New York 10011.

Bhaktivedanta Book Trust, 3764 Watseka Avenue, Los Angeles, California 90034 (For addresses of local ISKCON centers see any issue of the magazine *Back to Godhead.*)

Sathya Sai Baba Society, 305 West First Street, Tustin, California 92680.

Meher Spiritual Center, P. O. Box 487, Myrtle Beach, South Carolina 29577.

Eckankar, P. O. Box 27300, Minneapolis, Minnesota 55427.

Chapter 8: The East in the Golden West

The Zen Center, 300 Page Street, San Francisco, California 94102.

The Zen Center, 7 Arnold Park, Rochester, New York 14607.

Naropa Institute, 2130 Arapahoe, Boulder, Colorado 80302.

Nyingma Institute, 1815 Highland Place, Berkeley, California 94709.

Nichiren Shoshu Academy, 525 Wilshire Boulevard, Santa Monica, California 90406.

National Spiritual Assembly of the Baha'is of the United States, 536 Sheridan Road, Wilmette, Illinois 60091.

Subud USA, 13701 Bel-Red Road, Suite B, Bellevue, Washington 98005.

The Unification Church, 4 West 43rd Street, New York, New York 10036.

INDEX

277.3
E14
1988

80056